PRICING STRATEGY

Setting Price Levels, Managing Price Discounts, & Establishing Price Structures

Tim J. Smith

Wiglaf Pricing

Australia • Brazil • Mexico • Singapore • United Kingdom • United States

Pricing Strategy: Setting Price Levels, Managing Price Discounts, & Establishing Price Structures
Tim J. Smith

Vice President of Editorial, Business: Jack W. Calhoun

Editor-in-Chief: Melissa Acuña

Executive Editor: Mike Roche

Developmental Editor: Kayti Purkiss

Marketing Manager: Gretchen Swann

Sr. Content Project Manager: Tamborah Moore

Media Editor: John Rich

Print Buyer: Miranda Klapper

Sr. Marketing Communications Manager: Jim Overly

Marketing Coordinator: Leigh Smith

Production Service: MPS Limited, a Macmillan Company

Sr. Art Director: Stacy Jenkins Shirley

Cover and Internal Designer: Itzhack Shelomi

Cover Image: iStock Photo

Rights Acquisitions Specialist, Text: Mardell Glinski Schultz

Text Permissions Researcher: Karyn Morrison

Rights Acquisitions Specialist, Images: John Hill

Photo Researcher: Josh Brown/Prepress PMG

Library of Congress Control Number: 2010938896

ISBN-13: 978-0-538-48088-8

ISBN-10: 0-538-48088-2

Cengage
20 Channel Center Street
Boston, MA 02210
USA

Cengage products are represented in Canada by Nelson Education, Ltd.

Printed in Mexico
Print Number: 03   Print Year: 2019

Though we live in an infinite universe that is constantly expanding, and we are all increasingly infinitesimally small by comparison, if we have a good stick and a well-placed fulcrum, we can move the world. To the next generation, may your questions be your stick and your wisdom define your fulcrum.

Brief Contents

Table of Contents

Table of Exhibits

Foreword by Janice D. Chaffin

Pricing isn't sexy.

I know my teenage daughters don't think I'm on the leading edge of pop culture, but I'm confident I'm right about this.

I bet you've never heard anyone say, "We just hired a Top 10 MBA grad from Stanford and we're putting her in charge of pricing."

There are no books about pricing on the best-seller list; they are never displayed beside *Good to Great* or *The Fifth Discipline*. While there's a new book about how to sell effectively every few weeks, there are hardly any books on the discipline of pricing effectively.

While pricing isn't sexy, it is strategic. That's why I'm hoping you'll pick up and read this valuable book.

Why is pricing strategic? I can think of three reasons.

Pricing moves customers (and market share). And despite what you may hear from salespeople as the end of a quarter approaches, lower prices do not necessarily mean more sales, or more profit.

Pricing moves markets. If you'll permit me to paraphrase Marshall McLuhan, pricing is the message. In an age when "Free" is a viable business strategy, more than ever pricing decisions communicate important things about your brand, your business model, and your product.

Pricing moves stock prices. Witness the gyrations in Apple's stock price when it announces whether or how much it's cutting the price of the last generation of hardware. Even changing pricing on our Norton products can cause Wall Street analysts to make assumptions about our future business.

That's the power of pricing. But too many managers and executives think of pricing as just a finance issue. Increasingly I see business leaders who think pricing is entirely out of their hands; they perceive themselves as helpless in the face of market forces.

When I first joined the Consumer Business Unit at Symantec, the organization didn't fully realize the pricing power that we had—and how we could use pricing as a way of gaining strategic advantage in a very competitive market. Tim Smith helped us change the way pricing is perceived throughout the organization.

We engaged Tim as a consultant to help us take a fresh look at pricing and, critically, our pricing management practices. Given Symantec's global presence and the multitude of channels we work through, pricing decisions involve local, regional and channel-specific sales teams, as well as finance and often a retail partner. At the time, there was no central management of pricing. This led to confusion and sometimes ad-hoc decisions but, worst of all, it meant decisions were often made without the necessary data and insight.

Tim's expertise helped us overhaul our pricing governance, set up a central pricing management team, and create the appropriate organizational structure and focus to advance our pricing practices and management capabilities. His suggestions have enabled our organization to benefit from improved analytics and coordination across markets and channels.

Good pricing governance doesn't mean taking the decisions out of the hands of the regional sales teams. No pricing strategy will work if the sales teams don't understand and support it. However, Tim also helped educate our global sales force so that they understood the pricing strategy, how to make pricing decisions, and the impact of those decisions on our bottom line.

The proof of the value of pricing management is visible right in our bottom line. The increased organizational focus we have placed on pricing management has delivered a 5% increase in profitability.

That's why I can highly recommend Tim's book. I've seen what treating pricing as a strategic issue can do. And although pricing may never make the cover of *US Weekly*, or even the business book best-seller list, I daresay that after reading this book you may start to think of pricing as sexy. (Probably not, but anything's possible.)

Janice D. Chaffin
Group President, Consumer Business Unit
Symantec Corporation

Preface

Pricing Strategy is a comprehensive text on pricing, examining pricing decisions with an aim to maximize a firm's profits through creating and capturing customers. With each price decision opportunity, this book highlights the stakeholder's importance of the decision, the key tradeoffs to consider in selecting between opposing outcomes, and the influences that should guide the decision.

Pricing Strategy directly addresses the major pricing decisions confronting today's executive, providing a comprehensive approach to managing the pressing price decisions. It goes more to the point than an economics text that focuses on industry-level dynamics, a marketing text that mentions price as just one of several levers under management, an accounting text that provides the mechanics of price-to-profit relationships but lacks insight necessary for making price decisions, or a strategy text that deals with industry and competitive dynamics.

Pricing Strategy has been written as a practical guide for making pricing decisions for the general MBA student or working professional. Students concentrating on marketing, economics, finance, strategy, or operations will all find the text approachable. It is designed for use within any competitive industry: business and consumer markets, durable and consumable markets, tangible and intangible markets. As such, working executives will also find *Pricing Strategy* highly beneficial in improving their decision making. Senior executives will value this text for its succinctly defined core concepts and techniques for managing prices. Similarly, specialized pricing practitioners who are primarily charged with managing prices will appreciate this text for its depth in defining models and enabling nuanced analysis.

Readers who want to understand a specific quantitative technique in pricing can use this text as a foundation. To equip readers to potentially compete within the field of pricing, specialized vocabulary is introduced throughout the text as necessary. Numerous case studies, examples, tables, and graphics further communicate the concepts contained within this text.

Pricing as a field spans many disciplines. *Pricing Strategy* leverages the best thinking in marketing, economics, competitive strategy, consumer behavior, and finance to deliver a comprehensive text on pricing. It is written primarily to better communicate well-documented existing knowledge, along with new ideas developed from logical insights, executive discussions, and mathematical proofs.

One of the larger challenges of communicating best practices in pricing is the issue of balancing quantitative skill sets with qualitative concepts. Students require familiarity with specific mathematical concepts and formulas to perform basic tasks in pricing. Yet pricing is not a purely quantitative field. Much of pricing, and the influences to price positioning, price setting, and price management, are conceptual in nature.

To strike the right balance of quantitative instruction, *Pricing Strategy* has been structured to allow latitude in choosing the level of quantitative instruction. The core text in the chapters is written at a level appropriate for any student familiar with basic algebra. For more advanced students, numerous appendices that require little more than an introductory level of calculus have been included.

Pricing is not a static field. New approaches are being developed constantly. It is hoped that this book will provide students of pricing with a solid foundation to build upon over their careers.

Acknowledgments

A book of this magnitude could not have been completed without the support of my family members, friends, and professionals, for which I am deeply grateful.

The development of this text is the result of a long journey that was informed by many outstanding individuals. I would like to draw attention to a few specific individuals who greatly influenced the path that led to writing *Pricing Strategy:* Jeffrey A. Cina of the University of Oregon, who taught me how to conduct research while a graduate student in physical chemistry; Ann L. McGill of the University of Chicago, who introduced me to the complex world of marketing; Puneet Manchanda of the University of Michigan, who introduced me to the value of using quantitative models for analyzing marketing decisions; Harry L. Davis of the University of Chicago, who led me to connect analytical decision to the challenge of organizational leadership; Eric Mitchell, founder of the Professional Pricing Society, for helping me connect the issues of sales and marketing with pricing; Enda O'Coineen of Kilcullen Kapital Partners for demonstrating the successful path of entrepreneurship; and Robert E. Cermak and James T. Berger for encouraging me to undertake this specific entrepreneurial endeavor.

I am very appreciative of the research resources available through DePaul University and extremely grateful to Suzanne L. Fogel, Chair of the DePaul Marketing Department, for providing me the opportunity to develop this text.

This book has also benefited from the contributions of many reviewers. I deeply appreciate the efforts of Michael Roche of South-Western in editing this text. Rebecca Wernis, a graduate of Whitney Young High School in the Chicago Public School system, painstakingly reviewed the math in this text to ensure it would be accessible to any business executive. My thanks go as well to the Fall 2009 Pricing Strategy students at DePaul University who reviewed an early manuscript to ensure clarity and comprehension: Jeffrey Garbaciak, James Henderson, Kevin Knight, Dariusz Nowak, William Salatich, Matthew Sheffer, Cody Smith, and Kevin Spinti. In addition, I am grateful to the panel of reviewers who also helped ensure the text would be useful in a college pricing course: John R. Birge (Booth School of Business, University of Chicago) Mickey Goodman (NYU Stern School of Business), Brett R. Gordon (Columbia University), Praveen K. Kopalle (Tuck School of Business, Dartmouth College), Mikhael Shor (Vanderbilt University), Steven R. Shook (University of Idaho), and Z. John Zhang (The Wharton School).

Finally, I give my extreme gratitude to sculptor Yvette Kaiser Smith, who provided unending support throughout this journey.

About the Author

Tim J. Smith is the managing principal of Wiglaf Pricing and an adjunct professor of marketing and economics at DePaul University.

At Wiglaf Pricing, Smith provides strategic pricing support for entrepreneurial and globally established firms in business and consumer markets. At DePaul University, Smith teaches undergraduate and graduate courses in marketing as well as undergraduate economics. He has presented seminars on pricing to executive audiences throughout the globe.

© Roman Černý (2010)

Smith began his career as a research scientist in quantum mechanics before his interest in transferring technological advances to societal implementations led to pursuits in business strategy. His focus on pricing is a natural culmination of his deep love of math and his orientation to capturing profitable customers.

In addition to *Pricing Strategy*, Smith has authored two other texts in marketing, hundreds of popular business articles, and is the chief editor of the *Wiglaf Journal*.

Smith is a member of the American Marketing Association and the American Physical Society. He has a bachelor's degree in physics and chemistry from Southern Methodist University, a bachelor's degree in mathematics from Southern Methodist University, a doctorate in physical chemistry from the University of Chicago, and a master's degree in business administration with high honors in strategy and marketing from the University of Chicago Graduate School of Business.

Introduction

An executive charged with managing prices must address four fundamental issues: (1) What should the price be? (2) When should discounts be granted and how can discounts be managed? (3) Will the structure of prices generate the highest profits? (4) How will competition and industry dynamics influence pricing decisions? To address these fundamental pricing challenges, we have structured *Pricing Strategy* into four parts: Setting the Price, Managing Price Variances, Establishing Price Structures, and Pricing Strategy.

Part 1: Setting the Price explores quantitative methods for and qualitative influences to price setting. The three most commonly used quantitative methods for determining list prices are exchange value models, economic price optimization, and consumer perception-based pricing. Each of these quantitative approaches to setting prices is founded on a common philosophical belief, that price should reflect value. As such, we explore the conceptual relationship between price and value directly through both qualitative models. Accepting that value is in the mind of the beholder, we then explore the many psychological and behavioral influences to the perception of value.

Part 2: Managing Price Variances examines price-discounting decisions. We treat discounts as a form of price segmentation, historically known as price discrimination. We begin by examining the reasons why a firm would grant a discount once they have already identified an optimal price, followed by an examination of the profit, consumer behavior, and organizational challenges created by discounting. To address these challenges, we discuss industry-leading accepted methods for monitoring and managing discount decisions. One of these methods for managing discount decisions, volume hurdles arising from a profit-sensitivity analysis, was developed earlier en route to revealing economic price optimization.

Part 3: Establishing Price Structures examines six different price structures. There are numerous pricing structures and business executives continue to explore new pricing structures and variants of historic price structures. We have attempted to focus on the most common and effective price structures, though acknowledge that the field is evolving. Each price structure is examined with respect to consumer behavior, profit optimization, economic analysis, and key managerial tradeoffs in selecting a specific price structure.

One of the oldest pricing structures is two-part pricing, where the purchase of one part of the offer enables the purchase of the second part of the offer. Two-part prices are common in utilities, membership structures, nightclubs, and many other industries.

Oftentimes, firms will sell a base product that can be enhanced through the purchase of accessories or add-on modules. In Add-ons, Accessories, and Complementary Products, we examine the interplay in pricing the base product and potential add-on products.

In contrast to marketing base products and enhancements separately, firms can create product versions, incrementally improving the benefits delivered by the product as the product versions improve from good, to better and best. In Versioning, we examine the drivers and limitations to versioning price structures.

Bundling is another approach to enhancing the benefits in an offer. In price bundling, two distinct products are sold simultaneously in a single transaction. Bundling creates profits for the firm that are different from other approaches through the effect bundles have on customer behavior and the optimization of their pricing structure.

A similar approach to pricing can be found in subscriptions, such as magazines and newspapers historically or Software-as-a-Service offers more recently. A key ingredient to proper subscription pricing is an understanding of customer lifetime value.

Alternatively, firms can practice dynamic pricing, of which yield management is one form. Yield management techniques have come to dominate pricing challenges in the airline and hotel industries.

Part 4: Pricing Strategy places pricing challenges in the context of a larger competitive, industry evolution, and legal frameworks.

This book takes an approach of raising decision challenges in pricing and deploying quantitative and qualitative models to inform the decision. As the book progresses, new models are introduced that build upon those presented earlier in the text. In building models for informing pricing decisions, we are acknowledging that flaws are inherent in every model and that there are areas in which decisions can be further improved. This is not to say that the models are useless, but rather that they are inherently incomplete.

In this sense, pricing is like physics. Beginning students of physics learn the Newtonian mechanics of force, mass, and acceleration. Although many strong predictions can be made, machines designed, and advances achieved from such simple seventeenth-century models, Newtonian mechanics began to show its shortcomings as scientists started to look more closely at the universe. As a result, in the twentieth century we discovered the beauty of quantum mechanics and relativity in explaining the laws of motion in greater detail.

Similarly in pricing, simple models can be constructed that guide executives toward better decision making; but like Newtonian mechanics, these simple models only inform decisions up to a point. As decision making improves, some of the simpler models must be relegated to the position of being merely informative as better models are deployed.

A new student of pricing may find it unsettling that quantitative approaches fail to deliver clear and final answers. However, pricing is not an engineering challenge, it is a strategic challenge. At some point, managers must make decisions in the face of uncertainty. The models presented provide guidance to managerial decision making, informing their consequences and potential outcomes of taking one action over another. However, a single quantitative model alone is insufficient for all pricing decisions. As such, we have strived to present a variety of insights and models for pricing, leaving room for managers to pick and choose the model that is most applicable to the decision confronting them at the time. As George E. P. Box stated, "all models are wrong, but some are useful."

PART 1

Setting the Price

Chapter 1

Boundaries of a Good Price

Nash Photos/Photographer's Choice RF/Getty Images

- Who is involved in pricing decisions?
- Why is pricing so important to the health of a firm?
- Can firms influence their pricing power?
- What is the nature of a good price?
- How relevant are marginal costs and consumer surplus in setting a good price?
- How should the comparable alternatives on the market influence the pricing of a product?
- How can exchange value models be used to set prices?
- Stretch Question: How are exchange value models related to market segments?

How should executives price a new product? Should they price the product the same as competing products? Should they price it low to grab market share? Should they price it high to grab greater profits with each individual sale? Perhaps they should take an accounting position and simply add a reasonable markup to the marginal cost of production. If so, what is that reasonable markup?

Pricing questions are perhaps the most vexing decisions facing an executive. Few other strategic decisions will have a greater impact on the profitability of the firm, the demand customers will have for its products, and the latitude that the firm will develop to adjust its competitive position. Pricing questions span organizational boundaries because of their strategic importance, crossing over into marketing, sales, finance, and operations. Each new functional executive contributing to a pricing decision will add a differing perspective that may only complicate the pricing challenge.

To address this challenging strategic decision and manage the competing organizational viewpoints, executives need a rational approach to setting prices. They need an approach to pricing that is grounded in the realities of the market environment, including issues of competition and customer preferences.

When thinking of prices, it is useful to consider price as the value that the firm captures in a mutually beneficial exchange with its customers. The reason for the firm's existence is to produce value for its customers in exchange for a price. All profits derive from delivering value to customers at a price that is greater than the cost of producing that value. Customers gain value when the benefits delivered to them through a product exceed the price that they pay for it.

This exchange is made freely between the firm and its customers. In a free market, customers choose whether or not to purchase a product or service. It is illegal, if not unethical, to coerce customer purchases in free and open markets. Even when customers may not like the price, they ultimately have the choice to decline the exchange in a free market. Hence, prices are the value that the firm captures in a mutually beneficial exchange with its customers.

We begin by demonstrating the impact of pricing and clarifying the challenge of making pricing decisions. We demonstrate the construction of an exchange value model as an initial means to make rational pricing decisions. Exchange value models reveal the boundaries of a good price that a firm should use to market a new product. In developing an exchange value model, we will reveal the importance of using the customer's perspective of value in pricing decisions.

Informing Price Decisions

THE IMPORTANCE OF PRICE

The importance of setting the right price cannot be understated. Pricing directly affects the profits of a firm. Even for nonprofit institutions, pricing decisions affect the resources of the firm and its ability to serve its constituents. For everyone involved, the costs of pricing errors are weighty. Whether the price is too high or too low, pricing errors destroy profits.

When goods and services are priced too high, many customers will refuse to purchase them. Not only will the firm cede market share to its competitors, but it will relegate itself as irrelevant to many potential customers. With few items sold, market traction is forfeited and potential and actual investors sour on expectations of financial returns from the firm. The firm will eventually find itself lowering its prices in an effort to regain market attention, though it may already be too late. Consumer sentiment may turn negative, potentially resulting in public relations challenges and regulatory ramifications.

When goods and services are priced too low, the firm will have forgone an important opportunity to earn profit in proportion to the value it is creating for customers. While prices are often set low to gain volume, firms often discover that the volume is simply not there. Moreover, entering a market with an extremely low price will set incorrect price expectations for the product category. Firms attempting to recover from such a mistake will face a headwind of customer expectations for the products to be priced low. In the worst case scenario, costs are not covered and the firm becomes insolvent.

Repeatedly, the wrong price yields lost revenues, lost profits, lost customers, and ultimately a strategically lost firm. There are numerous examples of firms executing bad pricing decisions. From Motorola's choice to decrease the price of its revolutionary RAZR mobile handset to gain market share to Pilgrim's Pride's failure to increase chicken prices while chicken feed costs were skyrocketing, bad pricing decisions have had disastrous effects. In most cases, not only are profits harmed, leading to potential bankruptcy, but employees are dismissed and customers switch to more competitive offerings. With insufficient profits to provide adequate resources to compete, firms are unable to invest in productivity improvement, much less in developing the next generation of products customers will demand. In the end, lost firms all too often become irrelevant and die.

CROSS FUNCTIONAL

Due to the high importance of pricing, executives will place a huge emphasis on getting pricing decisions right. Yet who should make pricing decisions?

From an organizational viewpoint, pricing decisions are a cross-functional challenge fraught with discord. Finance, sales and marketing, and even operations executives will each be in a position to contribute to pricing decisions. Each of these functional executives will bring valuable and unique vantage points and skill sets from which they can draw information. Unfortunately, functional executives are likely to be biased by the incentives by which their performance is measured.

Finance executives will likely be highly influenced by their accounting orientation in addressing pricing decisions. From an informational perspective, they should have a firm understanding of the costs to produce. With a strong grasp of break-even analysis and cost-plus pricing, finance executives tend to have a heightened understanding of the relationship between higher prices and higher profits, and in turn, higher shareholder value. Given their training and vantage point, finance executives frequently argue for higher prices and higher contribution margins. However, they are rarely in the best position to evaluate whether customers are willing to pay higher prices.

In contrast, the pricing decisions of sales and marketing executives are likely to be highly influenced by their customer orientation. From an informational perspective, sales and marketing executives are likely to be well informed about market share, competitive actions, and customer preferences. Given their training and experience in marketing, they are likely to understand both the potential and the limitations that a firm has in shaping customer preferences and willingness to pay. Sales and marketing executives are often rewarded based on their ability to take market share, meet revenue targets, or capture specific customers. Given this incentive bias, sales and marketing executives are unfortunately often encouraged to lower prices to grab customers. In the process, they may be forgoing opportunities to capture higher profits.

Even operations executives can contribute meaningfully to pricing decisions. Issues related to economies of scale, scope, and learning are well within their scope of responsibility and will influence pricing decisions. Like other functional executives, operations executives make decisions influenced by their incentives and performance measurements. In this case, performance metrics tied to average cost efficiencies may encourage operations executives to seek lower prices to drive up volume and improve capacity utilization.

In making pricing decisions, executives must take advantage of the benefits of the informational resources and skill set of each functional executive while countering the bias that each brings to pricing decisions. The needs for unit volume and market share must be tempered by the need for contribution margins, and information must be collected across functional boundaries to balance these needs. To make the right decision, many firms make pricing a chief-executive-level concern due to their breadth of responsibility. To aid their decision, many chief executives have developed a new organizational capability: the pricing professional.

Pricing professionals must bring a breadth of insight and skills to pricing decisions. They understand how customers perceive offerings and their willingness to pay for them. They also have a firm grip on issues related to marginal productions costs as well as the fixed incremental costs related to serving specific markets. From a marketing perspective, they will have a strong understanding of competitive actions, market share, and industry dynamics. Often, they have a deep understanding of economics and are able to both measure the elasticity of demand and understand the relationships among price changes, volume changes, and profit improvements. By nature and need, pricing professionals mix hard quantitative analytical skills with softer qualitative skills to inform pricing decisions meaningfully and enable action.

Pricing professionals often come from a finance, marketing, economics, or mathematical science background. Functionally, they typically report to either marketing or finance, depending on the nature of the pricing challenges they must address daily. For strategic pricing decisions, it is increasingly common for pricing professionals to report to the chief executive directly.

IMPACTING PROFITS

To demonstrate the importance of price, consider the standard profit equation of a firm

$$\pi = Q \cdot (P - V) - F \quad \text{Eq. 1.1}$$

where π is used to denote profit, Q denotes quantity sold, P denotes price, V denotes variable costs, and F denotes fixed costs.

To make accurate pricing decisions, we will consistently consider the variable costs to be the true marginal costs to produce related to the decision at hand. Many times, when firms calculate variable costs, they actually calculate average unit costs. Average unit costs are not variable costs because they include allocated overhead and other forms of fixed costs in their calculation. As such, average unit costs will decrease if volumes increase, and increase if volumes decrease. True marginal costs are the costs to produce one more unit of output and are therefore much lower than average unit costs in almost all circumstances. While many executives will approximate marginal costs as average unit costs, the result is an overly conservative understanding of the true boundaries of profitable prices potentially leading to lost profit opportunities.

In the profit equation of the firm (Eq. 1.1), all fixed costs should be captured in the term F. Fixed costs include many forms of overhead such as infrastructure (plant and equipment, allocated management, and in some situations, even line staff when labor costs cannot be truly varied in proportion to output).

Q, representing quantity or volume sold in Equation 1.1, can be measured in the millions for firms like Taiwan Semiconductor Manufacturing Company (TSMC) in producing silicon chips or McDonald's in producing hamburgers, or in the single digits for specialized industrial products. Similarly, P, standing for price in Equation 1.1, can be measured in fractions of a unit of currency or in the millions.[1]

If an executive can apply pressure to improve the profitability of the firm by adjusting any of the variables in the profit equation Equation 1.1 (variable costs, fixed costs, quantity sold, or price), which has the largest impact? To answer this question, let us conduct a simple quantitative analysis.

Suppose that a firm operates under the following conditions: Variable costs are $10 for each unit of production and fixed costs are $1 million per quarter. Currently, prices average $25 per unit and volumes are 80,000 units per quarter. Under these conditions, the firm earns $200,000 in profit per quarter. See Exhibit 1-1.

We can contrast this baseline performance with the outcome achieved by improving any one of the profit levers by 1 percent and holding all else constant. Investing in higher productivity to reduce variable costs by 1 percent will improve profits by a mere 4 percent. Likewise, reducing overhead or otherwise cutting fixed costs by 1 percent would

Exhibit 1-1 Profit Levers

		Last Quarter	1% Improvement for Next Quarter...			
			in Variable Cost	in Fixed Cost	in Volume	in Price
Price	P	$25.00				$ 25.25
Volume	Q	80,000			80800	
Variable Cost	V	$10.00	$ 9.90			
Fixed Cost	F	$1,000,000.00		$ 990,000.00		
Profitability	π	$200,000.00	$208,000.00	$210,000.00	$212,000.00	$ 220,000.00
Change in Profitability			$ 8,000.00	$10,000.00	$12,000.00	$20,000.00
% Profit Improvement			4%	5%	6%	10%

yield 5 percent higher profits. If the firm were to invest in better marketing to drive volumes up by 1 percent, it would still improve profits by only 6 percent. In contrast, increasing prices by 1 percent, either through changes in list prices or reductions in discounts, improves profits by a whopping 10 percent.

In comparison to any other variable under management, price has a larger and more immediate impact on profit than all other levers. The results of this hypothetical firm are not unique. Researchers have examined the average profit equation of 1,200 large publicly traded firms from around the globe and have likewise demonstrated that price changes have a larger impact on profit than any other variable under management control.[2]

However, the impact of price on the firm is a double-edged sword. Just as a small improvement in price delivers a large increase in profits, a small degradation in price is highly damaging to profits. As price has such a significant impact on profits, and because it directly influences customer behavior, it deserves all if not more of the executive attention that it receives.

INFLUENCING PRICE CAPTURE

As the executive-level attention given to pricing indicates and the example profit lever analysis suggests, getting the price right has a significant impact on the firm. Yet, these observations only underscore the challenge. What is the right price?

Recalling that price is the value that the firm captures in a mutually beneficial exchange with its customers, we discover that the right price is often not a single number, but rather a range of potential points that benefits both the customer and the firm. While some points are more beneficial to the firm and others are more beneficial to its customers, any point within this range will mutually benefit both the firm and its customers. Moreover, the price that a firm gets in the exchange is somewhat under its own influence.

For example, consider a simple negotiation exercise concerning Kenyan Coffee that I have regularly conducted at DePaul University with both undergraduate and graduate students with similar results. Suppose the coffee roaster can deliver Kenyan Coffee at a marginal cost of $3.20 per pound. Furthermore, suppose a retailer can resell the Kenyan Coffee and earn a profit so long as he or she buys it for less than $7.50 per pound. Any price agreed upon by the sellers and buyers between $3.20 and $7.50 leaves both parties better off and is therefore a good price. While lower prices favor the retailer at the expense of the roaster, higher prices favor the roaster at the expense of the retailer. However, any price within this range delivers a mutually beneficial exchange.

To arrive at the transaction price, sellers and buyers are asked to negotiate an agreement. In the basic experimental setup, all buyers are directed to purchase Kenyan Coffee for less than $7.50. All sellers are directed to sell Kenyan Coffee for more than $3.20, but half of the students are told some key selling points regarding Kenyan Coffee and the other

Exhibit 1-2 Kenyan Coffee Negotiation

	Brand Name	Reservation Price	Key Selling Points	Average Transaction Price
All Buyers	Yes	$7.50	No	
Price Sellers	Yes	$3.20	No	$3.82
Quality Sellers	Yes	$3.20	Yes	$5.33

Kenyan Coffee KSPs (Key Selling Points)

$7.50/lb

Kenyan coffee is among the best, if not the best, coffee grown on the planet.

Kenya, the birthplace of coffee beans, is the East African powerhouse of the coffee world. Their research and development is unparalleled. Their quality control is meticulous. Many thousands of small farmers are highly educated, and rewarded, in their agricultural practice for top level coffee.

Zone of Potential Agreement

In general, Kenyan coffee is a bright coffee that lights up the palate from front to back. A great Kenyan coffee is complex: interesting fruit (berry, citrus) flavors; sometimes alternating with spice; cherished winey flavor.

$3.20/lb

half are not. Thus, there is a Zone of Potential Agreements, or ZOPA in the negotiations literature, between $3.20 and $7.50. See Exhibit 1-2.

Invariably, sellers who have key selling points and discuss them during the negotiation strike a higher price than those who don't. In a typical experimental run, the average selling price of sellers without key selling points was $3.82, while that of sellers with key selling points was $5.33. The key selling points alone enabled sellers to achieve a 40 percent higher transaction price on average in that experimental run. Clearly, price is a profit lever that can be influenced. Moreover, it is influenced by information. Sellers who are informed of the value of their products and can communicate it to their customers are able to achieve higher transaction prices than those who are not.

Further investigations into the dynamics of these types of negotiations have demonstrated that the starting price greatly affects the negotiated price. Sellers who initiate the negotiation at a higher price routinely end up at a higher settlement price. Likewise, sellers who initiate the negotiation at a lower price routinely end up at a lower settlement price.

From this more detailed investigation, we learn that negotiations favor aggressive opening bids. Initiating the negotiation at a more favorable price and then slowly ceding price concessions enables the negotiator to discover the boundary price of their negotiating counterpart and thus settle upon a price that is more favorable.

In yet a third investigation, Kenyan Coffee buyers and sellers were told the average selling price of Colombian Coffee. This time, negotiated Kenyan Coffee prices almost always converged to a price point similar to that of stated Colombian Coffee. Reference prices greatly influence transaction prices.

In their entirety, the Kenyan Coffee experiments reveal three very strong prescriptions for achieving good prices. One, sellers must be well informed of and aggressively communicate the value of their products if they hope to achieve a better price. Two, sellers must price aggressively and grant discounts from these prices reluctantly. And three, reference prices greatly influence transaction prices.

THE ART AND SCIENCE OF PRICING

Clearly, pricing is a quantitative field with a direct impact on profitability. However, as the negotiation experiments reveal, pricing is equally a qualitative field where the actions of the firm affect the price that they can achieve. Good pricing requires a tight connection between quantitative and qualitative insights.

The **science of pricing** refers to the act of gathering information, conducting quantitative analysis, and revealing an accurate understanding of the range of prices likely to yield positive results. Pricing data, like any other set of information that influences executive decisions, is rarely perfectly clear. Not only will there be uncertainties in the underlying data, but the appropriate price structure, price point, and price discount will vary over time, geography, and customer situation. The time and budget required to remove all uncertainty is beyond the patience and resources of almost every firm. Hence, prices must be set with some uncertainty. Despite the uncertainty, quantitative approaches can be used to improve the pricing decision, prevent grievous errors, and uncover new opportunities.

As the negotiation experiments demonstrate, the firm can take actions to influence its pricing power in ways that may be difficult to analyze using quantitative methods. These actions can either be value destroying (such as failing to communicate the value of the offering) or value creating (such as uncovering new applications for the offering that improves its value to customers).

It is important to remember that customers are not a monolithic group to consider when setting pricing policy. Some customers will value the product more than others. Consequently, the firm can price its products higher for some customers than others. Understanding variations in customer demands uncovers pricing opportunities.

The **art of pricing** refers to the ability to influence consumer price acceptance, adapt pricing structures to shift the competitive playing field, and align pricing strategy to the competitive strategy, marketing strategy, and industrial policy. It requires an understanding of consumer behavior and the influence of features embedded within the product, the perception of value, the expectations of customers, and the price structure itself. It also requires that pricing strategy support the firm's marketing strategy in light of the overall competitive and industrial environment of the market.

By taking a more creative approach, firms are better able to price in proportion to the value that customers perceive. Doing so will combine both quantitative and qualitative approaches. In many cases, quantitative approaches will be found to be highly informative but lacking in their ability to reveal nuances of customer behavior and therefore opportunities to improve pricing. Qualitative insights enable executives to fill these gaps. In doing so, executives are able to better align pricing strategy with other strategic decisions. Hence, pricing is both an art and a science.

Exchange Value Models

Accepting that the right price lies within some range shifts the challenge of pricing to identifying the boundaries of a good price. **Exchange value models** quantify the price boundaries.[3] Knowing the boundaries of a good price narrows pricing discussions to a reasonable range of potential price points.

Using exchange value models to manage pricing decisions shifts pricing challenges from the position of managing internal corporate politics or copying historic practices that may have little bearing on the challenge at hand, to one of focusing on the value created and the firm's ability to capture its fair share of that value.

Two sets of boundaries are uncovered from exchange value models. The extreme boundaries define the range of acceptable prices outside of which no rational buyer or seller would ever transact. The narrower boundaries which lie within these extremes define the range of prices that are most likely to encourage customer transactions and leave the firm in the most favorable position. While buyers and sellers will sometimes transact outside these narrower boundaries, it is not usually in their best interest to do so.

To illustrate the boundaries of a good price, we will examine the release of the Cypher drug eluting stent by Cordis, a Johnson & Johnson Company, in April 2003.[4] Stents are used to reopen clogged arteries leading to the heart after plaque has narrowed the passage and restricted blood flow. Prior to its release, the best alternative was a standard metallic stent made by a number of competitors. In mechanical construction, the Cypher drug eluting stent was similar. In laboratory tests, the addition of a pharmaceutical formulary coating the standard metallic stent was demonstrated to improve the patient's body's ability to accept the stent within the artery. With the unique addition of a patented formulary that was approved by the U.S. Food and Drug Administration (FDA), Cypher was a revolutionary new product when launched. No other product of its kind had been marketed. As such, Cordis executives could not simply copy a competitor's practices in pricing it. Rather, pricing would be a particularly daunting challenge for these executives.

To price a revolutionary product like Cypher, executives can construct an exchange value model. Exchange value models inform executives of the relative value that their product delivers to customers and therefore enables executives to price in proportion to its perceived value. For revolutionary products, exchange value models are a commonly used best-practice approach to identifying launch prices. Once an exchange value model has been used to set prices, it can then be repurposed as a sales tool to support the communication of value. As such, exchange value models are an important quantitative tool for setting prices and influencing price acceptance.

EXTREME BOUNDARIES

At the extremes, the price should lie between the marginal cost to produce and the full consumer utility. Any transaction outside these extremes would leave the seller or buyer worse off after the transaction than before, and therefore it cannot be expected to occur between rational buyers and sellers.

Marginal Costs Define the Extreme Lower Boundary

Marginal costs constitute the seller's bottom line. Any price below marginal costs leaves the seller worse off than it would have been without the transaction. Any price above it leaves the seller better off. At times, sellers may choose to price very near marginal costs for tactical price purposes, but in general, sellers will seek to profit from their transactions. Failure to profit from transactions removes any motivation to participate in the trade; hence executives cannot be expected to price at this level.

Estimates vary widely on the marginal cost to produce Cypher and it is difficult to pierce the corporate veil to identify the true marginal costs. Some reports indicate that standard metal stents had an average unit cost near $150 at the time of launching Cypher. Coating a stent with pharmaceuticals is not an expensive challenge, and manufacturing the pharmaceuticals should add only a few dollars per stent. That said, some estimates indicate that Cypher had a fully loaded average unit cost of $375 at the time of its launch. While fully loaded average unit costs are likely to be much higher than marginal costs, we will accept this figure as a gross approximation of the true marginal costs of production for the sake of demonstrating an exchange value model.

Regardless of how low the true marginal costs are, Cordis should not price Cypher anywhere near this level. It would not be a fair exchange to expect Cordis to price the drug eluting stent near marginal cost. Developing Cypher required a tremendous amount of research and development—a risky investment made with the expectation of lofty rewards.

Not only should the firm desire prices to cover the investment costs of developing Cypher, but it should also seek to gain profits, which are necessary not only to reward investors, but also to invest in further research and development leading to the creation of new products that will be valued by consumers in the future. Furthermore, even after being first to market with a drug eluting stent, Cordis faces a business risk that other research and development efforts will develop new solutions for coronary heart disease long before the patent on Cypher has expired. Rather than using marginal costs as a guide to making pricing decisions, therefore, the executives of Cypher are better off using them as a bright line below which prices should not fall.

Marginal costs are simply a lower boundary on prices. They provide little guidance to what the price should be, outside of stating that the price should not be below this level. Importantly, internal cost accounting considerations of marginal costs fail to incorporate the value that the product delivers to customers. Without connecting the price to the value that the product delivers, sellers have little insight into their pricing potential. Failing to understand value from the customer's perspective may tempt executives to price very high to recover sunk costs or opportunistically profit from uninformed customers, yet doing so will quickly make the firm irrelevant to the market as customers refuse to purchase. Or, equally pernicious and far more prevalent, the failure to understand the customer's perspective of value leaves the seller to cleave to its marginal costs and price a new product too low, denying the firm its well-deserved reward for the hard work that it takes to develop a new product and deliver its value to customers. As we saw in the negotiation experiment, marginal costs are simply one of two extreme boundaries.

Consumer Utility Defines the Extreme Upper Boundary

If marginal costs are the seller's bottom line, customer utility is the buyer's bottom line. The **customer utility** is the value a customer gains from having the product. All customers would be worse off after a transaction if they paid more for the product than they gained in utility, and they would be better off if they paid less for the product than they gained in utility. The value that buyers place on a product is the utility that they derive from the product. The **consumer surplus** is the difference between the overall customer utility and the transaction price. So long as the consumer surplus is positive, customers will value the product.

Customers gain utility from a product directly from the benefits that the product delivers. These benefits have been categorized into four fundamental types. **Form** utility derives directly from the intrinsic properties of the product itself, such as the value that customers place on extending their lives with a stent, the enjoyment that customers experience when drinking a tasty beverage, or the production value of a turbine to an electricity merchant generator. **Place** utility derives from the ability to acquire the product in a desired location, such as having the stent available at a nearby hospital, drinking the beverage at a local cafe, or receiving the turbine at the merchant generator's power plant. **Time** utility derives from the ability to access the product at a convenient moment, such as receiving the stent when coronary heart disease has been detected, drinking the beverage when thirsty, or getting the turbine at the right time in the construction process of the merchant generator's power plant. **Ownership** utility is gained from possessing the *rights* to the value of the product even if the possession is never actually taken, such as the value of insurance coverage that would pay for the implant of the stent when and if needed, the value of holding a beverage which can either be drunk or resold, or the value of holding rights to a turbine to be delivered in the future.

While customers derive utility from an improved stent from all four fundamental types, in pricing Cypher, Cordis should focus on the form utility. The most significant value created in producing Cypher is that which is most closely related to the value that customers gain in extending their lives. Yet, what is the value of extending life?

Life is exactly what is at stake with coronary heart disease. Coronary heart disease increases the strain on the heart and deprives the heart of the oxygen and blood flow that it needs to function properly. Without corrective action, patients suffering from coronary heart disease will have a much reduced life expectancy, an increased likelihood of a heart attack, and potentially sudden death.

Economists have attempted to quantify the value of a life. In a somewhat accepted although ethically questionable practice, economists often value a life as the present value of the future lifetime earnings. Not only does this approach fail to adequately consider potential career changes during a person's lifetime, but more importantly, it is a woefully inaccurate calculation of the value that individuals place on their lives. It doesn't begin to capture the value that people attach to spending more time with their spouse, seeing their children and grandchildren mature, attending the weddings and baby showers of loved ones, or being able to accomplish one more lifetime goal. Put in these terms, we quickly understand why many philosophers will argue that all life is equally valuable and perhaps immeasurable.

As with many decisions in pricing, we must accept our inability to perfectly quantify everything and rather work with the best estimates and commonly accepted practices that we have. As such, let us estimate the value that people place on their lives as the present value of future earnings. In addition, while the wages and duration of future productivity vary between individuals, let us estimate that the present value of the lifetime earnings of a coronary heart disease patient is $500,000 on average.

No doubt, many readers will argue that that is a ridiculously low value for a person's life. However, if the customer utility of a stent is near $500,000, should Cordis launch Cypher near this level? Quickly we realize that such a price would be absurd. If Cordis did price Cypher anywhere near this level, most customers would find it unattainable. Moreover, customer sentiment would likely sour on Cordis, leading to retaliation, claims of unfair pricing practices, and protests that Cordis was charging too much or that Cordis was only serving the rich elite. In such an environment, governments might force Cordis to forgo its patents and allow other firms to produce copycat products. Clearly, pricing near the customer's utility is not a very informed or advisable approach.

Customer utility is simply an upper boundary on prices. It provides little guidance to what the price should be outside of stating that the price should be below this level. Customer utility is the mirror image of marginal costs. Just as firms should avoid pricing near marginal costs, customers should avoid accepting prices near customer utility. As we saw with the negotiation experiment, customer utility is simply the second of two extreme boundaries.

Marginal Costs and Customer Utility Are the Extremes

At this point, we have examined two of the most discussed issues related to pricing in any introductory economics textbook. What they reveal is that marginal costs are the seller's bottom line (and hence the lower extreme boundary on the potential price), and that customer utility is the buyer's bottom line (and hence the upper extreme boundary on the potential price). Neither reveals the right price by itself, but combined, they reveal the hard boundaries of potential price one might, in one's wildest dreams, imagine for launching Cypher.

Unfortunately, the range of prices between these boundaries is quite wide. Conservatively estimating marginal costs at $375 and customer utility at $500,000 leaves a range of potential prices that is far too wide for any meaningful decision making. The two extreme boundaries are separated by more than a factor of 1,000. Even for physicists, stating that some physical value lies somewhere within a factor of 1,000 is of little use in all but the most advanced astronomy or particle physics research questions. From these boundaries,

Cordis executives would be unsure if the launch price of Cypher should be $400, $4,000, $40,000, or $400,000.

Executives need a tighter set of boundaries than those provided by marginal costs and customer utility for pricing decisions. Even reducing the dispersion of potential prices to a single factor of 10 would be far more useful than that developed by considering the extreme boundaries alone. For a revolutionary product, executives may accept reluctantly a somewhat broad range of a factor of 10 but will give no credence to a method that leaves three orders of magnitude in uncertainty. For more evolutionary products, they are likely to demand pricing guidance that narrows the range to within a few percentage points.

NARROWER BOUNDARIES

Executives looking for guidance in pricing decisions clearly need a narrower and more relevant set of boundaries than those identified by considering marginal costs and customer utility. To identify these boundaries, we need to think strategically about prices.

As the discussion on customer utility reveals, products are valued because they enable a customer to do something. Customers value products because they enable them to accomplish a goal. Prior to the launch of a new product, customers have usually found alternative ways to accomplish the same or similar goals. No product enters a complete vacuum. Life doesn't start with the introduction of a new product, but it may get better. After the launch of a new product, customers can accomplish their goals easier.

Rather than painstakingly quantifying the full and accurate value of accomplishing a goal, the more relevant question is, What is the value of accomplishing that goal in the presence of the new product compared to its absence? That is, what are the alternative means to accomplishing a goal? What is the price of these alternatives? How much more value is created by accomplishing that goal with the new product? What other goals can be accomplished with the new product that were difficult to accomplish before?

Strategically, prices should reflect the value to customers of accomplishing their goals in comparison to alternative means. Higher prices reflect the ability of a product to fulfill a need better than the alternatives. Lower prices reflect the ability of a product to fulfill a subset of the needs as well as the alternatives. This is the nature of strategic pricing: to price in proportion to the value delivered in light of the comparable alternatives.

The narrower price boundaries are defined by the comparable alternatives and differential value.

Comparable Alternatives

Comparable alternatives are solutions that customers may have to accomplish the same or a similar set of goals. They may be directly **competitive offers** or indirect **substitute** solutions to the challenges facing customers. Competing alternatives can usually be identified within the marketplace and will have an existing transaction price. As such, they can inform the pricing decision.

For Cordis, the nearest comparable offer to the Cypher drug eluting stent was the standard metal stent. The standard metal stent was not a perfect solution to coronary heart disease. Roughly 25 percent of the patients who received the standard metal stent suffered from the complication of restenosis, or reclogging of the artery. Clinical trials demonstrated that Cypher reduced the probability of restenosis to around 5 percent. Hence, the Cypher drug eluting stent was a superior alternative to the existing products on the market at the time of its release.

Comparable alternatives are sometimes more challenging to identify, but they will always exist. For revolutionary products, the comparable alternative is usually a substitute offer. For instance, prior to the introduction of the Internet in the 1990s, there were postal services, billboards, telephone books, telephones, newspapers, magazines, radio, and television. Prior to the introduction of the desktop computer in the 1980s, there were typewriters, calculators, and cellulose slides. And, prior to the railroad of the 1800s, people walked, rode horses, and travelled in stagecoaches.

There are more distant comparable alternatives to Cypher. Before the development of the metal stent, patients suffering from coronary heart disease would often be treated with cardiac bypass surgery. Cardiac bypass surgery is only one of the substitute solutions on the market. Other substitute solutions might include pharmaceuticals, bed rest, and the directive to change one's eating habits and exercise regimens.

In formulating pricing guidance, it is best to use the most closely comparable offer on the market. Customers are more likely to evaluate their willingness to pay in relationship with a closely comparable solution than they are with some distant alternative. As such, executives should use the closest competing or substitute solution when identifying potential price points.

At the time of launching Cypher, the standard metal stent was the most common, effective, and cost-efficient approach to addressing coronary heart disease. Therefore, the standard metal stent will be the basis for creating our narrower price boundaries. The standard metal stent is clearly an inferior alternative to Cypher because it is associated with a higher rate of restenosis.

Inferior alternatives are any competing alternatives that deliver similar benefits to the one under consideration with less overall consumer utility. Inferior alternatives define the narrow lower bound for pricing decisions.

This narrow lower boundary is a soft lower boundary. In general, executives should price products higher than their next nearest inferior alternative because their new product will deliver more value. In some cases, executives may price below this boundary if they expect to tap into a new market that was inaccessible with existing offers at their current prices. When they do so, they must still price above the hard lower boundary set by marginal costs. In general, though, pricing below an inferior alternative implies the firm is forgoing some profit potential.

Cordis produced a standard metal stent priced at roughly $1,050 prior to its launch of Cypher.[5] Using this data point to guide a pricing decision and the fact that the Cypher drug eluting stent is superior to a standard metal stent implies that Cypher should be priced at or above this level. But how much higher? To determine how much higher to price Cypher than the standard metal stent, we need to determine the value of its superiority.

Differential Value

Differential value is the change in customer utility that a product delivers in comparison to the alternative. If the new product is superior to its comparable alternatives, the differential value is positive. If the new product is inferior to its comparable alternatives, the differential value is negative.

The economic **exchange value** of a product is the price of the nearest comparable alternative adjusted for the differential value of the product. (Eq. 1.2) It is the price that customers would pay for its nearest comparable offer plus the value of the increased (or decreased) benefits of the improved (or degraded) new product.

$$\text{Exchange Value} = \text{Price of Comparable Alternative} + \text{Differential Value} \quad \text{Eq. 1.2}$$

For a given product, rational customers should be willing to pay any price up to that determined by the exchange value. Hence, the exchange value is the upper narrow boundary on price for products superior to their nearest comparable alternative.

A new product priced at the exchange value would, on average, leave customers indifferent between the new product and the nearest comparable alternative. Some customers may value the new product more and thus be willing to pay more, while others will value it less. Thus, the exchange value is a soft upper bound on the narrower range of potential prices. Executives may price higher than the exchange value but usually find it more beneficial to price slightly lower. Any price below the exchange value will, on average, leave customers better off with the new product than they would be with its comparable alternatives, and definitely better off than they would be without the product at all, and therefore would be a good price.

To quantify the differential value, we must create a model. As with any model developed within the timescale of human existence, it will be incomplete. Yet the model will provide executives with better quality information than they would achieve in its absence, and therefore it will be highly useful for providing pricing guidance.

To construct a model of the differential value of a new product to its comparable alternative, executives should attempt to quantify the value of the change in benefits. One of the more useful approaches is to conduct an "as is" and "to be" description of the situation. The "as is" description elucidates the current means that a customer will use to achieve a goal with the current comparable alternatives, the value of that approach, and its shortcomings. The "to be" description elucidates the future means that a customer will use to achieve a goal with the new product, the value of that approach, and its shortcomings.

The specific quantitative model that will describe the benefits will change depending on the nature of the benefits. In creating the model, pricing professionals will demonstrate some artistic license in their quantitative analysis. No single model captures the value of every type of benefit. Time savings, labor savings, asset utilization improvements, revenue capture improvements, risk reductions, enjoyment improvements, health improvements, and many other types of benefits can be quantitatively modeled to some degree. The best quantitative model that describes the value of the benefits and the change in value will depend upon the nature of the pricing challenge at hand.[6]

Cypher clearly delivers more benefits than standard metal stents to cardiac care patients; therefore, we should expect the differential value to be positive. In comparison to the standard metal stent, the major increase in benefits comes from the reduction in the rate of restenosis. As a starting point for providing pricing guidance, we will model the differential value created by reducing the rate of restenosis.

Stents are not used in isolation but rather as a component of a larger procedure. To implant a stent and relieve some of the challenges created by coronary heart disease, patients must undergo surgery. The price of the operation, including the hospital stay, operating room costs, doctors, nurses, postsurgery hospital monitoring, and other components can be estimated at $12,000.[7]

Of the total operation price, the standard metal stent is only a $1,050 component. If a procedure fails 25 percent of the time when a standard metal stent is implanted, we can expect that the cost of failure to be equal to, if not greater than, the cost of the original stent implantation. When restenosis occurs, doctors must address the issue with pharmaceuticals, angioplasty, a second implant, and perhaps even cardiac bypass surgery. We can use these insights to estimate the differential value of a drug eluting stent such as Cypher.

To construct a model of the differential value, let us first calculate the expected total costs of using a standard metal stent using a probability tree. According to the data collected, we know that patients undergoing a metal stent implantation must pay the initial $12,000 surgery price 100 percent of the time; 25 percent of the time, we believe they must pay a similar $12,000 price to rectify the challenge of restenosis; and 75 percent of the time, no further action is required and the patients can return to their normal life. Using these insights, we can calculate the expected total cost of using a standard metal stent to be $15,000. See Exhibit 1-3.

Exhibit 1-3 Expected Total Costs for Standard Metal Stent Implantation

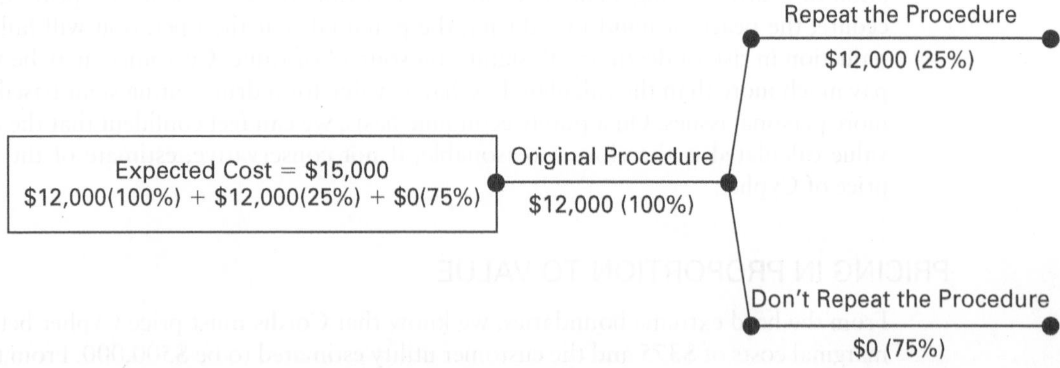

$$\begin{aligned}\text{Expected Costs} &= \text{Cost of Original Procedure} \times \text{Frequency}\\ &\quad + \text{Cost of Repeat Procedure} \times \text{Frequency}\\ &\quad + \text{Cost of Not Repeating Procedure} \times \text{Frequency}\end{aligned}$$

$$\text{Expected Costs} = (\$12{,}000)(100\%) + (\$12{,}000)(25\%) + (\$0)(75\%)$$

To calculate the differential value of Cypher in comparison to a standard metal stent, we can repeat the calculation after adjusting for the change in the rate of restenosis using the price of the stent as an unknown while holding the expected total cost constant. In this case, the total expected cost is still $15,000. We use the same total expected cost because we are attempting to identify the price of Cypher that will leave customers indifferent between the new product and its nearest comparable alternative. We have identified the price of a single surgical implant procedure with a standard metal stent at $12,000, of which the standard metal stent constitutes $1,050. Thus, the cost of the procedure not including the choice of stent is $10,950 ($10,950 = $12,000 − $1,050. Because we don't know the potential price of the drug eluting stent, let this be the unknown that we are trying to solve for and denote it with *X* in Exhibit 1-4.

After a little algebra, the probability tree analysis reveals the exchange value of the drug eluting stent to be $3,340. If the exchange value is $3,340 and the comparable alternative is priced at $1,050, we can calculate the differential value to be $2,290 ($2,290 = $3,340 − $1,050).

Exhibit 1-4 Exchange Value for Drug Eluting Stent

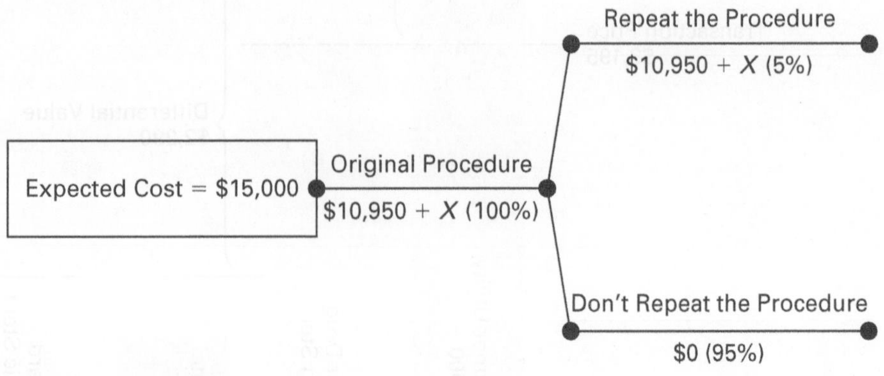

$$\begin{aligned}\text{Expected Cost} &= \$15{,}000\\ &= (\$10{,}950 + X)(100\%) + (\$10{,}950 + X)(5\%) + (\$0)(95\%)\end{aligned}$$

This model does not include many of the other sources of value delivered by the creation of a drug eluting stent. The value of lost time to the patient in repeating the procedure, the peace of mind in reducing the potential that the operation will fail, and the reduction in risk of death are all significant sources of value. Customers may be willing to pay much more than the calculated exchange value for a drug eluting stent based on these more personal issues. On a purely economic basis, we can feel confident that the exchange value calculated is therefore a reasonable, if not conservative, estimate of the potential price of Cypher.

PRICING IN PROPORTION TO VALUE

From the hard extreme boundaries, we know that Cordis must price Cypher between the marginal costs of $375 and the customer utility estimated to be $500,000. From the softer narrow boundaries, we suspect that Cordis should price Cypher higher than its nearest comparable alternative at $1,050 because it will deliver more value. From a simple exchange value model, we suspect that any price below $3,340 should be appealing. See Exhibit 1-5.

By strategically considering comparable alternatives and their differential value to calculate the exchange value, we have reduced our uncertainty in pricing from a factor greater than 1,000 to something closer to 3. Clearly, exchange value models grounded in considerations of comparable alternatives and differential value are far more useful for providing pricing guidance than simple considerations of marginal costs or customer utility. In fact, for many pricing decisions, marginal costs and customer utility have relatively little use in setting prices. Identifying competing products and substitutes and understanding why customers will judge them to be inferior or superior is a far more accurate approach to pricing.

Exhibit 1-5 Price Boundaries for Superior Goods: Cypher

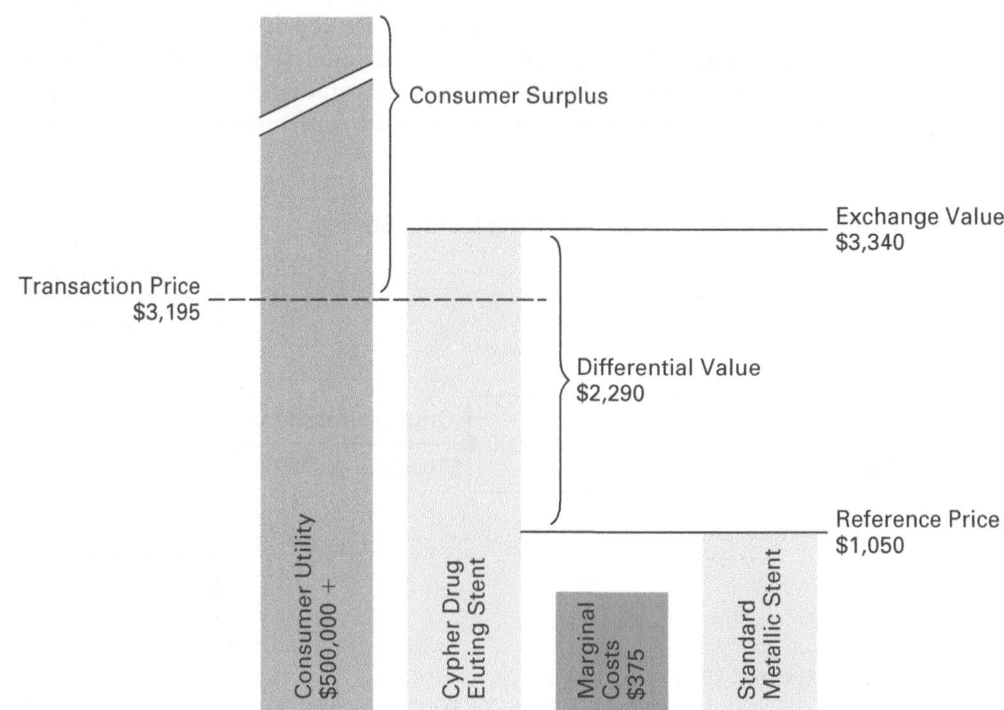

At what price did Cordis executives release Cypher? As a compromise to the needs of insurers and government bodies and the needs of the firm, Cypher was released with a list price of $3,195.[8]

At $3,195, Cypher was priced much higher than its marginal costs and much lower than the consumer utility delivered. Likewise, $3,195 is higher than Cypher's nearest comparable inferior alternative and lower than its exchange value.

Priced at $3,195, Cypher was roughly three times the price of its competitors. Did customers balk at this new price? Not at all. In the nine months after its release, the Cypher stent raised Cordis's market share from less than 10 percent to more than 60 percent in the U.S. market.[9,10]

Financially, Cypher was a runaway success for Cordis, earning the firm billions of dollars. Clearly, pricing anywhere near marginal costs would have forfeited a tremendous profit opportunity, reducing the required income to continue developing blockbuster innovations. At the opposite boundary, researchers have examined the pricing decisions of highly successful entrepreneurs and found they tend to price as near to the exchange value as possible, much as the executives of Cordis did with Cypher.[11]

The release price of Cypher represents an acceptable compromise of the needs of Cordis, insurance companies, and governmental bodies. At this price, the circle of stakeholders has been improved. Investors are rewarded for their risk taking. Employees are rewarded for contributing the talents and initiative to developing new solutions to customer needs by continued employment and potentially bonuses. Finally, not only do customers have a slightly more cost-effective treatment of coronary heart disease, but patients can be expected to enjoy longer, healthier lives.

Setting Prices

For revolutionary products like Cypher, exchange value models have proven to be highly cost-effective and time-efficient means of determining the boundaries of a good price. Executives are plagued with a dearth of information and customers lack the insight necessary to make informed comments about pricing decisions for revolutionary products. As such, exchange value calculators create clarity in an otherwise informational abyss. The form of the exchange value model will change depending on the benefits delivered by the product, yet the overall approach of identifying comparable alternatives, understanding the differences in benefits, and calculating the differential value can be repeated for almost any pricing challenge.

For more evolutionary products or even mature commodity products, exchange value models fail to provide a sufficiently narrow range of prices for decision making. With these types of products, research-based techniques that more directly measure customer preferences and other economic factors are required.

In all cases, the range of a good price is bound at the extremes between marginal costs and consumer surplus, and bound in a narrower sense by the exchange value determined by comparable alternatives adjusted for its differential value. A price that lies within these boundaries will leave all stakeholders better off, and that is the mark of a good price.

Summary

- Pricing is a strategic challenge with a direct impact on profitability. It requires a breadth of information and the right perspective, as well as the ability to balance competing agendas.
- The **science of pricing** refers to the act of gathering information, conducting quantitative analysis, and revealing an accurate understanding of the range of prices likely to yield positive results.

- The **art of pricing** refers to the ability to influence consumer price acceptance, adapt pricing structures to shift the competitive playing field, and align pricing strategy to the competitive strategy, marketing strategy, and industrial policy.
- Good prices are those that leave both the firm and its customers better after the transaction than before. The extreme range of good prices is bound by **marginal costs** from below and **customer utility** from above. A narrower range of prices is bound by the price of the nearest **inferior alternative** from below and the **exchange value** from above.
- **Differential value** is quantified from the increase or decrease in benefits delivered by the product under investigation in comparison to those delivered by the comparable alternative.
- The **exchange value** is the price of the comparable alternative plus the differential value.
- For revolutionary products, simple exchange value models are often the most efficient means of quantifying the boundaries of a good price.
- Equipped with quantified price boundaries, executives are able to combine their desire for profits with an understanding of the value that they deliver to customers to make better pricing decisions.

Exercises

1. Assume that a firm produces an industrial product at a variable cost of $8,500 and has fixed costs of $25,000 per week. Currently, the firm sells 20 units per week priced at $10,625 per unit.
   a. What is the current profitability of the firm?
   b. What is the improvement to profitability if variable costs are reduced by 1 percent, holding all else constant?
   c. What is the improvement to profitability if fixed costs are reduced by 1 percent, holding all else constant?
   d. What is the improvement to profitability if units sold are increased by 1 percent on average, holding all else constant?
   e. What is the improvement to profitability if the price is increased by 1 percent, holding all else constant?
   f. In isolation, improving which aspect of the firm will have the largest positive impact on profits—variable costs, fixed costs, units sold, or price?
2. Assume that a firm produces a consumer product at a variable cost of $7.25 and has fixed costs of $75,000 per month. Currently, the firm sells 14,000 units per month priced at $14 per unit.
   a. What is the current profitability of the firm?
   b. What is the harm to profitability if variable costs rise by 1 percent, holding all else constant?
   c. What is the harm to profitability if fixed costs rise by 1 percent, holding all else constant?
   d. What is the harm to profitability if units sold decreases by 1 percent, holding all else constant?
   e. What is the harm to profitability if the price falls by 1 percent, holding all else constant?

   f. In isolation, failing to manage which aspect of the firm will have the greatest harm on profits—variable costs, fixed costs, units sold, or price?

3. Old Product is sold at $5 and Improved Product delivers $2 more in value to customers than Old Product. Improved Product costs $3 per unit to make.
   a. What is the price of the nearest comparable alternative for Improved Product?
   b. What is the differential value of Improved Product in comparison to Old Product?
   c. What is the exchange value of Improved Product?
   d. What range would you suggest to executives for pricing Improved Product?
4. Old Product is sold at $27 and Reduced Product is less functional than Old Product, to the point that it delivers $6 less value to customers than Old Product. Reduced Product costs $10 to make.
   a. What is the price of the nearest comparable alternative for Reduced Product?
   b. What is the differential value of Reduced Product in comparison to Old Product?
   c. What is the exchange value of Reduced Product?
   d. What range would you suggest to executives for pricing Reduced Product?
5. A competitor sells heavy machinery priced at $14,000. Your firm has been working to enter the heavy machinery market and has developed a new product with a marginal cost of $8,500. Your firm's new machine is superior to its competitors in some ways and inferior in other ways. Its speed is limited, which reduces the value to customers by $1,000 per engine. However, it requires less maintenance, delivering labor savings of $3,500 per engine.
   a. What is the price of the nearest comparable alternative for New Product?
   b. What is the differential value of New Product in comparison to Old Product?
   c. What is the exchange value of New Product?
   d. Where range would you suggest to executives for pricing New Product?
6. In 2005, GE released its Evolution Series locomotive engine, which delivered revolutionary savings in fuel over the lifetime of use. It has been estimated that fuel savings were roughly 1,000,000 gallons per year. At the time of its release, GE and other competitors were selling numerous locomotives priced near $2 million.
   a. What is the price of the nearest comparable alternative for the GE Evolution locomotive?
   b. If diesel is priced at $2.50 per gallon, what is the value of fuel savings of the GE Evolution locomotive in the first year alone?
   c. Based on the fuel savings in the first year alone, what is the exchange value of a GE Evolution locomotive?
   d. If Union Pacific operates locomotives for 20 years and uses a discount rate of 8 percent, what is the present value of fuel savings of operating a GE Evolution locomotive over 20 years?
   e. If customers face additional maintenance costs with a GE Evolution locomotive of $200,000 per year, using the same 8 percent discount rate what is the present value of the additional maintenance costs of a GE Evolution locomotive over 20 years?
   f. Based on the fuel savings over the lifetime of operation and the increased maintenance costs, what is the differential value of a GE Evolution locomotive in comparison to existing locomotives? What is the exchange value of a GE Evolution locomotive?

7. In the 1990s, Itron introduced new automatic meter reading (AMR) solutions to the North American utility market. AMR was a revolutionary product in the 1990s that completely changed the challenge of reading electric meters. Prior to AMR products, utilities were forced to read meters manually, at a cost of approximately $1 per meter read. After the release of AMR products, the cost of reading a meter went to roughly zero. Utilities faced steep switching costs for adopting AMR over manual meter reading methods. Installing an AMR module required a skilled technician to visit each home individually. Assume the cost to install an AMR solution is $50 per meter. For the sake of this exercise, assume the above estimates are accurate and the marginal cost to produce an AMR module is $12.
   a. What is the annual cost per meter to a utility for manual meter reading? For AMR?
   b. Assume that utilities use a 6 percent discount rate to evaluate new purchases. Over the 10-year life span of an AMR solution, what are the cost savings per meter?
   c. What is the price of the nearest comparable alternative to AMR for a utility?
   d. What is the differential value of AMR to its nearest comparable alternative?
   e. What is the exchange value of a standard AMR solution in North America?
   f. In most of Europe, utilities read their meters only once per year. What is the exchange value of a standard AMR solution in Europe? Should Itron have pursued the European market in the 1990s?
8. Given the information in the text, what is the price of a Cordis drug eluting stent that would make all standard metallic stents unprofitable to market?
9. Zipcar provides a car sharing service to its customers. For approximately $10 an hour, a customer can borrow a car. (The price includes all fuel, insurance, taxes, and car usage fees.) In contrast, the average American spends $3,000 per year in car payments and service, $2,000 per year for fuel, and $1,000 per year for car insurance and taxes.
   a. What is the total annual cost of car ownership for the average American?
   b. Consider an urban resident who uses a car 6 hours a week. What is the annual cost of Zipcar usage?
   c. Consider a suburban resident who uses a car 50 hours a week. What is the annual cost of Zipcar usage?
   d. Can Zipcar attract both urban and suburban residents given its current price structure? Who is Zipcar's primary target market?

Appendix 1 Inferior Goods

Assumed in the evaluation of the boundaries of a good price was that the nearest comparable alternative was, in some way, inferior. Often, however, the existing comparable alternatives are superior. When the existing products are superior to the new product, the approach to identifying the boundaries of a good price must be slightly altered.

Inferior products are developed and marketed routinely. In construction, some of the features and benefits of existing products are removed to make a cheaper alternative. Fortunes have been made by stripping out unnecessary benefits to deliver the product desired by customers, so it is worthwhile to consider the boundaries of a good price for these products as well.

The analysis of the boundaries is somewhat similar in the case of marketing an inferior good as it is in the case of marketing a superior good. The key difference is that the

Exhibit 1-6 Price Boundaries for Inferior Goods

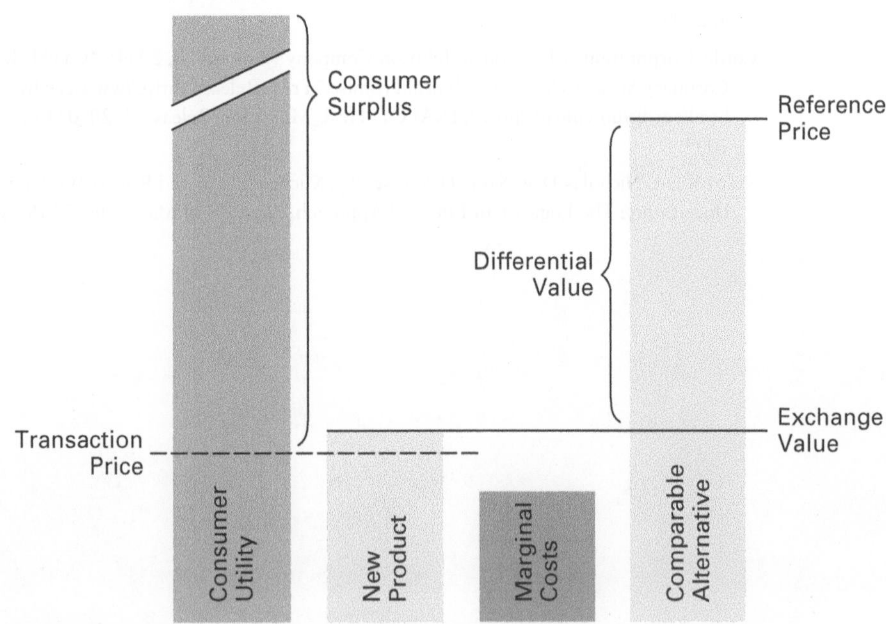

differential value is negative. Thus, the exchange value will be less than the price of the nearest comparable alternative. The hard boundaries of marginal costs and customer utility do not change in concept. With an inferior good, the boundaries of a good price now lie between the exchange value and the marginal costs. See Exhibit 1-6.

Notes

[1] Tim J. Smith, "The Transaction Landscape," *Hawks, Seagulls, and Mice: Paradigms for Systematically Growing Revenue in Business Markets*. Lincoln, NE: iUniverse, 2006: 6–27.

[2] Michael V. Marn, Eric V. Roegner, and Craig C. Zawada, "Introduction," *The Price Advantage*. Hoboken, NJ: John Wiley & Sons, Inc., 2004: 4–6.

[3] Exchange value models are discussed in a variety of settings including Robert J. Dolan, "Pricing: A Value-Based Approach," HBS No. 9-500-071 (Boston: Harvard Business School Publishing, 1999). Gerald E. Smith, Thomas T. Nagle, "A Question of Value," *Marketing Management* 14, No. 4 (July 2005): 38–43.

[4] U.S. Food and Drug Administration (April 24, 2003). "FDA Approves Drug-Eluting Stent for Clogged Heart Arteries." Press Release (http://www.fda.gov/bbs/topics/NEWS/2003/NEW00896.html), retrieved on January 4, 2009.

[5] Kurt Kruger, "Devices and Information Technologies," in Lawton R. Burns (Ed), *The Business of Healthcare Innovation*. New York: Cambridge University Press, 2005: 288–89.

[6] Tim J. Smith, "Communicate the Value," *Hawks, Seagulls, and Mice: Paradigms for Systematically Growing Revenue in Business Markets*. Lincoln, NE: iUniverse, 2006: 160–74.

[7] Reported total procedure costs vary from a low of $9,000 and a high of $30,000. The value that we are using in this text is acceptable for demonstrating the usefulness of an exchange value model in pricing. See Jason Ryan and David J. Cohen, "Are Drug-Eluting Stents Cost-Effective? It Depends on Whom You Ask," *Circulation* 114 (2006): 1736–44.

[8] "J&J Tells Doctors of Cypher Stent Clots," *Los Angeles Times* (July 9, 2003). (http://articles.latimes.com/2003/jul/09/business/fi-rup9.10), retrieved on January 4, 2009.

[9] Organ Gurel, "Drug-Eluting Stent Market: $5 Billion Turning on a Dime" *Midwest Business.com* (July 24, 2006). (http://www.midwestbusiness.com/news/viewnews.asp?newsletterID=15086), retrieved on January 4, 2009.

[10] Cordis Corporation, a Johnson & Johnson Company (January 20, 2004). "CYPHER Sirolimus-Eluting Coronary Stent: Delivers on Clinical Promise." Press Release (http://www.cordis.com/active/crdus/en_US/html/cordis/downloads/press/FINALCYPHER_Milestone_Release_1_20_041.pdf), retrieved on January 4, 2009.

[11] Stuart Read, Nicholas Dew, Saras D. Sarasvathy, Michael Song, and Robert Wiltbank, "Marketing Under Uncertainty: The Logic of an Effectual Approach," *Journal of Marketing*, 73 (May 2009): 1–18.

Chapter 2

Profit's Sensitivity to Price

Frances M. Roberts/Newscom

- How do price changes influence the ability to capture customers?
- How sensitive are profits to price changes when we include the influence of price on sales volume?
- When considering a price cut, what is the necessary increase in sales volume to improve the firm's profits?
- When considering a price increase, what is the allowable decrease in sales volume that will leave the firm more profitable?
- How does elasticity of demand enable executives to optimize prices?
- What are the limitations to using elasticity metrics alone for price-setting decisions?
- Stretch Question: How is elasticity of demand related to exchange value models for different customers?

In more-established markets, executives require stronger guidance in pricing decisions than that provided by exchange value models. They will require a clearer understanding of the customer's response to price. Through quantifying the relationship between sales volume and prices, executives can identify the profit sensitivity to price changes and optimize prices.

Economic price optimization is useful in some markets. Unlike the broad range of prices developed from exchange value models, economic price optimization can provide price guidance down to a fraction of a cent. In markets for mature, commonly purchased products such as milk, fuel, chickens, and iron ore, customers will switch suppliers to capture even the slightest price break. To capture and retain customers, executives need the higher level of accuracy provided through economic price optimization than that provided through exchange value models.

Despite the apparent ability of economic price optimization to pinpoint a price, it is not appropriate for all pricing decisions. Economic price optimization requires a highly accurate understanding of the relationship between prices and demand. One of the key differences between revolutionary products and more mature products is the availability of relevant information regarding the customer's response to price changes. In revolutionary markets, the product will have very little track record from which to quantify the customer response to price changes. In more mature markets, research and statistical approaches may reveal an accurate relationship between prices and demand.

A **profit sensitivity analysis** demonstrates the impact of a small change in price on profits. Price changes have both direct and indirect effects on profits. The direct effect is seen in linear relationship between profits and prices. The indirect effect derives from the influence of price changes on customer demand. In normal markets, higher prices lead to fewer purchases and lower prices lead to greater purchases.[1] Because profit depends on the quantity sold as well as price, and the quantity sold itself depends on prices, price changes indirectly affect profits through their influence on demand.

From the profit sensitivity analysis, we can uncover volume hurdles. **Volume hurdles** define the required demand increase to justify a price cut and the allowable demand sacrifice to justify a price hike. In strategic decisions to attack a specific market at a new price point, volume hurdles enable executives to quantify the required selling goals and compare them against their expectations of potential demand. In tactical pricing decisions, volume hurdles are a routine procedure in setting sales targets for price promotions and discount practices and for evaluating the profitability of price concessions at the end of the promotion.

The profit sensitivity analysis also lays the foundation for conducting economic price optimization. **Economic price optimization** is a method of identifying the price that maximizes profits. It will rely on quantifying the elasticity of demand, a measure of the relationship between price changes and sales volume.

In this chapter, we continue our exploration of rational approaches to setting prices and managing price decisions. First, we conduct a profit sensitivity analysis to construct volume hurdles. In doing so, we will highlight the importance of understanding the relationship between prices and demand leading to an exploration of elasticity of demand. With an understanding of the elasticity of demand, executives are in a position to conduct economic price optimization and understand profit's sensitivity to price.

Profit Sensitivity Analysis

A profit sensitivity analysis evaluates the impact of a small price change on profitability. It is a straightforward analysis of the expected profits earned at two different prices. With a profit sensitivity analysis, we can compare the expected profits to be earned at the current price against those which may be earned at a different price.[2]

Returning to our standard profit equation of a firm, we can see that price directly affects profits. Less obvious are the effects of prices through the other variables in the profit equation. Recall that

$$\pi = Q \cdot (P - V) - F \quad \text{Eq. 2.1}$$

where π, the Greek letter pi, denotes profit, Q denotes quantity sold, P denotes price, V denotes variable costs, and F denotes fixed costs.

Among the variables that determine profit, a pure price change influences the quantity sold but not the variable and fixed costs. For normal goods, price increases are associated with volume decreases and price decreases are associated with volume increases. Statistically, one would state that the price and quantity sold are negatively correlated in normal markets. A pure price change implies that the price increases or decreases without changing the product. Because the product itself isn't affected, it can be anticipated that the means of production, and therefore the variable and fixed costs, should not be affected by a pure price change.

To identify profit's sensitivity to price, let us compare the expected profit earned at the current price against the profit that may be earned at the future new price under consideration. Using π_i to denote the profits earned at the initial prices and π_f to denote the expected profits to be earned at the final price, we find from Equation 2.1 that

$$\pi_i = Q_i \cdot (P_i - V) - F \qquad \text{Eq. 2.2a}$$

$$\pi_f = Q_f \cdot (P_f - V) - F \qquad \text{Eq. 2.2b}$$

where P_i identifies the initial prices and P_f identifies the final price under consideration. Similarly, we denote the initial quantity sold with Q_i and the quantity that will be sold at the new price with Q_f. Variable and fixed costs are constant with respect to pure price changes; hence they do not vary between Equations 2.2a and 2.2b.

VOLUME HURDLES

Volume hurdles result from the requirement for price changes to leave the firm better off, if not at least as well off, after the price change than it was before. Based on the profit motive of the firm, we can state the requirement of price changes to improve profits as

$$\pi_f \geq \pi_i \qquad \text{Eq. 2.3}$$

Algebraic Analysis

Using Equations 2.2a and 2.2b and the requirement that any price change should improve profits in Equation 2.3, we can derive algebraically the required change in volume to deliver equal or higher profits from a price change. The resulting inequality defines the volume hurdle, or the minimum change in volume to associate with a change in price to improve profits:

$$\%\Delta Q \geq \frac{-\%\Delta P}{\%CM_i + \%\Delta P} \qquad \text{Eq. 2.4}$$

In Equation 2.4, $\%\Delta Q$ is the required percent change in quantity sold to justify a price change, $\%\Delta P$ is the percent change in price under consideration, and $\%CM_i$ is the ratio of the initial contribution margin to the initial price. Mathematically, these quantities are defined as

$$\%\Delta Q \equiv \frac{Q_f - Q_i}{Q_i} \qquad \text{Eq. 2.5a}$$

$$\%\Delta P \equiv \frac{P_f - P_i}{P_i} \qquad \text{Eq. 2.5b}$$

$$\%CM_i \equiv \frac{P_i - V_i}{P_i} \qquad \text{Eq. 2.5c}$$

Exhibit 2-1 Profit Sensitivity Analysis of a Price Reduction

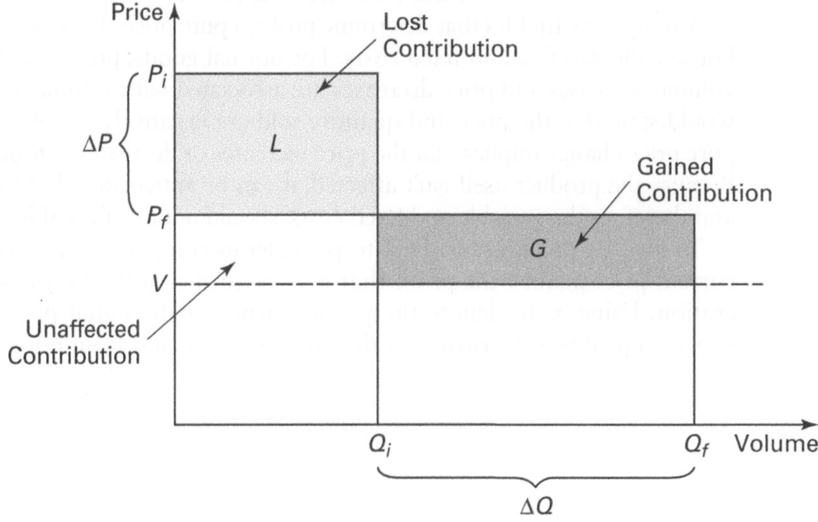

In accordance with the profit motive of the firm, the objective of any price change is simply to improve profitability. If the firm expects the volume hurdle to be met, then a price change may be in order. If the volume hurdle is greater than the expected change in sales, then the new price cannot be justified and the firm should consider alternative actions.

Graphical Analysis

With a graphical analysis, we can see that the volume hurdle results from requiring profit contributions gained through increases in volume at a lower price to be greater than those lost by the price reduction. See Exhibit 2-1.

The revenue gained at a given price is the area of a rectangle given by $P \times Q$. The profit contribution at a given price is the area of a smaller rectangle given by $(P - V) \times Q$. As before, a price change should be executed only if, at a minimum, the new price improves profits.

If G is the profit contribution gained through volume increases at a reduced price, and L is the profit contribution lost through the price reduction, the profit motive of the firm requires gains to be greater than losses, or

$$G \geq L \qquad \text{Eq. 2.6}$$

The profit contribution gained, G, is the area of the rectangle defined by the change in volume multiplied by the new contribution margin. The profit contribution lost, L, is the area of the rectangle defined by the change price multiplied by the old volume. Mathematically, we can state this as

$$G \equiv (P_f - V) \cdot (Q_f - Q_i) \qquad \text{Eq. 2.7a}$$

$$L \equiv (P_i - P_f) \cdot Q_i \qquad \text{Eq. 2.7b}$$

Inserting Equations 2.7a and 2.7b, which quantify the expected losses and gains, into Equation 2.6, which requires that gains should be greater than losses, we find that

$$(P_f - V) \cdot (Q_f - Q_i) \geq (P_i - P_f) \cdot Q_i \qquad \text{Eq. 2.8}$$

Dividing both sides of Equation 2.8 by Q_i and the quantity $(P_i - V)$ reveals

$$\frac{(Q_f - Q_i)}{Q_i} \geq \frac{(P_i - P_f)}{(P_f - V)} \qquad \text{Eq. 2.9}$$

Equation 2.9 reverts to the familiar volume hurdle Equation 2.4 after making the substitution of variables defined in Equation 2.5.

DECISION IMPLICATIONS

Executives can use the volume hurdle in considering either price increases or decreases before the price change has occurred. All the variables that define the volume hurdle in Equation 2.4 can be quantified with information internal to the firm. The current price and variable costs are all facts that executives can identify from their internal accounting records. The proposed price is up to the management's discretion. The result is a requirement on the change in volume associated with the chosen change in price. If the expected change in volume is greater than that predicted by the volume hurdle, then a price change may be in order. If not, then the price change will damage profits and should be averted.

For price reductions, the percent change in price, $\%\Delta P$, is negative, and therefore the right side of Equation 2.4 will be positive. This implies that the volume hurdle, $\%\Delta Q$, will be positive, or that volumes are required to increase if prices are reduced for the firm to profit from the price move. If the expected increase in volume associated with the price reduction under consideration will overcome the volume hurdle, the price reduction is predicted to improve profitability. If not, the price reduction is predicted to harm profitability.

Volume hurdles can also be created for considering price increases. For price increases, the percent change in price, $\%\Delta P$, is positive and therefore the right side of Equation 2.4 will be negative. In this case, the inequality will allow the change in volume, $\%\Delta Q$, to be negative. That is, volumes can decrease, but only up to a point. The expected volume decrease must be smaller than that determined by the volume hurdle for a price increase to improve profits. Price increases that can be expected to lead to volume reductions less than the volume hurdle are predicted to improve profitability. Those that don't are anticipated to damage profitability.

The volume hurdle depends on the size of the price change under consideration. Larger price changes require greater volume hurdles to be met, and smaller price changes are associated with smaller volume hurdles.

The volume hurdle also depends on the size of the contribution margin and therefore indirectly depends upon variable costs. In this case, larger contribution margins yield smaller volume hurdles. Smaller contribution margins yield larger volume hurdles.

Notice that fixed costs play no role in identifying the volume hurdle. It may surprise many executives, but fixed costs are irrelevant for marginal price change decisions. While firms must cover fixed costs to stay in business, fixed costs do not affect the optimal price. As an issue, fixed costs affect the investment decision to enter, stay in, or exit a business, but they should have no impact on pricing. If a firm determines that the optimal price is insufficient to cover fixed costs, executives may want to divest from that industry, identify means to reduce fixed costs, or take actions to improve its customers' willingness to pay. But, raising prices to cover fixed costs is simply not justified from a profit maximization viewpoint.

Put crudely, the firm's fixed costs are that firm's problem, not the customers'. Customers are not responsible for the firm's cost structure, but they are responsible for ensuring that the value they get from a product is greater than the price they pay. Prices define the way that value is shared between the firm and its customers. The profit sensitivity analysis focuses on the effect of price changes to both customer behavior and a firm's profits. Through it, we see fixed costs are irrelevant when optimizing price to improve profits.

The volume hurdle is a necessary condition for pricing actions to improve the profitability of the firm, but it is not a sufficient condition. Every time a price change is contemplated, volume hurdles should be the first line of analysis. No pricing action should be taken if the volume hurdle is unlikely to be achieved. However, there are times when executives may forgo a pricing action even though they expect the volume hurdle to be overcome. That is, even though executives may expect a pricing action to deliver volumes greater than those required by the volume hurdle, it may be in their best interest to avoid the price change due to other strategic factors. Volume hurdles provide an important first check on the pricing decisions, but not the final word.

Many strategic factors will guide executives to apply more requirements than the volume hurdle in considering a pricing action. Volume hurdles do not take into account long-term changes in customer demand that may be influenced by a pricing action. For instance, a price reduction may stimulate demand in the short term, which relaxes to its previous level only once the novelty has worn off. Likewise, volume hurdles ignore several significant tertiary effects of a price change, which would encourage executives to be more cautious of price changes than that determined by the volume hurdle alone. One of these tertiary effects is that a temporary price reduction can reset customer expectations, making it difficult to restore prices following a promotional period. Another tertiary effect can come from competitors who react to a price reduction with a matching offer, thus reducing the ability of a price promotion to draw volumes and lowering the overall industry price level. These and other more subtle effects will be considered in later chapters of this book, but they are mentioned here as a point of caution: Volume hurdles are only the first line of analysis for price changes and do not necessarily provide sufficient justification for taking a pricing action.

For tactical decisions, the volume hurdle can be used to evaluate the appropriateness of short-term price promotions and discounts. For strategic decisions, the volume hurdle can be used to consider both price reductions and increases. Price reductions may be necessary for entering a larger market at a lower price point. If the firm has sufficient assurance that the necessary volume will exist at a lower price point, it may benefit from pursuing this market. Price increases may be associated with entering a new market or distribution channel. They may also be possible when variable costs have been creeping up industry-wide and competitors feel a common pressure to improve prices. If the firm believes that customers will accept a price increase without an excessively negative volume impact, then the firm should expect to benefit from a price increase.

Price Cuts Hurt

The minimum required impact on unit sales of a price reduction for different types of business can be determined easily with the volume hurdle. We take up the case of a hypothetical retailer, manufacturer, and broker to demonstrate that price cuts are hard to justify.

Consider a retailer that marks up its products 100 percent. This retailer would be earning a 50 percent contribution margin with each sale (CM_i = 50 percent). A common 20-percent-off sales promotion might be used to drive store traffic and move merchandise ($\%\Delta P = -20$ percent). In this case, the temporary 20-percent-off sale would need to deliver more than 67 percent greater volume if the sale is to improve profitability ($\%\Delta Q \geq 67$ percent). That is, two-thirds more sales are required during the price promotion to justify a 20-percent-off sale.

Similarly, consider a manufacturer earning a healthy 25 percent contribution margin on each unit sold ($CM_i = 25\%$). A mere 5 percent discount extended to a particular customer would need to increase sales to that customer by more than 25 percent ($\%\Delta P = -5$ percent, $\%\Delta Q \geq 25$ percent). That is, one-quarter more sales are required from the customer to justify a 5 percent discount.

Finally, consider a broker earning a slim 1.5 percent contribution margin ($CM_i = 1.5$ percent). In this case, a 10-basis-point price decrease would need to deliver more than 7.1 percent greater volume to justify the "break" in the broker's commission ($\%\Delta P = -0.10$ percent, $\%\Delta Q \geq 7.1$ percent).

These volume increases are hard to achieve with a mere price decrease. Furthermore, the volume hurdle is only a necessary condition for executing a price cut. There may be other factors to consider prior to executing a price reduction. Because price cuts are hard to justify, executives are usually better served if they search for other means to increase sales.

Price Increases Are Challenging

The allowable impact on unit sales resulting from a price increase can also be determined from the volume hurdle. Once again, we consider a hypothetical retailer, manufacturer, and broker. A retailer earning a 50 percent contribution margin and considering a 20 percent price increase can lose up to 29 percent of its business and still increase profits ($CM_i = 50$ percent, $\%\Delta P = +20$ percent, $\%\Delta Q \geq -29$ percent). A manufacturer earning a 25 percent contribution margin and considering a 5 percent price increase can allow for a 17 percent loss in unit sales and still profit from a price increase ($CM_i = 25$ percent, $\%\Delta P = +5$ percent, $\%\Delta Q \geq -17$ percent). Finally, a broker with a 1.5 percent contribution margin executing a 10-basis-point commission increase must lose no more than 6.3 percent of its sales. ($CM_i = 1.5$ percent, $\%\Delta P = +0.10$ percent, $\%\Delta Q \geq -6.3$ percent).

There are times in which price increases will have negligible effects on unit sales. In most markets, however, customers will take fierce advantage of any disparity in prices between competing firms. Thus, price increases are likely to drive many sales away and will be challenging to put into effect.

Price Changes Have Asymmetric Effects

A careful examination of this analysis reveals that the effects of a price change are asymmetric. For instance, the manufacturer considering a 5 percent price decrease or increase is either requiring unit sales to increase by at least 25 percent, or allowing unit sales to drop by no more than 17 percent, respectively. We can see the asymmetrical effects of price changes with a simple plot.

Exhibit 2-2 plots the volume hurdle as a function of price changes for our hypothetical manufacturer. We have used the economists' convention of plotting price on the vertical access and volume on the horizontal access. If the price change is associated with a volume change that is to the right of the curve depicting the volume hurdle, it will improve profits. If the price change is associated with a volume change that is to the left of the curve depicting the volume hurdle, it will harm profits.

The asymmetry of the volume hurdle as a function of price is also demonstrated by its curve. The volume hurdle rises more quickly when the price change is negative than it falls when the price change is positive. These results are common. For all firms, the volume hurdles associated with price increases are much smaller than those associated with price reductions.

Elasticity of Demand

While the profit sensitivity analysis reveals the volume hurdle that a pricing action must meet, it does not indicate what the volume will be. Management intuition informed through past experience may leave executives to suspect that the volume hurdle will be surpassed, but measured fact is a more reliable predictor.

Exhibit 2-2 The Volume Hurdle: *The Volume Hurdle as a Function of Price Changes for a Firm with a 25 percent Contribution Margin.*

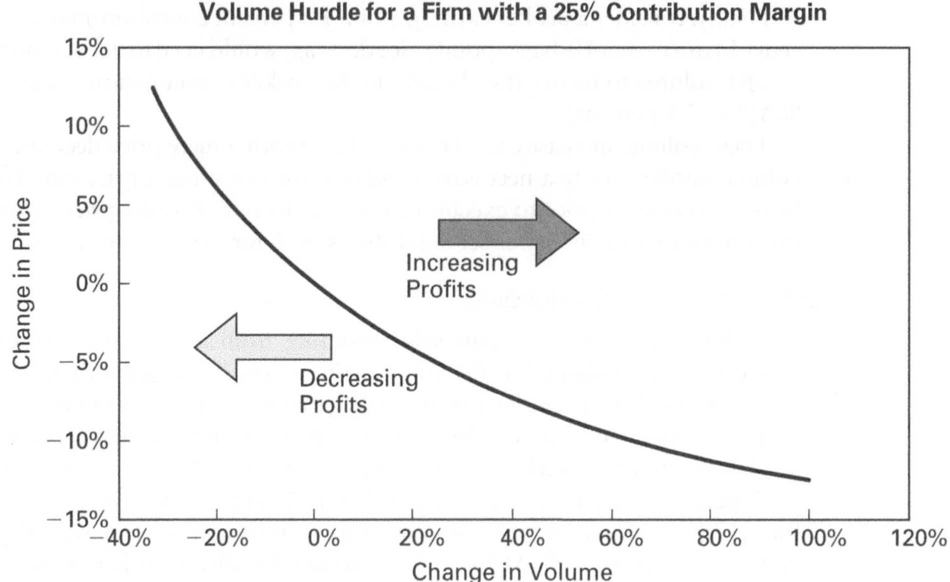

Elasticity of demand is a measure of the changes in volume delivered with a change in price. Formally, it is defined as the ratio of the percent change in volume to the percent change in price:

$$\varepsilon \equiv \frac{\%\Delta Q}{\%\Delta P} \qquad \text{Eq. 2.10}$$

We have used ε (pronounced "epsilon") to denote the elasticity of demand in accordance with economic conventions. Numerically, the elasticity of demand is negative for normal markets, implying fewer goods are sold at higher prices and more goods are sold at lower prices. By convention, economists tend to drop the sign in speaking about the elasticity of demand. Thus a large elasticity of demand is large in absolute value but negative in direction, and a small elasticity of demand is small in absolute value but also negative in direction.

Executives can use a measured elasticity of demand to predict the expected volume change resulting from a price change. For small price changes, the elasticity of demand can be approximated as a constant. Thus, the simple product of the percent change in price multiplied by the elasticity of demand will predict the change in volume that an executive should expect to result from a price change.

$$\%\Delta Q = \varepsilon \cdot \%\Delta P \qquad \text{Eq. 2.11}$$

Coupled with the volume hurdle, this simple metric is a highly powerful tool for informing pricing decisions. By comparing the volume hurdle identified in Equation 2.11 against the change in volume predicted from the elasticity of demand in Equation 2.11, executives can easily discriminate between price changes that improve profits and those which don't.

ELASTIC MARKETS

Markets are said to be elastic when a small change in price has a large effect on the quantity sold. Quantitatively, elastic markets are defined as markets with an elasticity of demand that is greater than 1 ($|\varepsilon| > 1$). Most firms face elastic demand curves, which means that a small change in price drives a large change in demand. This is a direct result of competition. In competitive markets, customers switch suppliers when price changes alter the disparity in offers between competitors.

In the short run, elastic markets tend to favor price cuts to improve profitability. A high elasticity of demand implies that a small price cut delivers a large enough volume increase to overcome the volume hurdle. We can see this by overlaying the change in volume predicted from the elasticity of demand (shown by the gray curve in Exhibit 2-3) with the volume hurdle (the black curve). From Exhibit 2-3, we see that the predicted change in volume is greater than the volume hurdle for a wide range of potential price cuts. However, for any price increase, the predicted change in volume is greater than the allowable volume hurdle. Thus, elastic markets favor price reductions.

INELASTIC MARKETS

Markets are said to be inelastic when a large change in price has only a small effect on the quantity sold. Quantitatively, inelastic markets are defined as markets with an elasticity of demand that is less than 1 ($|\varepsilon| < 1$). Many industries face inelastic demand curves. Meaning, at the industry level, demand changes little when prices across the market change greatly. However, as implied previously, only a few firms face inelastic demand curves.

Inelastic markets tend to favor price increases to improve profitability. A small elasticity of demand implies a large price increase can be expected to yield negligibly small reductions in volume, and thus it will leave demand above the allowable volume hurdle.

Exhibit 2-3 Volume Hurdle and Demand Curve for Elastic Markets: *An Elastic Demand Curve ($\varepsilon = -10$) is Plotted in Gray. The Volume Hurdle for a Firm with a 25 percent Contribution Margin is Plotted in Black.*

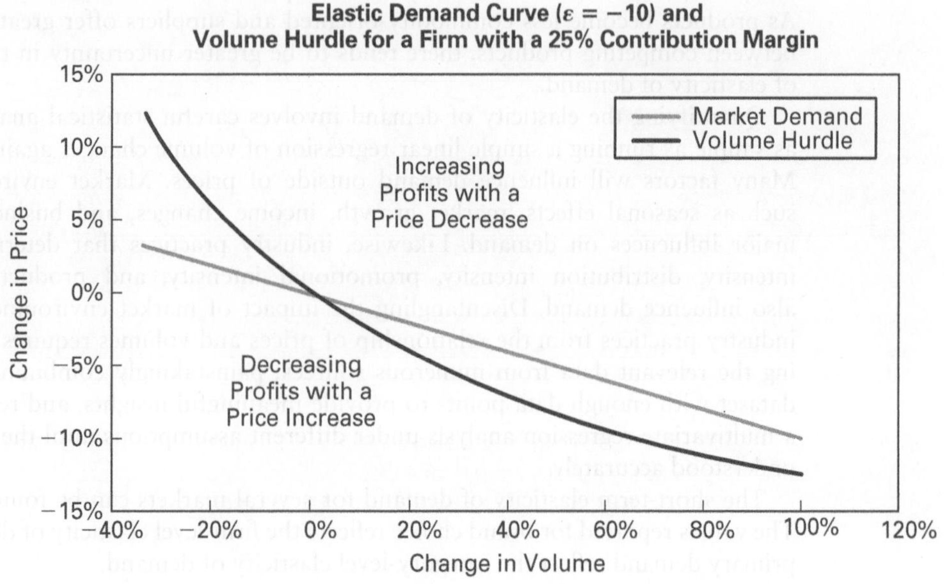

Exhibit 2-4 Volume Hurdle and Demand Curve for Inelastic Markets: *An Inelastic Demand Curve (ε = −0.5) is Plotted in Gray. The Volume Hurdle for a Firm with a 25 percent Contribution Margin is Plotted in Black.*

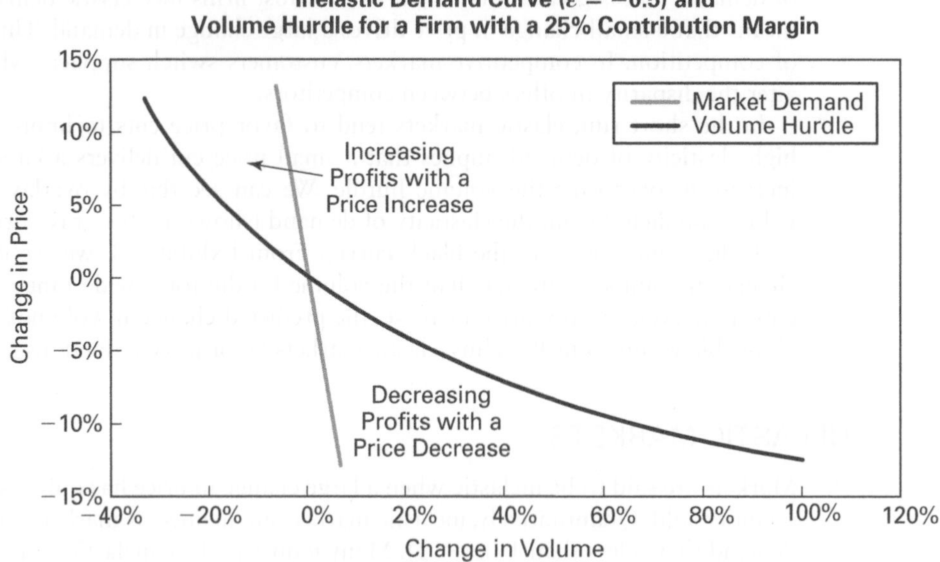

Overlaying the change in volume predicted from the elasticity of demand with the volume hurdle in Exhibit 2-4, we can compare predictions and requirements once again. In this case, we see that the predicted change in volume is less than the allowable volume hurdle for a wide range of potential price increases. However, for any price cut, the predicted change in volume is less than the volume hurdle. Thus, inelastic markets favor price increases.

MEASURED ELASTICITY OF DEMAND

In many mature markets, the elasticity of demand can be routinely measured and used to inform pricing decisions. In general, historic metrics of the elasticity of demand are better quantified for more commodity-oriented products than they are for branded goods. As products become less commodity-oriented and suppliers offer greater differentiation between competing products, there tends to be greater uncertainty in the measurements of elasticity of demand.

Quantifying the elasticity of demand involves careful statistical analysis. Rarely is it as simple as running a simple linear regression of volume changes against price changes. Many factors will influence demand outside of prices. Market environmental factors such as seasonal effects, market growth, income changes, and business cycles are all major influences on demand. Likewise, industry practices that determine competitive intensity, distribution intensity, promotional intensity, and product evolutions will also influence demand. Disentangling the impact of market environmental factors and industry practices from the relationship of prices and volumes requires carefully collecting the relevant data from numerous sources, painstakingly combining it into a single dataset with enough data points to provide meaningful insights, and repeatedly running a multivariate regression analysis under different assumptions until the market has been understood accurately.

The short-term elasticity of demand for several markets can be found in Exhibit 2-5. The values reported for brand choice reflects the firm-level elasticity of demand. Those for primary demand reflect the category-level elasticity of demand.

Exhibit 2-5 Measured Elasticity of Demand[3]

Category	Brand Choice	Primary Demand
Bacon	−1.25	−0.32
Margarine	−2.22	−0.12
Butter	−1.24	−0.74
Ice Cream	−1.89	−0.68
Paper Towels	−4.00	−0.74
Sugar	−4.03	−0.57
Liquid Detergents	−3.95	−1.70
Coffee	−1.65	−1.42
Soft Drinks	−2.66	−0.42
Bath Tissue	−3.85	−0.80
Potato Chips	−2.50	−0.88
Dryer Softeners	−4.08	−1.19
Yogurt	−1.57	−0.35

Notice that in all cases, the firm-level elasticity of demand is greater than or equal to that at the category level. This is reflective of customer behavior. When the price of an individual brand increases, customers readily switch brands to a lower-cost alternative. However, when the prices on all brands in the category increase, customers have to reduce their purchases to save money. Category-level switching is far more difficult than brand-level switching; hence, the elasticity of demand at the category level will be less than that at the brand level.

The short-term elasticity of demand is often lower than the long-term elasticity of demand. In the short term, customers are often locked into a particular purchasing pattern. In the long term, however, customers may uncover substitutes or change their lifestyle to reduce their need for the product. For example, the price of gas in the United States jumped from $1.27 to $4.11 between 2000 and 2008, but the demand changed very little. The measured elasticity of demand was less than −0.04. Consumers grumbled about the higher prices, but their consumption patterns could not change instantly because they still required fuel to commute to work, go shopping, and meet other transportation needs. In those intervening years, however, some consumers bought bicycles, increased their use of mass transit, and switched to more fuel-efficient cars in response to the price change. Thus, the long-run elasticity of demand has been estimated to be slightly higher, perhaps around −0.06.

NECESSARY, BUT INSUFFICIENT

In reviewing the reported elasticities of demand, we also notice that demand at the firm level is often elastic, while that at the category level remains inelastic. Executives should take notice of this observation. This result derives directly from the nature of competition. In a perfectly competitive market, individual firms face infinitely elastic demand regardless of the elasticity of demand for the industry as a whole. For pricing decisions, this has a very strong implication. Managers should be very cautious of pricing actions that may reduce the overall industry-level prices.

The fact that the brand-level elasticity of demand is lower than the category-level elasticity of demand reveals a key reason why volume hurdles are a necessary condition for evaluating a price change but not a sufficient condition for judging a pricing action as healthy.

For instance, consider the potential sequence of events that could arise from a price cut guided solely from a volume hurdle and volume prediction made from the elasticity of demand. Executives may predict that the price cut will increase profits and therefore believe that it is in their best interest. However, by failing to consider competitive reactions, the decision may be misguided. If the increase in volume associated with a price cut comes at a competitor's expense, the firm should expect that competitor to react. If the competitor's response is to match the firm's price cut, all temporary gains in volume will be lost and both the firm and its competitor will be pricing their product at a new, lower price point. The result would be to lower the overall industry-level prices, thus harming industry profits.

Most firms would earn greater profits by being a middling firm within a healthy industry than a leading firm within a hemorrhaging industry. Hence, many firms will be better served by seeking to raise or at least maintain their prices to promote overall industry health, rather than lowering them to take a greater share but damage the industry as a whole.

We see evidence that these kinds of event sequences are not only possible, but probable in the measures of elasticity of demand. As noted before, elastic markets favor price cuts and, as observed, most brands face elastic markets. Therefore, executives at individual firms face a strong incentive to lower their prices. However, we also should examine the value of price change at the industry level. As noted before, inelastic markets favor price increases and, as observed, many industries face inelastic markets. Therefore, executives within most industries would be, in aggregate, better off if the industry-level prices increased. These insights can be explained easily by the actions of individual firms that have reduced prices to take market share, only to find that they have been matched by their competitors and left the industry impoverished overall.

The competitive reaction to price cuts and the potential for destroying profits industry-wide is one of the more convincing reasons that volume predictions from the elasticity of demand and volume hurdles are insufficient guidelines for pricing decisions. Both of these quantitative approaches ignore competitive reactions. They also fail to consider the differences between long-term changes in consumer behavior and short-term predictability. Executives should require expectations for the volume hurdle to be surpassed as a first-line evaluation of a potential price cut, but they cannot stop their analysis there. Further considerations must be included in their analysis. Often the next steps in the analysis will be less concretely quantitative in nature and more qualitative, but pricing is not a simple engineering challenge—it is a strategic challenge.

Economic Price Optimization

From the profit sensitivity analysis, we see that raising prices can increase profits directly by improving contribution margins and decrease profits indirectly through their moderating effect on demand. These insights imply that there is some price that balances the opposing influences and delivers the maximum profits. Economic price optimization is an approach to identify the profit maximizing price. Any price above the optimum will damage profits by depressing demand sufficiently to destroy gains created by improving margins. Any price below the optimum will damage profits by decreasing margins more than the gains earned in improving volumes.

We have been able to quantify the required volume hurdles for a price change to improve profits from the firm's profit equation. We have also been able to quantify the expected volume change associated with a price change from the elasticity of demand. Economic price optimization builds on these approaches to identify further the optimal price that delivers maximal profits.

Exhibit 2-6 Price Optimization

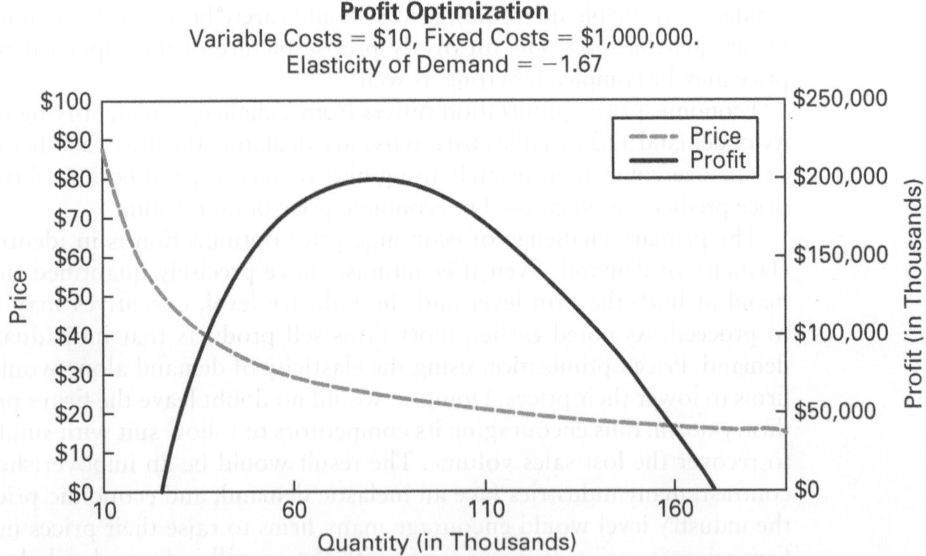

Demand decreases along with price increases for any normal good. If we plot the demand at a given price given an understanding of the overall demand and the elasticity of demand, we will find a downward-sloping curve much like that in Exhibit 2-6. Because price predicts volume through the elasticity of demand, we can also identify the profits earned from the product at any volume. As seen in Exhibit 2-6, profits exhibit a typical inverted parabola-like curve when plotted against volume. At the peak of this parabola-like curve, profits will be maximized.

Exhibit 2-6 depicts the prices and profits associated with a specific volume sold for a hypothetical firm. We have modeled the firm to have fixed costs of $1 million per quarter and variable costs of $10 per unit. To model demand, we used a constant elasticity of demand equal to −1.67 (a value representative of many firms in many industries) and set the overall demand equal to 368,000 units per quarter if the product was priced at marginal costs. (In general, demand models require identifying the demand at a particular price and the elasticity of demand around that price.) Given these figures, the price is optimized for this product at $25. At this optimal price, the firm would sell 80,000 units and earn $200,000 per quarter. See also Exhibit 1-1.

To derive the optimal price from the elasticity of demand and the known demand at a particular price requires a little calculus. Interested readers can follow the derivation in Appendix 2.B. Assuming that the elasticity of demand is constant over the range of prices under consideration, we can express the relationship between prices and volumes as

$$Q = AP^{\varepsilon} \qquad \text{Eq. 2.12}$$

The optimal price is found simply by substituting in this expression for quantity sold into the firm's profit equation and maximizing profits with respect to prices. We find

$$\hat{P} = \frac{V\varepsilon}{(1 + \varepsilon)} \qquad \text{Eq. 2.13}$$

After arriving at the equation for the economically optimal price, one might be tempted to say "Voila, so this is how we should price." But beware: Economic price optimization produces a false sense of accuracy. Despite the inherent attractiveness of getting an exact price based on historic metrics of elasticity of demand, marginal costs, and other independently verifiable quantities, prices should rarely be set in this manner. Its quantitative beauty provides not only an overly precise picture of the supposed right price, but the price may be completely wrong as well.

Economic price optimization suffers from a challenge in identifying the relevant elasticity of demand and variable costs to use in calculating the price. Neither of these challenges can be overcome appropriately using historic metrics, and both lead to wildly inaccurate price predictions when used in economic price optimization.

The primary challenge of economic price optimization is in identifying the relevant elasticity of demand. Even if economists have precisely quantified the elasticity of demand at both the firm level and the industry level, executives may be uncertain how to proceed. As noted earlier, most firms sell products that individually face an elastic demand. Price optimization using the elasticity of demand alone would encourage most firms to lower their prices. Doing so would no doubt leave the firm's prices below the industry norm, thus encouraging its competitors to follow suit with similar price decreases to recover the lost sales volume. The result would be an impoverished firm overall. In contrast, many industries face an inelastic demand, and economic price optimization at the industry level would encourage many firms to raise their prices in aggregate. If one firm raises its prices in accordance with the overall industry-level elasticity of demand, but other firms did not, customers would switch brands quickly, and again the firm would be impoverished overall. Hence, neither of these elasticities of demand is useful in finding the optimal price.

The secondary challenge of economic price optimization is in uncovering the relevant marginal costs. The relevant marginal costs depend on the time frame under consideration. In the narrowest sense, short-run marginal costs may include little more than raw materials as the production capacity must be maintained from one second to the next. In the medium run, marginal costs would expand to include other factors such as labor, facilities, and equipment. In the long run, the decision to invest or divest from production capacity and marketing activities depends on the expected units to be sold, and therefore it can influence the meaning of marginal costs.

Because of the challenges inherent in price optimization through purely economic arguments, executives are wise not to use this approach. Only in rarified and idealized cases can prices be optimized solely through historic metrics of the elasticity of demand and the cost accountant's interpretation of variable costs. For almost every firm, this is a highly dubious approach.

Accepting these challenges, executives may use economic price optimization to create a range of potential prices. From the industry-level price elasticity, they may be able to identify a higher price that would improve the firm's and industry's profits overall. From the firm-level price elasticity, they may identify the minimum price to charge if all other competitive actions were thwarted and customers behaved in a consistent manner.

Profit Sensitivity Analysis with Changing Cost Structures

The analysis considered so far is that of a pure price change in the absence of any cost changes. In many cases, executives face the issue of making a price change in response to a change in the product. Quality-oriented manufacturers often make product improvements with the expectation that a higher price can be earned with a higher-value good. Likewise, cost-oriented manufacturers may seek to reduce costs in the belief that a larger market may exist at a lower price point. In either case, cost changes are often associated with price changes. In a similar manner as that used in the case of a pure price change, we can also examine the profit sensitivity to concurrent changes in costs and price.

We can define volume hurdles for a product under the relaxed constraint of allowing for both a price and variable costs. Using the same generalized profit equation, but this time allowing for changes in variable costs, we find the new volume hurdle to be

$$\%\Delta Q \geq \frac{-\Delta CM}{\Delta CM + CM_i} \quad \text{Eq. 2.14}$$

where V_i represents the initial variable costs and V_f the final variable costs, and define the following equations:

$$\Delta CM \equiv (P_f - V_f) - (P_i - V_i) \quad \text{Eq. 2.15a}$$

$$CM_i \equiv (P_i - V_i) \quad \text{Eq. 2.15b}$$

The volume hurdle under changing variable costs, Equation 2.14, is highly dependent on the effect of changes in the contribution margin. We can see this in Exhibit 2-7. In Exhibit 2-7, we have returned to our hypothetical firm with a $15 initial contribution margin.

A negative change in contribution margin may arise from increasing the variable costs less than a commensurate increase in price, or decreasing variable costs less than a commensurate decrease in price. If the change in the contribution margin is negative, the volume hurdle will be positive. In this case, the volume hurdle will indicate the required increase in sales to justify the product improvement without a price increase.

Negative changes in contribution margins can be anticipated to harm profits in general. For instance, consider a product enhancement that costs more to deliver than the price can be increased. In this case, the contribution margins will be squeezed even though the prices are higher. In general, a firm should expect to sell fewer, not more, units at a higher price point unless competitive pressures or other factors have worked to redefine the price to quality tradeoffs for customers. Thus, in most cases, a price increase smaller than the variable cost increase would decrease both contribution margins and volumes, collectively harming profits.

A positive change in the contribution margin may arise from an increase in price greater than the commensurate increases in variable costs, or decreasing variable costs more than

Exhibit 2-7 Volume Hurdle with a Changing Contribution Margin

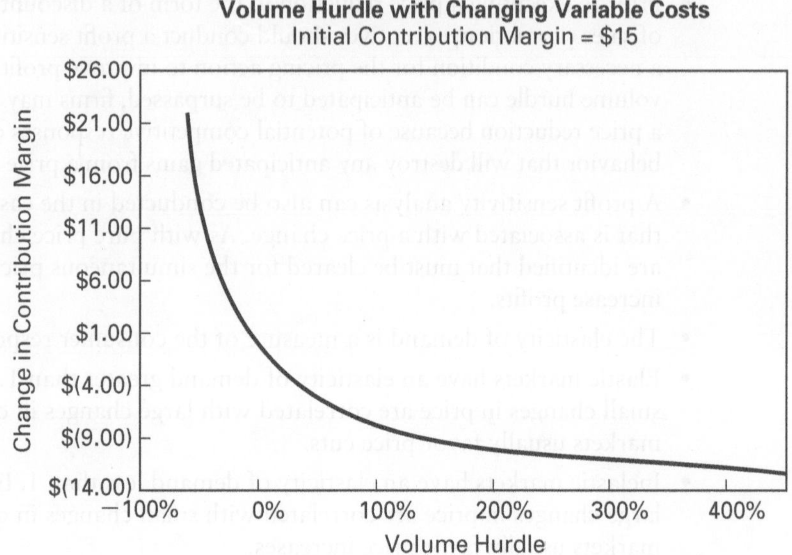

decreasing price. If the change in contribution margin is positive, the volume hurdle will be negative. In this case, the volume hurdle will indicate the allowable drop in sales, which would improve profits when the price and marginal costs increase.

Positive changes in contribution margins can be anticipated to improve profits in general. For instance, consider a product refinement that both strips out costs and is targeted to sell at a lower price point but with an overall increase in contribution margins. In this case, the contribution margins may be higher even though prices are lower. In general, a firm should expect to sell more units at a lower price point. Thus, in most cases, this strategic action would improve both contribution margins and volumes, and thus collectively improve profits.

Just as we have conducted a profit sensitivity analysis for the case of changing variable costs, we can also conduct one for the case of changing fixed costs. Firms may face changes in their fixed costs when expanding to a new market, improving production, altering distribution, or making other operational changes in response to a strategic opportunity. In this case, we find

$$\%\Delta Q \geq \frac{\Delta F}{CM \cdot Q_i} \quad \text{Eq. 2.16}$$

where F_f is the final fixed-costs and F_i the initial fixed costs, and ΔF equals $F_f - F_i$. The increase in volume required equals the ratio of the increase in fixed costs to the existing marginal profits.

Summary

- Anticipating the customer's response to price changes empowers executives to analyze the profit sensitivity to price changes and improve prices.
- In a profit sensitivity analysis, volume hurdles are identified. For a pure price reduction, the volume hurdle will be positive and will identify the minimum required volume increase needed for a price cut to improve profits. For a pure price increase, the volume hurdle will be negative and will identify the allowable volume decrease for the price hike to improve profits.
- Profits are asymmetrically sensitive to price changes. A price decrease is associated with a larger volume hurdle than an equivalently sized price increase is with an allowable volume decrease.
- Prior to executing a price reduction in the form of a discount, coupon, or other form of sales promotion, executives should conduct a profit sensitivity analysis to uncover a necessary condition for the pricing action to improve profitability. Even if the volume hurdle can be anticipated to be surpassed, firms may be wise to refrain from a price reduction because of potential competitive responses or changes in consumer behavior that will destroy any anticipated gains from a price reduction.
- A profit sensitivity analysis can also be conducted in the case of a cost change that is associated with a price change. As with pure price changes, volume hurdles are identified that must be cleared for the simultaneous price and cost change to increase profits.
- The elasticity of demand is a measure of the consumer response to price changes.
- Elastic markets have an elasticity of demand greater than 1. In elastic markets, small changes in price are correlated with large changes in quantity sold. Elastic markets usually favor price cuts.
- Inelastic markets have an elasticity of demand less than 1. In inelastic markets, large changes in price are correlated with small changes in quantity sold. Inelastic markets usually favor price increases.

- Brand-level elasticity of demand typically is higher than industry-level elasticity of demand.
- Price optimization through a basic economic model depends only on the elasticity of demand and variable cost to produce.
- A reduction of prices below the optimal price leads to insufficient gains from volume increases to cover the greater losses from the contribution margin decrease. An increase in prices above the optimal price leads to insufficient gains in contribution margins to cover the greater losses from decreased volumes. The optimal price balances these gains and losses to deliver the highest potential profit.
- Despite their beauty, economic price optimization usually identifies the wrong price. The primary challenge to economic price comes from identifying the relevant elasticity of demand for pricing decisions. The secondary challenge comes from identifying the relevant variable costs. Economic price optimization may be useful for some pricing questions, but it is a highly dubious approach to pricing in general.

Exercises

1. Consider a retailer considering a 33-percent-off sale on blenders currently priced at $54. The retailer pays $29 per blender from the manufacturer.
   a. What is the initial contribution margin?
   b. What is the proposed sale price and the percent change in price captured per unit sold?
   c. What is the volume hurdle that must be achieved for the sale on blenders to improve profits through the sale of blenders alone?
   d. Suppose that instead of having this sale, a young pricing expert suggested that the price of blenders be increased to $59. What would be the allowable loss in sales of blenders that would still leave the retailer in a more profitable position?
2. Consider a Scandinavian wind turbine manufacturer attempting to understand the profit impact of a price change on turbines. Currently, a 1.5-megawatt (MW) wind turbine has a total price of $1.7 million to an electric generator but faces only a $1.3 million in marginal cost to deliver. The Scandinavian wind turbine manufacturer has a 35 percent market share.
   a. What is the initial contribution margin?
   b. If the wind turbine manufacturer considered dropping the price by 3 percent, what would be the new price, and what volume hurdle must be cleared for the price change to improve profits?
   c. If the wind turbine manufacturer considered raising the price by 3 percent, what would be the new price, and what would be the allowable volume loss for the price change to improve profits?
   d. Discussion Question: A U.S. competitor sells comparable wind turbines for $1,675,000 and has 25 percent market share. Given this information, should the Scandinavian wind turbine manufacturer raise or lower prices by 3 percent? What is the reasoning behind your suggestion?
3. Consider a firm with a current contribution margin of 30 percent.
   a. What is the volume hurdle associated with a 1 percent price decrease? What is the allowable volume loss associated with a 1 percent price increase?
   b. What is the volume hurdle associated with a 5 percent price decrease? What is the allowable volume loss associated with a 5 percent price increase?

c. What is the volume hurdle associated with a 10 percent price decrease? What is the allowable volume loss associated with a 10 percent price increase?

d. What is the volume hurdle associated with a 20 percent price decrease? What is the allowable volume loss associated with a 20 percent price increase?

4. For a firm with a current contribution margin of 50 percent, plot the volume hurdle as price goes from a decrease of 40 percent to an increase of 40 percent. Are profits more sensitive to price increases or price decreases?

5. For a consumer product, the manufacturer's suggested retail price (MSRP) is $49. The manufacture's price to the retailer is $25. The manufacturer faces a marginal cost of $15 per unit to produce.

   a. What is the current contribution margin for this product at the retail level if priced at the MSRP? What is the current contribution margin for this product at the manufacturer level? What is the current contribution margin for this product for the value chain if priced at the MSRP?

   b. What is the volume hurdle associated with a 15-percent-off sale at the retail level to leave the overall value chain more profitable?

   c. Assume that the retailer seeks to share the burden of a price discount with the manufacturer such that its promotional price is reduced by 15 percent while the price its pays for the product also decreases by 7.5 percent. What is the volume hurdle faced by both the retailer and manufacturer under this scenario?

   d. What decrease in manufacturer price to the retailer would deliver the same volume hurdle to both the retailer and manufacturer as a 15-percent-off sale at the retail level?

6. For a consumer product, the MSRP is $19. The wholesale price from the manufacturer to the retailer is $12.50. The manufacturer faces a marginal cost of $8.50 per unit to produce.

   a. What is the current contribution margin for this product at the retail level if priced at the MSRP? What is the current contribution margin for this product at the manufacturer level? What is the current contribution margin for this product for the value chain?

   b. What is the volume hurdle associated with a $2-off sale to leave the overall value chain more profitable?

   c. Assume that the retailer seeks to lay the entire burden of the sale on the manufacturer, such that its promotional price is reduced by $2 and the price that it pays the manufacturer for the product decreases by $2. What is the volume hurdle faced by both the retailer and manufacturer under this scenario?

   d. What decrease in manufacturer price to the retailer would deliver the same volume hurdle to both the retailer and manufacturer as a $2-off sale at the retail level?

7. The short-run elasticity of demand for a consumer product is measured from NPD data at $\varepsilon = -2.9$.

   a. What is the expected unit sales increase to result from a 10 percent price decrease?

   b. If the contribution margin for the value chain is 60 percent, what is the volume hurdle for a 10 percent price decrease?

   c. Should the value chain expect a 10-percent-off sale to improve its profits?

8. The short-run elasticity of demand for chicken breasts is measured by the National Chicken Council to be $\varepsilon = -0.75$.
   a. What is the expected unit sales decrease from a 10 percent price increase?
   b. If the contribution margin for the value chain is 30 percent, what is the allowable volume loss for a 10 percent price increase?
   c. Should the value chain expect a 10 percent price increase in chicken breasts to improve profits?
9. A computer maker is considering improving its product. It currently produces a desktop computer at a marginal cost of $249, and the computer sells for $289. The improved version of its product would have a new marginal cost of $289 and would be priced at $359. What volume hurdle does this manufacturer face?

Appendix 2.A A Discrete Demand

While economic texts usually assume that demand is a continuous function of price, in many cases, it isn't. In many industries, demand is nonlinearly dependent upon price. At certain price points, a product may have a large change in demand as customers find a new use for the product and the product displaces a substitute.

For instance, consider the aluminum industry.[4] In the 1930s, aluminum had five major applications: aircraft sheet bodies, metallurgy, cooking utensils, electric cables, automotive parts. Each use for aluminum had a different value to its customers and would displace a different substitute material.

The most valuable use of aluminum in the 1930s was in the manufacturing of aircraft. Although the aircraft sheet body market represented only 10 percent of the output of Alcoa in 1930, it was highly valuable. Few realistic alternatives to lightweight and structurally sturdy aluminum could be used in the development of commercial and military aircraft. Moreover, the demand for aircraft sheet body aluminum was derived from the overall demand from the air transport industry, and hence it was highly inelastic.

Metallurgical application of aluminum was in the development of sheet metal. In 1930, 8 to 10 percent of Alcoa sales were for metallurgical purposes. Prices for aluminum in the metallurgical market could be somewhat high, though not as high as they could be in the aircraft industry. Moreover, demand in the metallurgical market was largely inelastic because aluminum represented a small portion of the cost of producing sheet metal and the demand depended upon the overall demand within the larger steel industry.

The other markets for aluminum were significantly more elastic. Aluminum sold for cooking utensils represented about 40 percent of the volume in 1940. Although superior over other material in lightness, resistance to chipping, and ease of cleaning, customers could easily substitute enamel cookware for most aluminum cookware. Aluminum sold for electric cables represented 10 to 15 percent of volume by 1940. Aluminum cables were inferior to copper cables in conductivity but superior in lightness, and hence they were found to be of value only in specific applications. Aluminum sold for electrical purposes typically was discounted to stimulate sales. Automotive sales of aluminum represented 17 percent of Alcoa's sales in 1930 and were related to the use of aluminum in machine parts. The automotive market was also highly elastic because manufacturers could use steel in many applications instead of aluminum.

If aluminum were sold to all markets at one price and the price were set in proportion to the willingness to pay of the aircraft sheet body market, only aircraft manufacturers would purchase it, and there would be little or no demand from the metallurgical market or other areas. Not until the price of aluminum became competitive to its substitutes for the metallurgical market would that market purchase. At that point, the overall demand would increase sharply. Thus, the cumulative demand curve for aluminum, if priced at one price to all markets, would have numerous inflection points corresponding to the prices at which aluminum became competitive for specific industries. See Exhibit 2-8 for a qualitative understanding of the price-to-demand relationship.

To segregate these markets and price in proportion to each market's willingness to pay, Alcoa forward-integrated into specific industries and sold aluminum ingots of varying quality. This enabled Alcoa to improve its ability to price aluminum differently depending on its application. Alcoa's pricing practice was altered only after 1937, when the U.S. Department of Justice filed a Sherman Act civil suit.[5]

When a product has multiple applications where each application has a different value to its customers and the product is sold to all customers at the same price, the demand can be better thought of as coming in discrete chunks rather than as a continuous function of price. That is, the cumulative demand at any one price is the sum of the demand of all markets up to that price. Once the price of the product makes it competitive to a substitute, a new market application becomes economically viable, and demand will increase sharply.

Executives considering repricing a product to serve a new market application should consider the willingness to pay of that market and its potential demand volume. As with continuously varying demand curves, a profit sensitivity analysis will reveal the required volume to justify a price resetting designed to attack a new market application.

Attempts at pricing the same product at two different levels for two different market applications may fall foul of legal restrictions, as Alcoa discovered. Even in cases where legal restrictions don't apply, enterprising individuals will commonly develop means of buying products designed and sold to one market and resell them to the second, higher-value market, pocketing the price differential as their own profit. The result is what is commonly called a *gray market*. Many industries have learned how to work with gray markets and manage them, but gray markets are generally a source

Exhibit 2-8 Demand for Aluminum (1930–1950)

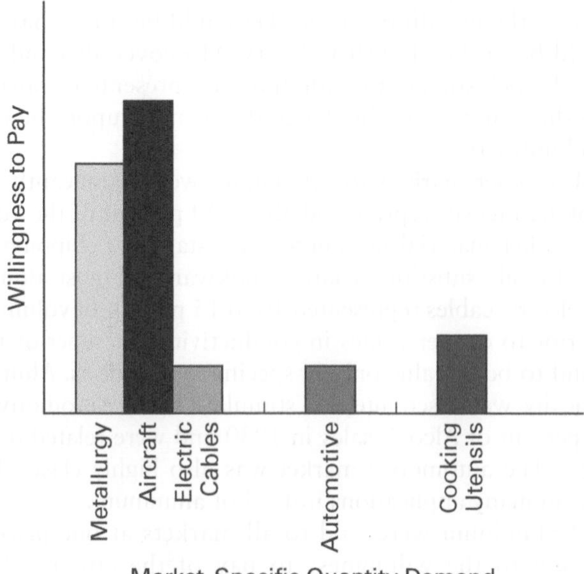

of consternation. One method of minimizing both the legal and gray-market risk is to reengineer the product such that it becomes sufficiently differentiated for each market application. In these situations, executives can optimize the price independently for each individual market.

Appendix 2.B Derivation of Economic Price Optimization

In Equation 2.13, we provided the economically optimal price given the variable costs and elasticity of demand. The derivation of Equation 2.13 is a direct result of the definition of the elasticity of demand and the firm's profit equation.[6]

The optimal price is that which maximizes profits. At the maximal profit, the slope of the profit curve with respect to deviations in price is zero. Using calculus, we can find this price by setting the first derivative of the profit equation to zero. From Equation 2.1 for the firm's profit, we find the first derivative of profit with respect to price to be

$$\frac{\partial \pi}{\partial P} = \frac{\partial Q}{\partial P}(P - V) + Q \qquad \text{Eq. 2.17}$$

where we have assumed that demand (Q) depends on price while variable costs (V) and fixed costs (F) are constants with respect to price changes.

The optimal price can be found at the point where the first derivative of profits with respect to price is equal to zero. Thus, setting the first derivative of profits in Equation 2.17 equal to zero, we find the optimal price to be constrained by the condition

$$0 = \frac{\partial Q}{\partial P}(\hat{P} - V) + Q \qquad \text{Eq. 2.18}$$

Equation 2.18 requires an understanding of the partial derivative of the quantity sold with respect to price ($\partial Q/\partial P$). Changes in demand with respect to price are defined in the continuously differential form of the elasticity of demand:

$$\varepsilon \equiv \frac{\%\Delta Q}{\%\Delta P} = \frac{\Delta Q/Q}{\Delta P/P} \Rightarrow \varepsilon = \frac{\partial Q/Q}{\partial P/P} \qquad \text{Eq. 2.19}$$

Thus, we can make the following substitution for the partial derivative of the quantity sold with respect to price ($\partial Q/\partial P$):

$$\frac{\partial Q}{\partial P} = \varepsilon \frac{Q}{P} \qquad \text{Eq. 2.20}$$

Substituting Equation 2.20 for the partial derivative of demand with respect to price in Equation 2.18, we identify the optimal price in the case of elastic markets ($\varepsilon > 1$) to be

$$0 = \varepsilon \frac{Q}{\hat{P}}(\hat{P} - V) + Q \qquad \text{Eq. 2.21a}$$

which simplifies to

$$\hat{P} = \frac{V\varepsilon}{(1 + \varepsilon)} \qquad \text{Eq. 2.21b}$$

Equation 2.21b is the same as Equation 2.13 for the optimal price.

The elasticity of demand captures the relationship between prices and volume. From the definition of the elasticity of demand, the demand curve can be found. Rewriting Equation 2.19 as

$$\varepsilon = \frac{\partial \ln Q}{\partial \ln P} \qquad \text{Eq. 2.22}$$

and under the assumption that the elasticity of demand is a constant, we can integrate Equation 2.22 to find the volume sold for a given price. The result is

$$\ln Q = \alpha + \varepsilon \ln P \qquad \text{Eq. 2.23}$$

Using the property that $e^{\ln X} = X$ on both sides of Equation 2.23, we identify the quantity sold at any price to be

$$Q = AP^{\varepsilon} \qquad \text{Eq. 2.24}$$

where constant A is simply a redefinition of the constant $\exp(\alpha)$. We find the maximum profit earned by substituting the expression for the optimal price (Eq. 2.21b) into that for the quantity sold (Eq. 2.24) and the firm's profit equation (Eq. 2.1).

Notes

[1] Economists use the term Giffen good to describe a good that violates the law of demand.... Giffen goods are inferior goods for which the income effect dominates the substitution effect. Therefore, they have demand curves that slope upward. Have any actual Giffen goods ever been observed? Some historians suggest that potatoes were a Giffen good during the Irish potato famine of the 19th century. Potatoes were such a large part of people's diet that when the price of potatoes rose, it had a large income effect. People responded to their reduced living standard by cutting back on the luxury of meat and buying more of the staple food of potatoes. Thus, it is argued that a higher price of potatoes actually raised the quantity of potatoes demanded. N. Gregory Mankiw, "The Theory of Consumer Choice," *Principles of Economics*, Sixth Edition (Mason, OH, Cengage Learning, 2012): 453–454.

[2] For a similar examination of a profit sensitivity analysis, see Thomas T. Nagle and Reed K. Holden, "Financial Analysis: Pricing for Profit," *The Strategy and Tactics of Pricing: A Guide to Profitable Decision Making*, 3rd ed. (Upper Saddle River, NJ: Prentice Hall, 2002): 37–39. See also Robert J. Dolan and Hermann Simon, "Price, Costs, and Profit: Economic Underpinnings of Pricing," *Power Pricing: How Managing Price Transforms the Bottom Line* (New York: Free Press, 1996): 17–41.

[3] David R. Bell, Jeongwen Chiang, and V. Padmanabhan, "The Decomposition of Promotional Response: An Empirical Generalization," *Marketing Science* 18, No. 4 (Autumn 1999): 504–26.

[4] Martin K. Perry, "Forward Integration by Alcoa: 1888–1930," *Journal of Industrial Economics* 29, No. 1 (September 1980): 37–53.

[5] Robert W. Crandall and Clifford Winston, "Does Antitrust Policy Improve Consumer Welfare? Assessing the Evidence," *Journal of Economic Perspectives* 17, No. 4 (Autumn 2003): 3–26.

[6] For a similar examination of economic price optimization, see Robert L. Phillips, "Basic Price Optimization," *Pricing and Revenue Optimization* (Stanford, CA: Stanford Business Press, 2005): 49–55.

Chapter 3

Customer Perception–Driven Pricing

Martin Lee/mediablitzimages (uk) Limited/Alamy
Martin Darley, 2010/Used under license from Shutterstock.com
Gerrit Buntrock/PhotoLibrary

- How can the perceptions of customers be used to set prices?
- How can intangible value be quantified and used for pricing?
- What is conjoint analysis, and how does it use customer perceptions to inform pricing?
- How does conjoint analysis compare to the other methods of price setting?
- Which method of price setting is found to be the most useful, and for which kinds of pricing challenges?
- Stretch Question: What is the value of a brand in monopolistic competition?

Given the tools defined up to this point, executives might be greatly dismayed at the inability of the basic quantitative means of identifying a good price. On one hand, exchange value models provide pricing guidance that is accurate but perhaps too wide. On the other hand, economic price optimization provides pricing guidance that is highly precise but often misleading. To set prices, executives require an approach that is both accurate and precise. Using customer perceptions directly is a proven means of guiding pricing decisions with both acceptable accuracy and precision.

Customer perception–driven pricing has become the dominant approach to pricing in many industries. Through market research, the willingness of customers to pay is identified, either directly or indirectly. The most common methodology for using customer perceptions to set prices is conjoint analysis.[1] Conjoint analysis is marketed under many different trade names and will vary in form; however, all these forms and trade names share a common foundation. Conjoint analysis reveals the tradeoffs that customers make in purchasing decisions and therefore identifies the best price that can both encourage customer purchases and deliver profits. Furthermore, conjoint analysis can be used to expand a pricing challenge beyond pricing a specific product to the more complex challenge of uncovering the willingness to pay for alternative variations of that product.

Conjoint analysis rose to dominate pricing challenges for evolutionary markets due to its precision and accuracy. As already discussed, exchange value models can identify a range of good prices. This range can be rather wide, however, driving executives to seek further clarity. Through conjoint analysis, executives can be much more precise in identifying the specific price most likely to optimize profits. On the other hand, economic price optimization allows executives to identify the predicted best price with extreme precision, but with little assurance that this price is indeed accurate, due to the inherent challenge of identifying the relevant metric of the elasticity of demand. Conjoint analysis overcomes this challenge and accurately identifies the best price for an individual product in the face of competition in many situations.

In this chapter, we provide an executive-level description of conjoint analysis and complete our exploration of rational approaches to setting prices. While the finer points of conjoint analysis can be found in texts dedicated to market research and statistical analysis, we will focus on an executive-level description of the approach. Every executive charged with pricing decisions should understand conjoint analysis at a managerial level to evaluate the merits of this approach for specific pricing decisions.

Despite the superior attributes of conjoint analysis, it is not the best approach for all pricing challenges. Exchange value models, conjoint analysis, and economic price optimization each has its place in guiding pricing decisions. Hence, we will also provide an analysis of the managerial tradeoffs in selecting one of the three dominant approaches to price setting.

Matching the Price-Setting Approach to the Market Stage

Exchange value calculators, economic price optimization, and conjoint analysis are the three dominant approaches to setting prices. Using any of these three approaches, executives can address an overwhelming majority of their price-setting challenges. Each of these approaches has been used in both business and consumer markets, services and tangible goods markets, and durable and consumable goods markets. Each also has its benefits and drawbacks in terms of accuracy and precision. Fortunately, there are clear differences in the appropriateness of these approaches in addressing the specific pricing challenge.[2] Executives may be able to select which approach should be used for their specific pricing challenge based on a few simple tradeoffs.

One of the key issues to align in selecting a price-setting approach is the market maturity. In revolutionary markets, where the product is defining a new product category and there are no directly competing offers, exchange value models tend to dominate the price-setting challenge. At the other extreme, in highly mature markets of commodity products where the difference between competing products is negligible, economic price optimization will dominate in price-setting questions. Between these two extremes, for established markets where products are evolving in both adding new points of value and finding new means of reducing costs, conjoint analysis is the dominate approach to setting prices.

REVOLUTIONARY MARKETS

In revolutionary markets, both executives and their customers lack sufficient critical information required to use most methods of price setting. Revolutionary markets are rare and unique. They are created by the introduction of the first product into a new market, such as the first electric-powered car, the first personal computer, the first railroad line, or the first mobile phone network. Truly revolutionary products are breakthrough initiatives that redefine the status quo, delivering dramatically different or totally new benefits to customers in a manner that had never before been considered. Compared to the alternative approaches, exchange value models are likely to be the best approach to setting prices in revolutionary markets.

The new product creates an entirely new market in a revolution. This revolutionary market will have no history from which one could even hope to identify the elasticity of demand through econometric means, and hence economic price optimization becomes a highly useless approach.

Furthermore, customers in this revolutionary market will have no experience with the product category. Product category experience is necessary for customers to learn the features and to inform them of the expected value of differing product configurations. If they lack the benefit of experience-based learning, customers may be unable to evaluate offers and make reliable tradeoffs. Because conjoint analysis fundamentally relies on customers making an informed decision regarding their preferences, it does not work well in revolutionary markets. One approach to overcoming this challenge is to provide the research subjects with an overwhelming amount of data regarding its value to them. At this point, many entrepreneurial firms will have been better off simply using the price determined by the exchange value model in the first place, and spending their limited marketing resources on selling it to customers rather than conducting research on them.

EVOLUTIONARY MARKETS

Evolutionary markets are common. They are markets in which products currently exist, customers currently purchase, and products are evolving. Product evolutions are found in subtle shifts in the features of products, such as adding chocolate chips to ice cream, power transmissions to forklifts, or faster customer service in banking. In comparison to the alternative approaches, conjoint analysis is typically the best approach to setting prices in evolutionary markets.[3]

By many measures, evolutionary products represent more than 98 percent of the new products on the market. By *evolutionary,* we mean products that make improvements to the status quo rather than disrupt the current evolution of products. The improvements in evolutionary markets typically derive from adding new features or benefits to existing products, whereas new products in revolutionary markets address customer needs in an entirely new manner.

In evolutionary markets, customers have experience with the product category. Through their experience, customers will have become aware of the existing products and their competition. They may also have developed sufficient insight to conceptualize different combinations of product attributes and predict their benefits. Therefore, in evolutionary markets, customers hold sufficient information that is critically required to make informed statements regarding their preferences, and therefore executives can reliably conduct conjoint analysis. Because evolutionary product enhancements are more common than revolutionary product creation, most marketing managers will rely heavily upon conjoint analysis.

Conjoint analysis is particularly appropriate and useful for brand managers. In evolutionary markets, not only will customers have familiarity with different features, products, and product categories, but they are also highly likely to be familiar with the existing brands. Marketing executives of branded goods can use this familiarity to identify price points for the product under different competing brand identifications, co-branding arrangements, and new brand introductions. As such, they can select the best brand association for a new product in an evolutionary market.

In comparison to exchange value models, conjoint analysis is more precise in most evolutionary markets. External customers tend to have better information than internal executives regarding the value the customers themselves will give to a product in contrast to its competitors in evolutionary markets. In contrast, internal product managers tend to have better information regarding the value of a product relative to its substitutes for revolutionary products. As such, conjoint analysis generally provides much deeper and more precise insights into the appropriate price in evolutionary markets, while exchange value models continue to be the workhorse in revolutionary markets.

A significant exception to this rule is found in small markets. Markets with few customers (that is, markets where the number of customers is on the order of magnitude of 10 to 100) are common in many industrial markets. Aircraft, nuclear generation, and paper manufacturing machines are good examples of markets with few customers. Because conjoint analysis relies on market research, and market research is itself reliant on the ability to collect data from a statistically relevant set of sample customers, conjoint analysis may become untenable in small markets.

Compared to economic price optimization, conjoint analysis is not only more accurate but also more relevant in evolutionary markets. Executives managing a product are far more interested in the best price for their particular product formulation rather than the product category as a whole. The best measures of elasticity of demand, a necessary input for economic price optimization, are usually found at the industry level. The industry-level elasticity of demand combines all the product features, attributes, and brands into a single metric. This prevents the ability of product managers to identify which features add value to the product and which can be dropped to improve profits.

MATURE MARKETS

For pure commodities sold to highly mature markets, economic price optimization is often used to guide pricing decisions. There is little product differentiation in commodity markets; thus, there is little to guide the price differentials required for an exchange value model to add value to the decision. Likewise, customers may be unable to differentiate between the values of competing commodity products, and therefore conjoint analysis is unlikely to reveal significant information. As such, economic price optimization continues to dominate pricing discussions for commodity products, and products tend to be sold at the market clearing price.

Conjoint Analysis

In conjoint analysis, researchers measure customer preferences between products.[4] Products are treated as a bundle of attributes, features, and benefits, where price can be one of those features in a conjoint analysis study. By measuring their preferences, researchers can detect how customers make tradeoffs and use these tradeoffs to decompose a product valuation into the sum of the values that customers assign to specific attributes, features, and benefits. In this manner, executives can determine how customers value specific product formulations and quantify the source of pricing power within their product.

In identifying the value that customers place on specific product attributes, features, and benefits, conjoint analysis creates a part-worth utility function. Because a specific product is the collection of a set of attributes, features, and benefits, the value of that product to a customer, or its customer net utility, is the sum of their part-worth utilities.

By decomposing a product value into its part-worth utilities, executives can ask "what if" questions. They can posit alternative variations of product formulations, each with its own cost structure, and identify which product formulation could be priced the highest, priced the lowest, capture the largest contribution margin, or capture the highest sales volume at a given price. Even product formulations that currently don't exist can be valued through conjoint as the sum of a product's part-worth utilities. The richness of these results enables executives to uncover new product compositions and potential prices to identify which specific product formulation at a specific price is likely to deliver the highest profit.

Conjoint analysis is a market research technique, and as such, the quantification of value comes directly from the customers' perspective. This is very important. Recall, in the exploration of the range of a good price, one of the key ingredients of capturing a better price is knowing how customers value a product. The closer a firm can price its products to a point just below the value customers place on that product, the higher the price the firm can capture. While exchange value models enable the firm to estimate the value that customers will place on a product, conjoint analysis will measure it.

Customer valuations will vary between customers, and conjoint analysis will reveal these variations. The dispersion in valuations can lead to an understanding of the expected demand at a given price even before a product is launched. From this anticipated demand curve, executives can use some of the techniques explored in economic price optimization in identifying the price most likely to deliver the highest profits, but with much greater accuracy and relevance.

If consumer dispersion in valuations of specific features can be aggregated into meaningfully different groups, conjoint analysis can form the basis of highly valuable market segmentation. The dispersion in valuations may derive from customers having alternative uses for a product that were not originally intended by the producer, or from satisfying a need greater than was anticipated. Market segmentation through product design requires this understanding of how some segments of customers prefer a certain product composition while other segments prefer an alternative composition. Executives can use these results to identify which product formulations might be attractive as an entry-level product into the category and which might serve as higher-value products to capture the more-demanding customers.

As with any market research technique, conjoint analysis shows only a snapshot of customer desires. New product concepts that may have not been considered in the research design may dramatically change the product valuations. Likewise, changes in the economic climate can alter the willingness to pay. In a rapidly evolving market, the outcomes from conjoint analysis may become dated before the product ever reaches the market. For slowly evolving markets, the changes within the market environment are manageable challenges to the outcomes of a conjoint analysis study.

Conjoint analysis can be done in a variety of forms and the market name for the approach varies with the form, such as discrete choice, tradeoff analysis, external analysis, or conjoint itself. The underlying principles and mathematics are similar across the differing forms. In purpose, each form attempts to reveal the structure of customer preferences that are ascribed in terms of levels of different attributes.

USING CUSTOMER PREFERENCES TO REVEAL PART-WORTH UTILITIES

In a conjoint analysis study, researchers ask participants that are representative of the target market to identify their preferences between different products. The products that customers choose between are themselves compilations of specific sets of features, attributes, and benefits. After customers make selections, the responses are analyzed with statistical methods. (Commercially available, off-the-shelf software can be used to automate the research design and data analysis.) The results from this analysis are the customers' part-worth utility functions.

To demonstrate how conjoint analysis can reveal a customer's part-worth utility function, we will use a simplified example with mango juice. This example will use hypothetical attributes and measurements and is not intended to be representative of fact but rather for elucidating the process of conducting a conjoint analysis.[5]

Fresh mango juice is common in tropical regions but is harder to find in latitudes farther north. As the world's population becomes more mobile, however, many peoples in northern climates are familiar with mango juice, either from their travels abroad or from their familiar roots in a tropical climate. Drink makers have increasingly become aware of the potential demand for mango juice in northern climates and have recently been making products to serve the growing demand. However, mango juice is relatively expensive to produce, transport, and distribute to northern climates. In response, many producers have chosen to offer mango juice blends rather than pure mango juice. In mango juice blends, the beverage is made mostly of non-mango juices such as grape, orange, and apple, but will contain some mango or an additive to impart a mango flavor.

For concreteness, consider a hypothetical 32-ounce container of mango juice. The producer can either offer pure mango juice or a mango fruit blend, and the product can be sold under a well-known national brand or a new premium niche brand. The executives would like to know the potential prices of the different formulations of mango juices marketed under different brand names.

In this hypothetical example, there will be three attributes under investigation: ingredients, brand, and price. Each attribute will be investigated at two different levels for this simplified example, but more attributes and levels could be explored in a more realistic investigation. The two ingredient levels are pure mango juice and mango fruit blend. The two branding levels are a well-known national brand and a premium niche brand. The price levels under consideration are \$4 and \$7. See Exhibit 3-1 for a 2 × 4 matrix depiction of the eight different potential product attributes and levels.

In the conjoint analysis study, participants are asked to rank the potential products in order of preference. For our example, consider a participant that most prefers pure mango juice with a national brand priced at \$4 and least prefers mango fruit blend priced with a premium niche brand price at \$7. Continuing to rank the products, from 1 being the most preferred to 8 being the least preferred, the participant exhausts the potential product formulations. See Exhibit 3-2 for this particular participant's rankings.

The participant's ranking of potential products is a measure of the utility that he or she places on each specific product formulation. Those with the highest utility were ranked

Exhibit 3-1 Mango Juice Attributes

	Price			
	Ingredient		Ingredient	
Brand	Pure Mango Juice Premium Niche \$7	Mango Fruit Blend Premium Niche \$7	Pure Mango Juice Premium Niche \$4	Mango Fruit Blend Premium Niche \$4
	Pure Mango Juice National \$7	Mango Fruit Blend National \$7	Pure Mango Juice National \$4	Mango Fruit Blend National \$4

Exhibit 3-2 Mango Juice Rankings

	Price			
	Ingredient		Ingredient	
Brand	Pure Mango Juice Premium Niche $7	Mango Fruit Blend Premium Niche $7	Pure Mango Juice Premium Niche $4	Mango Fruit Blend Premium Niche $4
	Rank = 6	Rank = 8	Rank = 2	Rank = 4
	Pure Mango Juice National $7	Mango Fruit Blend National $7	Pure Mango Juice National $4	Mango Fruit Blend National $4
	Rank = 5	Rank = 7	Rank = 1	Rank = 3

first, while those with the lowest utility were ranked last. The researcher can use this to prepare the data collected from this participant for evaluation by scoring it from 0 to 7, where the lowest score is that which yields the lowest utility and the highest score yields the highest utility. See Exhibit 3-3 for the researcher's data preparation.

These product scores can be used to evaluate the part-worth utility function of this participant. The part-worth utility of a specific attribute level is found by averaging the scores of the products that have that particular attribute level. For simplicity, we will measure part-worth utilities with a metric called utils, an economist's unit of utility. See Exhibit 3-4.

To find the participant's utility for a specific product formulation, we simply add the part-worth utilities associated with the specific attribute levels. We can see that the utility valuation from the sum of part-worth utilities reproduces the same rankings as the participant reported in the survey. See Exhibit 3-5.

Because price was one of the attributes being measured in the conjoint analysis, we can place a monetary value on the unit of utils. Specifically, the ratio of price disparity in the study design to util disparity between the two price points found from the customer preferences reveals the dollar value per util. Because the price ranged from $4 to $7 and the calculated part-worth utilities ranged from 5.5 to 1.5 utils, we find the valuation of $0.75/util. See Equation 3.1.

$$\$0.75/\text{util} = \frac{(\$7 - \$4)}{(5.5 \text{ utils} - 1.5 \text{ utils})} \qquad \text{Eq. 3.1}$$

Exhibit 3-3 Mango Juice Scores

	Price			
	Ingredient		Ingredient	
Brand	Pure Mango Juice Premium Niche $7	Mango Fruit Blend Premium Niche $7	Pure Mango Juice Premium Niche $4	Mango Fruit Blend Premium Niche $4
	Score = 2	Score = 0	Score = 6	Score = 4
	Pure Mango Juice National $7	Mango Fruit Blend National $7	Pure Mango Juice National $4	Mango Fruit Blend National $4
	Score = 3	Score = 1	Score = 7	Score = 5

Exhibit 3-4 Mango Juice Part-Worth Utility

Attribute	Level	Average Score	Part Worth Utility (utils)
Ingredient	Pure Mango	(2 + 3 + 6 + 7)/4	4.5
	Fruit Blend	(0 + 1 + 4 + 5)/4	2.5
Brand	Premium Niche	(2 + 0 + 6 + 4)/4	3.0
	National	(3 + 1 + 7 + 5)/4	4.0
Price	$7	(2 + 0 + 3 + 1)/4	1.5
	$4	(6 + 4 + 7 + 5)/4	5.5

Exhibit 3-5 Mango Juice Utilities

Product	Utility (utils)	Ranking
Pure Mango, Premium Niche, $7	4.5 + 3.0 + 1.5 = 9.0	6
Mango Fruit Blend, Premium Niche, $7	2.5 + 3.0 + 1.5 = 7.0	8
Pure Mango, Premium Niche, $4	4.5 + 3.0 + 5.5 = 13.0	2
Mango Fruit Blend, Premium Niche, $4	2.5 + 3.0 + 5.5 = 11.0	4
Pure Mango, National, $7	4.5 + 4.0 + 1.5 = 10.0	5
Mango Fruit Blend, National, $7	2.5 + 4.0 + 1.5 = 8.0	7
Pure Mango, National, $4	4.5 + 4.0 + 5.5 = 14.0	1
Mango Fruit Blend, National, $4	2.5 + 4.0 + 5.5 = 12.0	3

Armed with this information, we can calculate the preference value that this participant places on different attribute levels. For instance, Exhibit 3-4 shows that the difference in utility of a national brand versus premium niche brand is 1 util, or $0.75. For this participant, the premium niche brand detracts value from the product with respect to a national brand. Likewise, Exhibit 3-4 shows that the difference in utility of pure mango juice versus a mango fruit blend is 2 utils, or $1.50. Purity in mango juice adds value for this participant.

We can also use the attribute-level valuations to compare different products that could be made. For instance, a new entrant to this market promoting a premium niche brand of pure mango juice competing against an established national brand of mango fruit blend priced at $4 would have to market its product at a price less than $4.75 to attract this research participant. This product valuation is found by adding the part-worth utility differences between premium niche versus national (−1.0 utils) and that between pure mango juice and mango fruit blend (2.0 utils), which yields 1 util. This participant values 1 util at $0.75, so this product could attract this participant away from the $4 established brand only if priced at or below $4.75.

Different customers will have different rankings leading to different part-worth utility functions. The aggregate market's part-worth utility for specific attributes is the average of each individual participant's part-worth utility. Rather than finding the aggregate market's utility for a product formulation, it is often more insightful to identify the willingness to pay of each different product formulation for each research participant to create potential demand curves for the market of specific product formulations. If there are meaningful differences between the utility rankings of market research participants that can be aggregated, researchers can also segment the market and uncover the prices that different segments would be willing to pay for different product compositions.

STUDY DESIGN

Conjoint analysis is clearly a very powerful tool to gain insight into customer preferences, as the example described previously demonstrates. Its value to executives in understanding markets, evaluating products, and identifying prices has made conjoint analysis a routine technique of many market researchers to evaluate markets, products, and prices since its introduction in 1964. Along the way, the design of a conjoint analysis study has become codified.[6]

In essence, there are five basic steps in a conjoint analysis: (1) defining the attributes and attribute levels, (2) presenting the stimulus, (3) measuring the response, (4) setting the evaluation criterion, and (5) analyzing the data. Each of these will be examined in the following sections.

Defining the Attribute

One of the key values of conjoint analysis is its ability to identify the value that customers place on different attributes. To accomplish this task, researchers must clearly define the attributes under investigation and the levels of those attributes to be investigated. Conjoint analysis cannot identify the utility of attributes and levels that are not stated, hence the attribute and level lists need to be full, relevant, and executable.

In our mango juice example, the attributes considered included ingredients, brand, and price. To take another example, we could consider a commuter bicycle. A commuter bicycle could be described as a compilation of physical attributes, performance benefits, and psychological positioning. Physical attributes refer to tangible issues, such as the frame weight, or hardware features, such as tire width and braking system. Performance attributes are the benefits that the commuter bicycle will deliver, such as stopping distance under wet conditions, or the effect of frame weight and tire width on cycling speed or durability in handling potholes in the street. Psychological positioning refers to the feelings that the product could invoke, such as the emotional connection a brand might have to Lance Armstrong, or the assurance of stopping quickly in high traffic, or the desire to improve one's health and look more fit by commuting to work.

Attribute selection includes both the choice of which attributes will be investigated and the different levels of those attributes. For instance, with the commuter bicycle, the tires could be evaluated at three levels of width—narrow, medium, or wide—or the selection could be expanded to include five levels by adding extra wide and extra narrow widths. Likewise, the braking system could be evaluated as being either of disc or pivot type, or it could be expanded to include standard disc, high-performance disc, standard pivot, or high-performance pivot, making four different attribute levels for a second single attribute. Combined, the difference between using limited levels with these two attributes and using an expanded number of levels is one of investigating six ($3 \cdot 2 = 6$) different product compositions versus twenty ($5 \cdot 4 = 20$). For most pricing questions, researchers will have a far lengthier list of attributes, with a wide range of potential levels to be investigated.

Presenting the Stimulus

Products can be presented to research participants in a variety of ways, and the results of conjoint analysis may depend in part on the way in which the product in question is presented. The development of a survey is an art in itself, and pretesting is commonly used to investigate whether the survey questions reveal the facts that are needed to inform managerial decision making or fail to interpret the results with certainty. The more popular forms of stimulus presentation include verbal descriptions, paragraph descriptions, or pictorial representations.

In a verbal description of the product, the attribute is listed along with its level. Continuing with the hypothetical mango juice study, the attribute of brand was stated as either national brand or premium niche brand. Some of the key advantages to verbal descriptions are its simplicity in execution, efficiency in collection of data, and variety in number of attributes and levels that can be considered in a single study.

Paragraph descriptions are perceived by some researchers to provide a more realistic and complete description of the product, which would lead to more reliable measurements of results. A significant drawback of paragraph descriptions is that the total number of descriptions is limited to a small number, which may lead to an inaccurate understanding of the complexity in demand.

With both verbal and paragraph descriptions, care must be taken when preparing the stimulus to ensure that executives can interpret the results accurately. For instance, let us continue with our commuter bicycle example and the levels of braking system under consideration. The brake levels may be described as either pivot brakes or disc brakes. Pivot brakes, which are found on most racing and mountain bicycles, are more common. Disc brakes are far less common but are sometimes prized for their shorter stopping distances in wet conditions. As such, these same brake levels may alternatively be described as having a normal stopping performance or having a quicker stopping performance in wet conditions. In choosing between these two product descriptions, the researcher is evaluating a physical attribute versus a performance benefit. This choice may be guided by an understanding of the target market. For instance, a new bicycle purchaser may not understand the differences between pivot brakes and disc brakes but would be able to discriminate meaningfully between the value of the two performance descriptions.

Pictorial representations use various visual props or three-dimensional models in soliciting participant responses. They hold several advantages over verbal descriptions in that the stimulus can be more realistic, the pictorial representations are more likely to communicate the meaning of different attribute levels accurately, the participants are less likely to suffer from information overload in reviewing multiple lists of features, and the task itself is more interesting and less fatiguing. The primary disadvantage of pictorial representations is in the cost to prepare and present the stimulus.

Measuring the Response

While our mango juice example required participants to rank their preferences in order, preferences can be measured in many other ways. Measurements of preferences can use nonmetric means, such as rank ordering or paired comparisons. They can also use metric approaches, such as rating scales or ratio scales. Each of these approaches has been investigated with multiple variations.

In rank-ordering studies, participants typically are provided with a stack of cards where each card holds a product description or stimulus presentation. Participants are then asked to divide the cards into two piles, preferred and not-preferred, and then repeat the procedure starting with the preferred half, moving through the pile until the ranking is complete.

In a paired comparison approach, two products are presented at a time and the participant is asked to state her or his preference. See Exhibit 3-6. Its advantage over rank ordering is its increased reliability in producing results. It suffers, however, in terms of the time required to complete the task. A pairwise comparison of n products would require $n(n - 1)/2$ different choices. For a limited investigation of only five attributes at two different levels, a paired comparison would require each participant to make 45 choices—not the easiest way to assure choice accuracy. Designing a research survey with a large number of paired comparisons requires great care. At times, an approach known as *orthogonal design* can be used to reduce the number of paired comparisons greatly, while delivering similar accuracy.

Exhibit 3-6 Paired Comparison: *Which Commuter Cycle do you Prefer?*

Gray Disc Brakes 700 × 38C Street tires Made in China Well-known brand Price is several dollars more than average	OR	Black Pivot Brakes 26" × 1.95" Rugged tires Made in the United States Unknown brand Price is average

Metrics such as rating scales have been adapted by some researchers due to their ease of administration. With rating scales, participants are asked to rate their level of interest in a product. See Exhibit 3-7. The scale can be continuous, as shown in the exhibit, or discrete, such as giving a product a whole-number rating between 1 and 100. Functionally, researchers have shown that rating scales and rank ordering can yield similar results under many circumstances.

Setting the Evaluation Criterion

One of the more subtle issues in a conjoint analysis study is the criteria that participants are asked to use to justify their preferences. Two evaluative criteria commonly requested are either a statement of overall preference or intention to buy.

The evaluation criterion used may bias the results of the study inappropriately. For instance, consider two potential commuter bicycles: (1) Schwinn World GS, Disc Brakes, costing $499; and (2) Trek District, Alloy Dual-Pivot Brakes, costing $929. Research participants may, in some sense, prefer the Trek option but, due to lack of financial resources, may be more likely to purchase the Schwinn option.

In practice, both preference and likelihood to purchase are used as the evaluation criterion about equally. The intention to purchase evaluations have been identified to be particularly suitable for new product classes and services that consumers do not purchase currently. These studies help researchers estimate the potential market size for such items. When studying more established markets, preference evaluations have been identified to be more useful in estimating market shares.

Exhibit 3-7 Rating Scale

- Commuter Cycle
  - The cycle is *gray.*
  - The cycle has *disc brakes.*
  - The cycle is *better than average.*
  - The cycle costs *several dollars more than average.*
  - The cycle is made in *China.*
  - The label on the cycle is a *well-known brand.*
- Based on the information above, how likely is it that you would purchase this commuter cycle?

Not at All Likely ———————————————— Very Likely

Analyzing the Data

The type of data analysis that is conducted depends upon the prior decisions regarding response type. If rank ordering has been used, then it is appropriate to recognize that we don't really know by how much one alternative is preferred over another. We can only analyze the ordering of preferences through techniques such as monotone analysis of variance (MONANOVA), PREFMAP, or LINMAP. If paired comparisons have been used in which participants have been asked to state their probability of choice, LOGIT and PROBIT methods can be used to accommodate the fact that probabilities lie between zero and 1. If rating scores have been used, the partwise utility system is derived through regression analysis such as ordinary least squares (OLS) or minimum sum of absolute errors (MSAE).

Each of these procedures yields an estimate of the participant's part-worth utility functions. We will leave it to the interested reader to consult a market research text for greater detail about the nature of these data analysis techniques as we attempt to keep this text at a level appropriate for the general executive charged with pricing responsibilities.

Summary

- Customer perception–driven pricing has become the dominant approach to pricing in many industries. The most popular and academically sound approach to measuring customer perceptions of value is conjoint analysis.
- Conjoint analysis, exchange value calculators, and economic price optimization are the three dominant approaches to setting prices. Using these three approaches, executives can address an overwhelming majority of their price-setting challenges. Each of these approaches has been used in both business and consumer markets, services and tangible goods markets, and durable and consumable goods markets.
- One of the key issues in selecting a price-setting approach is the market maturity. Exchange value calculators tend to dominate price-setting challenges with revolutionary products. Conjoint analysis tends to dominate price-setting challenges with differentiated and evolutionary markets. Economic price optimization tends to dominate pricing discussions for commodity products in mature markets.
- In conjoint analysis, researchers measure customer preferences between products. The products themselves are treated as a bundle of attributes, features, and benefits. By measuring their preferences, researchers can detect how customers make tradeoffs and quantify the value of different attributes, features, and benefits.
- Part-worth utility functions are identified in a conjoint analysis. Each specific attribute, feature, or benefit has a part-worth utility. The overall utility of a product is the sum of its part-worth utilities.
- Dispersion between the part-worth utility functions that customers place on different attributes can be used to identify market segments and estimate market shares of products serving those market segments.
- Conjoint studies require identifying (1) attribute definition, (2) stimulus presentation, (3) response measurement, (4) evaluation criterion, and (5) data analysis.
- Attributes can include physical attributes, performance benefits, and psychological positioning.
- Products can be presented to participants in a variety of ways. The more popular forms of stimulus presentation include verbal descriptions, paragraph descriptions, or pictorial representations.

- Measurements of preferences can use nonmetric means, such as rank ordering or paired comparisons. They can also use metric approaches, such as rating scales or ratio scales.
- Two evaluative criteria commonly requested are either a statement of overall preference or an intention to buy.
- Data from a conjoint study is analyzed through a variety of statistical means to develop the part-worth utility functions.

Exercises

1. Consider the following items and the challenge of setting their prices. If selecting between exchange value models, economic price optimization, or conjoint analysis, which method would be most appropriate, and why?
   a. Coal
   b. A new software app for the iPad
   c. Ocean Spray laundry detergent
   d. A new fastener for the automotive industry
   e. A training seminar on treating patients with mental dementia
   f. A forklift with an automatic transmission
   g. Boneless chicken breasts sold to restaurants
   h. Branded boneless chicken breasts sold to consumers through a grocer
2. A new business product has been subjected to a conjoint analysis study. One respondent provided the following part-worth utilities for differentiating features A, B, C, and D of this product. A competing product currently is priced at $600. What is the perceived value of the product in comparison to the competing product?

Feature	Part-Worth Utility
A	+ $200
B	+ $25
C	– $75
D	+ $130

3. The Chicago Garden Dog is served with a Vienna beef wiener on a poppy-seed roll with sweet pickle relish, mustard, onions, tomato wedges, cucumber slices, sport peppers, and celery salt. A New York Dirty Water Dog is served with a natural-casing all beef frankfurter on a white-bread roll with sauerkraut, mustard, onions, and tomato relish. A researcher wants to investigate the pricing of a Chicago Garden Dog and a New York Dirty Water Dog. She collects the following rank order information regarding the perceived value of the different attributes of hot dogs, where 1 is most preferred and 8 is least preferred.

   Dog: Vienna Beef *OR* Natural Casing (all beef frankfurter with Natural Casing)

   Toppings: Garden (poppy-seed roll, sweet pickle relish, mustard, onions, tomato wedges, cucumber slices, sport peppers, and celery salt) *OR* Dirty Water (white-bread roll, sauerkraut, mustard, onions, and tomato relish)

   Price: $2.50 or $3.50

	Price			
	Topping		**Topping**	
	Garden Vienna Beef $2.50	Dirty Water Vienna Beef $2.50	Garden Vienna Beef $3.50	Dirty Water Vienna Beef $3.50
	Rank = 2	Rank = 6	Rank = 4	Rank 8
Hot Dog	Garden Natural Casing $2.50	Dirty Water Natural Casing $2.50	Garden Natural Casing $3.50	Dirty Water Natural Casing $3.50
	Rank = 1	Rank = 5	Rank = 3	Rank = 7

a. Score the hot dog offerings from 0 to 7, with 0 being the lowest-utility hot dog and 7 being the highest-utility hot dog.

b. Calculate the part-worth utility of each of the attributes at their different levels.

c. For each combination of hot dogs, toppings, and prices, what is the utility measured in utils?

d. Calculate the dollar value per util.

e. What is the utility difference between Garden toppings and Dirty Water toppings in utils?

f. What is the utility difference between Vienna beef dogs and natural-casing dogs in utils?

g. If a nearby established competitor offers a Chicago Garden Dog at $3, what would be an appropriate price for a natural-casing hot dog with Garden toppings? A natural-casing hot dog with Dirty Water toppings? A Vienna beef dog with Dirty Water toppings?

4. In designing a conjoint analysis study for pricing a coffeemaker, name three attributes and at least two different levels for each attribute that might be used in the study.

5. Which type of stimulus presentation would be best for evaluating the merits of a product package? Of a technical feature, such as reduced fuel consumption of a truck?

6. In measuring responses, why might researchers choose to use rank ordering over other methods? When might they prefer to switch to paired comparisons?

7. Which evaluation criterion would be suggested for the following conjoint analysis studies?

   a. Hellmann's mayonnaise with chili spice

   b. A 3-D gaming console

   c. A solar-powered automobile

   d. A Volvo heavy truck

8. In a conjoint analysis study of forklifts using two respondents, Respondent A valued an automatic transmission forklift at 18,000 euros, while Respondent B valued an automatic transmission forklift at 21,500 euros.

a. What percentage of the market might the company expect to capture if it sold automatic transmission forklifts priced at 21,500 euros?

b. What percentage of the market might the company expect to capture if it sold automatic transmission forklifts priced at 18,000 euros?

c. Draw the demand curve for these two respondents for an automatic transmission forklift, assuming that the entire market consists of Respondent A and Respondent B.

Notes

[1] Paul E. Green, Abba M. Krieger, and Yorum (Jerry) Wind, "Thirty Years of Conjoint Analysis: Reflections and Prospects," *Marketing Engineering* 31, No. 3 (May–June 2001): S56–S73.

[2] Kent B. Monroe and Albert J. Della Bitta, "Models for Pricing Decisions," *Journal of Marketing Research* 15 (August 1978): 413–28.

[3] Philippe Cattin and Richard Wittink, "Commercial Use of Conjoint Analysis: A Survey," *Journal of Marketing* 46, No. 3 (Summer 1982): 44–53. Dick R. Wittink and Philippe Cattin, "Commercial Use of Conjoint Analysis: An Update," *Journal of Marketing* 53, No. 3 (July 1989): 91–96.

[4] Paul E. Green and Vithala R. Rao, "Conjoint Measurement for Quantifying Judgmental Data," *Journal of Marketing Research* 8, No. 3 (August 1971): 355–63.

[5] A similar type of example and illustration of conjoint analysis can be found in C. Scott Greene and Japhet Nkonge, "Gaining a Competitive Edge through Conjoint Analysis," *Business* (Atlanta) 39 (April–June 1989): 14–18.

[6] Paul E. Green and V. Srinivasan, "Conjoint Analysis in Consumer Research: Issues and Outlook," *Journal of Consumer Research* 5, No. 2 (September 1978): 103–23.

Chapter 4

Price to Value

Jochen Luebke/Newscom

paul prescott, 2010/Used under license from Shutterstock.com

- What should we expect to find when we identify products on the price versus value plane?
- What does it mean to be priced to value? Value advantaged? Value disadvantaged?
- Are penetration pricing and skim pricing the only pricing strategies for launching a new product?
- When launching a new product, which competitors are most likely to be threatened?
- Stretch Question: When considering the use of price versus value to capture market share, which approach is more defensible?

For every price-setting technique that we have considered, the issue of value has had to be considered. In reviewing the results of negotiation exercises, we saw that negotiators who can transact at a price closer to the reservation value of their counterpart will capture a better price. From the exchange value models, we demonstrated the potential to estimate the value that customers will place on a product and argued for pricing at or just below the identified exchange value. Setting prices with conjoint analysis likewise requires measuring customer preferences to calculate their valuation of products and set prices accordingly. Even in economic price optimization, the issue of value from the customer's perspective is important. The demand at any given price is a count of the number of customers that value the product at, or more than, the price being considered. Thus value, from the customer's perspective, is the key to pricing.

The importance of pricing in proportion to value is so strong that, in many markets, the relationship between value and price is linearly correlated. Higher-valued products are sold at higher prices; lower-valued products are sold at lower prices.

From a broad perspective, we can see this relationship with automobile sedans. There is a large variation in prices for sedans, ranging from the Tata Nano at $2,500, the Chevrolet Malibu at $28,000, and the Bentley Flying Spur at $170,000, using rough estimates of 2008 prices. The difference between the lowest-price proposed sedan and the highest-price production sedan is nearly a factor of 70. What justifies this huge price difference? The answer is simple: the value delivered in the form of benefits. Although both the Tata Nano and the Bentley Flying Spur will transport a family of four from A to B, we would be hard-pressed to find anyone who thinks these two sedans are comparable in terms of benefits delivered. The Bentley Flying Spur simply delivers far greater benefits than the Tata Nano could hope to achieve.

Value-based pricing is not just the underpinning of the price-setting methods considered so far, it is also the starting point for all refinements to prices that we will consider in future chapters. Pricing to value is a guiding principle in many strategic and tactical pricing actions. When launching a new product, repositioning an existing product, or tactically discounting a product to capture a specific segment, value from customers' perspectives can act as a guide to evaluating the profitability of the action. Moreover, as we will see in Chapter 5, firms have some influence over customer perception of value, and therefore over their prices.

In this chapter, we will explore pricing to value using a price-to-benefits map. From this map, we will demonstrate the importance of pricing to value, the potential to price in alternative positions, challenges that arise when benefits or prices are unclear, and opportunities for launching a new product within a crowded competitive market.

Price-to-Benefits Map

In a price-to-benefits map, products are positioned according to their perceived prices on the vertical axis against their perceived benefits on the horizontal axis.[1] It is a visual representation of how customers perceive the value tradeoffs.

Price-to-benefits maps are directly related to both exchange value models and conjoint analysis. In constructing an exchange value model, executives are estimating the differential values of products in comparison to relevant competing alternatives. Price setting from exchange value models is a simple exercise of identifying a price that approaches the management agreed-upon exchange value from below. Likewise, using conjoint analysis, executives can detect the differential value of both exiting products and potential new product formulations. Moreover, conjoint analysis can reveal how customers perceive the value of various attributes, features, and benefits. Price setting with conjoint analysis is an exercise of identifying the price that customers perceive as leaving them with sufficient value after the transaction to encourage their purchase. Both these techniques encourage firms to price in proportion to benefits. Price-to-benefits maps add to these other price-setting techniques by providing executives with a strategic vantage point into the position of their product compared to all the relevant competition.

We can demonstrate a price-to-benefits map with the automobile sedan market. In designing and positioning the Tata Nano, executives at Tata Motors have deliberately attempted to market a sedan that provides little more than basic transportation. Customers can be expected to perceive the Tata Nano as having both the fewest benefits and the lowest price of sedans on the market. In contrast, executives at Bentley have deliberately strived to deliver the most luxurious sedan on the market with the Flying Spur. They have worked to give the Flying Spur superb performance, handling, comfort, sound, and automation, to name a few dimensions of benefits. Customers of the Bentley Flying Spur may even perceive that this sedan confers status upon them because of its impressive features. It can be expected that customers would perceive the Bentley Flying Spur as having not only

Exhibit 4-1 Sketch of Price to Benefits for Sedans

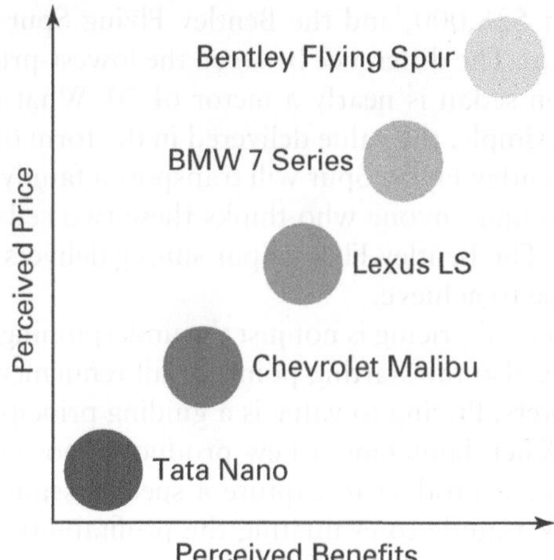

one of the highest prices on the commercial market, but also the highest level of benefits that can be had in a commercially available sedan. Between these two extremes, there are several other sedans such as the Chevrolet Malibu, Lexus LS, and BMW 7 Series. Each of these sedans offers different levels of benefits in terms of safety, performance, luxury, and status. If we were to measure the perceived benefits of these sedans and plot them against the perceived prices, the results are likely to resemble Exhibit 4-1.

VALUE EQUIVALENCE LINE

In our sketch of the perceived price against perceived benefits in the sedan market, products are positioned along a line. This line is called the *value equivalence line.* See Exhibit 4-2.

For products positioned along the value equivalence line, the benefits delivered by a product increase in proportion to the prices. Goods that deliver greater benefits can be

Exhibit 4-2 Price-to-Benefits Zones

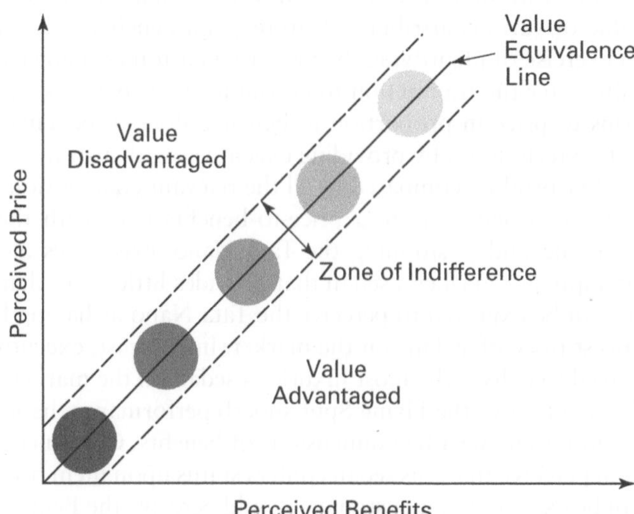

priced higher, while goods that deliver fewer benefits can only capture a lower price. The value equivalence line shows the correlation between perceived benefits and prices for competing products within a market.

The value equivalence line is depicted as lying along a 45-degree angle, but it need not be. The angle is somewhat arbitrarily dependent upon the metric of benefits. Moreover, the value placed on different levels of benefits varies between markets. Even within a single market, different segments will value the benefits differently, causing the slope of the value equivalence line to be different between the segments.

More interesting than the absolute value of the angle of the value equivalence line are changes in the slope of the value equivalence line. Changes in the slope of the value equivalence line indicate shifts within customer demand. Market evolutions where new products are offered that deliver a different set of benefits may affect the perceived tradeoffs between prices and benefits. When these market evolutions drive a change in the slope of the value equivalence line, executives of existing products face a challenge in repositioning their products and an opportunity to uncover the nature of the new demanded benefits and deliver an offer that meets customer desires.

In the simplest approach, executives will use observed market prices and specific product attributes to define the benefits metric in constructing a price-to-value plot.[2] Often however, more thorough effort is required to construct a price-to-value plot. In the common situation of executives attempting to resolve a current pricing challenge, many researchers suggest using market research to identify the benefits metric that is best correlated with average selling prices or perceived prices. In less-common situations, where executives are searching for subtle changes in customer tastes, some researchers have found that using expert opinions gleaned from product reviews is useful for identifying the set of benefits that account for the greatest proportion of variation in price and the variation of this set of benefits over time.[3] The most appropriate technique for drafting the price-to-value plot will depend on the strategic question being addressed and the availability of data. Regardless of the technique used to identify the metric of perceived benefits, the qualitative concept is similar. Prices tend to increase in proportion to benefits.

ZONE OF INDIFFERENCE

Small variations in perceived price or benefits around the value equivalence line often have negligible effects on sales volume. Hence, there is a zone of indifference around the value equivalence line. Prices of products may be able to increase slightly above the value equivalence line without having a measurable effect on sales. For some firms, this can serve as a costless means to improve profitability.

The zone of indifference may arise due to the inability of products to exhaust the value equivalence line and challenges in customer purchase decisions. In making a purchase, customers may be benefit-bracketed or price-bracketed. Benefit or price brackets can prevent them from easily switching products when alternatives are distant in their position to one another on the price-to-benefits map.

Benefits brackets may arise from customers demanding a particular set of benefits that are delivered through only a subset of the products within the market. A benefit floor may arise from customers requiring a minimal level of benefits from the product category to warrant a purchase. For instance, a customer may believe that accounting software must be able to produce a profit and loss report or perceive it as having no value over an Excel spreadsheet. A benefits ceiling can arise from customers who are unable to take advantage of certain product features; for instance, some customers may feel that discounted cash flow analysis is unnecessary within their accounting software.

Examples of issues that can give rise to price brackets are budget constraints or credibility issues. Budgetary constraints may force customers to purchase items below a certain level even if they agree that they would gain greater benefits if they purchased a higher-priced product. Customers suffering from budgetary constraints may be forced to "make do" with the best available product below a certain price point. Products can also suffer from a credibility challenge. Low-priced products may be perceived as having very little credible value to warrant any investigation into their benefits. High-priced products may be perceived to be unable to provide sufficient credible benefits to warrant the price, and hence they are also discarded. For many purchasing situations, products are evaluated with respect to a zone of credibility.

If the next nearest competitor in terms of benefits delivered is much higher or lower than the product under consideration, or if the next nearest competitor in terms of price is much higher or lower than the product under consideration, then the price of the product may be changed somewhat without having many customers defect to the competing offer due to their benefits brackets.

Not all products within all markets will fall within the zone of indifference. Outside of the zone of indifference lie the value-advantaged zone and the value-disadvantaged zone. Products lying in the value-advantaged or -disadvantaged zones are either priced significantly lower or higher than the corresponding levels of benefits, as perceived by customers.

VALUE ADVANTAGED

Products that deliver far more benefits than the price extracted are said to be *value advantaged*. Value-advantaged products can be created when firms choose to price aggressively, thus providing more benefits than expected at a given price, or when a product is enhanced with added features and benefits but the price is not changed. In either case, positioning a product in the value-advantaged area on the price-to-benefits map implies that the product provides an expected excess value in comparison to the price.

Researchers sometimes refer to products positioned in the value-advantaged area as being priced with *unharvested value*. These researchers believe that positioning a product in the value-advantaged area implies that the firm could have priced their offering higher. Thus, the executives will have failed to harvest the value that they deliver and may have committed a pricing error, which failed to maximize profits. Examples of unharvested value may be found in theatrical performances when tickets for front-row seats are sold below that which customers are willing to pay in secondary markets.

Alternatively, positioning a product as value advantaged is sometimes purposely executed to take market share. By providing more benefit than competing products at a given price, customers will have an incentive to select that product.

Despite the potential to improve volumes and market share, executives should reflect carefully on the consequences of positioning a product as value advantaged before executing this strategy. Deliberately positioning a product as value advantaged can have some negative consequences.

When competitors identify a product as value advantaged, they are likely to react in various ways. One form of reaction might be to launch a similar product priced at a similar level of benefits to negate the price-to-benefits differential of the value-advantaged products. Fortunately, to bring a new product through the product development cycle and into a market launch requires time; so the threat of a competitor reacting with the launch of a new, similarly benefit-oriented product may be relatively benign. The more common reaction of competitors is simply to drop their prices on existing products, potentially initiating an all-out price war. Price wars are not just bad for individual firm-level profits; they tend to harm overall industry health for an extended period as well.

In technology-driven markets, certain product categories may evolve rapidly with sequential improvements in benefits delivered per price paid, a pattern known as *hypercompetition*.[4] For instance, DRAM memory costs per kilobyte decrease each time a new photolithography technique becomes available. LCD TVs, computer processors, software, and nanotech products have all been found to demonstrate similar trajectories. Hypercompetitive markets are like a bare-knuckle brawl. Firms will price new technology that offers significant cost advantages aggressively over legacy technology; that is a common trait in these markets. Executives who have performed well in them have focused their firms on speed of delivery in launching improvements, often relying on a hard learning curve for imitators to provide strategic room for maneuvering.

In general, firms should not position their product as value advantaged unless they hold a concurrent cost advantage or perceive that the action will deliver a future cost advantage in the form of an economy of scale, scope, or learning. When the firm has a cost advantage over its competitors, it may endure a price battle with greater health than the industry's average competitor, enabling it to emerge from a temporary skirmish in a better position. Even when executives perceive that they hold a cost advantage, they should take actions to minimize the price skirmish, as discussed in Chapter 15.

VALUE DISADVANTAGED

Products that are priced high relative to the benefits they deliver are value disadvantaged. Value-disadvantaged products can be created when the firm positions a product with many features and benefits at a high price, but customers perceive little value from these new attributes. Value-disadvantaged positioning can also arise from changes in the competitive landscape that leave a product misaligned in terms of price and benefits. A product positioned in the value-disadvantaged area typically suffers from lost market share.

Researchers sometimes refer to products that are value disadvantaged as suffering from missed opportunities. These researchers believe that positioning a product as value disadvantaged implies that the firm could have sold more units if their prices were more in line with the expectations of the market. Thus, the executives will have missed the opportunity to capture market attention and may have committed a pricing error that fails to maximize profits. Examples of missed opportunities may be found with media sales situations where advertising space goes unsold because its price is too high in comparison to the value that it delivers for a segment of potential advertisers.

Alternatively, products may be deliberately positioned as value disadvantaged due to a market segmentation strategy. Some segments within the market may prefer a certain combination of benefits that are not valued by others. A firm may attempt to capture that segment profitably by offering a product with those benefits and pricing it in proportion to the value that the chosen target segments deem worthy of purchase, and yet the market overall deems the position to be out of line. For example, both the Bentley Silver Spur and the Porsche 911 GT2 are priced relatively high—about \$170,000 and \$194,000, respectively. The Porsche would be value disadvantaged for a sedan customer while the Bentley Silver Spur would be value disadvantaged for the coupe customer. When the market can be segmented along the lines of different benefit categories, it is often best to generate specific price-to-benefits maps for the independent market segments rather than just one for the market as a whole to better identify product positioning.

Customer Perceptions

Because it is customers who purchase products, it is often best to consider product positions from a customer's perspective. If customers perceive a product to be priced to value, then it will sell in proportion to the number of customers who are willing to pay the stated price for that level of benefits. If they perceive it to be value advantaged or value disadvantaged, then the product is likely to capture market attention or find it waning, respectively. Customer perceptions matter.

Different customers may hold wildly different perceptions regarding product positions. This dispersion may arise from a segmentation strategy, but it often arises due to challenges in positioning a product. Products that are poorly positioned may fail to capture the intended market segment, leaving customers who purchase dissatisfied and disinclined to repurchase and failing to gain the customers who would have been highly satisfied and become loyal to the brand in the future. Both dispersions in perceived price and dispersions in perceived benefits can be a direct result of a failure to manage perceptions. When it is, executives may have an opportunity to address the challenge and therefore improve their profitability.

DISPERSION IN PERCEIVED PRICE

When different customers hold contrasting beliefs regarding the price of a product, there is a dispersion in perceived price. See Exhibit 4-3. Variations in price perceptions may be deliberate due to strategic or tactical decisions, or they may arise from an inability to communicate prices accurately. When actual prices are above expected prices, customers may delay purchases due to sticker shock, resulting in fewer sales. When actual prices are below perceived prices, the level of sales that executives may have hoped to achieve may fail to materialize. Keeping price perceptions aligned with actual prices tends to improve profits.

Structurally, the price of a product might vary widely between different customers. For instance, phone tariff structures are often designed to extract a higher price from high-usage customers than low-usage customers. Likewise, distribution channels and purchase locations may drive differences in the price of commonly purchased goods such as carbonated beverages. Structural price variations that support segmentation strategies will drive dispersion in the perceived price, but this dispersion in prices usually results in a profit enhancement rather than a positioning challenge.

Tactically, the price of a product may also vary. Promotional prices and discounting policies are ways of refining market segmentation efforts through tactical means. Customers purchasing at the list price will pay a much higher price than those purchasing at a sale or discounted price. Tactical price variations that support segmentation efforts may

Exhibit 4-3 Dispersion in Perceived Price

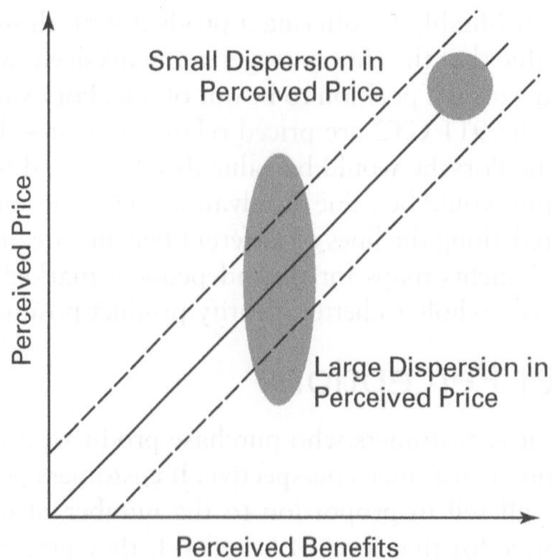

also result in profit enhancements. Overused, these tactical price variations can lead to positioning challenges as well.

The more persistent challenge in price positioning results from time delays between purchasing opportunities. Customers who purchase from a product category infrequently may hold inappropriate beliefs regarding the price of products within that category. When the prices within a product category are changing rapidly, it will be difficult to keep price expectations of customers in line with reality. Periods of high inflation or dramatic changes in production costs can lead to price expectations that are misaligned with market realities.

DISPERSION IN PERCEIVED BENEFITS

When different customers hold different beliefs regarding the benefits of a product, there is dispersion in perceived benefits. See Exhibit 4-4. The dispersion in perceived benefits may result from a structural variation within the market or from a failure of communication. When actual benefits delivered are greater than those perceived, customers may place inadequate value on a product and select a competing alternative. When the benefits are less than what are perceived, the firm may be able to capture some sales opportunistically, only to find customers defecting quickly to competitor products in future purchasing situations.

The benefits of a product may be grounded in functional, process, or relationship issues. **Functional benefits** derive from the physical nature or performance characteristics of the product itself, such as the square footage of a home, the clarity and size of a gemstone, or the ability of a financial software package to create customized invoices. **Process benefits** derive from reducing transactional costs by making the product available when and where customers desire or reducing search costs in identifying products. **Relationship benefits** accrue to customers through their mutually beneficial relationship with the seller and may be created through an emotional connection to the brand or sales representative, loyalty programs, or information provisions.

Because different customers may seek a different set of benefits from a product category, they may also perceive products themselves to hold a different overall level of benefits. For instance, risk-averse customers may seek assurance and greatly discount the claimed benefits of a new product. Less-risk-averse customers, however, may value

Exhibit 4-4 Dispersion in Perceived Benefits

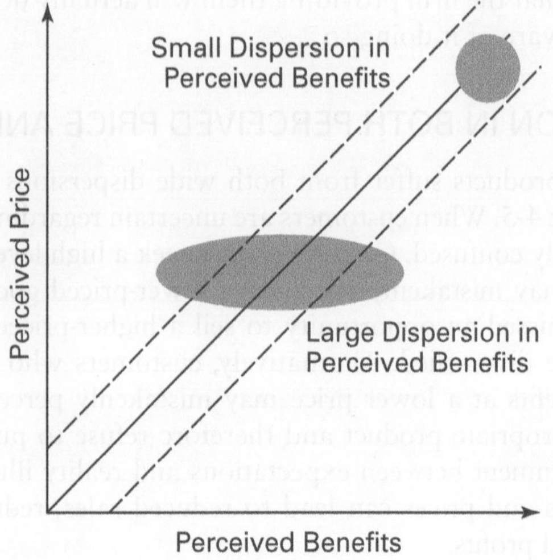

the benefits within a new product precisely because they bring about change. Variations in risk aversion have been well observed in technology markets and can result in a time-dependent segmentation strategy. Similarly, attitudes towards risks vary between senior executives and mid-level managers. Senior executives tend to seek dramatic improvements in productivity, while mid-level managers tend to seek stability and steady career improvement.

Perceptions of benefits may vary between customers due to poor marketing communications. When different marketing communications efforts tout different sets of benefits, customers may have a hard time developing a common understanding of the benefits delivered through a product. When a wide disparity in perceived benefits is indicative of customer confusion, executives may have the opportunity to clarify their marketing communications and increase the level of communications to drive sales and profits.

Wide dispersions of perceived benefits are more common with experience and credence goods than search goods. **Search goods** are items that allow for a functional comparison between competing products during the shopping experience itself. For instance, prior to purchasing an automobile, customers can compare engine size, tires, entertainment systems, suspensions, braking systems, and other features to predict the benefits of the automobile. Bicycles, home appliances, and some software products are all examples of search goods. Through feature descriptions and promotional statements, customers can make comparisons between products prior to purchase with search goods. **Experience goods** are items in which the full knowledge of the benefits can be gained only from past experience with the product. For example, with newspapers, it is hard to tell the value of the content until after the news is read, and only through experience with the brand can a customer form meaningful expectations of the newspaper's value. Entertainment and other forms of media, along with some forms of beverages and branded clothing, are examples of experience goods. **Credence goods** are items in which the benefits are unknown and may never be known. For instance, the purchase of insurance is done with the expectation that reimbursement will come following a disaster. However, few customers of insurance products hope for a disaster, and most try to avoid them. If the insured disaster never comes, the insurance policy will expire and go unused, thus the buyer will never truly know if the policy was worth anything. Other credence goods includes prepurchased funerary service (it is hard to evaluate the benefits of a service provided after the customer is dead), prostate cancer care (it is difficult to ascertain whether slow-growing prostate cancer will kill the patient or some other disease will first), and product warranties. People purchase credence items on the belief that the firm providing them will actually deliver the benefits, even if the customer is unaware of it doing so.

DISPERSION IN BOTH PERCEIVED PRICE AND PERCEIVED BENEFITS

Some products suffer from both wide dispersions in price and benefits perceptions. See Exhibit 4-5. When customers are uncertain regarding the position of a product, the market is simply confused. Customers who seek a high level of benefits and are willing to pay for them may mistakenly purchase a lower-priced good. In this case, not only will the firm have missed an opportunity to sell a higher-priced product, but also the customer may become dissatisfied. Alternatively, customers who would be satisfied with a lower level of benefits at a lower price may mistakenly perceive that the market does not provide an appropriate product and therefore refuse to purchase any product. As both types of misalignment between expectations and reality illustrate, a wide dispersion in perceived benefits and prices can lead to reduced sales, reduced customer loyalty, and ultimately reduced profits.

Exhibit 4-5 Uncertain Value Proposition with Multiple Products

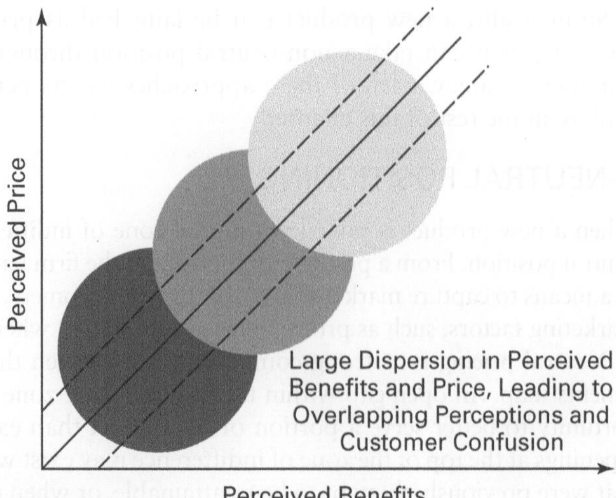

New Product Positioning

Executives can use the price-to-benefits map to identify opportunities for launching a new product within an existing market.[5] Potential positions within the price-to-benefits map can be considered. With each position, the price-to-benefits map will reveal the customer-addressable horizon to executives. The customer-addressable horizon is the source of the customers for the new product. Some of the new customers would have been previously purchasing a product at a higher price-and-benefits position; others would have been purchasing a product at a lower price-and-benefits position. Identifying the customer-addressable horizon can be used to estimate the market share and sales volume for the new product.

Uncovering the customer-addressable horizon can also be used to anticipate competitor reactions. Any new product that takes sales away from competing products can encourage a competitive response. Executives can be prepared to address a competitor's response by considering the circumstances under which they will accommodate the competitive maneuver, respond to the competitive action, or withdraw from the market.

There are eight major factors that can be evaluated to gauge the likelihood of a competitive response to a new product.[6] (1) Competitors with a **strategic intent** to stay in the market due to a strong profit margin on a product that is threatened by the new entry are more likely to defend their position than those who may be looking for a way out of the industry. (2) Competitors that have made **recent investments** within the industry are likewise likely to respond to an encroachment upon their price-to-benefits position. (3) In contrast, competitors whose **range of options** for responding is limited due to cost challenges or inability to match the new entry's benefits may be unlikely to respond. (4) Likewise, firms in strong **financial health** may perceive that they can be patient in responding to measure the true effect of the new entry. (5) In general, the greater the **level of threat** a competitor perceives the new entry to represent, the greater the response will be. New entries will threaten products that are nearer in position more than they will those who are more distant. (6) Similarly, the overall **market position** of existing competitors will also affect their decision to respond. Competitors that are already value disadvantaged face a greater urgency in responding than those who are value advantaged. Other factors that may indicate the likelihood and type of competitive response include industry maturity and tradition. (7) Competitors with greater **maturity** will have experienced multiple business cycles and might be expected to respond more appropriately. (8) Similarly, **industry tradition** may reveal patterns of competitive actions, such as a tendency to innovate or avoid price wars or conversely to defend share aggressively. Such patterns can be anticipated to be repeated.

Strategically, a new product can be launched as price neutral with respect to other products, or it can take a non-neutral position through a penetration-pricing or price-skimming strategy. Each of these approaches has its benefits and drawbacks, as we will explore in the rest of this chapter.[7]

PRICE-NEUTRAL POSITIONING

When a new product is priced within the zone of indifference, the firm has taken a price-neutral position. From a price-neutral position, the firm has negated the potential to use price as a means to capture market share. To capture customers, executives place pressure on other marketing factors, such as promotion or distribution, when positioned as price neutral.

Neutral pricing is a strong competitive move when there is an opening in the price-to-benefits map. An open gap within the middle of the zone of indifference may imply an opportunity to better serve a portion of the market than existing products have done so far. Openings at the top of the zone of indifference may exist when new benefits become possible that were previously thought to be unattainable, or when the market expands sufficiently to warrant further segmentation. For instance, the fortunes of Robert Mondavi Winery have tracked the growing interest in wines within the United States for more than forty years since the 1960s by continually focusing on improving the quality of their wines and pricing them appropriately to the upper end of the market. Alternatively, openings at the bottom of the zone of indifference may become available when customers begin to seek greater simplicity in their purchases, as U.S. consumers did in the aftermath of the 2008–2009 Great Recession.

Positioning a new product as price neutral is generally the safest approach to avoiding a negative competitive response. When a competitive response is made to a price-neutral launch, it is most likely to be from a competitor that markets a product positioned closest to the new entry. See Exhibit 4-6. Positioning a product at the bottom or within the middle of the zone of indifference is subject to the potential of a competitive response in the form of a price decrease on existing products. The likelihood of a price response is tempered by the need for competitors to maintain contribution margins, not just volumes. Entering a product category positioned at the top of the zone of indifference usually grants the firm some leeway in that a competitive response will be slowed due to the challenges faced in delivering a product with similar benefits.

Exhibit 4-6 Neutral Pricing

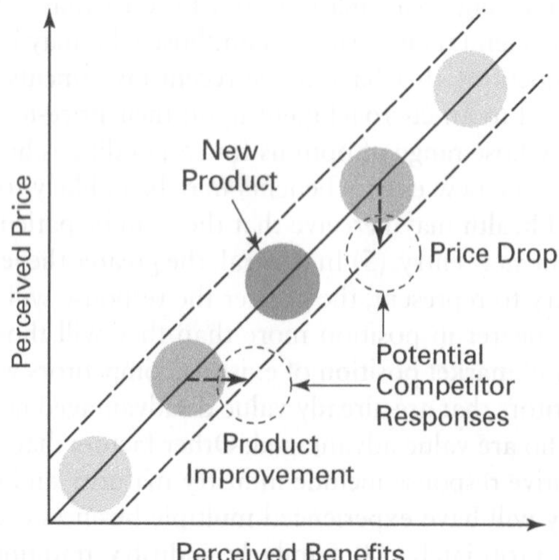

Exhibit 4-7 Penetration Pricing

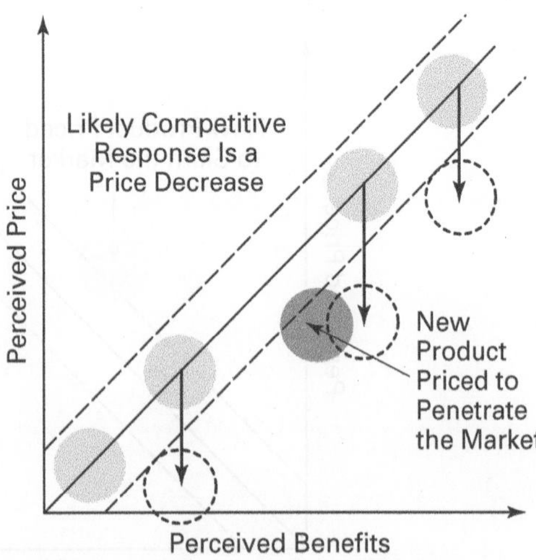

PENETRATION PRICING

If a new product is launched within an existing market at a low price in comparison to the benefits that it delivers, the firm is executing a penetration-pricing strategy. See Exhibit 4-7. Penetration pricing is undertaken to gain market share quickly. It is risky in many cases because there may be little to prevent existing competitors from dropping their prices as well to thwart the new entrant from gaining a foothold. Executives who choose to practice penetration pricing when launching a new product are often wise to treat it as a tactical price promotion for introducing the new product rather than a strategic resetting of the price level.

Often, in rapidly evolving high-tech industries, penetration pricing arises from increasing the level of benefits while leaving the price unchanged. This occurs due to cost advantages being gained concurrent to benefits improvements with the adoption of new manufacturing techniques. If executives can sustain a rate of improvement greater than its competitors' for several release cycles, penetration pricing may enable the firm to capture a dramatic amount of share.

From a promotional perspective, penetration pricing obviously generates customer interest. However, this position may be deleterious for the firm, not only in failing to capture potential contribution margins but also in strongly encouraging a competitive response. The most likely direct response is a price decrease by competitors to bring all products back to parity within a price-to-benefits tradeoff.

PRICE SKIMMING

If the new product is launched within an existing market at a high price in comparison to the benefits that it delivers, the firm is executing a price-skimming strategy. See Exhibit 4-8. Price skimming is undertaken to capture profits from early customers with the expectation of lowering prices at a future time. It is unlikely to incur any competitive response because the new entry will be perceived as relatively benign. However, such a position is usually the result of a pricing error that results in lower sales volumes and forgone profits.

Products launched under a price-skimming strategy fail to provide most customers with sufficient motivation to purchase given the alternatives; hence, they may not gain market attraction. Firms may use this strategy to explore a market strategically, but few executives should expect this initial thrust to deliver significant results.

Exhibit 4-8 Price Skimming

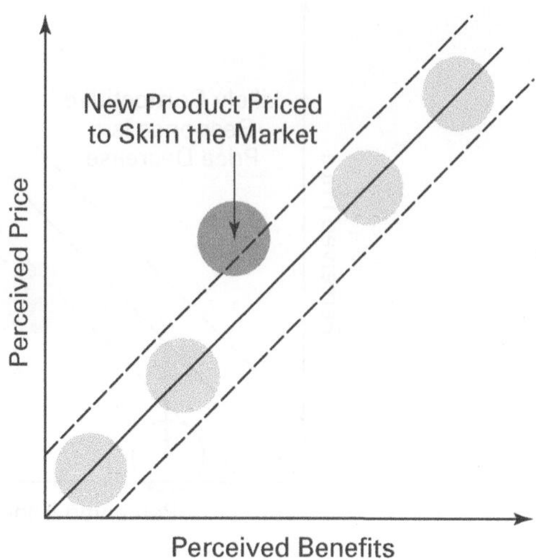

SUMMARY

- A price-to-benefits map plots the position of the competing products with respect to perceived price and perceived benefits.
- Products in which perceived price increases with perceived benefits lie on the value equivalence line. Around the value equivalence line may lay a zone of indifference where small changes in price have a negligible effect on demand.
- Products that are perceived to provide excess benefits with respect to price are said to be value advantaged. Value-advantaged positioning is usually undertaken to take market share, but it represents a choice to leave some value unharvested.
- Products that are perceived to provide insufficient benefits with respect to their perceived price are said to be value disadvantaged. Value-disadvantaged positioning usually comes at the cost of missed opportunities and reduction in market share.
- Dispersion in perceived price can be driven by strategic and tactical variations in price or misperceptions of price.
- Dispersion in perceived benefits can be driven by different segments placing different importance on different benefits, or misperceptions of benefits delivered.
- Large dispersion in perceived price, benefits, or both can lead to customers purchasing suboptimally, leading to both missed profit opportunities and customer dissatisfaction.
- To launch a new product within the zone of indifference is to assume a price-neutral position. Price-neutral positioning tends to apply pressure on the remaining marketing levers of promotion and distribution.
- Launching a new product at a low price in comparison to its benefits is penetration pricing. Penetration pricing tends to use price itself as a means to gain market share.
- Launching a new product at a high price in comparison to benefits is price skimming.

Exercises

1. Consider the following Dayton 220 V hazardous location exhaust fans offered by Grainger. Position the products on a price-to-benefits plot using cubic feet per minute (CFM) as the metric of benefits.
   a. Which exhaust fans fit on the value equivalence line?
   b. Are there any exhaust fans that are value advantaged? Value disadvantaged?
   c. How would you explain the variations in price among the exhaust fans?

Item	CFM	Blades	Price
Dayton 3GPA3	1217	Cast aluminum	$999
Dayton 3GPA5	3247	Hardened steel	$1,127
Dayton 3GPA6	4438	Hardened steel	$1,368
Dayton 3GPA8	6267	Hardened steel	$1,558

2. Consider the following wall-mounted sculptures by Yvette Kaiser Smith. Calculate the size of the sculptures in square inches. Position the sculptures on a price-to-benefits plot using square inches (sq in) as the metric of value.
   a. Which sculptures on the value equivalence line?
   b. Are there any sculptures that are value advantaged? Value disadvantaged?
   c. How would you explain the variations in price among the sculptures?

Sculpture	Height (in)	Width (in)	Price
Clique	43	49	$1,500
White	50	51	$2,000
Porphyrin Ring	55	31	$3,000
Immurement	75	96	$6,000
Weave	116	92	$8,500
Blue Line	107	131	$11,000
Pi	61	283	$11,000
Construct 10	103	157	$13,000

3. In Chapter 3, we evaluated the part-worth utility function of mango juice. If we add the part-worth utility of an ingredient with the brand, we can find the partial utility of an offering of mango juice. Similarly, we can complete the evaluation of conjoint-derived prices relative to a $4 national brand of mango fruit blend. See the following chart.
   a. Complete the chart for the partial utilities.
   b. Plot the partial utility of mango juice offerings relative to the conjoint-identified prices.
   c. Where do the conjoint-identified prices lie relative to perceived value? On the value equivalence line, value advantaged, or value disadvantaged?

Formulation	Ingredient Part-Worth Utility	Brand Part-Worth Utility	Partial Utility	Conjoint-Identified Price
Pure Mango, National Brand	4.5	4.0	8.5	$5.50
Pure Mango, Premium Niche Brand	4.5	3.0		$4.75
Mango Fruit Blend, National Brand	2.5	4.0		$4.00
Mango Fruit Blend, Premium Niche Brand	2.5	3.0		$3.25

4. In the Chapter 3 exercise, we evaluated the utility and optimal prices for different hot dog offers. Calculate the partial utility of a Vienna Beef Garden Dog, Vienna Beef Dirty Water Dog, Natural Casing Garden Dog, and Natural Casing Dirty Water Dog. Use the prices found from conjoint analysis to construct a plot of price vs. hot dog utility for the different configurations of hot dogs.
5. Consider the following price vs. value positioning plot of products A, B, and C. If a new product is positioned at NEW, answer the following questions.
   a. From which products is it most likely to steal share?
   b. If the other products are sold by competitors, which competitive product is likely to be most affected? Which competitive product is likely to be least affected? What reaction should the company expect? How would the reaction vary between the products?

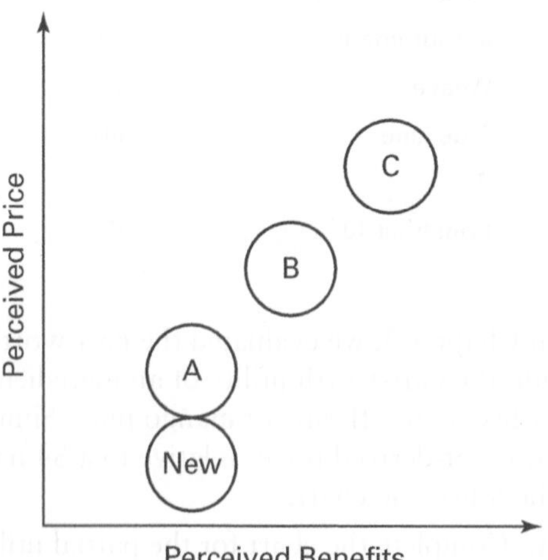

6. In 2010, Apple released an iPad that some observers perceived to be a far superior electronic reading device compared to other similar products on the market.

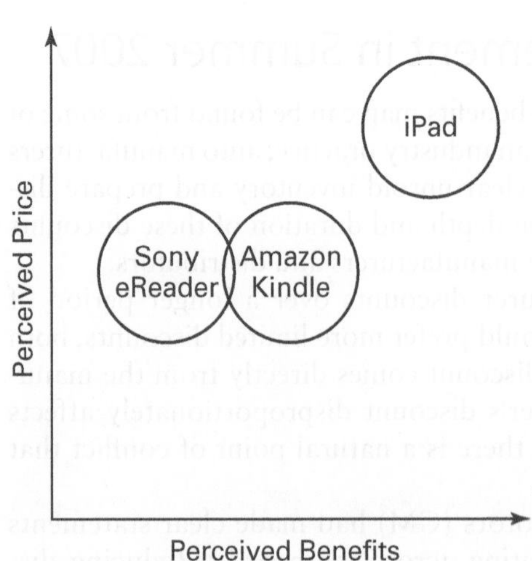

Consider the following plot of the iPad, Kindle, and Sony eReader. If the iPad is positioned at iPad, answer the following questions.

a. From which products is the iPad most likely to steal share?
b. What immediate reaction should Sony take to the release of the iPad?

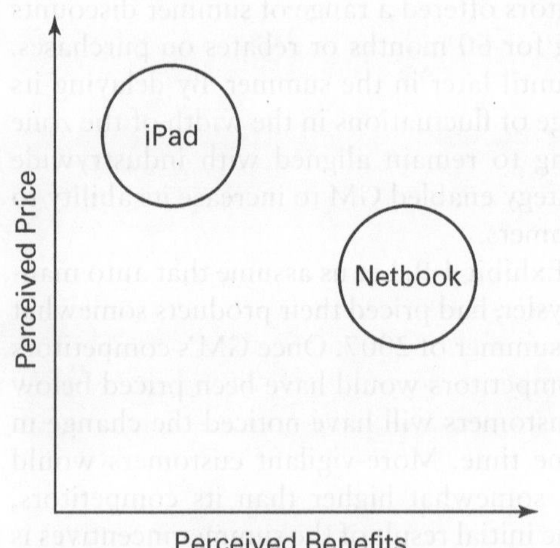

7. In 2010, Apple released an iPad that some observers perceived as far inferior to a netbook. Consider the following plot of iPad vs. Netbook. What immediate reaction should netbook producers take to the release of the iPad?

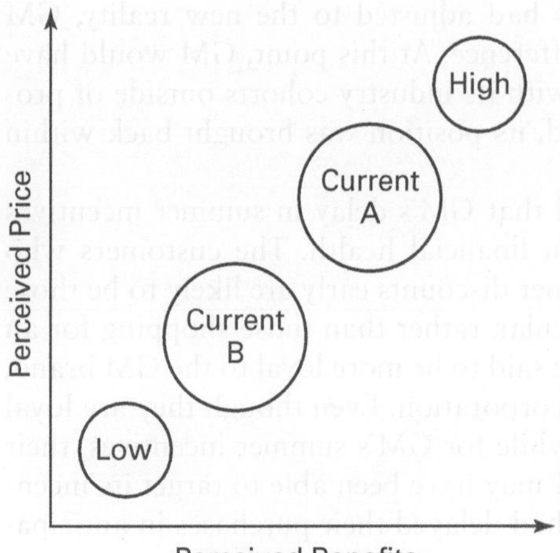

8. A product manager is considering investing in a new product. The firm currently markets two products on the market with equal unit sales, identified on the price-to-benefits plot as Current A and Current B. What are the costs and benefits of designing a new product for position High? For position Low? If prices tend to be twice the variable cost of production, which position should the product manager seek to develop and why? What relative market shares between product A and B would imply that the product manager should invest in developing a product for position High? For position Low?

Appendix 4 General Motors: Price Management in Summer 2007

An illustration of the strategic value of a price-to-benefits map can be found from some of the pricing dynamics in the U.S. auto industry. As an industry practice, auto manufacturers have offered summer incentives to customers to clear unsold inventory and prepare distribution channels for the next year's models. The depth and duration of these discounts have implications for the profitability of both the manufacturers and distributors.

Distributors should prefer deeper manufacturer discounts over a longer period of time to increase sales volume. Manufacturers should prefer more limited discounts, both in duration and depth, because the cost of the discount comes directly from the manufacturer's profitability. Because the manufacturer's discount disproportionately affects the manufacturer's profit over the distributors', there is a natural point of conflict that requires negotiation.

Going into the summer of 2007, General Motors (GM) had made clear statements regarding its strategic intent to reduce discounting across the board.[8] Reducing discounts, however, cannot be confused with eliminating discounts. GM did provide discounts, but the duration of its summer discounting was shorter than that of its industry cohorts.

Early in the summer of 2007, GM's competitors offered a range of summer discounts like those from Toyota for 0 percent financing for 60 months or rebates on purchases. GM, however, delayed its summer incentives until later in the summer. By delaying its incentives, GM may have been taking advantage of fluctuations in the width of the zone of indifference while simultaneously managing to remain aligned with industrywide pricing practices. It can be argued that this strategy enabled GM to increase its ability to target its discounts toward its more loyal customers.

Conceptually, we can show this dynamic in Exhibit 4-9. Let us assume that auto manufacturers, such as GM, Toyota, Ford, and Chrysler, had priced their products somewhat along the value equivalence line going into the summer of 2007. Once GM's competitors had released their summer incentives, those competitors would have been priced below the value equivalence line. However, not all customers will have noticed the change in the price-to-benefits of all vehicles at the same time. More-vigilant customers would have noticed that GM was effectively priced somewhat higher than its competitors, while the less vigilant may not have noticed. The initial result of the summer incentives is a temporary broadening of the zone of indifference as some customers perceive the price change and others fail to notice. This temporary broadening of the zone of equivalence created some leeway for GM to delay its summer incentives.

Eventually, all customers will have noticed that GM had not yet provided any summer discounts. Once the customer perceptions had adjusted to the new reality, GM would have been priced above the zone of indifference. At this point, GM would have had few other options for staying competitive with its industry cohorts outside of providing similar summer incentives. Once GM did, its position was brought back within the new zone of indifference.

From a strategic viewpoint, it can be argued that GM's delay in summer incentives might have been able to improve its long-term financial health. The customers who would have noticed that GM did not offer summer discounts early are likely to be those who were shopping for a GM product in particular, rather than those shopping for an automobile in general. These customers could be said to be more loyal to the GM brand, and hence they were more valuable to the GM corporation. Even though they are loyal customers and may be willing to wait a short while for GM's summer incentives, their patience would not be infinite. By delaying, GM may have been able to target its incentive program to its more loyal customers, who had delayed their purchases in anticipation of the summer incentives.

Exhibit 4-9 Dynamics in Price to Benefits During Summer Incentive Periods in the Automotive Industry

Step 1
Prior to summer incentives.

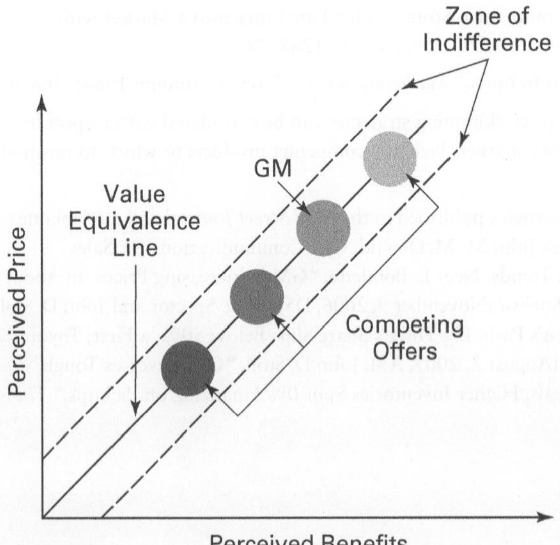

Step 2
Immediately following competitor summer incentives. Zone of Indifference broadens as customers adjust to new pricing expectations.

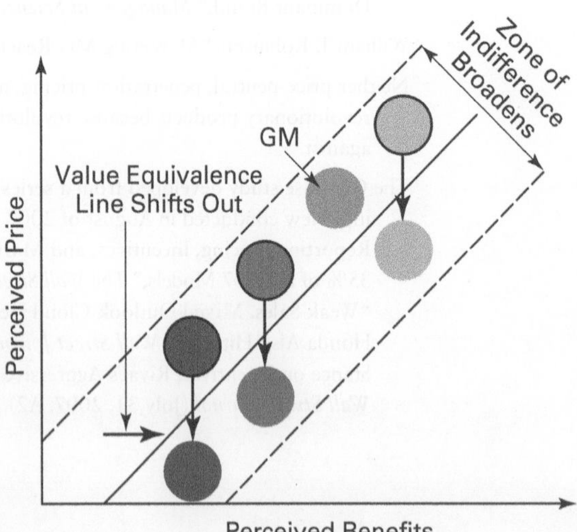

Step 3
Zone of Indifference narrows as customer expectations relax to new Value Equivalence Line.

Step 4
GM adjusts to new Value Equivalence Line to remain competitive.

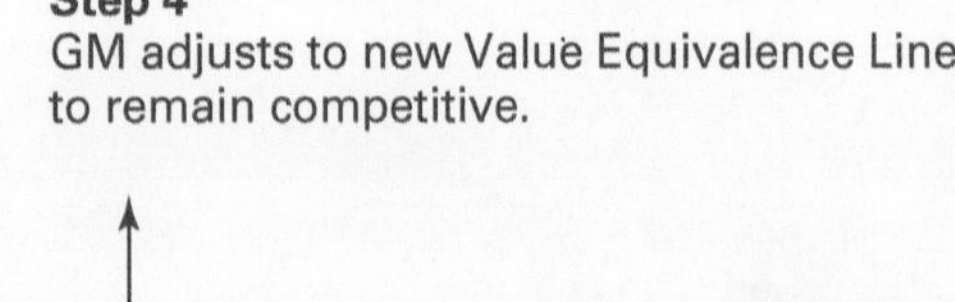

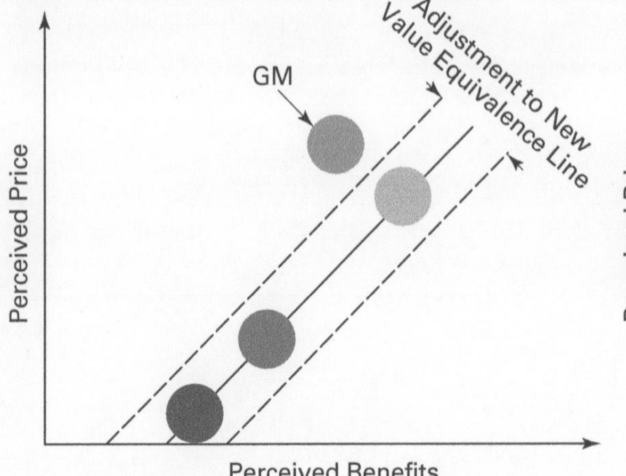

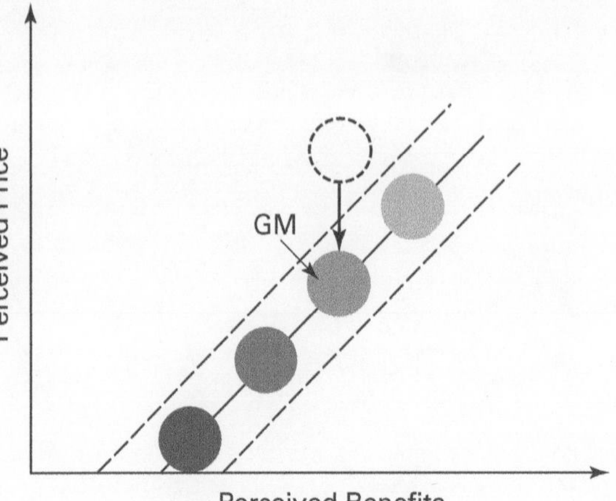

Notes

[1] Price-to-benefits maps can be found in most strategic pricing texts. Michael V. Marn, Eric V. Roegner, and Craig C. Zawada, "Product/Market Strategy," *The Price Advantage* (Hoboken, NJ: John Wiley & Sons, Inc., 2004): 74–82. Thomas T. Nagle and Reed K. Holden, "Pricing Strategy," *The Strategy and Tactics of Pricing: A Guide to Profitable Decision Making*. 3rd ed. (Upper Saddle River, NJ: Prentice Hall, 2002): 152–56. Robert J. Dolan and Hermann Simon, "Pricing and Competitive Strategy," *Power Pricing: How Managing Price Transforms the Bottom Line* (New York: Free Press, 1996): 83–90.

[2] Benson P. Shapiro and Barbara B. Jackson, "Industrial Pricing to Meet Customer Needs," *Harvard Business Review* 56, no. 6 (November–December 1978): 119–27.

[3] Richard A. D'Aveni, "Mapping Your Competitive Position," *Harvard Business Review* 85, no. 11 (November 2007): 110–20.

[4] Richard A. D'Aveni, "How Firms Outmaneuver Competitors with Cost-Quality Advantages," *Hypercompetition: Managing the Dynamics of Strategic Maneuvering* (New York: Free Press, 1994): 39–70.

[5] Gregory S. Carpenter, and Kent Nakamoto, "Competitive Strategies for Late Entry into a Market with a Dominant Brand," *Management Science* 36, no. 10 (October 1990): 1268–78.

[6] William T. Robinson, "Marketing Mix Reactions to Entry," *Marketing Science* 7, no. 4 (Autumn 1988): 368–85.

[7] Neither price-neutral, penetration-pricing, nor price-skimming strategies can be considered with respect to revolutionary products because revolutionary markets lack any competing products to which to position against.

[8] The GM case study developed from a series of articles published in the *Wall Street Journal* and a telephone interview conducted in August of 2007 with John M. McDonald, GM Communications for Sales Reporting, Pricing, Incentives, and Market Trends. Neal E. Boudette, "GM Is Increasing Prices on About 35% of its 2007 Models," *The Wall Street Journal* (November 9, 2006, D5). Mike Spector and John D. Stoll, "Weak Sales, Mixed Outlook Cloud Detroit's Path: Big Three's Share Slips Below 50%, a First; Toyota, Honda Also Hit," *The Wall Street Journal* (August 2, 2007, A3). John D. Stoll, "GM Reverses Tough Stance on Incentives; Rival's Aggressive Deals, Higher Inventories Spur 0% Financing on Pickups," *The Wall Street Journal* (July 31, 2007, A2).

Chapter
5

Psychological Influences on Price Sensitivity

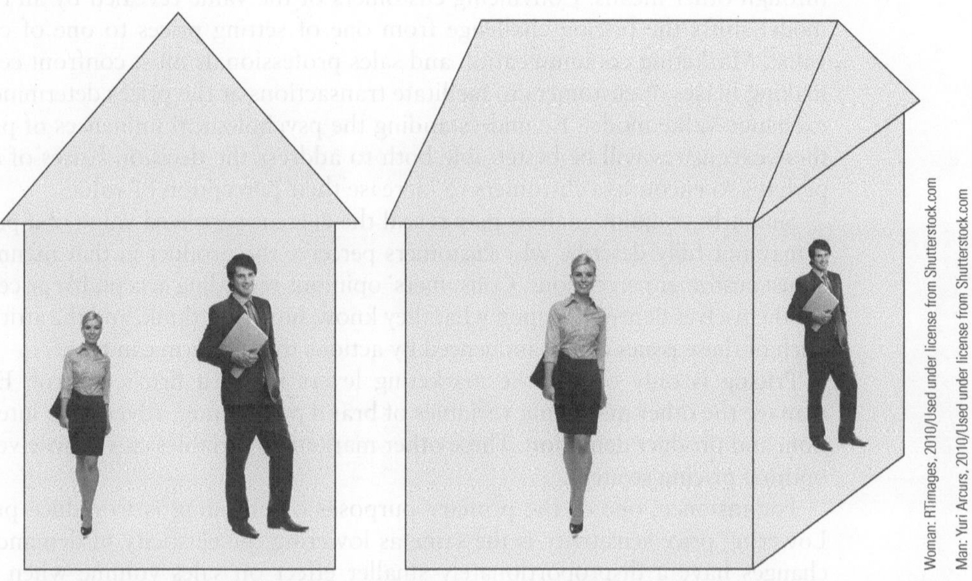

Woman: RTimages, 2010/Used under license from Shutterstock.com
Man: Yuri Arcurs, 2010/Used under license from Shutterstock.com

- Why do prices end in 9?
- If private transactions are just that—private—why do customers care what others paid?
- How do customers perceive prices and offerings?
- Are there inherent biases that influence the perception of value and price?
- Can a firm influence a customer's perception of the value?
- Stretch Question: Is the best price always the one that accurately reflects value?

In many ways, value is a subjective matter. The perception of value is inherently dependent upon how the customer perceives the product, the benefits it offers, and their alternatives. This perception of value and to some extent the perception of price are subject to many psychological influences. Executives who understand these influences can better gauge the limits of their pricing power and the responses of customers to price actions. Moreover, they may be able to uncover means of influencing customers' perceptions of value and price and therefore improve their pricing power.

The dominant approaches to setting prices that we explored have each been built upon the common pillar of value. Prices should be set in proportion to the value that customers perceive a product delivers. However, these approaches have not fully addressed how customers perceive value.

Consider exchange value models as an example. Exchange value models inform executives of the potential value within a product based on the benefits that executives quantify. An incomplete list of benefits would lead executives to believe that they must charge a lower price, while a list of benefits that the market does not perceive as relevant would lead them to price the product higher than what the market will bear. Determining which benefits should be quantified and determining the best means to quantify the value of a specific benefit can be improved by understanding the needs of customers, but will remain, to some extent, a subjective decision. Furthermore, once an exchange value model has identified the range of a good price, it leaves the challenge of convincing customers that the value of the product is near the price revealed by the exchange value model to be managed through other means. Convincing customers of the value revealed by an exchange value model shifts the pricing challenge from one of setting prices to one of communicating value. Marketing communication and sales professionals must confront certain decision-making biases of customers to facilitate transactions at the prices determined through the exchange value model. By understanding the psychological influences of price sensitivity, these executives will be better able both to address the decision biases of customers and perhaps to encourage customers to increase their perception of value.

Similarly, conjoint analysis may reveal the current perceived value of a product, and yet it may not fully describe why customers perceive the product in that manner nor how to adjust customer perceptions. Consumers' opinions regarding acceptable prices for a product are themselves dependent upon what they know, how they think, and the attitudes they hold. Each of these issues can be influenced by actions that the firm can take.

Pricing is only one of the marketing levers under a firm's control. Executives also manage the other marketing variables of brand positioning, advertising intensity, distribution, and product definition. These other marketing variables can themselves influence the optimal pricing strategy.

For instance, one of the primary purposes of branding is to reduce price sensitivity. Lowering price sensitivity is the same as lowering the elasticity of demand; that is, price changes have a disproportionately smaller effect on sales volume when customers are less price-sensitive than when they are more price-sensitive. We have seen that products facing a lower elasticity of demand can increase prices to improve profitability. Thus, good branding can lead to better prices.

In contrast, increased price sensitivity is the same as increasing the elasticity of demand. We have also seen that firms facing elastic demand have an incentive to lower prices to increase profitability and have argued that such actions tend to lead to price wars between competitors, which lower overall industry profitability. Very few firms can profit in an unhealthy industry. Therefore, executives should be aware of the influences that may increase price sensitivity and avoid actions that may give rise to their importance.

Numerous factors influence how customers perceive value and price.[1] While some of these factors are more properly considered economic in nature, many arise from deeper, psychological influences, and perhaps even arise from evolutionary biological forces in their development and expression in human behavior.

Executives can use a deeper understanding of these psychological influences to overcome decision-making biases of themselves and their customers. In some cases, pricing professionals can use an understanding of decision-making biases in purchasing behavior to clarify the limits of their pricing power and uncover new approaches to pricing, which reduces psychological dissonance within customers and therefore improves the acceptance of their pricing practices by the market.

The psychological influences on price sensitivity may be as much a result of how the brain works as it is a result of cold rational factors regarding economic welfare. Recent studies that examine brain activity during economic decisions have led to a neuroeconomic understanding of how customers make purchase decisions.[2] Some of these studies indicate that these psychological influences are not simply a function of customers misunderstanding the economics of an offer but rather derive from evolutionary biological forces.[3]

In one model of the human psychology of purchase decisions, the brain is viewed as a prediction machine that continuously generates predictions about what to expect in the environment. These continuous predictions are extremely rapid and depend on similarities between novel inputs and the closest familiar representations stored in memory. For example, if you see a chair that you have never seen before, you can still determine what it is, its function, approximate weight, expected price, and other nonvisual characteristics. To derive these expectations rapidly, we rely on surprisingly little information. Neural circuits may mediate the vital mental skills that translate information into impressions, preferences, judgments, and predictions.[4]

Many psychological influences on price sensitivity can be derived from the tendency for human beings to be cognitive misers who develop heuristics for accelerating decisions. As cognitive misers, we attempt to store as little information as possible and make decisions with as little information as possible. To improve our decisions with minimal effort, we develop heuristics, or decision shortcuts, that have a tendency to be accurate—although, at times, they are completely inaccurate.

While these models of human psychology are extremely intriguing and create excellent fodder for understanding purchasing behavior, our understanding of these effects is still in its nascent stages. Moreover, executives require a more distilled description of these influences than those provided by pure neuroeconomics. As we understand these forces more deeply, we can expect pricing to become even more nuanced and their influence on pricing decisions to become more codified.

In this chapter, we will examine some of the better-researched influences and consumer behavioral effects on price perceptions. Some of the factors will lead to an increase in price sensitivity, while others will decrease it. Some of the factors can be influenced by the firm's actions, but others may not. All will help executives understand their pricing power, and therefore may help guide pricing decisions.

While some researchers have attempted to collect all of these influences in a unified theory, these approaches have fallen short of providing sufficient breadth to capture the breadth of influences. As an alternative, we group influences as being related to true economic costs, related to perceptual challenges, encapsulated in prospect theory, or related to prospect theory. While we accept that this grouping is likely to be imperfect, we believe that it will enable better understanding.

True Economic Costs

There are several effects that are often discussed with respect to human psychology and can be properly placed within the context of a rational decision maker making an economic decision. As we will see, these effects derive from implicit economic costs that come in form of opportunity costs or hidden costs.

SHARED COST EFFECT

The shared cost effect denotes the reduction of price sensitivity found when customers use other people's money to pay for a product. For instance, business travelers often receive full reimbursement for travel expenses from their companies. Airline loyalty programs enable airlines to increase prices marginally because the price is paid by the business but the choice of airline is influenced by the traveler. To a lesser degree, rebates tend to lower price sensitivity due to the partial payment of the product through the rebate.

One way of describing the shared cost effect is that people spend from four funds of money.[5] (1) People spend their own money on themselves. When they do so, they pay high attention to gaining utility from the product and getting the most utility per dollar spent. (2) People spend their own money on someone else. When they do so, they are seeking to maximize the utility of the gift recipient as well as maximize their utility in giving the gift. Thus, they remain price-sensitive, but the definition of utility changes. (3) People spend someone else's money on themselves. In this case, customers will be more benefit-oriented, but less price-sensitive, than when spending their own money on themselves or someone else. (4) People spend someone else's money on someone else, such as when buying products for a business. In the absence of decision-making oversight and proper incentives, people spending someone else's money on someone else are neither very price- nor benefit-sensitive.

SWITCHING COSTS

When customers change brands or adapt a new technology, they will incur a switching cost. Switching costs arise from product-specific investments that buyers make.[6] Switching costs can be psychological, such as the value that customers place on remaining loyal to a trusted brand. More tangibly, switching costs can be fiscal in nature. For instance, customers may purchase complementary goods to enhance the benefits of a core product, and switching to a new brand may drive them to reinvest in new complementary products. Alternatively, business processes may need to be restructured to reap the benefits of a new technology. Similarly, customers may have to invest in learning a new technology to use it, and the time spent learning creates a further switching cost.

Firms that increase switching costs find that their customers will be less price-sensitive. Firms that reduce the switching costs of a competitor's customers may also find the market less price-sensitive toward their offer. Switching costs can be factored into exchange value models and segmentation studies from conjoint analysis to better understand the willingness to pay of existing customers and contrast it with that of potentially new customers.

EXPENDITURE EFFECT

Some researchers have argued that customers are more price-sensitive at higher prices due to economic incentive to identify savings.[7] For instance, people may shop more intensely for high-expenditure items than they do for low-expenditure items. This expenditure effect arises from opportunity costs. Shopping, comparing offers, and making decisions require the investment of time and effort, both of which could be used doing something else. These investments of time and effort are forms of opportunity costs. With high-expenditure items, the opportunity cost of shopping is a small portion of the total purchase cost. With low-expenditure items, the opportunity cost of shopping is a large portion of the total purchase cost. As such, an economically rational customer should spend more time shopping for expensive items than for inexpensive items.

In consumer markets, these researchers have argued that the magnitude of the expenditure as a proportion to the household income is a strong indicator of price sensitivity. Households with lower income will be more price-sensitive with large-expenditure items than households with higher income. In business markets, these researchers have argued that the magnitude of the expenditure effect is moderated by the absolute size of the purchase and the importance of the expenditure to the strategic direction of the business. Products that are correlated with the strategic direction of the firm are more likely to be subject to alternative discovery and price comparisons than those more related to standard business inputs. Likewise, products that require a higher absolute expenditure are subject to greater management scrutiny and are therefore also subject to higher levels of price sensitivity.

However, it is uncertain as to if customers are consistently more price-sensitive with high-expenditure products than they are for low-expenditure products. Some research has uncovered contradictory evidence which demonstrates that the expenditure effect is moderated by the manner in which savings are presented. For instance, compare the reaction to a $5 savings when shopping for a low-priced item such as a $39.99 microwave oven versus a high-priced item such as a $499.99 flat-screen TV. Telling customers that the same microwave can be found at a store 2 miles away for $5 less tends to encourage more customers to defect to the alternative outlet in comparison to telling customers that the same TV can be found 2 miles away for $5 less. This counter expenditure effect will be somewhat explained through prospect theory.

DIFFICULT COMPARISON EFFECT

The opportunity costs related to shopping also give rise to the difficult comparison effect. Firms can, at times, alter customers' perceptions of competing offers in their favor by making it difficult for them to compare prices or compare benefits.[8] There are three main areas where the difficult comparison effect can be found: Incumbent/New Entrant Rivalry, Brands vs. Generics, and Size Changes.

Incumbent/New Entrant Rivalry

The difficult comparison effect is often used by incumbents as a means of defending market share against new entrants. This strategy works to the incumbents' advantage for two reasons. First, by making comparisons difficult, the information-gathering requirements of potential product switchers is increased. By increasing the information-gathering costs of customers, product switchers have an economic incentive to stay with their current brand. Second, by making comparisons difficult, marketers can increase uncertainty within customers. Customers that are uncertain regarding the net benefits of switching products tend to stay with their current trusted brand rather than explore an uncertain new brand relationship. These two factors explain much of the effort by incumbents to obfuscate the price and benefits of their offerings. In contrast, new entrants tend to make price comparisons as explicit as possible to facilitate rational decision making and brand switching.

An example of the difficult comparison effect being used strategically by incumbents and being attacked by new entrants can be found in the 2002–2009 conflict between Vonage and AT&T. AT&T's basic residential telephone service was priced low, but any advanced services such as long distance calls, call waiting, call forwarding, caller ID, and three-way calling were available only through additional purchases. Customers selecting a calling plan based on the price that they should expect to pay for services would have a difficult time calculating their expected bill due to the numerous factors that determined a bill from AT&T. To some extent, AT&T's price structure may have been purposely designed to make price comparisons with alternative service providers difficult. By making comparisons difficult, reluctant brand switchers are encouraged to stick with AT&T rather than risk uncovering new, higher phone bills with an unknown Voice over Internet Protocol (VOIP) provider with uncertain call quality. In the years leading into 2009, Vonage has been advertising complete national home telephone service for a flat fee of $24.99, which includes many of the features that AT&T sells only through additional contracts. In these advertisements, Vonage has explicitly contrasted its simple, flat price structure with that of AT&T. Vonage has also touted the quality of its VOIP services. Vonage's attempt to make price and benefits comparisons as clear as possible has been necessary to facilitate brand switching.

Brands vs. Generics

At times, a nationally branded product and a generic or store brand product may be identical in every physical dimension except name and label. For instance, two pain relievers may be chemically identical in terms of active ingredients but are named differently. Likewise, table salt may be sold in both a branded form and unbranded form but fundamentally be the same entity. In many cases, customers will tend to purchase the branded form of these items, and moreover they will tend to be willing to pay more for the branded form of these items, even though they may rationally know that the two products are identical.

Brands imbue products with trust. Because of this trust, many customers will be reluctant to betray a brand in favor of its generic equivalent. Even though the generic equivalent provides the same physical benefits at a lower price, it fails to provide the emotional security sought by many customers and may be perceived as the riskier alternative. Hence, the brand itself makes comparisons between items difficult.

Recent inroads by hard discounters and improvements in generic offerings in general have reduced the value of many brands. As consumers increasingly learn to trust generics, the difficult comparison effect that enables branded goods to be priced higher than their generic equivalent will be reduced.

Size Changes

The third approach to using the difficult comparison effect is in obfuscating parity relationships by changing the size related to offers. For instance, at bars in Prague one orders beers by size and not brand for most bars offer only one brand of beer. A typical offering in 2006 was a large beer for 20 CzK or a small beer for 14 CzK. On the face of it, a small beer appears cheaper. However, a large beer provides 0.5 liters of beer, making the unit costs 4.0 CzK per deciliter, while a small beer is only 0.3 liters of beer, making the unit costs 4.7 CzK per deciliter. On a per deciliter basis, a large beer is less expensive than a small beer. In this case, the difficult comparison effect enables the supplier to provide the product at a higher per unit price but at a lower perceived price.

Perceptual Challenges

Some influences to the customer acceptance of prices arise from more purely psychological issues, such as the adherence to social norms or the misapplication of decision-making rules.

PRICES ENDING IN 9

One of the best understood influences in pricing is the tendency to end prices in the digit 9. If price endings were randomly distributed, we would expect that prices would end in each digit about 10 percent of the time. Observation alone would indicate that this is not the case. A frequency analysis of retail price endings from 0 to 9 reveals that prices overwhelmingly tend to end in 9, and less so in 5 and 0.[9] See Exhibit 5-1. Researchers have uncovered many psychological influences that explain why firms may profit from this tendency.

The psychological effects that lead to the tendency to bias price endings are so strong, they even extend well beyond the last, rightmost digit. For instance, consider the consumer market reaction to odd price points, such as the difference between pricing a product at $24.99, $28.59, or $29.99. While the lowest price, $24.99, tends to lead to more sales than either higher price, as predicted by a downward sloping demand curve, an odd observation is associated with the somewhat unusual middle price point, $28.59 in many consumer markets, versus the more culturally accepted normal price of $29.99. Products tend to sell better when priced at "normal" prices, like $29.99, over odd prices, like $28.59, even though the normal price is slightly higher than the odd price. This kink in the demand

Exhibit 5-1 Price Ending Frequency: *January 1965 Study by D. W. Twedt of Price Endings of 30,878 Products in 1,865 Supermarkets in 70 Cities.*

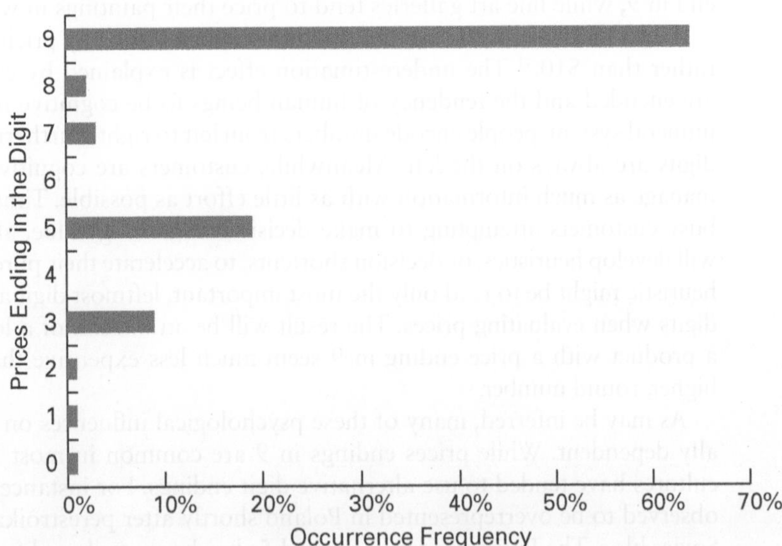

curve is a direct contradiction of standard economic theory and can best be explained by examining psychological influences.

The common, but discredited, hearsay reason for ending prices in 9 is due to a historical artifact relating odd pricing and shrinkage at the cash register. The belief was that even-priced merchandise would often be paid in cash with the exact amount, allowing clerks to pocket the cash. By using odd amounts, clerks would have to use the cash register to make change, thus making the pocketing of the customer receipts obvious to shoppers as well as bookkeepers who would later review the cash register tally. However, if this habit were only a bookkeeping tendency that stuck, then all odd price endings would be more common than the price endings with the digit 0. We see from the data that clearly there is more going on in price setting than would arise from a historical artifact.

The tendency to end prices in 9 may be influenced by the relationship between cognitive accessibility and comparative shopping. Round digits, such as 0 and 5, are easily stored and retrieved from memory due to their familiarity. Thus, prices that end in 0 and 5 will be more easily perceived, encoded into memory, and recalled during a comparison shopping effort. As such, round digits such as 0 and 5 may facilitate price comparisons while odd digits, such as 9s, may hamper efforts at price comparison. When customers compare prices between outlets, their increased ability to recall prices may also lead to increased price sensitivity. To reduce price sensitivity, shopkeepers may have intuitively learned the value of underrepresenting these round price endings and have chosen 9s instead.

Another source of encouragement for price endings in 9s may result from the perception of discounts that they tend to impart. Humans may frame a price ending in 9s as a small discount from the next higher round number. (The framing effect will be discussed in more detail later in this chapter in the "Framing Effect" section.) This discount represents a small gain in utility that may mildly encourage a purchase due to deeper psychological reasons.

Related to these prior insights is the issue of the meaning that the price ending imparts.[10] Prices ending in 9 tend to imply a relatively low price or a discounted price, thus stimulating demand. Unfortunately, prices ending in 9 may also communicate an unfavorable impression relating to quality due to the inferences that customers make regarding lower or discounted prices and their implication of lower quality. In contrast, prices ending in 0 are suspected to imply quality and tend to be used in retail outlets with a classier image. This observation partially explains the tendency for posters to be sold at prices that end in 9, while fine art galleries tend to price their paintings in whole numbers.

Much discussed is the underestimation effect invoked by pricing at levels such as $9.99 rather than $10.[11] The underestimation effect is explained by considering how numbers are encoded and the tendency of human beings to be cognitive misers. Within the Arabic numeral system, people encode numbers from left to right. Furthermore, the most important digits are always on the left. Meanwhile, customers are cognitive misers that attempt to manage as much information with as little effort as possible. Time-pressed and cognitively busy customers attempting to make decisions regarding value, alternatives, and tradeoffs will develop heuristics, or decision shortcuts, to accelerate their purchase decisions. One such heuristic might be to read only the most important, leftmost digit and discard the remaining digits when evaluating prices. The result will be an illusion of a lower price, which makes a product with a price ending in 9 seem much less expensive than the next nearest, and higher, round number.

As may be inferred, many of these psychological influences on price endings are culturally dependent. While prices endings in 9 are common in most Western countries, some cultures have tended to use alternative digit endings. For instance, prices ending in 5 were observed to be overrepresented in Poland shortly after perestroika liberalized much of the Soviet bloc. The Polish tendency toward 5s has been attributed to the confrontational bargaining position of an ex-Soviet Poland that led Polish consumers to perceive prices ending in 9 as a loss above the lower round number rather than as a gain from a higher round number.[12] In contrast, prices ending in 8s were found to be overrepresented in Asian countries, including Japan. For Asian cultures, the number 8 is associated with luck and prosperity, thus likely affording the product some attribution of good fortune as well.[13]

THE FAIRNESS EFFECT

In any transaction, customers expect to be treated fairly. Moreover, customers tend to feel as though they have been treated unfairly when the price that they are charged is different from the price that someone else may have to pay. While many have argued on philosophical grounds that the issue of fairness should be dismissed in a free market because free markets allow exactly that—freedom to participate—these arguments tend to go against the grain of human behavior and may be counter to our evolutionary biology.

Current economic theory is structured on the basis of self-interest as the primary motivator for any transaction. If the price of a product is higher than the benefits delivered, customers are free not to purchase it in a free market. Likewise, if it is too low for a business to profit, the firm is free not to offer the product. Between these two levels, any transaction price is deemed fair. However, such a cursory examination of fairness in pricing does an executive a grave disservice. It not only ignores many behavioral economic studies but can lead to a corporate disaster.

Findings in brain physiology, especially evolutionary neuroscience, show that the part of our brain that engages in commercial transaction decisions evolved from the interplay of our self-preservational (egoistic) and affectional (empathetic) neural circuitries.[14] Thus, sharing activities, such as those within families or those associated with gift giving to friends, and commercial activities, such as those involved in transactions, both rely upon the same physiological cognitive functions. The presence of sharing motives in commercial transactions may drive expectations of fairness with respect to prices.

A common way in which fairness affects pricing is that customers perceive prices as fair when they are within expectations based on past interactions with the category.[15] Large price increases can be perceived as "profit taking" on behalf of suppliers and producers, or as taking advantage of less-powerful customers. Likewise, prices that are perceived to vary randomly between customers are subject to the fairness effect as some customers feel discriminated against due to paying a higher price. This latter effect plagued Amazon in 2005 when customers uncovered price experimentation and discrimination at their website.[16]

Customers may not only expect that the price represents a sharing of the surplus benefits between the firm and the customer, but also expect that prices are fair in the sense that all customers are presented with the same options. When prices are out of line with these expectations, customers can call foul. Violating the concept of fairness may not only dampen immediate purchases, but it may spark customer outrage, leading to public relations crises. In these cases, marketing communication and public relations must be used to manage price variances that are perceived as unfair, and pricing practices may need to change.

The issue of fairness is not applied to all products equally. Fairness has a larger role in necessity goods than those related to discretionary purchases. Moreover, fairness issues are culturally dependent and can become the basis for ethical and legal challenges.

OVERCONFIDENCE OF CONTROL OVER FUTURE BEHAVIOR

Customers purchase many products with the expectation of modifying their behavior in conjunction with the use of the product. Unfortunately, human beings systematically overestimate their ability to modify their own behavior in a positive manner. For anecdotal evidence, just consider the number of slightly used exercise machines available in online peer-to-peer sales networks like eBay or Craigslist.

A significant revelation of the misalignment between expected behavioral modifications and actual behavior expressed was found in a study of customers at gyms. Researchers reviewed over 7,000 purchases in which customers were able to select their membership level from a menu of contracts in three U.S. health clubs.[17] It was found that members who chose a monthly subscription priced at $70 attended the gym on average 4.3 times per month, making a per-visit price of more than $17. These same members could have selected to pay $10 per visit using a 10-visit pass. Furthermore, customers who chose the monthly subscription were 17 percent more likely to stay enrolled past the first year than those who purchased an annual subscription, which is surprising because monthly members pay a higher fee for the privilege of canceling their contract at will. The inability of expressed behavior to match expected behavior was attributed to overconfidence by the customers with respect to their future self-control and future economic efficiency.

SMALL-PIE BIAS

Investigations into price negotiations have demonstrated that individuals suffer from a small-pie bias.[18] Consistently, negotiators will underestimate the size of the bargaining zone; that is, they will believe they are negotiating between a very small range of possible price points rather than the entire range that is possible. It is as if customers believe that the firm's costs are a large portion of the price they face, and firms believe that the value of their product is very close to the marginal costs. By implication, both customers and firms overestimate the share of the surplus that they capture in a transaction and fail to achieve the fullest possible surplus.

This effect is called the small-pie bias because both parties to a transaction believe they are making a decision regarding the size of the slice they will gain from a small pie, rather than understanding that the pie may be quite large, allowing for a much better deal.

To overcome the small-pie bias, researchers have suggested that sellers should formulate expectations of buyers' reservation price and then use conversations in the negotiation itself to seek disconfirming information that updates their beliefs of buyers' reservation price. The disconfirming information can be elicited by making initial offers that are outside of their expected buyer reservation price. In other words, start the opening bid at a level well above what the seller expects the buyer to accept and then allow the negotiation process to bring it back to the transaction range.

The need to overcome the small-pie bias is one of the reasons behind the earlier suggestion to initiate price negotiations with customers aggressively and provide concessions reluctantly. This generalized prescription must be tempered when price negotiations are not the sole purpose of the initial offer, such as when initial offers are solicited by buyers to screen sellers according to price expectations.

PROMOTIONAL INFLUENCE

Marketing promotions influence price sensitivity directly through the claims that they make and indirectly though the kind of customers who respond to promotions.[19] In other words, what the firm says about its products, and to whom it says it, strongly influences its ability to capture prices that reflect the value that it is delivering to customers. If a firm fails to communicate the value that it delivers to customers, the firm will find the task of capturing a decent price difficult. Alternatively, if it communicates the value that it delivers to customers, it at least has a fighting chance to capture a decent price. Furthermore, if the firm spends its communication resources on customers who have little value for its offering or are otherwise highly price-sensitive, it will have a difficult time capturing a decent price. Alternatively, if the firm focuses its communications resources on customers who are relatively less price-sensitive, it will improve its ability to capture a good price. These claims have been based not only on the experiences of many business-to-business salespeople, but also on research on consumer goods.

In comparing the effects of price-oriented communications versus benefit-oriented communications for consumer goods, it has been found that the message communicated in sales claims or marketing communications has a strong effect on price sensitivity. Price-oriented communications are those which identify a product or national brand with a price, usually a discounted price. Price-oriented communications are common within weekly store circulars, newspaper advertisements, and Internet promotional efforts and tend to be financed by both the local retail outlet and the original manufacturer. Benefit-oriented promotions are those that focus on the brand and the features or benefits of the product. Benefit-oriented promotions are commonly found in national advertising efforts such as television commercials and magazine advertisements and tend to be financed by the original manufacturer alone. While price-oriented promotions are designed to communicate the availability of a product at a particular outlet, their emphasis on price can lead to heightened price sensitivity. In contrast, benefit-oriented promotions tend to lead toward greater sensitivity to variations in benefits and concurrently lower price sensitivity.

A secondary effect of promotions on price sensitivity arises from the ability of advertising to increase the size of the addressable market. In consumer markets, customers attracted by advertising behave differently with respect to prices than those customers who are less influenced by advertising. Specifically, advertising-sensitive consumers tend to be more price-sensitive consumers. By bringing new customers into the market who are more price-sensitive than the market overall, advertising has an indirect effect of increasing the overall price sensitivity of the market.

Prospect Theory

An approach to encapsulating many of the psychological influences into a unified theory has led to the development of prospect theory, codified in a seminal paper by Khanamen and Tversky in 1979.[20] Many of the psychological effects explored later in this chapter can be described through prospect theory. Anchoring, the comparison set effect, the endowment effect, the end-benefit effect, order biases, and reference price effects are all, at least somewhat, related to prospect theory. As such, prospect theory is an important framework for understanding many psychological influences to price perceptions.

In construction, prospect theory examines how people make choices between prospective offers with risky outcomes. Because every purchase decision involves risk, prospect theory provides insightful explanations into customer behaviors and strong prescriptions for price management.

LOSSES WEIGH HEAVIER THAN GAINS

One of the key insights elucidated through prospect theory is that losses weigh heavier than gains in decision making. While paying for a product in itself represents a loss, other forms of losses might include paying a higher price than expected or receiving fewer benefits than expected. Likewise, the benefits delivered through a product represent a gain. Other forms of gain might include paying a lower price than expected or receiving more benefits than expected.

When making purchase decisions, customers tend to be more fearful of potentially losing through the transaction than they are happy about potentially gaining through the transaction. Colloquially, we can say that taking $10 away from a person causes more pain than giving that same person $10 causes joy. Thus, it can be conjectured that $10 in price paid weighs heavier in people's minds than $10 in benefits gained. Some research has even uncovered that losses weigh about two-and-a-half times heavier in decision making than gains. That is, for every $1 loss in price paid, the product may need to provide roughly $2.50 in benefits to leave customers emotionally neutral.

The effect of losses weighing heavier in people's minds than gains implies that promotional statements should heavily stress the benefits of the product over its price. By stressing the benefits, sales claims and marketing communications can help customers become more aware of the potential to gain through the transaction. Moreover, these claims must be sufficient to leave customers better off not only economically, but also in terms of the way in which they weigh benefits against costs. The goal of these promotional messages is to leave customers psychologically in a net-positive position.

INFLECTION AT THE POINT OF REFERENCE

In making any purchase, customers will compare offers against their point of reference. This point of reference may be their current level of satisfaction with their current endowment of products and wealth, the most recent prices seen in the market, or their most recent status prior to finding a product has expired and needs replacement. The point of reference can be thought of as the *perceived status quo*.

The fact that losses weigh heavier than gains in decision making implies that changes in status away from the point of reference will be evaluated differently. Losses away from the point of reference will be strongly avoided. Meanwhile, gains above the point of reference will be highly discounted. Combined, these effects lead towards a status quo bias, or tendency for customers to replace items with replicas of the last item purchased and avoid taking risks with new products and services.

DIMINISHING SENSITIVITY

As gains or losses increase away from the point of reference, people become less sensitive to the absolute magnitude of these gains or losses. That is, the difference between a $5 gain and a $10 gain is felt more strongly than the difference between a $490 gain and a $495 gain, even though the absolute value of these differences is the same $5 in both cases. Similar differences can be found in the way losses are felt. In general, people express diminishing sensitivity as losses or gains mount.

RISK AVERSION IN THE POSITIVE FRAME AND RISK SEEKING IN THE NEGATIVE FRAME

Another insight elucidated in prospect theory is the tendency towards risk aversion in the positive frame and risk seeking in the negative frame. Positive frame offers imply that a person will, in some sense, gain from the transaction. Negative frame proposals imply that the person will, in some sense, lose from the transaction.

Two offers made in the positive frame might be the 50 percent chance to gain $5,000 versus the sure gain of $2,000. When offers are presented in the positive frame, many people will choose the less risky proposal of a sure gain of $2,000 even though the 50 percent chance at gaining $5,000 has a greater net expected value.

Two offers made in the negative frame might be a sure loss of $2,000 versus a 50 percent chance of a $5,000 loss. When offers are presented in the negative frame, a higher proportion of people will choose the risky proposal of the 50 percent chance of a $5,000 loss over the sure loss of $2,000, even though the sure loss of $2,000 leaves the person better off than they should expect to be when taking the 50 percent chance at a $5,000 loss.

UTILITY FUNCTION FROM PROSPECT THEORY

The many insights into the mental calculus of customers have led to the development of an alternative utility function for describing purchase decisions. Rather than assuming that gains are traded off equally with losses, the utility function from prospect theory incorporates the decision biases of people when confronted with alternative offers. In Exhibit 5-2, the horizontal axis represents the actual loss or gain incurred in an offer, while the vertical axis represents the perceived value of that gain or loss within a person. The utility function plots the way losses and gains are perceived.

The fact that losses weigh heavier than gains is captured in this graph. Points A and B represent an equal magnitude of an actual gain or loss, respectively (the horizontal axis). In terms of perceived value (the vertical axis), point A is closer to the origin than point B. Thus, the utility function shows that a gain of equal magnitude to a loss has a smaller weight in decision making. Furthermore, the utility function demonstrates diminishing sensitivity as gains and losses mount, and an inflection at the point of reference.

PRESCRIPTIONS

Executives can use the insights gained from prospect theory in pricing. While the implications are far-reaching, three quick examples will suffice in demonstrating the power of prospect theory in providing prescriptions for better pricing.

Exhibit 5-2 Utility Function from Prospect Theory

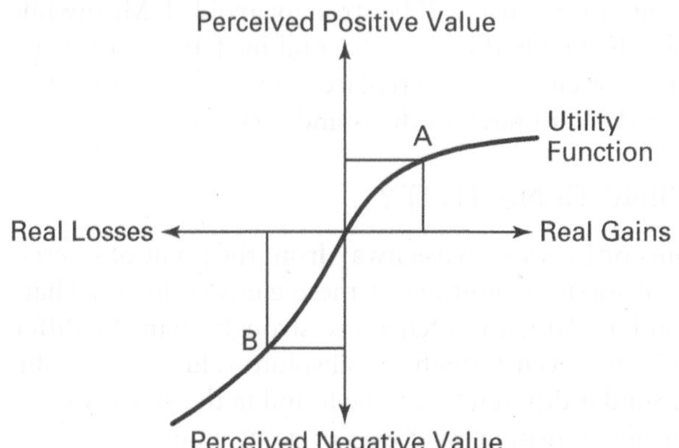

One prescription from prospect theory is to unbundle gains and bundle losses. As noted, losses weigh heavier than gains and both losses and gains are felt with diminishing sensitivity as one moves away from the point of reference. As such, unbundling gains into multiple smaller gains encourages the customer to perceive a greater gain than otherwise would be felt. In contrast, bundling all the losses into a singular event, the payment of the item, decreases the perceived pain involved in the transaction. In transactions, the unbundling gains and bundling losses can be executed by itemizing all the sources of benefits to heighten the sense of gain while providing only a single, total price into which to bundle the pain.

A second prescription from prospect theory is to avoid surcharges and provide discounts. Surcharges are perceived as a punitive loss, while discounts are perceived as a gain. To encourage customers to pay a higher price, the higher price should not be posed as a surcharge, but rather the "regular" price. Any discounts are perceived as an additional gain on top of gaining the product. Thus, credit card firms would strongly prefer that merchants raise prices and offer a 3 percent cash discount over implementing an equivalent credit card surcharge. Financially, these two offers can leave customers equally well off; however, surcharges are more likely to dissuade customers from using credit cards than the cash discounts.

The third prescription from prospect theory is to shift the pain from direct price paid to indirect opportunity costs. Many people associate less pain with loss of time and convenience than they do with direct and observable price payments. Shifting costs from the firm to customers by making them drive further for shopping, endure longer lines, or assemble their own products encourages purchases and lowers the perceived pain involved in the transaction. This third prescription may account for much of the success of superstores such as Wal-Mart, Tesco, and Carrefour, the furniture retailer IKEA, and discount airlines such as Ryanair.

Effects Related to Prospect Theory

Prospect theory encapsulates many influences on customer perceptions of prices and offers. Many of these influences were identified before prospect theory was codified and were studied in greater detail than can be described directly through prospect theory. What follows are some of the better understood effects that are related to prospect theory.

REFERENCE PRICE EFFECTS

Prospect theory identified the heightened sensitivity that people have in relation to their point of reference. One direct consequence of this is the reference price effect. In many markets, customers refer to the last price they paid in forming expectations regarding the price that they are willing to pay during the next purchasing situation. The manner in which past prices affect the perception of current prices is known as the *reference price effect.*[21]

The reference price held by customers is informed by the price that they currently see on a product and the price that they last saw on the product. Mathematically, we can write this as

$$\text{Reference Price} = \alpha\,(\text{Last Observed Price}) + (1 - \alpha)\,(\text{Currently Observed Price}) \qquad \text{Eq. 5.1}$$

where the moderating factor α (pronounced "alpha") describes the level of influence that past observed prices have on the current reference price. A large α implies that past prices largely determine the reference price that customers hold with respect to a product, while a small α implies that currently observed prices largely determine consumer reference prices. The size of α is itself influenced by many factors, such as the frequency of purchase within the category and the importance of price in making purchase decisions within the category.[22]

An example of the reference price effect can be found in the market for beef steaks. In 2008, the price of corn doubled in one year, driving an increase in the price of beef. Customers visiting restaurants infrequently were often shocked to see a sudden jump in the price of steaks in comparison to the price that they last saw in the market. This can be considered as a form of the reference price effect, and as a type of an anchoring effect. Customers expected one price and had a difficult time adjusting to new information regarding price levels. The result was a dampening of demand.

A traditional assumption concerning how prices influence buyers' purchasing behaviors has been that buyers know the prices of the products and services that they consider for purchase. However, empirical research during the past four decade repeatedly has revealed that buyers are routinely unable to remember the prices of items that they have recently purchased. Even though consumers don't have perfect recall of past observed prices, what recall they do have influences their willingness to pay, or the reference price.

When current prices are higher than past prices, the reference price effect drives an excess dampening in demand as current prices are above many consumers' willingness to pay. Price increases due to inflation or other economic factors are common, and the reference price effect predicts that demand will decline disproportionately as prices rise due to the need for customers to adjust their expectations to the new, higher price point.

A more insidious and common challenge for pricing professionals arising from the reference price effect comes from the use of promotional prices and discounts. During a price promotion, prices are lower than in the past, causing the reference price to be higher than the observed price. Thus, during the price promotion, sales will increase disproportionately. After the price promotion, however, prices will be higher than those observed during the last transaction. This drives their reference price to be higher than then observed prices during the non-sale period, thus dampening sales disproportionately. Consequently, during periods of price promotions, sales will sharply increase, and during regular price periods, sales will plummet. These dynamics may lead executives to believe that they must lower their prices to improve profits, when actually they simply indicate that they have been overly relying on price promotions to attract customers. The reference price effect is one of many reasons pricing professionals must go beyond purely quantitative analysis in managing price.

ENDOWMENT EFFECT

An intriguing psychological effect that can decrease price sensitivity is the endowment effect.[23] According to the endowment effect, people place more value in something once they possess it than they otherwise would. The endowment effect is strongly related in the heightened sensitivity uncovered around the point of reference in prospect theory.

The endowment effect was observed from experiments in which students were given coffee mugs and chocolate bars randomly and then allowed to make trades to optimize their gift. In the absence of any switching costs, it would be expected that about half of the students would switch products. Half of the coffee mug holders would prefer chocolate bars and vice versa, leading to half of the students trading gifts. However, experiments repeatedly show switching rates much lower than 50 percent. If the researcher asks students why they don't switch, they reply that they really like what they got. The claimed love of their randomly distributed gift has been attributed to the endowment effect.

The endowment effect is used in sales situations by many firms. At bazaars, for instance, vendors will quickly put a product in the hands of prospects to lower their price sensitivity.

Similarly, automobile dealers will encourage customers to take a test drive to increase their likelihood of purchase. Even trial offers benefit from the endowment effect by encouraging customers to adapt the new product once it has entered their endowment.

ANCHORING

Significant research into decision making has demonstrated that people create expectations based upon information gathered early in the decision-making process. Once a person has created an expectation from an initial set of information, changing the person's expectations will be difficult because it involves relearning or revealing new evidence that demonstrates the fallacy of applying expectations formed earlier to the current situation. The process of setting expectations early and changing them slowly is known as anchoring. Anchoring not only affects perceptions of prices as high or low but also affects perceptions of benefits as necessary or superfluous.

Examples of anchoring are very common in infrequently purchased, high-value business markets. Offers coming early in a purchase decision process are likely to set expectations for comparison to offers that are made later in the purchasing decision process. Prospects will anchor not just on the price of the offering, but also on the features, benefits, and value that they expect from buying from that category. Because of the power of anchoring to influence purchase decisions, many firms will hunt actively for prospects early in the purchase decision process and may even choose to ignore sales opportunities that come late in the purchase decision process.

Another example of anchoring can be found in negotiations. As any person who has experienced a few negotiations will tell you, people tend to anchor price expectations based on the first price they hear. This is the primary role of anchoring in pricing. Customers set their reservation price, or willingness to pay, early in the purchase decision process. Thus, beginning price conversations at higher levels tends to end price negotiations at higher prices than those which began at a lower level.

In price negotiations with an unprepared buyer, anchoring can be used by a seller to drive prices higher so long as the buyer perceives the value to be above the price communicated early in the process. Some sales literature even suggests that during a negotiation, salespeople should elicit the customer's acceptable purchase price first as a means to reveal the customer's willingness to pay. With more capable buyers, however, the anchoring effect of buyers around their willingness to pay is usually dissipated though structured learning and experience. In such cases, asking customers for their purchase price first can actually harm the potential to achieve higher prices by anchoring the salesperson around his or her own minimum asking price.

Anchoring creates a challenge for business markets with respect to budgetary prices. Budgetary prices are not actual transaction prices, but rather price ranges given to customers early in the sales process to determine their ability to purchase as well as the magnitude of the decision-making impact. From a sales perspective, the need to provide budgetary prices is related to the need to qualify customers early in the sales process with regard to their ability to purchase, timing of purchase, and scope of purchasing needs. In giving budgetary prices, many sales instructions will tell salespeople to give a wide range of potential prices and clarify that the actual price will depend on the specific product selected. They may furthermore suggest using higher figures than expected in the final price of the product. The logic behind this prescriptive suggestion is related to the challenge that anchoring creates, both in reducing the ability to charge a higher price and in driving a potential offer outside the consideration set. Giving prospects a higher price is suggested to anchor prospective customers towards higher price expectations, thus weakening their resolve in later price negotiations. The use of a wide range of prices is called for to keep the sale from being blocked by a failure to meet the relevant competitors in the sales process.

Anchoring may be related to aspects of prospect theory. Once people anchor on an initial piece of information, it forms a reference point. Moreover, the gains that they would receive by updating that information may be perceived to be too few in relation to the costs required to change their perceptions. As such, anchors once placed are hard to displace.

COMPARISON SET EFFECT

Just as initial offers will influence price expectations through anchoring, the price of comparable alternatives will also influence price expectations.[24] The product plus its comparable alternatives under consideration in a specific purchasing opportunity form a comparison set. When some of the products within the comparison set are priced low, price expectations of customers will tend to decrease. When some of the products in the comparison set are priced high, price expectations of customers will tend to increase.

Executives may be able to use the comparison set effect to influence price expectations. If the comparison set can be adjusted to include higher-priced items, customer price sensitivity can be reduced. For instance, when marketing a small car aimed at first-time car buyers in developing nations, automakers may find that their sales increase and prices get stronger when comparing the price of the small car to that of a larger, more expensive car rather than the price of a motorcycle, even though the small car has been developed and marketed specifically for families who would have purchased the motorcycle had the inexpensive car not become available.

The comparison set effect can also be used with the benefits under consideration to shift the dimensions of competition in a firm's favor. For instance, when customers are comparing durable goods, they may be tempted to compare only the upfront acquisition costs. Firms that offer products of higher quality, as measured by durability, efficiency, or productivity, should include these dimensions when encouraging customers to evaluate the merits of competing offers. By shifting the metrics of comparison, they may be able to capture both a higher price and more sales. In contrast, firms that offer an inferior product at a lower acquisition price would want to encourage customers to focus on the initial price only.

FRAMING EFFECT

How an offer is framed can affect the willingness of customers to accept that offer. In pricing, the framing effect can have dramatic influence on the price that customers are willing to pay.

A common example of the framing effect can be found in a behavioral experiment regarding the interaction between a person at the beach and a friend going to purchase beverages. The friend asks, "How much are you willing to pay for the drink? I will pay up to the amount you give me, but if the price is higher than that, I will not buy it." Using one frame, the friend then concludes the proposition by saying, "I am going to the pristine hotel bar." Using an alternative frame, the friend then concludes the proposition by saying, "I am going to a grungy convenience store." People regularly state a higher willingness to pay if it is associated with a hotel rather than a convenience store, even though the beverage is exactly the same and the benefits gained are exactly the same. Depending on the frame through which the offer is made (pristine hotel bar versus grungy convenience store), the person on the beach will change his or her willingness to pay.

The framing effect is related to many aspects of prospect theory. For instance, framing an offer in the positive frame will naturally make it more attractive than framing the same offer in the negative frame. Thus, rather than highlighting the price and the costs associated with using a product, firms are usually better off highlighting the benefits and the value derived from a product. Moreover, rather than lumping all the positive elements of an offer into a common frame, customers are usually more willing to purchase a product when all the positive elements of the offer are disaggregated and itemized.

ORDER BIAS

Pricing research has shown that the order of presentation of prices affects the selection of products and acceptable prices by customers.[25] Researchers have compared the dependence of the average transaction price on the order of price presentation. In general, when products are presented in decreasing price order (that is, from highest to lowest), customers select a higher price offer than when products are presented in increasing price order (that is, from lowest to highest). The order bias has been experimentally demonstrated with fast-moving consumer goods but remains suspect with more-expensive items and durable goods.

The order bias can be considered to be a result of anchoring upon initial offers and loss aversion coupled with a failure to adjust the frame of reference fully. When customers review a list of products in terms of both benefits and price, they may anchor their expectations of acceptable prices and benefits on the first item considered. When that first item delivers many benefits and is priced at a high level, they may be reluctant to forgo benefits to save a little by buying a lower-priced option. Hence they will tend to purchase a higher-priced item. In contrast, when the first item is priced very low and delivers somewhat fewer benefits, they may be reluctant to pay a higher price to gain a few benefits and thus will tend to purchase a lower-priced item.

The order bias influences sales and marketing communication efforts with respect to capturing better prices. When presenting a range of products within the same category, executives will present the highest-priced good first prior to exhausting all the possibilities by moving throughout the price points to lower levels. In selling automobiles, mattresses, and other consumer durables, it is common practice to show models starting from the most expensive item and moving downward from there. Similarly, in designing websites, many executives will showcase their most expensive items prior to revealing their cheaper alternatives.

END-BENEFIT EFFECT

Customers purchase products not because of their intrinsic features, but because they believe that the product will enable them to accomplish a goal. Sometimes, these goals are only tangentially related to the specific attributes of the product. Products that contribute a higher portion of the end-benefit sought by a customer are associated with lower price sensitivity than those that are ancillary to the end-benefit sought. Executives that help customers frame their products in relationship to the true desired end-benefit find their price sensitivity is somewhat reduced.[26]

For instance, families will tend to purchase entrance to an amusement park or museum not because of the benefits of riding a roller coaster or seeing a unique exhibit, but because of the hope they have in reconnecting with their family members during the event. Amusement park and museum executives therefore tend to position their offering as a means to create memorable family experiences to decrease price sensitivity and increase customer volume.

Similarly, successful diet food manufacturers have repositioned their offerings into weight-loss management systems. Moreover, much of the promotional material from these firms have moved one step further, not only tying their offering to successful weight loss, but connecting it to higher-level aspirational goals such as looking better, feeling healthier, or commanding a positive impression at social functions. When firms facilitate the connection between their core offering and a customer's aspirational goals, they can reduce price sensitivity.

The end-benefit effect influences not only prices, but also promotional messages. In promoting a product, executives should stress the relationship between their customers' goals and their products rather than simply focus on its features and attributes. In this sense, the end-benefit effect is a direct extension of the prescription from prospect theory to highlight gains and minimize losses. Framing a product as being a major contributor to the full end-benefit desired can make customers less price-sensitive.

Summary

- Many psychological influences to the perception of value arise from neurological functions, decision biases, and behavioral effects. Price management requires an understanding of the psychological influences on value perception.
- Customers are less price-sensitive when they are spending other people's money than when they are spending their own.
- Switching costs, both psychologically driven from brand devotion and fiscally driven from investments in complementary goods, business processes, or learning, can encourage customers to avoid changes from the status quo.
- Higher-expenditure product categories may be associated with greater price sensitivity as customers hold a strong economic incentive to compare offers by both price and benefits.
- By making price comparison difficult, firms can lower price sensitivity. The difficult comparison effect can be used by incumbents to halt the progress of new entrants, branded goods to halt the invasion of generics, and retailers to encourage customers to purchase a seemingly less expensive but actually more expensive item.
- The tendency for prices to end in 9 appeals to decision heuristics to pay attention only to the leftmost digit and uses cognitive accessibility challenges to discourage price comparisons when shopping. Price endings may also communicate a message, such as being priced cheaply or being lucky, depending upon culture influences.
- People expect fairness in transactions and can retaliate when their conception of fairness is breached. The fairness effect can dampen the ability of firms to increase prices, especially with necessity-oriented goods.
- Customers regularly suffer from overconfidence with respect to future behavior. Overly ambitious behavioral expectations can explain the tendency of customers to purchase packages greater than their needs.
- Both buyers and sellers routinely bias expectations to believe that they are negotiating over a smaller pie than they truly are. The small-pie bias leads to a tendency to accept smaller offers in sales situations.
- The message used to promote a product influences the value perceived in the product. Price-oriented promotions increase price sensitivity, while benefit-oriented promotions increase benefit sensitivity, thereby supporting higher prices.
- Prospect theory attempts to encapsulate many of the psychological influences on the perception of value. From prospect theory, we see that losses weigh heavier than gains, that the point of reference strongly influences the perception of an offer, sensitivity diminishes as losses or gains mount, and that people tend to be risk-averse in the positive frame while risk-seeking in the negative frame. A number of prescriptions for executives can be derived from prospect theory, such as unbundling gains and bundling pains, avoiding surcharges and providing discounts instead, and shifting direct sources of pain into indirect, less transparent pains.
- Reference prices are moderated by both the currently observed prices and the last observed prices. Price increases will yield prices above the reference price level, thus aggravating a drop in demand. Price decrease will yield prices below the reference price level, thus further stimulating a growth in demand.

- The endowment effect is the tendency of people to place more value in something once they possess it than they otherwise would. The endowment effect explains the ability to decrease price sensitivity and increase purchase rates simply by asking prospective customers to hold a product while making decisions.
- People have a tendency to anchor upon information gained early in the decision-making process. Anchoring can be used in selling situations to encourage customers to expect a higher price than what is finally determined, or can be overcome by salespeople by seeking disconfirming evidence during interactions and negotiations with clients.
- Customers formulate price expectations based upon the alternatives under consideration, or the comparison set. Lower-priced alternatives tend to heighten price sensitivity, and higher-priced alternatives tend to lower price sensitivity.
- The frame through which customers evaluate an offer affects their willingness to pay. Providing reasons to expect a higher price leads to less price sensitivity. Providing reasons to expect a lower price leads to greater price sensitivity.
- The order of offers can affect the average transaction price. Presenting a product lineup from the highest price down can bias selection towards higher-priced goods. Likewise, presenting the product lineup from the lowest price up can bias selection towards lower-priced goods.
- The greater portion that a product contributes towards the end-benefit sought by a customer, the lower price sensitivity customers will have with respect to that product.

Exercises

1. A study indicated that the optimal price for a consumer product is $32.45. Most products in the market sell for $29.99. What price would you suggest to retailers for selling the product, and why?
2. A haute cuisine restaurant is opening down the street, and its owner asks you for advice on pricing. Should you suggest that the restaurant price an appetizer at $6.99 or $7, and why?
3. The haute cuisine restaurateur has many appetizers in the range of $6 to $12 and many entrees in the range of $15 to $30. The chef has created a new vegetarian course and wishes to place it on the menu. Because the food costs are low on this dish, the restaurateur believes the proper price is $12, even though the course could be the main meal for the evening. On what part of the menu would you suggest placing the item and why?
4. Consider a grocer that offers double coupon redemptions and you are thinking about purchasing oatmeal with a $0.25 coupon. Now consider a furniture store that is offering a $0.50 discount on a dining room set. In which case are you more likely to travel to that specific store to receive the discount? Do you believe your response is rational? Explain.
5. A salesperson interacting with a corporate prospect believes she understands the challenge that the client is trying to address and quotes a project for $20,000 as a solution. A few days later, the corporate prospect begins to discuss many other aspects of the challenge that he is trying to address and asks for a proposal to be delivered. What is the nature of the pricing challenge that this salesperson has created, and how could she have prevented it?

6. IAR Systems has offered its software to engineers for writing tiny C code on embedded systems for free on a 60-day basis. Consider this sales process step in relationship to the endowment effect and switching costs. Is this a wise marketing move, or is IAR Systems forgoing revenue?
7. Consider the following scenario. You are shopping at the Silk Road Mall in Beijing and you notice a very nice leather bag that you would like to buy. You figure that a bag of similar style and workmanship would cost you about 150 euros in Germany. Furthermore, it is exactly what you want. You decide to bargain with the merchant and settle on a price of approximately 30 euros. Situation A: You later show it to a friend who reveals a similar bag purchased from the same merchant for 50 euros. Situation B: You later show it to a friend who reveals a similar bag purchased from the same merchant for 20 euros.
   a. In which case are you more likely to return to that merchant tomorrow to make another purchase?
   b. What effect(s) best describes this behavior?
8. Consider the following hypothetical. Situation A: You are at a drugstore when you notice a pair of sunglasses for $24.99. You like the sunglasses but believe the price is a little high for this kind of product. Situation B: You are at a high-end fashion store when you notice a pair of sunglasses for $24.99. You like the sunglasses but believe the price is a little high for this kind of product.
   a. In which case are you more likely to purchase the sunglasses?
   b. What effect(s) best describes this behavior?
9. Consider the following hypothetical. Situation A: You have gone to the theater to see a movie for $12. You have not purchased the ticket yet. Upon arrival, you discover that you have lost $12. You still can charge the admission to the movie. Situation B: You have gone to the theater to see a movie for $12. You had purchased the ticket on the Internet, but you forgot to bring the ticket and the movie theater is unable to track your purchase. You still can charge the admission to the movie.
   a. In which case are you more likely to purchase a second ticket to the movie?
   b. What effect(s) best describes this behavior?
10. Business schools tend to position the cost of tuition in comparison to the future earnings of people with MBAs. Identify the major psychological influence that is being used to influence the willingness of students to enroll in an MBA program, and explain why it improves enrollment.
11. When designing a course, professors select textbooks for students. Are professors likely to be price-sensitive to the price of a textbook? Why or why not?
12. How is each of these psychological effects related to prospect theory?
   a. Anchoring
   b. The comparison set effect
   c. The endowment effect
   d. The end-benefit effect
   e. The fairness effect
   f. Order biases
   g. The reference price effect
   h. Switching costs

Notes

[1] Kent B. Monroe, "Buyers' Subjective Perceptions of Price," *Journal of Marketing Research* 10, No. 1 (February 1973): 70–80.

[2] Colin F. Camerer, George Loewenstein, and Drazen Prelec, "Neuroeconomics: Why Economics Needs Brains," *Scandinavian Journal of Economics* 106, No. 3 (September 2004): 555–79. "Do Economists Need Brains?" *The Economist* (July 26, 2008): 13.

[3] "Science and Technology: The Triumph of Unreason?; Neuroeconomics," *The Economist* (January 13, 2007): 73. "Science and Technology: Money Isn't Everything; Neuroeconomics," *The Economist* (July 7, 2007): 86.

[4] Moshe Bar and Maital Neta, "The Proactive Brain: Using Rudimentary Information to Make Predictive Judgments," *Journal of Consumer Behavior* 7, No. 4/5 (July–October 2008): 319–30.

[5] Milton Friedman and Rose Friedman, "Cradle to Grave," *Free to Choose: A Personal Statement* (New York: Harcourt Brace, 1980): 116–17.

[6] Switching costs is largely discussed with respect to high-tech markets. Carl Shapiro and Hall R. Varian, "Recognizing Lock-In," *Information Rules: A Strategic Guide to the Network Economy* (Boston: Harvard Business School Press, 1999); 103–33. Geoffrey A. Moore, "High-Tech Marketing Enlightenment," *Crossing the Chasm* (New York: HarperCollins, 1991): 51.

[7] Thomas T. Nagle and Reed K. Holden, "Customers: Understanding and Influencing the Purchase Decision," in *The Strategy and Tactics of Pricing: A Guide to Profitable Decision Making*, 3rd ed. (Upper Saddle River, NJ: Prentice Hall, 2002): 93–94.

[8] Vicki G. Morwitz, Eric A. Greenleaf, and Eric J. Johnson, "Divide and Prosper: Consumers' Reactions to Partitioned Prices," *Journal of Marketing Research* 35, No. 4 (November 1998): 453–63. J. Edward Russo, "The Value of Unit Price Information." *Journal of Marketing Research* 14, No. 2 (May 1977): 193–201. Robert G. Docters, "Price Strategy: Time to Chose Your Weapons," *The Journal of Business Strategy 18*, No 5 (September/October 1997): 11–15.

[9] Dick Warren Twedt, "Does the '9 Fixation' in Retail Pricing Really Promote Sales?" *Journal of Marketing* 29 (October 1965): 54–55. Robert M. Schindler, "Consumer Recognition of Increases in Odd and Even Prices," *Advances in Consumer Research* 11, No. 1 (January 1984): 459–62.

[10] Robert M. Schindler, "Symbolic Meanings of a Price Ending," *Advances in Consumer Research* 18, No. 1 (January 1991): 794–801. Robert M. Schindler and Thomas M. Kibarian, "Image Communicated by the Use of 99 Endings in Advertised Prices," *Journal of Advertising* 30, No. 4 (Winter 2001): 95–99. Also studied with respect to restaurants in H. G. Parsa and Sandra Naipaul, "Price-Ending Strategies and Managerial Perspectives: A Reciprocal Phenomenon—Part I," Journal of Services Research 7, No. 2 (October 2007): 7–26.

[11] Keith S. Coulter, "Odd-ending Price Underestimation: An Experimental Examination of Left-to-Right Processing Effects," *The Journal of Product and Brand Management* 10, No. 4/5 (2001): 276–92.

[12] Adam Nguyen, Roger M. Heeler, and Zinaida Taran. "High-Low Context Cultures and Price-Ending Practices," *The Journal of Product and Brand Management* 16, No. 3 (April 2007): 206–14.

[13] Lee C. Simmons and Robert M. Schindler, "Cultural Superstitions and the Price Endings Used in Chinese Advertising," *Journal of International Marketing* 11, No. 2 (June 2003): 101–11.

[14] Gerald A. Cory Jr, "A Behavioral Model of the Dual Motive Approach to Behavioral Economics and Social Exchange," *Journal of Socio-Economics* 35, No. 4 (August 2006): 592–612.

[15] Margaret C. Campbell, "Perceptions of Price Unfairness: Antecedents and Consequences," *Journal of Marketing Research* 36, No. 2 (May 1999): 187–99. Lisa E. Bolton, Luk Warlop, and Joseph W. Alba, "Consumer Perceptions of Price (Un)Fairness," *Journal of Consumer Research* 29, No. 4 (March 2003): 474–91.

[16] Fred M. Feinberg, Aradhna Krishna, and Z. John Zang, "Do We Care What Others Get? A Behaviorist Approach to Targeted Promotions," *Journal of Marketing Research* 39, No. 3 (August 2002): 277–91. Anita Ramasastry, "Web Sites Change Prices Based on Customer Habits," *CNN.com* (June 24, 2005). http://www.cnn.com/2005/LAW/06/24/ramasastry.website.prices/ (accessed on January 19, 2009).

[17] Stefano Della Vigna and Ulrike Malmendier, "Paying Not to Go to the Gym," *American Economic Review* 96, No. 3 (June 2006): 694–719.

[18] Richard P. Larrick and George Wu, "Claiming a Large Slice of a Small Pie: Asymmetric Disconfirmation in Negotiation," *Journal of Personality & Social Psychology* 93, No. 2 (August 2007): 212–33.

[19] The influence of promotions on pricing is a closely studied issue. Lakshman Krishnamurthi and S. P. Raj, "The Effect of Advertising on Consumer Price Sensitivity," *Journal of Marketing Research* 22, No. 2 (May 1985): 119–29. Vinay Kanetkar, Charles B. Weinberg, and Doyle L Weiss, "Price Sensitivity and Television Advertising Exposures: Some Empirical Findings," *Marketing Science* 11, No. 4 (Fall 1992): 359–71. Anil Kaul and Dick R. Wittink, "Empirical Generalizations about the Impact of Advertising on Price Sensitivity and Price," *Marketing Science, Part 2* 14, No. 3 (July 1995): G151–G160. Sara Campo and María J. Yagüe, "Effects of Price Promotions on the Perceived Price," *International Journal of Service Industry Management* 18, No. 3 (2007): 269–86.

[20] Daniel Kahneman and Amos Tversky, "Prospect Theory: An Analysis of Decision Under Risk," *Econometrica* 47, No. 2 (March 1979): 263–91. Richard Thaler, "Mental Accounting and Consumer Choice," *Marketing Science* 4 No. 3 (Summer 1985): 199–214.

[21] Reference price effects are discussed in Richard A. Briesch, Lakshman Krishnamurthi, Tridib Mazumdar, and S. P. Raj, "A Comparative Analysis of Reference Price Models," *Journal of Consumer Research* 24, No. 2 (September 1997): 202–14. See also Kent B. Monroe and Angela Y. Lee. "Remembering Versus Knowing: Issues in Buyers' Processing of Price Information," *Academy of Marketing Science* 27, No. 2 (Spring 1999): 207–25.

[22] The moderator factor alpha in the exponential smoothing model of customer reference prices has been measured for some product categories. Greenleaf measured alpha (α) for peanut butter to be quite high, at 0.925 (1995), implying that customers strongly expect current prices to be similar to those last observed. Hardie measured alpha for orange juice at a similarly high level, at 0.83. See Eric A. Greenleaf, "The Impact of Reference Price Effects on the Profitability of Price Promotions," *Marketing Science* 14, No. 1 (Winter 1995): 82–104. Bruce G. S. Hardie, Eric J. Johnson, and Peter S. Fader, "Modeling Loss Aversion and Reference Dependence Effects on Brand Choice," *Marketing Science* 12, No. 4 (Fall 1993): 378–94.

[23] The endowment effect has been documented in a number of studies. Jack L. Knetsch, "The Endowment Effect and Evidence of Nonreversible Indifference Curves," *American Economic Review* 79, No. 5 (December 1989): 1277–84. John A. List, "Does Market Experience Eliminate Market Anomalies?" *Quarterly Journal of Economics* 118, No. 1 (February 2003): 41–71. Daniel Kahneman, Jack L. Knetsch, and Richard H. Thaler, "Experimental Tests of the Endowment Effect and the Coase Theorem," *Journal of Political Economy* 98, No. 6 (December 1990): 1325–48. Daniel Kahneman, Jack L. Knetsch, and Richard H. Thaler, "Anomalies: The Endowment Effect, Loss Aversion, and Status Quo Bias," *Journal of Economic Perspectives* 5, No. 1 (Winter 1991): 193–206.

[24] Nagle and Holden, "Customers: Understanding and Influencing the Purchase Decision," 112.

[25] Paula Bennett, Mike Brennan, and Zane Kearns, "Psychological Aspects of Price: An Empirical Test of Order and Range Effects," *Marketing Bulletin* 14 (January 2003): 1–8.

[26] Nagle and Holden, "Customers: Understanding and Influencing the Purchase Decision," 94–95.

PART
2

Managing Price Variances

Chapter 6

Price Segmentation

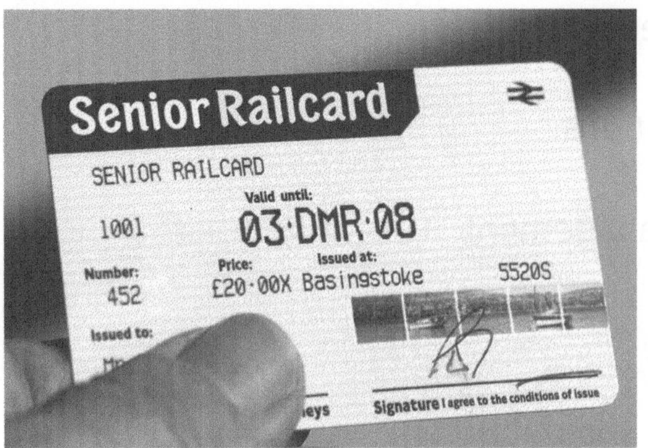

Peter Titmuss/Alamy

WORLDWIDE photo/Alamy

- What is price segmentation?
- When does price segmentation work?
- Is price segmentation good or bad?
- How do segmentation hedges enable a firm to price-segment the market?
- How should an executive design a price segmentation policy?
- Stretch Question: If a firm price-segments the market, what is the optimal set of prices and market shares for the different price segments?

While the best pricing techniques all share a foundation in guiding executives to price in proportion to value, they also share an opportunity, in that value is in the mind of the beholder and different minds will value a product differently. To seize this opportunity, firms will price-segment the market. Price segmentation is the method of pricing the same or similar products differently for different customer segments.

Within any market, different customers will value products differently, and therefore they will be willing to pay different amounts for that product. The diversity of individual customers within the collective market is a form of heterogeneity. Market heterogeneity can be seen in terms of brand affinity, benefits demanded, or willingness to pay. When we are describing differences between individuals in their willingness to pay, we are describing a form of heterogeneity in demand.

A simple thought experiment will demonstrate that almost every conceivable market exhibits heterogeneity in demand. Let us consider a market where every customer purchased only one unit.[1] The expressed demand at any given price is the number of customers who are willing to pay any price up to the one required. If the market was homogeneous and all customers had the exact same willingness to pay, the elasticity of demand would be zero until that critical price is reached. That is, the number of units sold would be constant with respect to price changes until the critical price is reached. At the critical price, the elasticity of demand would stretch to infinity as demand collapsed to zero. Overall market demand curves that are flat until a critical price is reached and then drop to zero at that critical price have not been reported in any markets to date. Therefore, we can conclude that heterogeneity in demand is the overwhelming norm for markets.

The drivers to heterogeneity in demand are multifarious. Some customers may derive greater benefits from the product compared to others with more modest requirements, and therefore they are willing to pay more. Some customers may have higher incomes, thus enabling them to pay more. Alternatively, some customers may have more time to price-compare and are therefore more price-sensitive. As we will uncover, even more issues may drive demand heterogeneity. The point is, demand is heterogeneous and this heterogeneity in demand creates the opportunity to practice price segmentation.[2]

Price segmentation, also known as price discrimination in economics, is charging different customers different prices for an otherwise identical or similar product. Firms can practice price segmentation by aligning prices to demand heterogeneity in an effort to extract a greater portion of the consumer surplus from the market in the form of profits. Factors that drive (or undermine) value for customers can be used to create a price segmentation policy in that the firm automatically charges more (or less) when and where the product delivers more (or less) utility. Alternatively, firms can practice price segmentation by aligning prices to cost factors to discourage profit-destructive behaviors. Factors that drive the cost to serve can be used to charge more automatically when there are predictably higher incremental costs for the seller. In either case, price segmentation enables the firm to increase profits.

A significant hindrance to price segmentation is the potential for aftermarket transference. Products priced with segmentation policies need to have ***limited transferability***—that is, once sold to a customer, that customer should find it difficult to resell it to another customer. If the product is easily transferable, then customers in the lower-priced segment are able to purchase the product and subsequently resell it to the higher-priced segment to their own advantage and not the firm's, and therefore price segmentation will fail to improve supplier profits. In the absence of limited transferability, price segmentation creates aftermarket trading alternatively named parallel or gray markets. Aftermarket trading remains a significant challenge for many products. Fungible products from tangible cigarettes and alcohol to intangible software and digital entertainment are all subject to aftermarket trading among consumers.

It is hard to discuss price segmentation without raising ethical and potentially legal issues.[3] However, pricing professionals need to be able to explore this area dispassionately if they are to be effective in their work. Price segmentation is a powerful tool for driving profits. It is practiced in many markets, cultures, and jurisdictions with neither popular indignation nor legal recourse. Indeed, governments themselves commonly practice price discrimination.[4] In fact, price segmentation can actually be beneficial to consumers in cases where the practice of price segmentation allows for a product to be sold to customers who otherwise would find the product unattainable. While we will examine ethical and legal issues of pricing in Chapter 17, for now we will take a more pragmatic viewpoint and address the issues of why and how.

Value of Price Segmentation

INCREASING PROFITS AND CUSTOMERS SERVED

Price segmentation enables two key developments within an industry. One, it can improve the firm's profits. Two, it can improve the number of customers served by actually lowering the market entry price for some customers. We can demonstrate these claims with a simple graph. (See Appendix 6 for a mathematical defense of these claims.)

In the absence of price segmentation, the firm will attempt to optimize a single price against the market's demand curve. Customers with a willingness to pay above the single price required will purchase, while those whose willingness to pay is below the single price will not purchase. The firm will earn profits in proportion to the difference between the optimal price and their variable costs multiplied by the number of customers who are willing to purchase at that price. See Exhibit 6-1.

With two-segment pricing, price segmentation aggregates the market into two groups: one that pays a higher price and the other that pays a lower price. Thus, the firm will now earn profits from two sources. See Exhibit 6-2. For normal markets, the optimal higher price in a two-price segment strategy will be greater than that of a single-price strategy, so the firm will enjoy a higher contribution margin from some of its customers. Moreover, for normal markets, the optimal lower price in a two-price segment strategy will be less than the price determined in a single-price strategy, allowing the firm to increase the units sold and expand its market. As such, price segmentation enables the firm both to increase its profits and increase the number of customers served.

We can illustrate the same concepts using a quantitative example. Recall that in Chapter 2, we explored the profit dynamics for a product given an elasticity of demand of −1.67 and overall demand of 368,000 units if priced at the $10 variable cost where the fixed costs were assumed to be $1 million. For this example product, we found that profit would be maximized at $200,000 per quarter at the optimal price of $25 and resulting volume of 80,000 units.

If we ran a similar analysis for a product sold to the same market with the same overall demand and elasticity of demand but under the condition of perfect price segmentation with two prices, we would find that the optimal high price is $47 and the optimal low price is $19.[5] With a perfect segmentation hedge, 28,000 units would be sold at the higher price to customers willing to pay $47 or more; and 98,000 units would be sold at the lower price to customers willing to pay $19 or more, up to $47. The total units sold would become 126,000, a full 46,000 more than under single-price optimization, or 58 percent more units, implying that 58 percent more purchasing opportunities leave customers better off when the firm price-segments the market into two groups rather than one. The resulting profit would be $918,000—360 percent higher profits with two price segments rather than one.

Exhibit 6-1 Single Price Profits

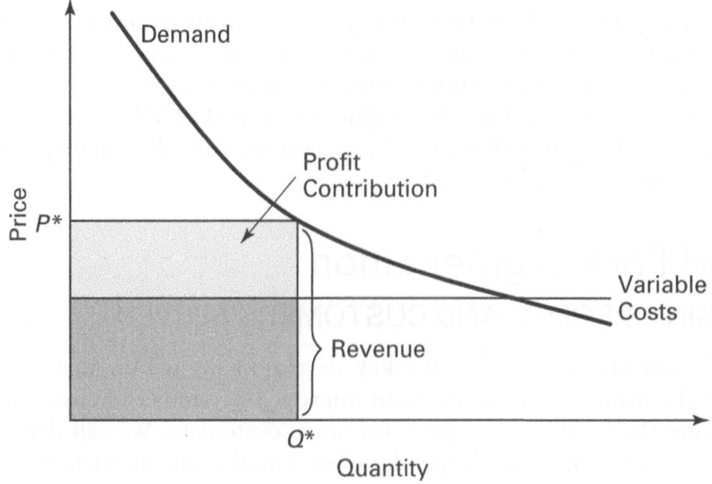

Exhibit 6-2 Dual Price Revenue and Profit

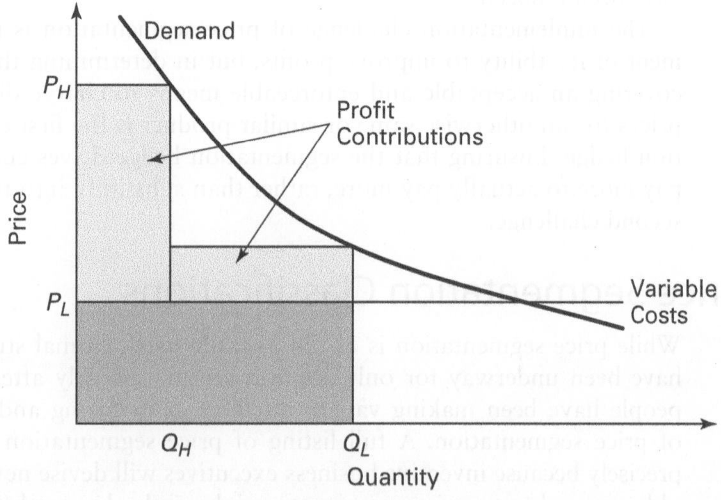

With a modicum of creative thinking, we can run the same analysis with three, four, or more prices under the same constraint of perfect price segmentation. Each time, we would find that the market entry price, or the price at which customers with the lowest willingness to pay will be charged, will decrease; and the premium price, or the price at which customers with the highest willingness to pay will be charged, will increase. With a lower market entry price, more units are sold and more customers or purchasing opportunities result in a transaction. Importantly, by improving the match between perceived value and price extracted, profits increase.

THE SEGMENTATION HEDGES KEY

The key to price segmentation is the ability to separate customers who are willing to pay more from those who are not. To accomplish this feat, firms construct **segmentation hedges** to segment the market according to willingness to pay. If the segmentation hedge is perfect, then all customers who are willing to pay a price greater than the higher price will purchase at that higher price, whereas any customer willing to pay more than the lower price but less than the higher price are allowed to purchase at the lower price. Importantly, a perfect segmentation hedge prevents any customer who is willing to pay more than the higher price to purchase at the lower price.

Of course, segmentation hedges are not perfect except in idealized cases. However, price segmentation with even imperfect segmentation hedges can improve the firm's profits and the number of customers served. Executives readily understand the value of executing price segmentation. It is an old, basic, freshman-level economic concept and forms the basis for many corporate, product, and pricing strategies.

If the segmentation hedges are very poor, however, price segmentation can actually harm profits. An ineffective segmentation hedge would prevent customers who would be willing to pay the higher price from masquerading as customers who will pay only the lower price. Consequently, no products would be sold at the higher price, and all products would be sold at the lower price. As discussed, the optimal lower price in most price segmentation strategies is actually lower than the optimal price in a single-price strategy. Thus, with poor segmentation hedges, all customers, both those with a high willingness to pay and a low willingness to pay, will purchase at the same low price, a price that is predicted to be lower than that optimal for the entire market, and the firm's profits will have been reduced.

The implementation challenge of price segmentation is not in convincing management of its ability to improve profits, but in determining the segmentation hedge. Uncovering an acceptable and enforceable means to charge different customers different prices for an otherwise same or similar product is the first challenge for any segmentation hedge. Ensuring that the segmentation hedge drives customers who are willing to pay more to actually pay more, rather than substitute into the lower-priced level, is the second challenge.

Price Segmentation Classifications

While price segmentation is as old as trade itself, formal studies of price segmentation have been underway for only about a century. Shortly after the advent of economics, people have been making valiant attempts at itemizing and categorizing all the forms of price segmentation. A full listing of price segmentation techniques is unattainable precisely because inventive business executives will devise new approaches and twists on old approaches to price segmentation inherently due to the profit-making potential of improving the technique. However, there are three popular classification strategies for price segmentation.

FIRST-, SECOND-, AND THIRD-DEGREE PRICE DISCRIMINATION

In 1920, Arthur Cecil Pigou released his treatise on economics of welfare in which he defined three types of price segmentation.[6] Perfect price discrimination, or first-degree price discrimination, is charging every customer at the price that matches their willingness to pay. In perfect price discrimination, all consumer surplus is captured by the producing firm. In practice, perfect price discrimination is impossible because it requires the seller to know exactly each customer's willingness to pay.

Second-degree price discrimination is charging different customers different prices according to the quantity purchased. Classic, quantity-based second-degree discrimination implies that larger orders are available at a lower unit price than smaller orders. Second-degree price discrimination, unlike perfect price discrimination, is common, although Pigou himself doubted its long-term efficacy.

Third-degree price discrimination is charging different markets or market segments different prices. An update to classic third-degree price discrimination has been to include benefit-based price segmentation in which products are designed to serve different market segments, where those with greater benefits cost a higher price than those with fewer benefits.

COMPLETE, DIRECT, AND INDIRECT PRICE SEGMENTATION

The approach to defining price segmentation categories has since been updated from Pigou's ordinal system. An alternative practice is to classify price segmentation techniques according to the information required to execute them.[7]

Complete discrimination is used to define pricing practices in which each purchase is made at a price wherein the marginal benefits to the customer equal the price charged, which is equivalent to first-degree price discrimination. Complete price discrimination, as noted with first-degree price discrimination, requires complete information of all customers' willingness to pay in all situations, a feat that is likely to cost more to achieve than would be rewarded through profit increases.

Direct segmentation defines price variances based upon specific attributes of the customer, such as age, gender, or location. Direct segmentation is relatively easy to implement and is a common practice of public institutions, nonprofits, and for-profit firms alike.

Indirect segmentation defines price variances based upon a proxy that correlates to customer segmentation based on willingness to pay. The proxy can be the use of coupons, package size, usage quantity, or any other variable that encourages price-sensitive customers to self-identify while discouraging customers who are willing to pay more from purchasing at the lower price point.

STRATEGIC OR TACTICAL PRICE SEGMENTATION

A third approach to defining price segmentation categories is simply to separate price segmentation practices that are tactical and short-term in nature from those that are strategic and longer-term.

Tactical price segmentation approaches are those that are used to capture marginal and sometimes even specific customers in unique situations. Tactical price segmentation techniques may form a part of the normal approach to business, but the decision to grant a tactical price variance is always grounded in the specifics of a situation. In consumer markets, coupons, price promotions, and rebates can all be said to be tactical approaches to price segmentation. In business markets, meet-the-competition pricing, volume discounts, and customer-specific price variances are also tactical price segmentation techniques.

Strategic price segmentation approaches are those in which the definition of the price structure itself enables different customers to pay different prices. Multipart tariffs, complement and add-on pricing, versioning, bundling, subscriptions, and yield pricing are all forms of strategic price segmentation. In some situations, even simple unit pricing can be considered a form of strategic price segmentation because it charges high-consuming customers a higher total price than it charges low-consuming customers.

Designing Segmentation Hedges

Segment hedges are barriers that prevent customers who are willing to pay a higher price from paying a lower price. If the segmentation hedge acts as a sieve rather than a barrier, it can actually damage profits. While it is doubtful that any practical segmentation hedge can deliver perfect price segmentation, executives can often improve their current pricing policy by improving their segmentation hedges. The four requirements for effective segmentation hedges derive from its **correlation** with customers' perception of value, the **information** needed for its implementation, its **enforceability**, and its cultural **acceptability**.

The primary requirement for segmentation hedges is that they must sort customers or customer segments efficiently according to their willingness to pay.

Segmentation hedges that are highly correlated to customers' willingness to pay are better than those that are weakly correlated to customers' willingness to pay in improving the ability of the firm to profit from a price segmentation strategy. Often, executives accept a convenient segmentation hedge that may or may not be well correlated with willingness to pay. Pricing executives will have a large impact if they can improve the relationship between the segmentation hedges and actual customer willingness to pay. Uncovering customer metrics that are highly correlated to willingness to pay requires understanding the drivers of value within the market.

A related requirement for segment hedges is that they should require minimal information gathering about specific customers on the part of the supplier to segment the market in an economically efficient manner. It cannot be expected that at the point of transaction, each customer will provide a complete profile of him- or herself to identify the price to be charged. Many segmentation hedges require only one piece of information to group customers according to their willingness to pay. Some popular segmentation hedges elicit specific behaviors that reveal customers' price sensitivity, effectively making the information-gathering effort invisible. Detailed customer profiles are constructed in only a few circumstances, mostly those related to industrial products or high-value consumer products.

From an operational standpoint, segmentation hedges also need to be enforceable, which usually results in constructing hedges with objective criteria. Managers need clear indicators of when a price variance should be granted and when prices should be kept high, leading to a need for clear, objective criteria for setting prices. Furthermore, price segmentation policies based on objective criteria are useful for discouraging potential abuse. Unscrupulous salespeople may abuse price segmentation policies to grant better prices to favored customers while making other customers pay higher prices regardless of their actual willingness to pay. Likewise, price segmentation policies provide incentives for customers to masquerade as customers with a lower willingness to pay, regardless of their true propensity. Objective criteria both improve clarity in setting prices and thwart abuse in managing prices, leading to better enforceability of price segmentation policy.

Finally, from the viewpoint of corporate citizenry, consumer desirability, and public relations, segmentation hedges must be culturally acceptable—or at least not observably culturally repulsive. We cannot overlook the fact that price segmentation treats some customers differently than others, and it can appear unfair, unjust, and unethical (if not illegal) to customers in the higher-paying category. There are price segmentation policies in practice that, if they were made aware to the public and regulators, would be scuttled quickly. Other price segmentation policies are considered to be culturally acceptable even though the true economics of the situation would imply an unfair, if not regressive, approach to pricing. In many cases, however, price segmentation policies are not only culturally acceptable and fully legal, but even desired by customers themselves. To navigate this labyrinth of potential social, cultural, and legal land mines, executives must calibrate and manage the acceptance of a segmentation hedge carefully.

Common Price Segmentation Hedges

Price segmentation is highly common due to its potential to improve profits.[8] We can find examples of price segmentation in consumer and business markets as well as government-supplied products and services. Organizations use price segmentation with services and goods, tangibles and intangibles, and durables and consumables. While we will explore tactical and strategic price segmentation in more detail in coming chapters, it is useful to review some simple examples of segmentation hedges in building a foundational understanding of price segmentation.

CUSTOMER DEMOGRAPHICS/FIRMOGRAPHICS

Customer demographics, such as age, gender, and income, are often used for the development of segmentation hedges. Customer demographics are objective and easy to identify criteria, hence they meet two of the requirements for forming a sound segmentation hedge. For some products, demographic information even correlates with willingness to pay. While price segmenting based on demographic information may at first appear to be philosophically reprehensible, it is amazing how culturally acceptable the practice is.

Similar to demographic segmentation used in consumer markets, firmographic price segmentation has been used in business markets. Like demographic segmentation, firmographic segmentation relies upon objective criteria such as location, industry, employment base, revenue base, and occasionally the company's customer base.

Age

In accordance with the four design requirements, age can be a good segmentation hedge with many products. Consider senior citizen and children discounts. With senior citizen and children discounts, age is used as the segmentation hedge.

Age is both an objective and easy-to-identify criteria based upon government-issued identification (driver's licenses and passports, for example). Moreover, both senior citizens and families with children are susceptible to having higher price sensitivity than other customer segments, though the underlying driver to their price sensitivity may be different. Families with children often have budget constraints, leading them to more frugal behavior and higher price sensitivity. While some seniors are likewise constrained by their budgets, a significant driver of their price sensitivity is the abundance of leisure time that retirees enjoy, which enables them to price-compare between offers.

Regardless of the driver, the status of being a senior citizen or a child is correlated with price sensitivity in many product categories, and thus age meets the most critical requirement of segmentation hedges: it discriminates customers based on willingness to pay. Finally, framing has much to do with the cultural acceptability of age as a segmentation hedge. Most cultures accept the concept of providing price discounts to seniors and children and even view firms that offer them as being more progressive and kind. In contrast, these same cultures would be outraged if the same pricing policy was reframed as a price surcharge for non-seniors or non-children.

Gender

Ladies' Night is a common practice at drinking establishments worldwide, including, until recently, the United States.[9] During Ladies' Night promotions, discounted entrance fees and drinks are provided to women to encourage more women to attend the entertainment venue and better balance the ratio of men to women. Although the correlation of willingness to pay to gender for beverages and entertainment is dubious, it is hard to argue with the results. Ladies' Night proved to be an effective promotional tool for many establishments in driving traffic and subsequent beverage sales. The loss of this promotional tool has caused much consternation by both establishment managers and many of their male and female customers. The practice of Ladies' Night remains common in most nations.

An alternative form of gender-based price segmentation that has yet to be dismissed is found at the local hair salon. A man and a woman who both want a haircut will often pay very different prices, even for the same short-haired style. The practice is defended on the grounds that women's hairstyles require greater skill and time than men's, even as this claim is becoming more dubious with the entry of the metrosexual male. In general, though, women continue to have a higher willingness to pay for beauty than men.

Comparing gender against the four design criteria, we find that it is (1) objective, (2) easily identifiable in most cases, (3) somewhat correlated with willingness to pay in certain categories, and (4) questionably culturally accepted. As such, it can act as a segmentation hedge.

Income

Price segmentation on income is practiced by many nonprofit institutions under the umbrella of financial aid. Colleges and universities will set high prices for tuition, but they provide financial aid to select students. Financial income is often a determining factor in granting financial aid. Presumably, students from a wealthy background have more financial resources to pay and therefore have a higher willingness to pay. Meanwhile, students from less well-to-do backgrounds, yet of high academic quality, require financial aid to pay for the learning experience. By charging high tuition and selectively granting financial aid, schools are in effect extracting prices from customers based on the value they place on going to that school.

TIME OF PURCHASE

Time of purchase is an inherently objective criterion. In addition, it does not require any specific customer information, but rather it indirectly tracks customer behavior that is suspected to be correlated with willingness to pay. Matinee prices, lunch specials, early-bird discounts, and seasonal pricing are all examples of using time of purchase as a segmentation hedge.

Matinee prices and early-bird discounts both exploit time of purchase as an indicator of leisure time. Customers viewing movies in the middle of the day or eating dinner prior to the end of a business day are likely not to be subject to the time constraints associated with employment. With greater leisure time, these customers can search for alternatives and seek the lowest price, thus warranting the need for a price concession to attract their business.

Lunch specials are driven by a different consumer behavior than matinee prices and early-bird specials, however. Dinner crowds often seek an expanded set of benefits beyond that provided by tasty and nourishing food—they are also seeking an enjoyable restaurant experience. The dinner occasion is driven by the desire for entertainment, relaxation with one's family and friends, or impressing one's professional colleagues. In contrast, lunch crowds have fewer expectations of deriving enjoyment from dining. For some, their focus is solely on replenishing their energy prior to returning to work. Because dinner crowds seek and receive more benefits from the restaurant experience than lunch crowds, it can also be anticipated that dinner crowds have a higher willingness to pay than lunch crowds. Price segmentation in the form of lunch specials exploits the partial correlation between price sensitivity and time of purchase.

Seasonal factors can also act as price segmentation. For instance, vacationers tend to be less price-sensitive because their shopping time interferes with their other desired vacation activities. As such, summer vacation locations often find it beneficial to raise prices during the summer season to capture profits from vacationers while reducing prices during "off-season" to attract volume from the locals. Similarly, gift-giving seasons are not marked by the highest price sensitivity, but customers do have more price sensitivity during these times than during other times. We can see this in the common practice of having shallow pre-Christmas sales, followed by deeper post-holiday sales.

Moreover, many of these time-based segmentation hedges exploit an opportunity of the supplier to time-shift price-sensitive customers to off-peak periods. Time-shifting customers both increases the available supply during peak periods when less-price-sensitive customers arrive and improves capacity utilization during off-peak periods.

Matinee prices, lunch specials, and early-bird discounts are all framed as discounts from a higher "regular" price. Framing these price segments as discounts enables customers to perceive them as a new source of gain rather than the regular price as an unwanted higher form of pain; thus, they tend to be culturally acceptable.

An alternative form of using time of purchase as a segmentation hedge is found in yield management and other dynamic pricing mechanisms. Yield management is most commonly found in airline ticket prices, though is also used with hotels, container ships, and other products. With yield management, prices increase depending upon the time of purchase in relationship to the time of use. The price increases as the time of purchase approaches the time of use. In this case, customers purchasing at times closer to the time of use are suspected to have greater urgency in terms of using the product, and therefore a higher willingness to pay.

PURCHASE LOCATION

The same product can be priced at very different levels depending upon the location of the outlet. While some of the difference in price may be explained by cost-to-serve factors, much of the variation in prices between purchase locations is driven by pure heterogeneity in customer willingness to pay.

For example, consider a beverage purchased for consumption at the beach. Customers could bring their own beverages from home to the beach if they purchased them earlier at a grocery store. The customer could also purchase a beverage at a nearby convenience store on the way to the beach; or the customer could select a beach restaurant complete with service where beverages are brought to them by waitstaff. In each case, the price that these customers would expect to pay would vary greatly between the locations of purchase, even if the actual beverage consumed was identical. Much of this variation in price is correlated with differences in costs to serve, with grocery stores being the lowest-cost channel and the dining area with the waitstaff representing the highest-cost channel. However, part of the variation in price is also correlated to willingness to pay and the benefits sought. The customer ordering a beverage from a server is seeking a large set of benefits (service plus beverage) and is expressing a higher willingness to pay than one who brought a beverage from home.

Variation in prices based on purchase location can be driven purely by heterogeneity in willingness to pay. For example, grocery stores may price the same or similar set of goods at different prices between locations based upon competitive factors and consumer behavior.[10] Middle-class neighborhoods often have numerous grocery outlets serving customers with ample access to transportation (cars), which enables them to price-compare between outlets. Customers from higher-income neighborhoods place more value on their leisure time, making them less prone to price comparison; thus, they have a marginally increased willingness to pay. Meanwhile, customers in lower-income neighborhoods often suffer from lack of adequate transportation and less competition, enabling grocers to price products at a marginally higher level in lower-income neighborhoods than in higher-income ones. As such, grocery stores in middle-class neighborhoods often provide the lowest prices in comparison to those in either poorer or richer neighborhoods. While pricing products higher in higher-income neighborhoods is usually free from customer backlash, pricing products higher in lower-income neighborhoods is fraught with potential challenges.[11]

BUYER SELF-IDENTIFICATION

Price segmentation policies may also rely upon buyer self-identification of willingness to pay. Promotional sales, buyer's clubs, coupons, and rebates are all forms of price segmentation that rely upon buyer self-identification.

Hunting for sales, cutting out coupons, and mailing in rebates are all time-intensive activities for customers. Customers who are willing to invest the time in these activities are revealing their willingness to search for alternatives and find the lowest prices. Customers who forgo coupon clipping and similar activities are likewise revealing their willingness to pay full price to save on opportunity costs. Providing price-sensitive customers with access to lower prices through targeted discounts while leaving the majority of the market to purchase at the regular price can improve firm-level profitability.

Similarly, buyer's clubs create an effective price segmentation technique because they require customers to declare their price sensitivity outright through membership. Buyer's clubs require shoppers to pay a fee for membership in exchange for receiving a discount on all their shopping at that outlet. The size of the membership fee is set such that a casual shopper would not receive any financial benefit from the buyer's club, but the heavy shopper would experience significant savings over the course of the membership. These savings are provided to encourage greater loyalty, yet they also signal price sensitivity. Buyers' clubs can prove to be highly profitable price segmentation strategies in markets where high-purchasing customers generate a disproportionate amount of profits and customer loyalty is a significant driver of customer profitability.

PRODUCT-ENGINEERED

Segmentation hedges are often product-engineered, where some products deliver greater benefits than others and each product within the category is priced differently to reflect its added value. Product-engineered price segmentation relies upon the addition and subtraction of specific features to define the segmentation hedges. Customers seeking greater utility from a product within a particular category find that specific features and attributes are missing from lower-priced alternatives, and they are thus encouraged to purchase a higher-priced product or bundle of products within the category. Meanwhile, customers with minimal utility requirements and lower willingness to pay are enabled to purchase a feature-deprived product at a lower price.

With product-engineered segmentation policy, profit-seeking firms usually reap larger margins with higher-priced items than with lower-priced items. No profit-seeking firm has an incentive to add one iota in marginal cost unless it can gain more than that iota in price or an equivalent volume boost.

The logic behind the claim that higher-benefit products should also have higher contribution margins is rather straightforward. Higher-benefit products usually cost more to produce. With each marginal increase in cost, the firm should at least seek to price the product at a price greater than or equal to the marginal increase in cost, or else improving the product reduces profits. At a higher price and with downward-sloping demand curves, the benefit-rich product could be expected to attract fewer customers than a feature-deprived product. Combined, these factors imply that the higher-priced product is likely both to increase marginal cost to produce and attract diminished customer demand. To compensate for these combined factors, the firm should seek to reap larger margins on higher-priced products than they seek on lower-priced products.

There are times when increases in marginal costs for product improvements are matched with smaller increases in the marginal price. Competitive forces may drive a firm to increase features beyond the potential price increase. Likewise, some product improvements come without increases in marginal costs. Finally, some products require enhancements to attract a larger market, especially with newer product categories. In these cases, the diminished contribution margin should be compensated by increased unit volume sales.

The key challenge for constructing a product-engineered segmentation hedge is defining which features and benefits some customers are willing to pay more for, and which ones all customers demand. Those features that all customers expect of the product category must be included in the lower-priced product. Features which only a segment of the market will value form strong elements for differentiating products and creating a product-engineered segmentation strategy.

Add-on pricing strategies, versioning, and bundling are all forms of product-engineered price segmentation in which the addition and subtraction of tangible features create the segmentation hedges. Branding can also be considered as a form of product-engineered price segmentation, where brand-name products command a higher price than generic or store-brand products, even when both are produced by the same supplier.

QUANTITY PURCHASED

Quantity purchased, either in a single transaction or in multiple transactions, is also a common price segmentation hedge. Like other approaches to price segmentation, quantity purchased is objective and is based on easily identifiable information. Outside of a few very specific business markets, the practice of altering the price paid based on quantity purchased is highly accepted.[12]

Order Size

Customers ordering large quantities are often provided a discounted price in comparison to those purchasing smaller quantities. For example, bubble wrap used in packaging can be sold to individuals at package delivery outlets and to larger organizations direct from the manufacturer. Individual customers will usually pay a much higher price for bubble wrap than larger organizations, not only because of their choice of purchasing outlet but also because of the quantity that they purchase at one time. Customers buying large quantities have sufficient incentives to price-compare between suppliers, which lowers their willingness to pay. Customers purchasing smaller quantities have less incentive to price-compare, and thus have a higher willingness to pay. In these cases, quantity purchase is closely related to willingness to pay, making quantity-based segmentation hedges effective.

Frequent Purchases

Like purchase quantity, purchase frequency can be used as a means for price segmentation. As customers consume a product, their desire for an additional unit of product can decline in a predictable way, making them much less willing to purchase additional units than they were for the purchase of the first unit. Price segmentation on the basis of purchase frequency attempts to use the heterogeneity of demand within specific customers to improve profitability marginally.

CUSTOMER USAGE

Price segmentation based on product usage relies on the heterogeneity of value that customers place on a product in relation to their usage patterns. For instance, urban individuals with access to mass transit will drive a car sporadically and will have less need for that car than a suburban family that requires an automobile daily. Likewise, people entertaining business customers or dating partners may place a much higher value on an automobile than those who simply seek transportation to work. If automobiles could be priced separately based on lifestyle, automakers might find a new source of profits in pricing the automobile based on the miles driven and the purpose of the trip. Of course, automakers cannot price a car based directly on lifestyle. Cars purchased in suburban markets can be transferred easily to more urban locations, and entertainment cars can also be used for work-related transport. Instead, automakers make different models optimized for different buying needs. However, similar pricing strategies based on actual customer usage patterns are executed by some firms.

Tie-ins and Two-Part Tariffs

One approach to pricing based on usage is to break the product into two constituent parts, a durable part and a consumable part, and price the two parts separately. The effect is named tie-in pricing at one end of the spectrum and a two-part tariff at the other end. In both cases, the purchase of the consumable part is related to the purchase of the durable part. (Tie-ins and two-part tariffs are explored specifically in Chapter 9.)

For example, a razor handle is valuable to customers only if they also have razor blades. Razor handles are somewhat durable, while razor blades are far more consumable, becoming dull after roughly a month of usage. Moreover, razor handles are usually designed to hold only a single manufacturer's blade, making them non-interchangeable. Firms are able to price the razor handle differently than the blade. In a sense, the purchase of the handle gives permission to the customer to buy the blade because the blades have little other value without the handle. Therefore, the blade price can reflect usage and the handle price can reflect the willingness of the customer to participate in the market for blades.

The approach of pricing blades and handles separately in the razor market can be found in other markets. At one time, a copy machine maker would demand that all customers purchase their paper only from it. Such tie-in pricing has since been declared illegal in the United States, yet it demonstrates the potential for firms to price the durable part of a product separately from the consumable part. Utility firms, such as those providing natural gas and electricity, will bill customers a connection fee (alternatively named a *metering fee* or *service charge*), plus a consumption charge based on the amount of service consumed. As with razor handles and blades, the durable part is charged differently than the consumable part. Similarly, gaming firms will price the durable gaming console at one level, while the consumable gaming software is priced separately.

In tie-ins markets, the prices of the consumable versus durable parts are set based upon very different agendas. Because the durable part is used over many periods, and because customers are usually price-sensitive to initial purchase prices to participate in a new product transaction, the durable part is often priced low to attract customers in tie-in markets. Meanwhile, in tie-in markets, the consumable part is priced high and forms the basis for most of, if not all, the profit. Customers tend to be less price-sensitive to the consumable part of the transaction because they have purchased the durable part already and face switching costs if they seek an alternative.

The amount of the profit that can be shifted to the consumable part of the product is limited by anti-dumping regulations and by the anticipated consumer behavior as calculated in a customer lifetime value model. Customer lifetime value is highly dependent upon the frequency of repeat purchases and the duration of customer loyalty. We can see these effects with mobile phone operators. Durable handsets are often subsidized by the mobile phone operator to encourage customers to select their services; meanwhile, all profits are earned from the sale of connection time and data transfer. Only in a few markets where regulation prevents locking handsets with single mobile phone operators, such as in the Czech Republic and Slovakia, are handsets not subsidized by the revenues earned from phone calls and data transmissions.

In contrast, in two-part tariff markets, the prices of the durable part of the offer are set very high to capture profits while prices of the consumable part of the offer are set low. The demands of customers are very different in two-part tariff markets than they are in tie-in markets. Specifically, customers will tend to be more sensitive to the price of the consumable part of the offer than they are to the price of the durable part. Utility bills for residential customers are often set in accordance with the concept of a two-part tariff.

Enterprise Software Complexity Charges

Like other products, prices of enterprise software attempt to reflect the economic value of that software to the customers. The usage patterns that affect the value of the software for a specific customer may themselves depend on customer size and industry as well as the strategy of that particular customer. While the value of enterprise software is highly related to usage, software producers often find it disadvantageous to reveal their method of price calculation. One method of obfuscating the pricing formula is to use "complexity charges."

For example, one utility billing software firm used a pricing formula that not only reflected the number of bills the software would go on to produce, but also reflected the type of bill produced. Commercial and industrial utility bills are far more complex in their construction than residential bills. As such, the software was more valuable to utility firms that had a higher proportion of commercial and industrial customers than those with a greater percentage of residential customers. To capture this value differential, the utility billing software firm added a "complexity charge" to reflect the portion of their customer's revenue base that was derived from commercial and industrial customers.

NEGOTIATION

Finally, price segmentation can be executed through simple negotiation. Haggling for consumer products is found throughout the world. In business markets, negotiation over final price is a standard step within the sales process. In consumer markets, it is common for customers to haggle with suppliers over the price of almost all goods in many economies, ranging from premier cities, such as Dubai, to developing ones such as Mexico City, and even latent economies such as Abuja, Nigeria.

Negotiation is perhaps the most direct attempt at uncovering a specific customer's willingness to pay, and therefore reaches towards complete price segmentation, yet it lacks precision. Negotiations are fraught with many biases from both the seller's and the buyer's position. The results from a negotiation are greatly dependent upon the preparation of the individual negotiating partners, perhaps as much as they are on the price sensitivity of the buyer. Therefore, they only partially reveal price sensitivity. Due to their imperfection, negotiations are only a marginally valuable price segmentation approach.

Examples of Price Segmentation

BANK FEES

Banks have long structured their prices to discourage profit-destructive behavior.[13] Unlike price segmentation that is driven by customer heterogeneity in willingness to pay, cost-driven price segmentation is driven by customer heterogeneity in cost to serve. Bank fees tied to overdrafts and insufficient funds are constructed to discourage customers from attempting to withdraw more funds than they have available. Similar price incentives to discourage profit-destroying behavior can be found with customer support fees with call centers, late payment fees by utilities, cash advance fees by credit cards and, more recently, baggage fees by airlines.

Price segmentation strategies designed to discourage bad customer behavior yet end up forming the core source of profitability should raise concerns among managers. Customers finding themselves constantly subject to penalty fees will likely be less favorably inclined to the firm and thus more likely to switch suppliers once an alternative is made available. If customers paying penalty fees were otherwise unprofitable, losing their business may be a satisfactory outcome. However, if they become a major source of profits, the firm will effectively be encouraging its most profitable customers to defect and be making itself vulnerable to the competition.

Prices structured to discourage profit-destructive behavior are common in many industries. For instance, consider the increasingly common practice of industrial firms charging for items that they previously provided for free to discourage waste. Alternatively, milk vendors may increase bottle deposit charges to encourage returns.

TAVERN DRINKS

Neighborhood taverns may price beverages differently to price-segment those with a higher willingness to pay from those with a lower willingness to pay. For instance, consider the neighborhood tavern that sells both single malt scotch and beer on tap. Many jurisdictions place restrictions on the serving of alcohol, effectively giving those few establishments who have a license to sell tremendous pricing power over their patrons. In these taverns, the cost of scotch and beer represents only a small fragment of the price, and customer willingness to pay is the dominant driver to determining prices. Customers drinking single malt scotch tend to have a higher willingness to pay than those who will select a common tap beer. Thus, the lone bar selling both single malt scotch and common tap beer is able to attract a larger customer base and extract disproportionately larger profits from the sale of single malt scotch than from the sale of tap beer. The tavern example is one of using a common location but attracting and profiting from customers with differing temperaments of benefits sought and willingness to pay.

While drinking establishments are perhaps among the leaders in price segmentation policies, they are not alone. Retail outlets can also practice demand-specific price segmentation. The American Doll Place in Chicago sells dolls to many customers.[14] However, customers seeking a greater experience and a broader set of benefits can expand their relationship with the American Doll Place to include dining, doll repair, and even a doll beauty shop. (At one time, the American Doll Place also offered short theatrical productions featuring child actresses interacting with dolls.) As with taverns selling scotch and beer, the American Doll Place aggregates many customers to a single location and allows them to self-segment into different buying groups, thus enabling those with a higher willingness to pay for products the experience to do so.

AIRLINES

Few industries use as many segmentation hedges as airlines. For starters, airlines segment customers according to willingness to pay in three major classes: first class, business class, and coach. The basic benefit of speedy transit is provided by all classes, but further amenities and services are provided in the transition from coach to business and eventually to first class. This is one example of product-engineered segmentation hedges.

Further price segmentation is executed by airlines, even for the same city-pair trip, on the same day, with the same flight. Consider the use of Saturday night stayover requirements, advance notice requirements, and yield management practices. (Yield management is discussed in detail in Chapter 14.)

Saturday stayover requirements segment the weekend traveler from the business traveler. The assumption is that weekend travelers are traveling for pleasure, and the flight faces greater competition in the form of driving instead of flying, or even forgoing or delaying the trip altogether. Meanwhile, business travelers have little maneuverability in their schedule and are more pressed for time.

Advance notice requirements similarly attempt to segment the casual traveler from the more-time-pressed traveler. Customers who shop in advance of the trip have taken more time to consider their options and are thus likely to be more price-sensitive than those customers who plan their travel closer to the time of travel, and they also are perhaps more pressed to take the trip.

Time of day and seasonal issues also influence prices of air travel. Morning and evening flights are priced differently than midday flights under the assumption that a morning flyer has an afternoon meeting at the destination, with a returning flight that evening to avoid a hotel stay and enable a speedy return home. In contrast, transatlantic flights are cheaper in the early spring than in the midsummer vacation season or the winter holiday season. The seasonal variation in price is designed to target vacationers with less schedule flexibility, such as parents with children, and profit from their restrictions.

INDUSTRIAL MARKETS

Firms selling industrial products and inputs into other businesses' products will combine a number of different price segmentation strategies. Many of these price segmentation strategies, such as firmographics, complexity charges, usage patterns, purchase frequency, and order size, have already been discussed. Other more popular price segmentation hedges can be found in Exhibit 6-3.

Exhibit 6-3 Industrial Market Segmentation Hedges

• Total volume purchased	• Stocking selection	• Customer development/ focus
• Product mix	• Stocking level	• Dealer development
• Order size	• Resale price	• Quality of warranty/claims service to customers
• Order timing and frequency	• Competitor lines carried	• Returns behavior
• Freight mode	• Promotional behavior	• Distributor/dealer size and concentration
• Payment behavior	• Customer application support/ service	• Distributor as a buying group or co-op

Summary

- Price segmentation is charging different prices to different customers or groups of customers.
- Willingness to pay varies between individual customers. This heterogeneity in willingness to pay creates the opportunity for firms to improve profitability through price segmentation. In addition to heterogeneity in willingness to pay, price segmentation strategies require that products sold to one segment of the market have limited transferability to another segment in the market. Price segmentation improves profits by enabling the firm to capture a higher price from those customers who value the product higher and capture higher volumes at a lower price from customers with a lower willingness to pay.
- Price segmentation has been studied for many years. In its early form, it was described as either first-, second-, or third-degree price discrimination depending upon its economic efficiency. Later, authors categorized price segmentation strategies according to the information required as complete, direct, or indirect price segmentation. Yet a third approach has been simply to segregate those techniques that are used on a tactical basis from those used on a strategic price structure basis.
- Segmentation hedges are used to separate customers who must pay more from those who will pay less. Good price segmentation hedges should be highly correlated with customers' perception of value, require minimal information from customers, be enforceable based on objective criteria, and be culturally acceptable.
- Price segmentation hedges can be constructed on consumer demographic or industry firmographic data when these objective facts are correlated with willingness to pay.
- Time of purchase can signal willingness to pay, resulting in matinee prices, lunch specials, and early-bird specials.
- Purchase location can signal willingness to pay, as observed with beverage price differentials between grocers, convenience stores, and restaurants.
- Temporary promotional sales, coupons, rebates, and buyer's clubs are all forms of price segmentation wherein buyers self-identify through their actions of their price sensitivity and lowered willingness to pay.

- Product-engineered price segmentation uses the inclusion or exclusion of specific attributes, features, and benefits to define segmentation hedges. Utility-sensitive customers with a greater willingness to pay will be encouraged to higher-priced products than those who require only basic functionality and have a lower willingness to pay.
- Quantity purchased can form a segmentation hedge. The quantity purchased can be signaled either through a single order or through the frequency of repeat purchases.
- When customer usage patterns are correlated with perceived benefits, firms can price products according to intended use. Metering and tie-ins are one form of price segmentation based on customer usage.

Exercises

1. McDonald's sells Happy Meals for as low as $2.50 and Value Meals for as high as $5.50. How would you describe this pricing strategy? What segmentation variables are being used?
2. Many firms offer a "Buy 4, Get 1 Free" card to encourage customer loyalty.
   a. What are the price segmentation concepts that support such an offer?
   b. Which of the following types of firms is most likely to find a "Buy 4, Get 1 Free" offer to increase unit sales, and why? Gift card shop, coffee shop, hair salon, hardware store.
3. Both Best Buy and Dell.com have offered a Memorial Day sale on personal computers. Which computer outlet is likely to attract more customers with the Memorial Day sale and why do you make this claim?
4. Heineken sells beer in 12 packs for $13, in 24 packs for $25, and in 5-liter mini-kegs for $21. Assume that there is 0.355 liter per beer in a multipack.
   a. On a cost-per-liter level, which offers customers the best price?
   b. In comparing the price of a 24-pack to 12-pack on a per-liter basis, what kind of price segmentation is being used?
   c. In comparing the price of a 24-pack to 5-liter mini-keg, what kind of price segmentation is being used?
   d. Which psychological effects might drive customers to purchase a 5-liter keg?
5. An industrial firm has been offering a single standard flat price. The sales team has requested that the firm offer discounts to a select group of customers. In constructing the discounting policy, the pricing manager decides to consider changing the standard price as well. Should the standard price remain the same, be lowered, or be raised in the presence of discounting based upon the information given and nothing more?
6. Every Day Low Pricing (EDLP) has become a popular grocery store format. In contrast, some grocers have adhered to Hi-Lo pricing, in which the prices on specific products oscillate between a normal high price and a special discounted low price.
   a. Based on the principle of price segmentation with perfect segmentation hedges, which store format can be anticipated to be the most profitable?
   b. In many cases, EDLP formats have proven to be more profitable than Hi-Lo formats. What does this imply with respect to the effectiveness of "special discounted prices" in forming a price segmentation hedge?

7. A firm currently offers a single product within the product category. The product management team is considering the development of a new high-featured and high-priced offering.
   a. Should they expect the new higher-priced product to cannibalize sales from the existing marketed product?
   b. If so, why might the firm move forward with the new high-featured and high-priced offering?
8. A firm currently offers a single product within the product category. The product management team is considering the development of a new low-featured and low-priced offering.
   a. Should they expect the new lower-priced product to cannibalize sales from the existing marketed product?
   b. If so, why might the firm move forward with the new low-featured and low-priced offering?
9. After reading Appendix 6, consider a firm serving a market with a downward sloping demand curve as described by Equation 6.1. Let the maximum demand be 10,000 units and the maximum utility that any customer can derive from the product be $100. Furthermore, assume that the variable costs for a product are $5 and the firm's fixed costs are $100,000.
   a. What is the optimal price without price segmentation?
   b. What is the unit volume at the optimal price without price segmentation?
   c. What is the firm's optimized profits?
   d. What is the optimal low price with two price segments and a perfect segmentation hedge?
   e. What is the optimal high price with two price segments and a perfect segmentation hedge?
   f. How large is the discount (in percent) between the optimal high price and the optimal low price with two price segments and a perfect segmentation hedge?
   g. What is the total quantity sold at any price with two price segments and a perfect segmentation hedge?
   h. What is the quantity sold at the high price with two price segments and a perfect segmentation hedge?
   i. What is the quantity sold at the low price with two price segments and a perfect segmentation hedge?
   j. What are the volume shares of the low-priced offer and the high-priced offer with two price segments and a perfect segmentation hedge?
   k. What is the firm's optimized profits with two price segments and a perfect segmentation hedge?
   l. How much higher are the firm's optimized profits with two price segments and a perfect segmentation hedge than they are with a single price without price segmentation (in percent)?
   m. How many more units do customers consume with two price segments and a perfect segmentation hedge than they do with a single price without price segmentation (in percent)?
10. Repeat problem 9 with the following conditions: The maximum demand is 10,000 units and the maximum utility any customer can derive from the product

is \$100. The variable costs for a product are \$35 and the firm's fixed costs are \$100,000. In addition to problem 9's questions, answer the following:

a. When does price segmentation have a larger effect on profits under the condition of low marginal costs or high marginal costs?

Appendix 6 Economic Model of Unit Prices and Price Segmentation

A simple economic model can demonstrate the power of price segmentation to increase both profits and the number of customers served. To demonstrate, consider a downward-sloping demand curve and identify the optimal prices, their associated quantity sold, and resulting profit under the conditions of using a single price versus using two prices with a perfect segmentation hedge using a standard profit equation of the firm. The process is similar to that used in Appendix 2.B; it differs only in the form of the demand curve and the number of prices considered.

Let the demand be sloping downward linearly, as defined by

$$Q = Q_{max} \cdot \left(1 - \frac{P}{S}\right) \quad \text{Eq. 6.1}$$

S is the maximum utility that any customer can derive from the product and therefore is the highest price that can be charged. When the price equals the maximum utility ($P = S$), no units are sold. Similarly, Q_{max} is the maximum units that the market can purchase. When the price is zero ($P = 0$), the demand is maximized ($Q = Q_{max}$). See Exhibit 6-4.

With a single price, we can use the familiar profit equation of the firm of

$$\pi_1 = Q \cdot (P - V) \quad \text{Eq. 6.2}$$

where π is profit, Q is quantity sold, P is price, and V is the variable costs. We have set fixed costs to zero to keep this example simple without losing generality. To find the optimal price, we take the first derivative of profits with respect to price and set it equal to zero. The first derivative of profits with respect to price is, from the firm's profit equation (Eq. 6.2),

$$\frac{\pi_1}{P} = \frac{Q}{P} \cdot (P - V) + Q \quad \text{Eq. 6.3}$$

Exhibit 6-4 Single-Price Optimization

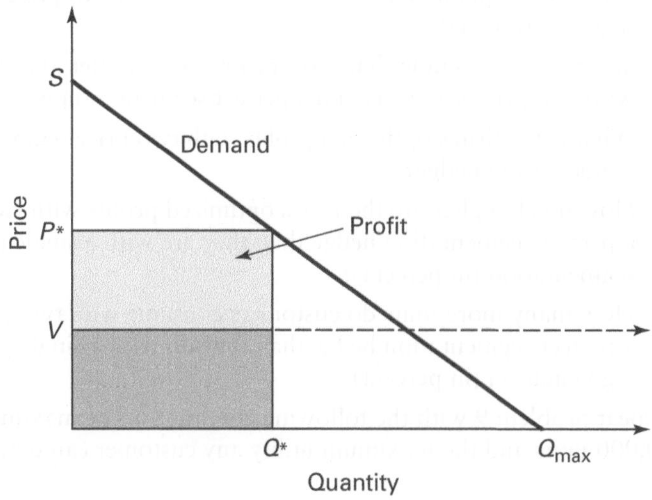

We find from the demand curve (Eq. 6.1)

$$\frac{Q}{P} = -\frac{Q_{\max}}{S} \qquad \text{Eq. 6.4}$$

Substituting Equation 6.4 into Equation 6.3 and taking the first derivative of profits with respect to price and setting this equal to zero, we find the optimal price to be the average of the maximum utility of any one customer and the firm's variable costs:

$$\hat{P} = \frac{1}{2} \cdot (S + V) \qquad \text{Eq. 6.5}$$

At this price, the firm will sell the number of units defined by

$$\hat{Q} = \frac{Q_{\max}}{2S} \cdot (S - V) \qquad \text{Eq. 6.6}$$

and earn a profit defined by

$$\hat{\pi}_1 = \frac{Q_{\max}}{4S} \cdot (S - V)^2 \qquad \text{Eq. 6.7}$$

Equations 6.5 to 6.7 define the optimal price, units sold, and profits earned under the condition of selling all units at the same price.

With two prices and a perfect segmentation hedge, the firm will earn profit from two sources. (1) Profits will be gained from customers who purchase at a higher price. (2) Profits will be gained from customers who purchase at a lower price. In this case, we must optimize both prices simultaneously. See Exhibit 6-5.

In this case, we modify the familiar profit equation of the firm to read

$$\pi_2 = Q_H \cdot (P_H - V) + (Q_L - Q_H) \cdot (P_L - V) \qquad \text{Eq. 6.8}$$

Q_H is the quantity sold at the higher price P_H; and Q_L is the quantity sold that would be sold at the lower price in absence of a segmentation hedge. Hence $Q_L - Q_H$ is the quantity sold at the lower price under the assumption of marketing the product with two prices and having a perfect segmentation hedge. The variable costs (V) are assumed to be unchanged

Exhibit 6-5 Dual-Price Optimization

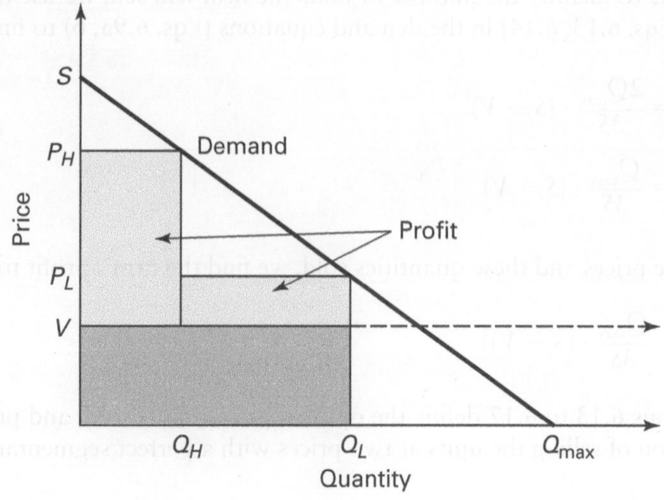

with respect to selling the product at two prices versus one. Assuming that the demand curve does not change simply through price segmentation (Eq. 6.1), we further find

$$Q_L = Q_{max} \cdot \left(1 - \frac{P_L}{S}\right) \quad \text{Eq. 6.9a}$$

$$Q_H = Q_{max} \cdot \left(1 - \frac{P_H}{S}\right) \quad \text{Eq. 6.9b}$$

To find the optimal prices under price segmentation, it is easier to define a new variable. Let R be defined as

$$R \equiv P_H - \frac{P_L}{2} \quad \text{Eq. 6.10}$$

Using P_H in terms of the variable R and using the demand found in Equation 6.9, we find the profit equation for the firm using price segmentation can be expressed as

$$\pi_{w2} = \frac{Q_{max}}{2} \cdot \left[-\left(R - \frac{S}{2}\right)^2 - \frac{3}{4}\left(P_L - \frac{1}{3}(S + 2V)\right)^2 + \frac{1}{3}(S - V)^2\right] \quad \text{Eq. 6.11}$$

From 6.11, we can optimize profits with respect to R and P_L by taking the partial derivative of Equation 6.11 with respect to R and P_L separately, and setting each derivative equal to zero. We find

$$\hat{R} = \frac{S}{2} \quad \text{Eq. 6.12}$$

$$\hat{P}_L = \frac{1}{3}(S + 2V) \quad \text{Eq. 6.13}$$

Using 6.12 and 6.13 in Equation 6.10, we find

$$\hat{P}_H = \frac{1}{3}(2S + V) \quad \text{Eq. 6.14}$$

Equations 6.13 and 6.14 define the optimal prices under a two-price segmentation strategy. To identify the number of units the firm will sell, we use the optimal price equations (Eqs. 6.13, 6.14) in the demand equations (Eqs. 6.9a, b) to find

$$\hat{Q}_L = \frac{2Q_{max}}{3S} \cdot (S - V) \quad \text{Eq. 6.15}$$

$$\hat{Q}_H = \frac{Q_{max}}{3S} \cdot (S - V) \quad \text{Eq. 6.16}$$

At these prices and these quantities sold, we find the firm's profit to be

$$\hat{\pi}_2 = \frac{Q_{max}}{3S} \cdot (S - V)^2 \quad \text{Eq. 6.17}$$

Equations 6.13 to 6.17 define the optimal prices, units sold, and profits earned under the condition of selling the units at two prices with a perfect segmentation hedge.

Interestingly, we can contrast the units sold under the condition of using a single price versus that of using two prices. With two prices, the firm will sell Q_H units at the higher price and $Q_L - Q_H$ units at the lower price, for a total of Q_L units. Comparing the optimal units sold under at two prices (Q_L^* in Eq. 6.15) to the optimal units sold at a single price (Q^* in Eq. 6.6) we find

$$\hat{Q}_L = \frac{4}{3} Q^* \qquad \text{Eq. 6.18}$$

The firm will sell fully one-third more units with two price segments than it will sell with a single price when prices are optimized against a downward-sloping, linear demand curve. Hence, optimal price segmentation is predicted to enable a product to be more widely purchased and used than without it.

Similarly, we can contrast the firm's profits under the condition of using a single price versus that of using two prices. Comparing Equations 6.7 to 6.17 we find

$$\hat{\pi}_2 = \frac{4}{3} \pi_1^* \qquad \text{Eq. 6.19}$$

The firm likewise earns one-third higher profits with two price segments than it earns with a single price when prices are optimized against a downward-sloping, linear demand curve. Hence, optimizing prices with multiple price segments is predicted to improve a firm's profits over that which can be achieved with a single price.

As for price, the unit volume–weighted average price at which a unit is sold using two prices and perfect segmentation is the same as it is when the product is sold at only one price when prices are optimized against a downward-sloping, linear demand curve. Price segmentation does not need to raise prices overall to improve profits and increase the number of customers served—it needs only to segregate those who are willing to pay more from those who are not.

Notes

[1] Modeling market dynamics with the restriction that every customer purchases only one unit is a simplifying assumption. It has little results on the conclusion of the thought experiment, but it makes the discussion easier.

[2] For an exposition on variance in willingness to pay and demanded benefits, see Rafi Mohammed, "Differential Pricing," in *The Art of Pricing: How to Find the Hidden Profits to Grow Your Business* (New York: Crown Business, 2005): 123–43.

[3] For a particularly pointed argument in favor of price discrimination, see Ronald J. Baker, "The Consumer Surplus and Price Discrimination," in *Pricing on Purpose: Creating and Capturing Value* (Hoboken, NJ: John Wiley & Sons, Inc., 2006): 175–96.

[4] In 2001, Anssi Vanjoki was assessed a $103,600 fine for speeding in Finland. The inordinately large size of the fine was determined according to Mr. Vanjoki's income in accordance with Finland's state practice. The approach to fining different violators in proportion to their income can be reframed as charging different road users different fees according to their willingness to pay—in effect, price discrimination. Steven Landsburg, "Highway Robbery," *Wall Street Journal Eastern Edition* (February 11, 2002): A.22.

[5] Optimizing two prices with a perfect segmentation hedge can be done with a spreadsheet analysis that jointly examines the profits earned at an array of prices.

[6] Arthur Cecil Pigou, "Discriminating Monopoly," in *The Economics of Welfare* (London: Macmillan, 1920).

[7] Ivan Png and Dale Lehman, "Pricing," *Managerial Economics* (Malden, MA.: Blackwell Publishing, 1998): 225–58.

[8] An examination of price discrimination practices is a standard component of any economics course. See for example N. Gregory Mankiw, "Monopoly," *Principles of Economics,* Sixth Edition (Mason, OH, Cengage Learning, 2012).

[9] Ladies' Nights in the United States are on their way to becoming virtual history since a recent slew of lawsuits. See Brittany Bacon, "Ladies' Night: Lawsuits on the Rocks? The Age-Old Tradition Is Threatened by Lawsuits Nationwide," ABC News (July 25, 2007). http://abcnews.go.com/TheLaw/Story?id=3412561&page=1 (accessed January 24, 2009). John E. H. Sherry, "Sex-Based Price Discrimination: Does It Violate Civil-Rights Laws?" *Cornell Hotel and Restaurant Administration Quarterly* 35, No. 2 (April 1994): 16–17.

[10] Price disparity related to neighborhood income was noted by John Kane, "The Supermarket Shuffle," *Mother Jones* 9 (1984): 7.

[11] The claim of "supermarket redlining" is often raised. See Elizabeth Eisenhauer, "In Poor Health: Supermarket Redlining and Urban Nutrition," *GeoJournal* 53, No. 2 (February 2001): 125–33.

[12] The Robinson-Patman Act restricts price segmentation in some business markets under specific circumstances. We will return to this issue in Chapter 17.

[13] For a discussion on pricing and influence of customer behavior, see Michael V. Marn, Eric V. Roegner, and Craig C. Zawada, "Pricing Architecture," in *The Price Advantage* (Hoboken, NJ: John Wiley & Sons, Inc., 2004) 193–206.

[14] Nina Diamond, John F. Sherry, Jr. Albert M. Muñiz, Jr. Mary Ann McGrath, Robert V. Kozinets, & Stefania Borghini, "American Girl and the Brand Gestalt: Closing the Loop on Sociocultural Branding Research," Journal of Marketing 73, No. 3 (May 2009): 118–34.

Chapter

7

Price Promotions

Patti McConville/The Image Bank/Getty Images

- How does a price promotion improve profitability?
- Do price promotions mostly grow the market or grow the share within the existing market?
- Are price promotions a good means of price segmentation?
- What customer behavior and psychological influences are affected by price promotions, and are these good for the firm?
- How should a price promotion be designed?
- What are common examples of price promotion?
- How should an executive evaluate the economic efficiency of a price promotion?
- Stretch Question: How many price promotions are just one too many?

Customers ask for a discount almost immediately after prices have been set, and executives face the challenge of making price concessions through discounts and price promotions. As a source of price variance, or pricing at points other than that determined in the price-setting process, price promotions are the most common challenge facing executives. Furthermore, price promotions can improve profits, but they can also harm profits, adding complexity to the challenge of their management.[1] Because of their frequency and complexity, few other issues will occupy a pricing professional's time more than that of managing price promotions.

Price promotions come in many forms. In their most discrete form, price discounts may be granted to specific customers to secure their purchase. In a broader sense, coupons, trial offers, trade deals, promotional sales, promotional discounts, promotional bundles, rebates, and specially marked packages can all be treated as price promotions.

Designed well, price promotions will improve profitability through their ability to price-segment the market. They capture sales from customers who have a lower willingness to pay at a lower price point, while leaving those customers who are willing to pay the full price to do so. If they are designed poorly, price promotions will harm profitability. As a form of price segmentation, price promotions tend to be "leaky," in that customers with a higher willingness to pay may benefit from a price promotion even though a price concession is not needed to secure their purchase. Left unchecked, poorly designed price promotions fail to act as a segmentation hedge and end up providing unnecessary, profit-destructive price concessions.

Because of their ability to improve profits, price promotions have become highly popular. At the time of this writing, the corporate expenditures on promotions have far exceeded outlays on advertising. For instance, in 1990, over 90 billion coupons were distributed. Since the advent of the Internet, online coupons and price promotions have only multiplied.

To make better decisions, managers need to understand the tradeoffs involved in price promotions. Like other aspects of pricing, price promotions have both quantitative and qualitative dimensions. Executives should consistently temper their desire for volume and the results of a profit sensitivity analysis with an understanding of the ability of a specific price promotion to act as a segmentation hedge. Price promotions that fail to act as a segmentation hedge should be discarded and replaced with a more targeted format.

Let us examine some of the positive and negative aspects of price promotions before comparing a few of the more popular formats side by side.

Positive Effects of Price Promotions

Price promotions have many attractive attributes for an executive looking to boost the top line. Price promotions can enable price segmentation effectively, thus both increasing the reachable market and potentially enabling an overall increase of the list price to capture higher prices from those with a higher willingness to pay. They also have an immediate impact on volume sold by both encouraging new customers to participate in the category and encouraging customers to try the promoted brand and potentially realign their loyalties.

PRICE SEGMENTATION

Positioning price promotion in the context of price segmentation hedges helps us reveal many of the positive aspects and methods of improving price promotions.[2] We have seen that price segmentation can improve profitability by enabling the firm to charge a higher price to those with a higher willingness to pay, and increase volume of product sold by charging a lower price to those with a lower willingness to pay. Therefore, the efficiency of price promotions as a segmentation hedge is largely determined by how well they segment the market according to willingness to pay.

A pricing policy that uses highly targeted price promotions improves profitability through the same mechanisms as those found with other segmentation hedges. First and most directly, price promotions are best at capturing marginal customers and encouraging them to purchase, thus increasing the volume sold (albeit at a lower price). Second, through indirect effects, price promotions can actually enable the firm to increase the "normal" price—that is, the price extracted through non-promotional transactions.

The effect of having a lower promotional price, even if it is only temporary and used by a small portion of the market, is to enable those customers with a low willingness to pay to purchase at a lower price. Once they have purchased, the remaining market will see an increase in the representation of customers with a higher willingness to pay. As such, the firm may be able to price the product slightly higher, in proportion to the marginal increase of the remaining customers' average willingness to pay.

If price promotions are simply a form of price segmentation, a curious reader might ask why price segmentation related to temporary price actions are nearly always posed as "discounts." After all, the effect of many price promotions is to toggle the price level between two different prices, one being the "normal price" and the other being the "discounted price." Why not rename the lower price as "normal" and the higher price as the "premium" price (or some other acceptable name)?

Prospect theory provides a simple explanation. Recall from prospect theory that people feel the pain of losses more than they feel the joy of gains. Price increases, either in surcharges or in temporary price hikes, are interpreted by customers as a loss from an earlier lower price. Price decreases, either through discounts or sales, are always seen as a gain from an earlier higher price. As such, price toggling between a "normal" and "discount" price will have less effect of depressing demand during the high-price period than those that toggle between a "premium" and "normal" price level. Even though the actual price levels may be the same, the framing effect implies that the name used to describe the low- and high-price levels affects customer response.

MARKET SIZE AND SHARE

During a price promotion, sales can increase substantially. For the manufacturer, increased sales come from two different sources: market size increases and brand switching.[3] For the retailer, increased sales come not only from those related to the promoted product, but also from other products at the store, especially complementary products.

Market size increases, or increased category-level spending, can occur because a price promotion may potentially lower the price required to participate in the market. The lower price draws marginal customers, customers who otherwise would not purchase from that category of goods, into the market. In this manner, price promotions can increase the size of the market.

Brand switching occurs because the specific product on promotion has improved its value proposition in relation to competing products within its category.[4] While price promotions lower the cost to purchase, they do not lower the benefits gained in purchasing, and they may even increase them due to the effect of a discount being perceived as a gain. Customers who are marginally loyal to a competing product may calculate that their overall utility will be greater by switching brands and purchasing the promoted product. This can induce brand switching during the promotion, the trial of competing products, and perhaps even the capture of customers who are now loyal to the new brand. When price promotions lead to the capture of new brand-loyal customers, they can have a very high impact on overall market share and profitability.[5]

We have seen evidence that price promotions both increase category-level purchases and encourage brand switching from the examination of elasticity of demand. Recall that category-level elasticity of demand is regularly observed to be less than brand-level elasticity of demand. The difference can be attributed to the fact that category-level elasticity of demand reflects the ability of a pricing action to increase the size of the market alone, while brand-level elasticity of demand reflects the ability of a pricing action both to increase the size of the market and to induce brand switching. The difference implies that, for most price promotions, sales increases come primarily from brand switching and secondarily from market size growth.

Negative Effect of Price Promotions

Much of the positive impact of price promotions, however, can be misleading. For instance, short-term sales data may indicate that a price promotion increases profitability, yet long-term sales and revenue data can contradict that. To make sense of the conflict, let's look at some of the negative impacts of price promotions.

IMPERFECT SEGMENTATION HEDGE

Price promotions are, at best, an imperfect segmentation hedge. Although they can induce some customers who would not otherwise buy to do so, they also can provide unnecessary price concessions to otherwise loyal customers.[6] Promotional design has a significant impact on the ability of a price promotion to discriminate between those with a higher willingness to pay and those with a lower willingness to pay, as we will see in future sections.

A potential source of sales increases during price promotions is the acceleration of purchases by customers who would have purchased anyway.[7] If customers are purchasing excess quantities for consumption, the price promotion will lead to an overall growth of the market and therefore improve profits. However, if customers are using price promotions to stockpile products, the sales that occur during a price promotion will come from those sales that would have occurred during a future period without a price promotion. This is one of several routes in which a price promotion can actually decrease demand during regular-priced periods.

CUSTOMER CHURN

As noted, price promotions can encourage brand switching. While encouraging brand trial will improve sales during the price promotion, one of the key metrics of the long-term success of a price promotion is the ability of the product to capture brand-loyal customers during regular price times. If consumers switch back to competing products following the firm's price promotion or during a competitor's price promotion, much of the potential gains derived from a price promotion will be lost quickly. Industries plagued with numerous and frequent price promotions may also be creating their own customer churn, encouraging customers to switch between brands during a promotion and failing to foster any long-term brand commitment. Customer churn has its own set of profit-damaging consequences.

Price promotions can have asymmetric effects on profitability between competing firms, where those products that are able to engender stronger brand loyalty are at a strategic advantage. The asymmetric effect of price promotions in delivering profitability to the firm with higher brand loyalty is one of the progenitor factors that encourage marketing managers of branded goods to favor price promotions when battling the encroachment of generic or store-brand products.

Cross-elasticity of demand between products is a strategic metric of the ability of a price promotion to take and keep market share. The cross-elasticity of demand measures the ability of a specific product to take market share from a competing product. The higher a product's cross-elasticity of demand, the stronger that brand is compared to other products. If the price promotion takes market share from a product with a weaker brand loyalty, it may improve market share in the long term. If, however, the price promotion takes market share from products with strong brand loyalty, it is unlikely that customer trial will translate into a realignment of brand loyalty.

REFERENCE PRICE EFFECT

Though price promotions as a part of a price segmentation policy can lead to higher "regular" prices during non-promotional periods, many marketing executives find that raising prices after a price promotion is very difficult.[8] As discussed with respect to the reference price effect, one model of how customers perceive prices shows an exponential smoothing of price expectations. In this model, the current price that customers expect to pay is informed by the last price observed. Following a price promotion, prices return to their regular level from the latest promotional level. However, at this regular price, customers may perceive the price to be too high because it is above what they last paid.

The strength of exponential smoothing on price expectations is reinforced by the depth and frequency of price promotions. Frequent price promotions reinforce the expectation of lower prices and thus encourage customers to expect lower prices.[9] Likewise, deep price promotions are likely to have greater saliency within customers' minds and thus also lead to lower price expectations.

LOSS OF PRICE CREDIBILITY

One way of speaking about the negative effect of price promotions on regular prices is the concept of losing price credibility. When the price fluctuates wildly between promotional levels and regular levels, and customers begin to notice the wide differential, they may simply stop buying at full price. The full price simply becomes non-credible as an acceptable price for purchasing, and all customers will hunt for the next outlet or the next sale date to purchase unless they are facing an emergency.

Many firms in industrial markets have lost list price credibility. From office supplies to enterprise software, even the smallest business can find routes around paying full list prices. Discounts are so numerous that it is hard to avoid them. Furthermore, purchasing managers know that industrial products can be purchased at a discount, and many are actually rewarded by the discount they receive below the list price. When it becomes common knowledge that "no one pays full price," suppliers must conclude that the list price has lost all credibility.

An old joke about price promotions goes as follows: "Our normal price is $1,000, but right now it has a $999 discount." If customers even come close to perceiving this about a firm's list prices, then that firm can be assured that it has lost all pricing credibility.

INCREASE OF PRICE SENSITIVITY

Perhaps the largest long-term challenge of price promotions derives from their focus on price itself. Price promotions, by their very nature, draw attention to price. When they do this, price promotions can take attention away from the issue of product value, the features and attributes that give rise to benefits from which customers derive utility. Research has demonstrated that benefit-focused promotions can improve the perceived value of a product, while price-oriented promotions increase price sensitivity. Firms seeking to improve their leverage over prices are encouraged to pay less attention to couponing and price promotions and instead focus on other methods of driving sales.

Managing Vagueness

At issue in price promotion with relationship to price credibility and pricing power is a challenge of vagueness. Vagueness is a philosophical issue deriving from the Sorites pardox. The name "sorites" derives from the Greek word *soros*, meaning "heap," and refers to a thought puzzle known as "the heap." "The heap" thought puzzle goes as follows: How many grains of wheat does it take to make a heap? Would you describe a single grain of wheat as a heap? Of course not. Would you describe two grains of wheat as a heap? Again, no. . . . Yet, you must admit the presence of a heap sooner or later as you add grains of wheat. So, how many grains of wheat does it take to make a heap? Alternatively, let's try it from the opposite direction. If you have a heap of wheat and take one away, is it still a heap? Yes. Would you describe it as a heap if you take two grains of wheat away? Again, yes. . . . Yet once more, you must admit the absence of a heap sooner or later as you take grains of wheat. So, which grain of wheat makes the difference between a heap and a non-heap?

In a similar manner, it is clear that price promotions can improve profits by driving marginal sales from customers with a lower willingness to pay. However, it is also clear that excess price promotions can have a negative impact on profits by decreasing price credibility and encouraging loyal customers to buy on price rather than value. Questions like "How many price promotions are too many?" and "How deep a price promotion is too deep?" are somewhat vague. It is hard to say that the last price promotion was exactly one too many, but at some point, there clearly were too many price promotions. When there are too many price promotions, taking just one away won't make it right.

To determine if a specific price promotion should be used, executives typically deploy a profit sensitivity analysis as a first step. A priori, volume increases are forecasted in conjunction with a specific price promotion, along with redemption rates and other cost factors depending on the format of the promotion. Then, after quantitatively defining volume hurdles, executives determine if a specific price promotion is likely to improve profits. See Chapter 2 to refresh the details.

While this method can prevent managers from executing the most egregious errors in price promotions, it fundamentally fails to address the subtle challenge of how many is too many. Further models are required to differentiate between price promotions that enhance profits and market share and those that negatively affect price credibility or excessively draw sales from those that would have occurred in the absence of a price promotion. Often, a more-complete quantitative model requires much more managerial effort and facts that can be gathered only through market research efforts. Due to the high popularity and frequency of price promotions and the effort required to execute price promotions, many executives conclude that a detailed quantitative analysis beyond a profit sensitivity analysis of specific price promotions is economically inefficient. Instead, they resort to periodic reviews of the overall promotional policy. In the absence of a detailed quantitative analysis on specific price promotions, many executives find that a well-constructed qualitative analysis that considers both the positive and negative effects of price promotion policy fruitful and economically efficient.

One such method for quantitatively evaluating price promotions has been proposed by Neslin and Shoemaker specifically for couponing in consumer markets.[10] The model considers the actions of manufacturers, retailers, and customers, and furthermore includes decisions taken both before and after the price promotion period. While the details of this model are beyond the scope of this text, an overview of the interactions and issues included their coupon promotion model is provided in Exhibit 7-1. From the coupon promotion model diagram alone, one can determine that numerous factors must be considered to manage the vagueness regarding how many price promotions are too many.

Price Promotion Design

In addition to the quantitative guidelines provided through a profit sensitivity analysis, managers can rely on four general qualitative rules to price promotions: Make them targeted. Make them temporary. Make them special. Make them irregular.

TARGETED

Targeted price promotions are better at price segmentation than more-diffuse price promotions. For a price promotion to act as a strong price segmentation hedge, it should specifically encourage marginal customers to purchase. Marginal customers are those who would have chosen not to purchase in the absence of the promotion, but otherwise desire to purchase. Without the price promotion, marginal customers may have purchased a

Exhibit 7-1 Coupon Promotion Model

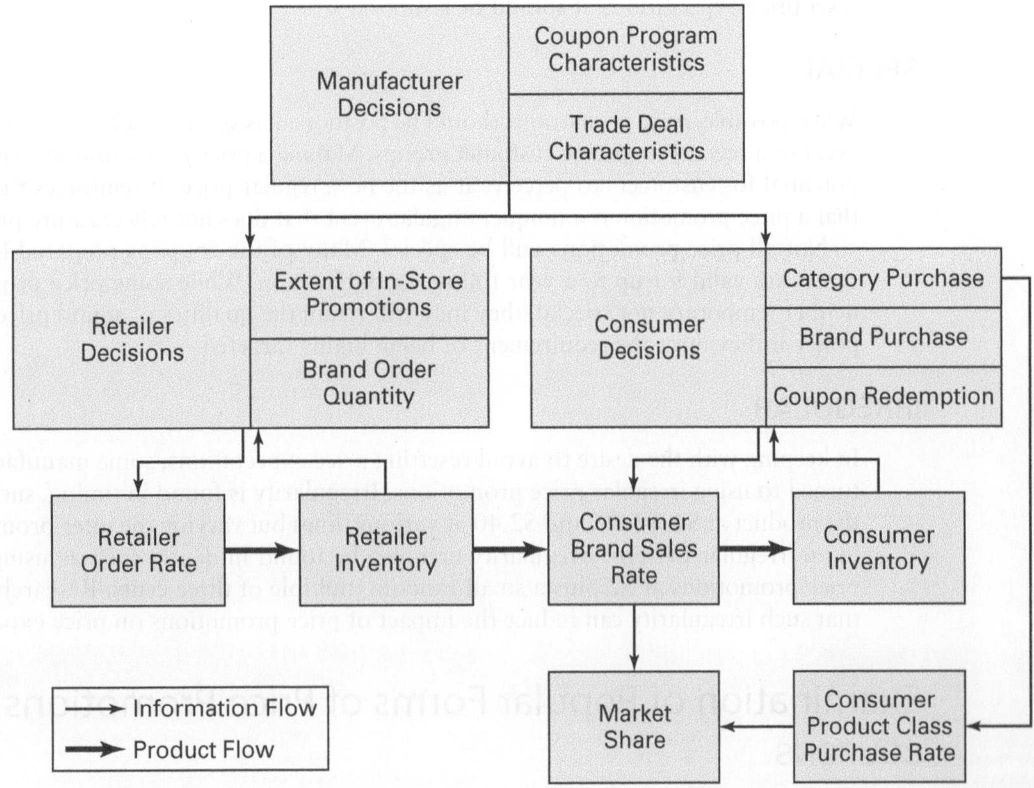

competing brand, delayed their purchase and reduced their consumption, or simply not have participated in the market at all. Customers who would have purchased anyway without the price promotion should be avoided, if possible, in a price promotion campaign.

The importance of targeting marginal customers can override many simpler metrics of price promotional effectiveness such as coupon redemption rates and volume increases. If the targeted price promotion selectively attracts only a few customers, but they are specifically those who otherwise would not purchase, it may be more efficient as a marketing tool than a promotion that is widely and indiscriminately used by both brand-loyal and marginal customers alike. Identifying promotions that target marginal customers may require examining data beyond that of redemption rates and into data that reveals buyer pre- and post-purchase intentions.

TEMPORARY

Price promotions should be temporary and time-dependent. One of the positive aspects of price promotions is their ability to increase sales immediately. They are, in nature, temporary marketing efforts that involve pricing actions that encourage customers to purchase. In contrast, a long-running price promotion will eventually fail to maintain the quality of being temporary and therefore morphs into the quality of being a new price level.

Recall that one of the negative effects of price promotions is the potential for resetting reference prices, or customer-expected prices. Long-running price promotions have greater saliency. They increase the likelihood that customers will remember the lower price paid during the promotion and make it easier for customers to recall that lower price. Short, temporary price promotions are more likely to stay in short-term memory and less likely to be stored in long-term memory. Thus, to reduce the potential for a price promotion to reset price expectations, it should be temporary.

SPECIAL

When possible, price promotions should be positioned as special, such as related to a unique event or a reward to specific customer groups. Making a price promotion special reduces the potential for customers to perceive it as the new, regular price. It reinforces the perception that a price promotion is a unique, singular event that does not reflect future prices.

Not all price promotions will be special. Many of the coupons prepared by manufacturers are valid for up to a year following publication. While some price promotions are neither temporary nor special, they may still retain the qualities of sound price promotion policy if they meet the requirement of being highly targeted.

IRREGULAR

In keeping with the desire to avoid resetting price expectations, some manufacturers have turned to using irregular price promotions. Irregularity is found in timing, such as pricing the product at $2, $2.20, and $2.40 at various times but varying the inter-promotion delay in an irregular pattern. Irregularity can also be found in depth, such as using successive price promotions at $2 plus a small random multiple of three cents. Research has shown that such irregularity can reduce the impact of price promotions on price expectations.[11]

Examination of Popular Forms of Price Promotions

COUPONS

Manufacturer coupons are perhaps the most proliferative form of price promotions, but not all coupons are equally valuable for the firm. Manufacturer coupons can appear on product packages, in direct mail, in newspaper cutouts, on websites, and within email. Retailers themselves provide direct-mail coupons, repeat-purchase coupons, receipt coupons, and in-store coupons, and the formats of coupons change daily. Depending on their format, different coupon programs have different efficiencies in their ability to price-segment the market and in their effectiveness in increasing promotional period sales.

To demonstrate some of the decision tradeoffs that are embedded in any price promotion using coupons, let us consider manufacturer coupons specifically. Manufacturer-supported coupons can be coordinated with specific retailers in a coordinated marketing effort, or they can be distributed directly by the manufacturer to consumers. Each choice represents a tradeoff.

When coupons are coordinated with retailers, the effect is that of a double-edged sword. On the positive side, coordinating with retailers greatly improves the effectiveness of the coupons in increasing sales volume and may enable the manufacturer to negotiate better shelf space and in-store displays. On the negative side, promotions coordinated with retailers can increase the proportion of coupon-using customers who would have purchased without the coupon, thus decreasing the economic efficiency as a price segmentation hedge.

To reduce the negative profit impact of providing unnecessary price concessions to otherwise-willing-to-pay customers, manufacturer-retailer price promotions should be highly temporary. The temporary nature of these promotions acts as a form of segmentation hedge. Those who are searching for a discount should find it available only in limited locations and for a limited time. In forcing customers to shop at a particular moment and place so they can receive the discount, customers with a higher willingness to pay and alternative priorities may find the offer inconvenient, while marginal customers with a lower willingness to pay may find the offer sufficient to encourage purchasing.

Manufacturer coupons placed within packaging will attract a higher proportion of repeat customers and, as such, might have a different kind of beneficial influence. If these repeat customers are accelerating their consumption of the product in relation to the coupon on the packaging, the coupon will have the beneficial effect of marginally increasing the market. Alternatively, if the coupon in the packaging reduces the likelihood of brand switching to competitors, the manufacturer can anticipate that the couponing strategy will improve brand loyalty.

Alternatively, direct-mail, web, newspaper, and magazine coupons can have the beneficial aspect of reaching a broader audience. Though typically more expensive to distribute, the broader audience reached by these communication channels implies the potential of reaching a higher proportion of prospective customers who otherwise would have little interaction with the brand. If the coupon distributed through these broader communication methods induces a higher portion of sales to new, brand-switching customers, manufacturers may find them more efficient even though the redemption rate is lower.

In general, coupons are a decent, although imperfect, price segmentation hedge. Customers who use coupons are signaling their lower willingness to pay through the action of identifying, collecting, and redeeming their coupons. Meanwhile, customers with a higher opportunity cost of time or with a higher willingness to pay for other reasons may find the couponing process inordinately wasteful.

TRIAL OFFERS

Trial offers are simple price promotions that the seller uses to induce trial of its product. Trial offers are made in the form of free samples, small packages priced at a significantly lower price point, or leased services and software as a service wherein the cost to enter the market is greatly reduced from the full, regular price.

In some formats, trial offers make it clear that the trial price is discounted from the regular price. In other formats, the benefits of the trial offer are reduced from that provided with the regular offer by shrinking the package size, automatically curtailing functionality, or simply providing only partial functionality. Because these trial offers are clearly not intended for regular use nor represent the regular price, they mitigate some of the challenges of inappropriately setting the reference price too low.

When targeted to new customers, they can effectively act to increase the market overall and, more specifically, increase the trial of the manufacturer's brand. A buyer's first purchase is not just incremental revenue; it is the first opportunity to educate the buyer on the value of the product. With experience goods, use enables customers to learn the benefits of the product that could not be fully comprehended through another process, and therefore trial offers greatly facilitate market penetration.

Trial offers as a means of introducing products to new customers should be used with products that will be purchased frequently, have a low incremental production cost, and have benefits that are self-evident after one use.

REBATES

Rebates provide a monetary incentive to purchase, like other forms of price promotion. They provide advantages in their ability to be highly targeted in the type of customers who redeem rebates and to whom the rebate is extended.

When rebates are extended, redemption rates may be low. Even with low redemption rates, the rebate may have a strong positive effect on profitability. Many customers find rebate offers attractive at the time of purchase and are encouraged to purchase because of the rebate, and yet these same customers will often fail to redeem the rebate. Failure to redeem can be attributed to many factors, yet mostly they represent opportunity costs on behalf of the customer. It takes time to complete the rebate forms, attach receipts, and mail them in. Customers failing in any one of these steps before the expiration of the rebate offer are effectively signaling their higher willingness to pay. In this sense, rebate offers are highly effective in segmenting customers by willingness to pay.

Rebates do not have to be extended to all customers. They can be targeted at repeat customers only as a means of fostering brand loyalty, or at new customers only as a means to encourage product trial. In some cases, rebates will be targeted specifically to customers who "trade in" a competitor's model, though the economic profitability of such deals are highly dependent on future purchases and customer longevity. In this sense, rebates should be related to accomplishing a specific strategic marketing goal.

PROMOTIONAL BUNDLES

Firms can use promotional bundles to disguise price promotions. Promotional bundling, like bundling in general, is the sale of two or more distinct products in a single transaction and at a single price. The bundled price of the two or more products is lower than the total prices of the individual constituent products. Unlike strategic bundling, promotional bundles are temporary in nature, related to a specific tactical marketing effort.

Research has found that promotional bundles are more effective at encouraging brand switching among marginal customers than in encouraging new customers to purchase the product. Further research has examined whether customers who purchase a promotional bundle view their savings as (1) being associated with an individual or dominant item within the bundle or (2) being associated with the entire bundle, where no specific product was perceived as providing the brunt of the price reduction. Encouragingly, the promotional bundle is perceived primarily as granting savings on the entire bundle, not on a single product. As such, bundles should have less effect on resetting price expectation of any individual product compared to other price promotion formats.[12]

Tradeoffs between Popular Price Promotions

There are a number of common discount approaches. When executives are choosing between different price promotions, they should consider the tradeoffs involved. Competing forms of price promotions can be evaluated according to the ability to segment customers according to willingness to pay and the fit with the overall price promotion design suggestions. For example, we compare newspaper versus in-store coupons, mail-in versus instant rebates, and Every Day Low Pricing (EDLP) versus Hi-Lo pricing formats.

NEWSPAPER VERSUS IN-STORE COUPONS

Guided by redemption rates and improved sales volumes alone, many marketing managers may be led to believe that in-store coupons are more efficient than those distributed by newspaper, direct mail, or other means to customers. Coupons sent to individuals tend to have a low redemption rate, not unlike the low conversion rate found with other direct-mail approaches. Conversion rates of 1 percent to 2 percent are common with direct-mail efforts, making direct mail an expensive promotional effort for firms. In contrast, in-store coupons have a very high redemption rate related to the fact that in-store coupons are closer to the point of purchase. If redemption rates alone were the metric of choice, many marketers could believe in-store coupons to be more efficient than those distributed through newspapers or other channels. Yet redemption rates are not the entire story. Marketers should also consider the targeting efficiency and the associated costs.

Many customers who redeem an in-store coupon are the same customers who would have purchased the product at full price. In contrast, those who redeem coupons delivered by newspaper cutouts, direct mail, web, or email tend to be more marginal customers, customers with a lower willingness to pay who would not purchase without the incentive.

The targeting inefficiency of in-store coupons may make them actually less economically efficient for the manufacturer than those distributed to a larger audience.

Couponing is always associated with a cost. Not only is the face value of a redeemed coupon a reduction in the price captured, but other costs also are involved, including those associated with printing and distributing coupons and coupon-processing fees. Low redemption rates and high distribution costs can increase the costs of couponing dramatically. In contrast, high redemption rates and low distribution costs can make the couponing appear efficient.

To incorporate both the effects of targeting efficiency and total couponing costs, one should calculate the break-even incremental unit sales per redemption.[13] Incremental unit sales per redemption measure the number of incremental sales generated by the coupon divided by the number of coupons redeemed. The break-even incremental unit sales per redemption define the required percentage of coupons redeemed to have come from incremental sales, or sales that would not have happened in the absence of the coupon.

In Exhibit 7-2, we present a sample calculation of the break-even incremental unit sales per redemption of a branded good manufacturer distributing a \$0.50 coupon with a \$0.09 processing fee per coupon when considering the distribution of coupons via the newspaper or an in-store display. Assume that the product has a manufacturer-to-retailer price of \$3, with a 40 percent manufacturer's profit margin.

If distributed via newspapers, we might anticipate the distribution of 1 million coupons at \$10 per thousand coupons with a 5 percent redemption rate, yielding a total of 50,000 coupons at a distribution cost of \$10,000. In contrast, the same branded-good manufacturer could distribute 62,500 in-store coupons at cost of \$100 per thousand with an 80 percent redemption rate to yield the same total of 50,000 coupons redeemed for only \$6,250 in distribution cost.

Exhibit 7-2 Break-even Incremental Unit Sales per Redemption

Coupon Face Value	\$0.50	
Processing Fee	\$0.09	
Price	\$3.00	
Margin	40%	
	Newspaper	**In-Store**
Coupons Distributed	1,000,000	62,500
Cost/1000 Distributed	\$10	\$100
Distribution Costs Coupons Distributed × Cost/1000 Distributed	\$10,000	\$6,250
Redemption Rate	5%	80%
Coupons Redeemed Coupons Distributed × Redemption Rate	50,000	50,000
Redemption Costs Coupons Redeemed × (Face Value + Processing Fee)	\$29,500	\$29,500
Total Campaign Costs Distribution Costs + Redemption Costs	\$39,500	\$35,750
Cost per Buyer Total Costs/Coupons Redeemed	\$0.790	\$0.715
Total Campaign Profit Coupons Redeemed × Price × Margin	\$60,000	\$60,000
ROI (Incremental Profit − Total Costs)/Total Costs	52%	68%
Break-even Incremental Unit Sales per Redemption $\frac{\text{Campaign Costs}}{\text{Campaign Profit}}$	66%	60%

Both approaches would have the same redemption costs, or costs associated with redeeming and processing. At $0.59 per coupon redeemed ($0.50 coupon + $0.09 processing fee), 50,000 coupons would have a $29,500 redemption cost. If we add the distribution costs to the redemption costs to find the total coupon campaign costs, we would find the total campaign costs associated with newspaper distribution to be $39,500 and the total campaign costs associated with in-store distribution to be $35,750. Dividing the total costs by the number of coupons redeemed, we find the cost per buyer to be $0.79 for newspaper distribution and $0.715 for in-store distribution. On the face of costs alone, we might conclude that in-store distribution is more efficient. However, such a conclusion would be premature.

We could also calculate the campaign profit generated from the couponing effort to determine the return on investment for the campaigns. Given that 50,000 coupons are redeemed in both cases, and that the product is priced at $3 with a 40 percent profit margin, the profit from either campaign is $60,000. The return on investment is the campaign profit generated minus the campaign costs, and then divided by the campaign costs. For newspaper distribution, the return on investment for the campaign is 52 percent. For in-store distribution, the return on investment for the campaign would be 68 percent. Again, on the face of return on investment alone, we might conclude that in-store distribution is more efficient—but such a conclusion remains premature.

Cost is not the only factor to consider when evaluating couponing. Rather, the efficiency of couponing should be evaluated based on its ability to generate new sales—sales that would not have occurred in the absence of the coupon. Fundamentally, we desire the portion of the campaign profit that can be attributed to incremental sales to be greater than the campaign costs (Equation 7.1).

$$\text{Campaign Profit} \cdot \text{Percent Associated with Incremental Sales} > \text{Campaign Costs} \qquad \text{Eq. 7.1}$$

We can rearrange Equation 7.1 to find the break-even incremental unit sales per redemption (Equation 7.2):

$$\text{Break-even Incremental Unit Sales per Redemption} = \frac{\text{Campaign Costs}}{\text{Campaign Profit}} \qquad \text{Eq. 7.2}$$

For coupons distributed via the newspaper, we find the break-even incremental unit sales per redemption to be 66 percent, meaning that 66 percent of the sales associated with the coupon must come from customers who would not have purchased in the absence of the coupon. If research indicates that newspaper coupons are good at targeting incremental sales, such that 70 percent of coupon users come from incremental sales, the manufacturer may conclude that newspaper coupon distribution is the efficient approach.

In contrast, we find break-even incremental unit sales per redemption to be 60 percent for in-store coupons. The lower break-even point for in-store coupons over newspaper coupons is a direct result of the higher redemption rates. Yet, if research indicates that in-store coupons are poor at targeting incremental sales, such that only 30 percent of coupon users come from incremental sales, the manufacturer may conclude that in-store coupon distribution is an inefficient approach.

Clearly, calculating the break-even incremental unit sales per redemption is useful for decision making. It also heightens the importance of selecting coupon distribution channels not only based on the effective cost per coupon redeemed, but also the effectiveness of coupons in attracting new sales. Much research has cast serious doubt on the belief that firms routinely achieve incremental sales in excess of the break-even point.

Where customers make purchase decisions, either at home or in the store, influences the optimal choice between direct-to-customer or in-store coupons. Products whose purchase is driven by a predefined need and that are selected by customers coming to the store with a list are likely to receive a more significant and lasting profit boost through direct-mail coupons or other broadly circulated coupon distribution methods. In-store coupons may provide a significant and lasting profit improvement when placed near the product, when they are used to promote trial or brand switching, and when purchasing decisions are made mostly at the point of sale.

MAIL-IN VERSUS INSTANT REBATES

Similar to direct mail versus in-store coupons, mail-in versus instant rebates differ widely on their redemption rates and targeting efficiency. Instant rebates are a poorer segmentation hedge than mail-in rebates, in that they are extended to customers with high and low willingness to pay alike. Mail-in rebates, through their requirement of completing a form, attaching a receipt, and mailing in the rebate request, are a better segmentation hedge to target than those with a lower willingness to pay. Experience has shown that mail-in rebate redemption rates vary between 5 percent and 50 percent, depending on the magnitude of the rebate, while in-store rebates regularly reach redemption rates of 100 percent.

Because of the lower segmentation efficiency of instant rebates in comparison to mail-in rebates, it is suggested that the value of an instant rebate should be less than that of a comparable mail-in rebate after adjusting for its lower redemption rate (Equation 7.3).

$$\text{Instant Rebate Value} < \text{Mail-in Rebate Value} \cdot \text{Mail-in Rebate Redemption Rate} \qquad \text{Eq. 7.3}$$

As with coupons, consumer behavioral factors that may sway the choice to use lower values for instant rebates than for mail-in rebates are those that indicate that product selection between competing offers is made in-store as opposed to at home when preparing a written list.

HI-LO VERSUS EDLP

Hi-Lo shopping formats and EDLP shopping formats attract very different types of consumer behavior. Hi-Lo formats, where coupons and price promotions are used frequently to drive sales, tend to cycle prices on specific products between high "regular" levels and low "sales" levels. EDLP formats eschew price promotions in favor of holding prices at a consistently low level. While some retailers are blatantly Hi-Lo channels, others advertise an EDLP strategy even though they tend to participate in some, albeit less frequent and shallower, Hi-Lo price promotions. Moreover, manufacturers themselves may, at times, announce a move towards EDLP.

EDLP retailers disproportionately attract customers with a lower willingness to pay, while full-service retailers tend to attract customers with both low and high willingness to pay.[14] Because EDLP formats tend to attract more marginal customers, many manufacturers find that granting these channels price concessions is an effective means to improve profits while having a minimal impact on sales through alternative channels to customers with a higher willingness to pay. Furthermore, because EDLP channels position themselves as a discount retailer to attract price-conscious customers, price actions through EDLP channels are somewhat, though not completely, isolated from those at other channels.

As mentioned, Hi-Lo and EDLP retailers attract different kinds of customers in other dimensions as well. For instance, EDLP formats also tend to attract big-basket shoppers who buy a wider variety and greater number of goods on a single shopping trip, than do Hi-Low formats. Other differences relate to the effect of reference prices and requirements for service.

In terms of reference price effects, EDLP shoppers tend to have a stronger expectation about prices than Hi-Lo shoppers, perhaps because EDLP shoppers routinely see the same price. Oddly however, EDLP shoppers tend to be less sensitive to short-term discounting than Hi-Lo shoppers—exactly those kinds of price changes related to a price promotion.

These incongruous claims may be due to EDLP store formats lulling customers into expecting low prices, thus encouraging them not to search elsewhere for discounts.[15]

If EDLP retailers have a consistent price and Hi-Lo retailers have a fluctuating price between high and low levels, which format tends to have lower prices on average? It is economically efficient for specific Hi-Lo prices to be lower than EDLP prices on a temporary basis. On average, however, prices in Hi-Lo retail outlets are higher than prices in EDLP retail outlets.[16]

EDLP channels often require manufacturers to provide them with the lowest prices consistently. This can create strain for manufacturers in dealing with their other channels. One strategy to mitigate this conflict of interest is to offer different versions of the product to EDLP and Hi-Lo retail channels. Through variation in size, packaging, or even features, EDLP and Hi-Lo channels can distribute different products. Because Hi-Lo channels capture more customers with a higher willingness to pay, it can further be argued that the EDLP channel should receive feature-deprived or larger-packaged products to act further as a segmentation hedge.

At the retail level, EDLP store formats tend to forgo many of the sales and customer support activities that are available at other stores. They tend to be low-touch channels. By providing less in-store sales support, EDLP stores are able to reduce costs and earn a profit at a lower price.

Some products should avoid EDLP channels and instead seek high-touch channels. Retail salespeople need not be simply clerks and shelf-stockers; they can be a strategic part of the marketing process. For instance, complex products—those whose features and attributes cannot be summed up in a simple promotional statement—require salespeople to communicate and explain the benefits of competing offers. Likewise, products whose benefits are hard to predict prior to purchase, or whose benefits are not visually obvious, have improved sales through the interaction of salespeople with customers. Furthermore, salesperson interactions benefit sales of products that require learning on behalf of customers. These include products that have a long time between purchases and are therefore difficult for customers to learn the differences and benefits of competing products, as well as complex products whose dimensions of features and attributes evolve with time. Finally, high-priced products whose purchase represents a significant portion of the customer's spending money benefit from salespeople interactions, due to the high risk of making a bad purchase decision.

Summary

- Price promotions are a form of price segmentation in which prices are reduced for those with a lower willingness to pay and regular prices are offered to those with a higher willingness to pay.
- Price promotions generate increased sales primarily through encouraging brand switching and secondarily through increasing the size of the market.
- From prospect theory, we understand that part of the power of price promotions to drive sales derives from consumers perceiving price reductions as a form of added gain on top of receiving the product, in exchange for the pain of payment.
- Price promotions can have asymmetric effects on profitability between competing firms where those products that are able to engender stronger brand loyalty are at a strategic advantage.
- The reference price effect, wherein customer price expectations are based on prior observed prices, can drive sales troughs following a price promotion and dampen the ability to raise prices thereafter.
- Deep and frequent price promotions can reduce price credibility, causing customers to stop believing that the full regular price is the appropriate price to pay.
- Because price promotions focus the customer's attention on price, they can also increase price sensitivity.

- While a profit sensitivity analysis to reveal volume hurdles can prevent the most egregious managerial errors with respect to price promotions, they fail to identify the more subtle challenges of "How many are too many?" and "How deep is too deep?" These questions suffer from the common philosophical challenge of vagueness. At some point, executives know that they have breached a limit, but it is difficult to identify which promotion crossed the line. To address this challenge, executives should conduct periodic reviews of the overall price promotion policy using more insightful qualitative and quantitative analysis techniques.
- In general, price promotions should strive to be targeted towards marginal customers. Other design criteria for price promotions include a desire for them to be temporary, special, and irregular.
- Price promotions take many forms, including specially marked packages, coupons, trial offers, trade deals, promotional sales, discounts, promotional bundles, and rebates. Each format of a price promotion has its strengths and weaknesses in targeting specific types of customers and achieving different marketing objectives.
- In contrast to Hi-Lo store formats, in which price promotions oscillate between high and low price levels, some retailers have executed an EDLP format, wherein everyday low prices are used. EDLP formats attract a higher proportion of customers with a lower willingness to pay, partially because their lower level of overall service discourages customers with a higher willingness to pay to patronize stores with such formats. To manage both Hi-Lo and EDLP retail channels, manufacturers often find it beneficial to market a feature-deprived or larger packaged version of their product in EDLP channels and full-feature, normal-size versions in Hi-Lo channels.

Exercises

1. Consider a price promotion with respect to two different products: a handheld video communicator (a new-to-the-world product) and a toothpaste made with all natural ingredients (a new-to-the-category product). In which case do you believe the price promotion will be more effective at increasing the market size? Increasing the market share?
2. Consider a price promotion with respect to two different diapers: a currently marketed form of Huggies and a new and improved form of Huggies.
   a. In which case is the price promotion most likely to induce trial among new customers, and why?
   b. In which case is the price promotion most likely to affect the perceived reference price, and why?
   c. In which case is the price promotion most likely to reduce price credibility, and why?
   d. In which case is the price promotion most likely to increase the price sensitivity of the market, and why?
3. Consider the following forms of price promotions according to their effectiveness at targeting customers for an existing, well-known, often-purchased, branded good. Rate them as either poorly targeted, targeted toward loyal customers, or targeted toward new customers.
   a. Newspaper
   b. Local retail store coordinated direct mail campaign
   c. Online coupon distributed by the manufacturer
   d. In-store coupon within a flyer

e. A coupon within product packaging applying to the next purchase
f. An on-package coupon for immediate redemption
g. An on-package coupon for mail-in redemption

4. General Motors (GM) regularly provides summer discounts to U.S. auto buyers. Consider the metrics of targeting, temporary, special, and irregular promotions. Are summer discounts a good form of price promotions for GM? Why do you make this claim? What would you want to know before determining if the summer discounts are a good form of price promotion?
5. Quaker Oats often, but not always, puts coupons within the package of a box of Quaker Oats for redemption on the next purchase. These coupons provide discounts not only on the product purchased, but also on other Quaker Oats products. Consider the metrics of targeting, temporary, special, and irregular promotions. Are the in-package coupons a good form of price promotion for Quaker Oats? Why? What would you want to know before determining if in-package coupons are a good form of price promotion?
6. A branded coffee manufacturer is considering a nationwide coupon campaign distributed via the newspaper. Complete the following chart to evaluate the effectiveness of the effort.
   a. Distribution Costs
   b. Coupons Redeemed
   c. Redemption Costs
   d. Total Campaign Costs
   e. Cost per Buyer
   f. Total Campaign Profit
   g. ROI
   h. Break-even Incremental Unit Sales per Redemption
   i. Do you believe that this campaign will be effective? Why or not?

Coupon Face Value	$0.40
Processing Fee	$0.07
Price	$2.40
Margin	30%
Coupons Distributed	30,000,000
Cost/1000 Distributed	$10
Distribution Costs	
Redemption Rate	7%
Coupons Redeemed	
Redemption Costs	
Total Campaign Costs	
Cost per Buyer	
Total Campaign Profit	
ROI	
Break-even Incremental Unit Sales per Redemption	

7. A veterinarian's office is considering a direct-mail local coupon campaign. After purchasing a list of local residents and removing all current customers, the veterinarian's office offers a $30-off coupon. Complete the following chart to evaluate the effectiveness of the effort.
   a. Distribution Costs
   b. Coupons Redeemed
   c. Redemption Costs
   d. Total Campaign Costs
   e. Cost per Buyer
   f. Total Campaign Profit
   g. ROI
   h. Break-even Incremental Unit Sales per Redemption
   i. Do you believe that this campaign will be effective? Why or not?

Coupon Face Value	$30
Processing Fee	$0
Price	$97
Margin	90%
Coupons Distributed	1,700
Cost/1000 Distributed	$882.35
Distribution Costs	
Redemption Rate	2%
Coupons Redeemed	
Redemption Costs	
Total Campaign Costs	
Cost per Buyer	
Total Campaign Profit	
ROI	
Break-even Incremental Unit Sales per Redemption	

8. Best Buy has decided not to distribute mail-in rebates, but it does want to distribute instant rebates. Adobe has typically used mail-in rebates of $200 on its Creative Suite software as a form of price promotion. Only 60 percent of those who qualify and receive the mail-in rebate coupon actually redeem the coupon. What is the best offer Adobe should make to Best Buy with respect to redeeming instant rebates? If Adobe chooses to exceed this value, identify three concessions Adobe might desire in return.

9. Before conducting a price promotion, executives of a well-known branded good decide to conduct an analysis of the break-even incremental unit sales per redemption. They then determine that the price promotion is highly likely to overcome this hurdle. Why might they still decide against the price promotion?

Notes

[1] For a detailed examination of the effect of price promotions on profitability, see Shuba Srinivasan, Koen Pauwels, Dominique M. Hanssens, and Marnik G. Dekimpe, "Do Promotions Benefit Manufacturers, Retailers, or Both?" *Management Science* 50, No. 5 (May 2004): 617–29.

[2] Chakravarthi Narasimhan, "A Price Discrimination Theory of Coupons," *Marketing Science* 3, No. 2 (Spring 1984): 128–47.

[3] For an overview of the effectiveness of price promotions to drive volume, see Robert C. Blattberg, Richard Briesch, and Edward J. Fox, "How Promotions Work," *Marketing Science, Part 2 of 2: Special Issue on Empirical Generalizations in Marketing* 14, No. 3 (1995): G122–G132.

[4] Promotional effects of national brands competing against generic brands were examined in Ram C. Rao, "Pricing and Promotions in Asymmetric Duopolies," *Marketing Science* 10, No. 2 (Spring 1991): 131–44. Rajiv Lal, "Price Promotions: Limiting Competitive Encroachment," *Marketing Science* 9, No. 3 (Summer 1990): 247–62.

[5] J. Morgan Jones and Fred S. Zufryden, "Relating Deal Purchases and Consumer Characteristics to Repeat Purchase Probability," *Journal of the Marketing Research Society* 23, No. 2 (1981): 84–99.

[6] Alfred A. Kuehn and Albert C. Rohloff, "Consumer Response to Promotions," in *Promotional Decisions Using Mathematical Models*, ed. Patrick J. Robinson (Boston: Allyn and Bacon, 1967): 71.

[7] Hi-Lo pricing practiced to shift inventory was discussed by Robert C. Blattberg, Gary D. Eppen, and Joshua Lieberman, "A Theoretical and Empirical Evaluation of Price Deals for Consumer Nondurables," *Journal of Marketing* 45 (Winter 1981): 116–29.

[8] Kamel Jedidi, Carl F. Mela, and Sunil Gupta, "Managing Advertising and Promotion for Long-Run Profitability," *Marketing Science* 18, No. 1 (1999): 1–22.

[9] João L. Assuncão, and Robert J. Meyer. "The Rational Effect of Price Promotions on Sales and Consumption," *Management Science* 39, No. 5 (May 1993): 517–35.

[10] The model shown in Exhibit 7-1 is from Scott A. Neslin and Robert W. Shoemaker, "A Model for Evaluating the Profitability of Coupon Promotions," *Marketing Science* 2, No. 4 (Autumn 1983): 361–88. An alternative model can be found in Praveen K. Kopalle, Carl F. Mela, and Lawrence Marsh, "The Dynamic Effect of Discounting on Sales: Empirical Analysis and Normative Pricing Implications," *Marketing Science* 18, No. 3, Special Issue on Managerial Decision Making (1999): 317–32.

[11] Eric A. Greenleaf, "The Impact of Reference Price Effects on the Profitability of Price Promotions," *Marketing Science* 14, No. 1 (1995): 82–104.

[12] Bundled promotions were examined in Bram Foubert and Els Gijsbrechts, "Shopper Response to Bundle Promotions for Packaged Goods," *Journal of Marketing Research*. 44, No. 4 (Nov 2007): 647–62.

[13] This model is very similar to that found in Scott A. Neslin, "A Market Response Model for Coupon Promotions," *Marketing Science* 9, No. 2 (1990): 125–45.

[14] Research into the ranking of competitive, demographic, and retail store format on discount sensitivity has been undertaken by Peter Boatwright, Sanjay Dhar, and Peter E. Rossi, "The Role of Retail Competition, Demographics, and Account Retail Strategy as Drivers of Promotional Sensitivity," *Quantitative Marketing and Economics* 2, No. 2 (June 2004): 169–90.

[15] For an analytical examination of reference price effects in Hi-Lo vs. EDLP channels, see Prafeen V. Kopalle, Ambar G. Rao, João L. Assuncão, "Asymmetric Reference Price Effects and Dynamic Pricing Policies," *Marketing Science* 15, No. 1 (Winter 1996): 60–85.

[16] Field studies demonstrated the profit-enhancing capability of Hi-Lo pricing over EDLP pricing in a number of products. See Stephen J. Hoch, Xavier Drèze, and Mary E. Purk, "EDLP, Hi-Lo, and Margin Arithmetic," *Journal of Marketing*, 58, No. 4 (October 1994): 16–27.

Chapter 8

Discount Management

Andersen Ross/Stockbyte/Jupiterimages

- How should discount decisions be managed?
- Why might some executives push for more discounts, while others push for fewer?
- What is the best way to connect explicit knowledge with implicit knowledge when managing discount decisions?
- How can senior executives monitor and manage thousands of individual discounting decisions at a high level?
- What are the carrots and sticks that can be used to encourage better discounting decisions?
- Stretch Question: Should every discount decision be made routine through quantitative analysis and checklists?

It has often been said that discount management is a game of improvement by inches that delivers miles of better performance. Many seemingly small decisions have incrementally small effects on the firm's performance, and yet the sum of these decisions can lead to overwhelmingly strong results. Because discounting decisions can either improve or harm profits, because they arise frequently and with great variety, and because they tend to suffer from the difficulty of telling how much is too much, firms will often dedicate tremendous resources towards managing discount decisions.

An organizational challenge arises when you have to determine how discounting decisions should be managed and who should make discounting decisions. Discount management is a natural source of conflict within any organization due to the differing objectives and beliefs that executives hold. To improve decision-making regarding discounting, firms have developed techniques for monitoring discounts, managing decisions, and aligning organizational incentives. In this chapter, we begin by exploring the source of organizational conflict with respect to discount management before turning to some of the systems and structures executives have developed as solutions for managing discount decisions.

Challenges in Discount Management Policy

Discounting decisions have challenged organizational cohesion and design for decades. One of the most common discount management challenges facing organizations is the disparity in incentives and knowledge between field and centralized executives.

FIELD EXECUTIVES PUSH FOR MORE DISCOUNTS

Salespeople and marketing communications executives in the field are encouraged to pursue market share. Their incentives, which take the form of bonuses and promotions as well as peer recognition, are often tied to their ability to increase sales volume and achieve targets. In fact, at one time it was common to set bonus structures for field executives in direct proportion to the volume they sold; this practice still continues in some firms today. With these kinds of incentives, it is not uncommon for field executives to move quickly toward discounts to achieve volume targets.

To meet lofty sales goals, field executives are faced with some unpalatable options. They may undertake the herculean task of uncovering more sales opportunities and simultaneously communicate the value to prospects to increase the volume of units sold and capture better prices. Most firms hire field executives to achieve precisely these goals. However, discounts can appear as a quicker and easier way to capture volume and at least deliver on some of these objectives. Moreover, the lofty sales goals given to field executives are sometimes unrealistic in the absence of discounting.

If sales require distributors, field executives must increase the number of distribution sites and the willingness of those distribution outlets to support the product to meet their volume targets. Manufacturer-financed price promotions and discounts are two tools that can help them achieve both greater distribution and stronger distribution support. In many situations, these tools are not just price concessions but necessary techniques to gain channel support and improve profitability.

Especially in high-value single sales situations, the needs of an individual field executive and those of the firm may be misaligned due to differences in risk bearing. When a salesperson faces the possibility of losing a valuable sale, the risk borne by the salesperson of losing that specific sale is greater than the risk borne by the firm, which typically manages multiple sales opportunities at a time. The firm can diversify its sales risk by pursuing multiple high-value single sales opportunities at a time. Salespeople at these firms often can do so only limitedly, if at all. Therefore, the salesperson may bear more risk than the firm with respect to a specific sales opportunity. To improve the probability of closing a single sales opportunity, it is not unnatural for the salesperson to feel a greater pressure than the firm to provide customers with price concessions.

Given these incentives, a firm can find itself in a disastrous situation if it abdicates all discounting authority to field executives alone. Even in businesses where incentives for field executives are more in line with the organizational goals, there is still a need to manage discounting decisions to avoid abusive price concessions.

CENTRALIZED EXECUTIVES PUSH FOR HIGHER PRICES

At corporate headquarters, product managers and other centralized executives often focus on capturing the highest price possible while expecting the volume to simply be delivered. Incentives for these centralized executives, which take the form of compensation, promotions, and peer respect, are often correlated with their ability to create products with a strong demand at a high price. After all, higher prices and larger market projections are strategies that senior executives and investors are very likely to support. Lower-priced items and low–market penetration ideas are routinely met with little interest. Given decision-making authority over strategic issues of product design and pricing, centralized executives may focus on marketing high-value products while holding expectations for field executives to extract high prices from their customers. As such, discounts often contradict the basic decision paradigm to extract a high price from the market in every transaction.

From either economic value models, customer perception–based research, or econometric price optimization methods, executives will identify prices that are appropriate on average, but in some circumstances will be higher than the willingness of specific customers to pay. These methods of identifying the market's willingness to pay often lump the entire market (or at least entire market segments) into a homogeneous group. However, price promotions and discounts may allow for finer market segmentation—market segmentation at a level that could not be predicted easily from a higher-level analysis, which in turn can account for disparity in willingness to pay between individual customers within the market. Centralized executives often lack the necessary tacit knowledge of the market required to make proper discounting decisions.

DISPARITY ABOUNDS

The disparity in incentives and knowledge between field and centralized executives leads to a natural conflict between them regarding discounts. Field executives will commonly call for greater discounts, while centralized executives will argue for fewer, if not zero, discounts. As we have seen, neither decision is optimal in all situations.

If discount decisions are yielded to field executives alone, the firm can expect to find a wide and growing disparity between list prices and actual selling prices. If all discount decisions are made centrally, the firm may be missing out on profit-enhancing price segmentation opportunities. Senior executives must narrow the disparity between these two outcomes to improve profits, but the path to narrowing this disparity requires the development of new organizational capabilities.

EXECUTIVES REACT

To halt the potential downward spiral in prices through discounting, some executives take a knee-jerk response and halt all discounts. Such a move is not only disruptive, it is also unprofitable. As has been discussed earlier, discounting is a form of price segmentation. If properly executed, price segmentation can improve profits. A profit-maximizing firm should not necessarily seek to halt all discounts; rather, it should seek to ensure that the discounts granted are those that meet the design requirements of price-segmenting the market and improving profitability.

As an intermediate move, some senior executives have sought to remove all discount decision-making authority from the field and manage it centrally. Unfortunately, even this intermediate move has often been found to be untenable for many firms. The productivity improvements created by reassigning decisions to those executives closest to the situation and possessing the most facts are real. In a large organization with hundreds of salespeople interacting with multiple channel partners or customers every day, senior executives are unable to devote the necessary intellectual capacity to the hundreds of discounting decisions that are made every day within the organization. Even if senior executives could spend the required time for every discounting decision, they would lack much of the required implicit knowledge required to make the optimal decision—knowledge that is held by the field executives and generated by their direct interaction with customers and channel partners. One of the key reasons to hire field executives is to make field decisions, including discounting decisions.

Discounting policy is naturally dispersed through various levels within an organization precisely because different parts of the organization bring different insights into the decision-making challenge. Centralized senior executives bring value to discount decision-making through their ability to aggregate multiple sources of data into a cohesive understanding. Meanwhile, decentralized field executives bring value to decision-making through uncovering specific facts and points of information regarding a particular decision-making challenge. In setting discount policy, one of the goals is to combine the power of these disparate sources of value-added decision-making insights, centralized oversight and field-gathered facts, to foster better decisions.

One might describe this as the challenge of marrying explicit knowledge to tacit knowledge. Explicit knowledge is knowledge that can be codified and transferred from one individual to another. It is knowledge that can be made explicit and be shared easily. Tacit or implicit knowledge is knowledge that is held by the knower and is difficult to trace to its source. With tacit knowledge, the knower is often unaware of the knowledge he or she possesses or how it can be valuable to others. Transferring tacit knowledge requires extensive communication. The tacit aspects of knowledge are those that cannot be codified; they can be transmitted via training or gained through personal experience, but not easily by any other means. Transference of tacit knowledge involves learning and skills, but not in a way that can be written down efficiently.

By interacting directly with customers or channel partners, field executives hold tacit knowledge that is valuable in making decisions regarding discounts. At the same time, centralized executives use explicit knowledge to make decisions and support field executives' actions. To marry the tacit knowledge of field executives to the explicit knowledge of centralized executives, many firms have adopted a common set of routines, analysis, and incentives to ensure that both field executives and centralized managers are aligned in working towards a common goal.

Identifying Discounting Management Opportunities

The three key analysis tools commonly used to measure, understand, and manage discounts explicitly are the net price band, the relationship between net prices captured and market variables, and the price waterfall. The net price band enables executives to grasp the level of discounting within the firm quickly. The relationship between net prices captured and market variables enables executives to uncover potential drivers to discounting, some of which may reflect competitive pressures while others may reflect opportunities for improved management. The price waterfall enables executives to identify the magnitude of the impact of specific types of discounts and potentially uncover a means of reshaping discounts to improve their profit impact. Combined, these three discount-monitoring tools provide a high-level aggregated picture of the firm's discounting practices that enables a quick executive review of price discounting and the potential for improving profitability.

The net price band, price to market variable, and price waterfall discount-monitoring tools have been developed mostly within industrial markets due to the unique nature of customer transactions and the magnitude of discounting within these industries. However, to illustrate the power of these monitoring tools for informing discount decisions, we will use a hypothetical firm working in a consumer market, because most readers are more aware of the specifics of consumer markets than industrial markets. SoftCo is a representative example of a consumer software product firm that distributes its products through consumer retail channels. While the specifics of this example are unique to consumer software firms, the overall approach described here can be used in any market. Consumer and business markets, tangible and intangible products, and products ranging from commodity to differentiated to niche all benefit from the application of these three analytical monitoring tools.

NET PRICE BAND

One of the most basic analytical tools for developing a high-level understanding of discounts is identifying the net price and plotting the net price band.[1] The net price is the actual price paid by customers after accounting for all forms of discounts, including on-invoice and off-invoice discounts. Firms use the net price rather than the average selling price as some forms of discounts are made obvious to customers by placing them on the invoice itself, whereas other forms of discounts are not necessarily on the invoice itself. Off-invoice discounts affect the actual transaction price, but are not on the invoice at the time of sale for various reasons. For instance, channel performance rebates may reduce the total invoice on future invoices but will not appear at the time of sale. Other items related to shifting costs from the buyer to the seller can also be conceptualized as discounts, and thus would reduce the net price paid by the customer. See Exhibit 8-1 for an example list of discount forms and their positions as "on-" or "off-invoice".)

The strategic informational value of net price band plots is in uncovering price heterogeneity and identifying unprofitable transactions. Some of the difference in net price paid may be driven by a true underlying form of market heterogeneity, or differences in willingness to pay between customers. In this case, a net price band plot can signal to senior executives the potential to identify which customers are more profitable, the opportunity to encourage behavioral changes among less-profitable customers, or the potential need to redirect chronically unprofitable customers. Unprofitable transactions identified from the net price band signal the need to make determinations to either eliminate or reduce such transactions.

For example, SoftCo's consumer product has a manufacturer's suggested retail price (MSRP) of $39.99. In selling through various retail channels, SoftCo offers a variety of discounting mechanisms, where the largest one accounts for retailer margin. Yet even after accounting for retailer margin, the net price captured by SoftCo varies from transaction to transaction. To show how the net price varies, we construct a net price band, a bar-plot of the volume of units sold within a specific price band. See Exhibit 8-2.

From the net price band, SoftCo discovers that there is significant variance in the magnitude of discounts within the market. Some of this variance can be properly attributed to price segmentation techniques that capture marginal customers and improve marginal profits, while other portions may be due to improper discounting practices. Before we detect the drivers of the price variance, let us first examine how the net price band alone informs decisions.

Variations in net price between different transactions are not uncommon; indeed, they are the norm. Moreover, observed variations in net price tend to be quite wide. For instance, in consumer products, a lighting fixture manufacturer observed a variance in net price of 60 percent and a computer peripherals supplier observed a variance in net price of 70 percent. In business products, a specialty chemical firm observed a variance in net price of 200 percent and a fastener supplier observed a variance in net price of 500 percent.

Exhibit 8-1 Price Discounts and Concessions

Typical On-Invoice Items

- Standard dealer/distributor discounts: industry-standard trade terms for specific channel arrangements
- Order size discount: discounts given based on order size or order volume
- Multiple SKU discount: discount allocated to an item based on channel partners stocking a larger variety of items
- Competitive discount: discounts given specifically to win business that would have gone to a competitor in the absence of the discount
- Exceptional discounts: other forms of discounts that are specific to that customer or channel partner

Typical Off-Invoice Items

- Cooperative advertising: an allowance paid to channel partners to support local advertising of a manufacturer's brand
- Slotting allowance: an allowance paid to retailers to secure a set amount of shelf space and product positioning
- Market-development funds: a discount to promote sales to a specific market segment
- Coupon redemption: reimbursed funds for redemption of manufacturers' coupons
- Off-invoice promotions: a marketing incentive that would, for example, give retailers an additional rebate for each unit sold during a specific promotional time period
- Consignment costs: the costs of funds when a supplier provides consigned inventory to a retailer or wholesaler
- Stocking allowances: a discount paid to wholesalers or retailers to make large purchases into inventory, often just before a seasonal increase in demand
- User rebate: a rebate paid to a retailer for selling a product to a specific customer (often a large or national customer) at a discount
- Quarterly volume bonus: an end-of-quarter bonus paid to channel partners if preset purchase volume targets are met
- Receivables carrying costs: the cost of funds from the moment an invoice is sent until payment is received
- Cash discounts: a deduction from the invoice price if payment is made quickly, for instance within fifteen days
- Freight: the supplier's costs of transporting goods to a customer
- Online order discount: a discount offered to customers ordering over the Internet
- Performance discount: a discount that the seller agrees to give buyers if the seller meets performance targets, such as quality levels or delivery times

Some of the variance in net price paid is due to true underlying differences in the ability to capture higher prices within the market arising from a variation between customers or market segments. For example, firms regularly take on low-margin business to satisfy certain large-volume customers who improve capacity utilization, while also serving numerous low-volume customers who purchase at a higher net price. Examining net price by market variables may uncover strategic insights into which customer segments are truly more profitable and which are not.

If the variable cost to produce SoftCo's product was $14, SoftCo would identify quickly from the net price band that roughly 5 percent of the units sold were actually unprofitable. In this case, SoftCo can take steps to eliminate these transactions immediately, either by correcting poor discounting decisions or by requiring those customers to pay a higher price.

A wide net price band informs executives of opportunities for improvement. Dropping a few sales in the lowest net price band and adding a few in the highest net price band

Exhibit 8-2 Net Price Band

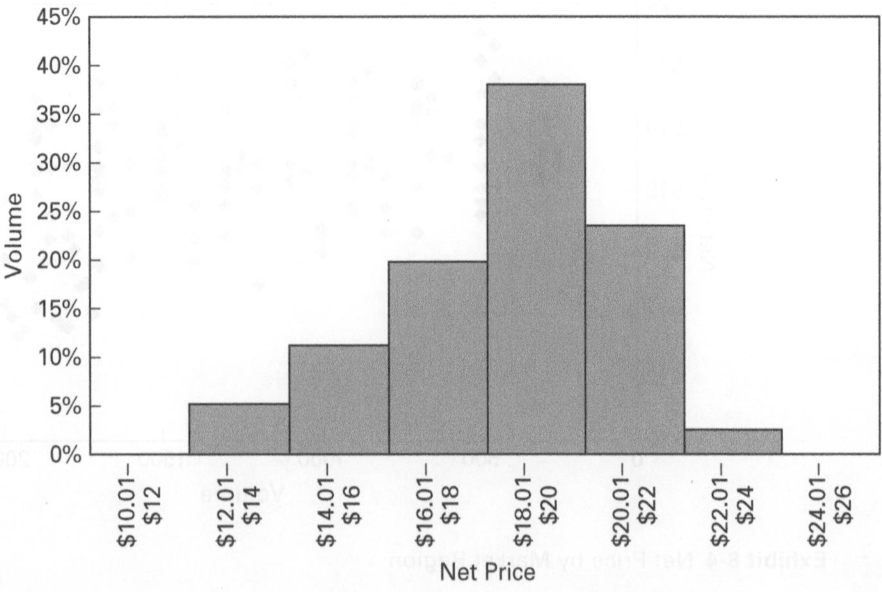

can improve profitability dramatically. To do this, firms can seek to move customers to the more appropriate and profitable discount levels while also acquiring new customers who fit the profile of those most likely to pay a higher price.

NET PRICE BY MARKET VARIABLE

If the net price band is wide and executives conclude that there is sufficient room for improvement, their next step is typically to examine the net price paid by certain market segments. This is the net price by market variable. This approach enables senior executives to identify quickly whether there is slack in sales management and potential to improve discounting practices within the firm or if there are true differences between market segments.

Differences in net price paid are often driven by some underlying segmentation variable within the market.[2] Examining the net price paid by various market segmentation variables may uncover the driver of price variations. Alternatively, examining the net price paid by sales territory may identify specific salespeople who may require better training and oversight when it comes to discounting, or it may reveal the potential to transfer best practices between sales leaders and sales followers so that the firm can capture higher prices.

Returning to the example of SoftCo, senior executives suspected that price variances may be related to volume discounts. To examine this suspicion, they plotted net prices against volume sold to various channels. The plot appears in Exhibit 8-3. If net prices had been related to sales volume, the scatter plot would demonstrate an overall downward trend where higher volumes would be related to lower prices. For SoftCo, this trend was unobserved. Higher-level statistical analysis may reveal a relationship between sales volume and net price, but the plot alone yielded sufficient evidence for the management of SoftCo that the valuable source of price variances may be another driver.

Another suspected driver of price variation was the region served. To examine this factor, net prices were plotted according to the market region. See Exhibit 8-4. The large

Exhibit 8-3 Net Price to Sales Volume

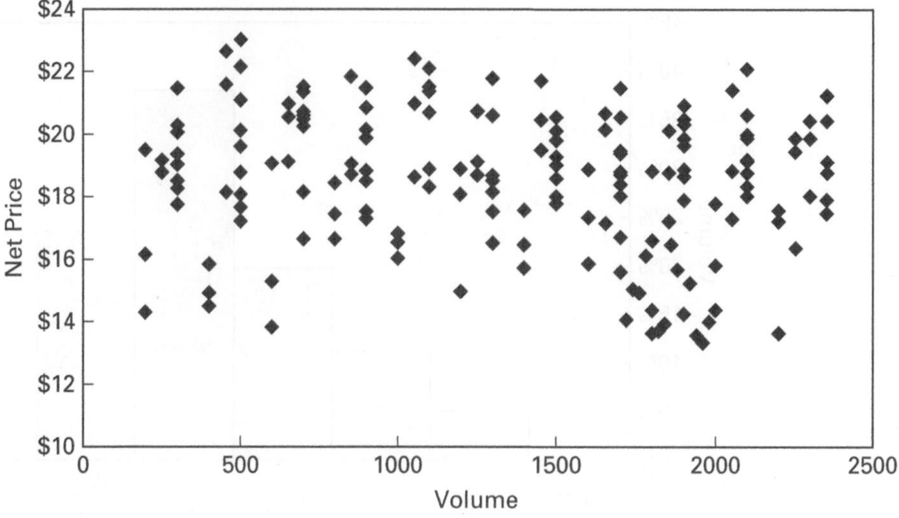

Exhibit 8-4 Net Price by Market Region

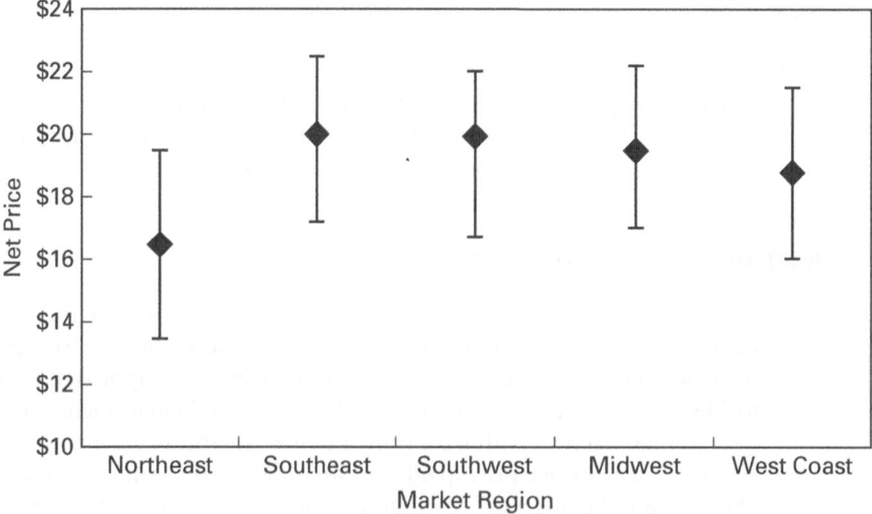

diamonds identify the average net price in various regions, while the upper and lower bars identify the range of prices within that region. From this plot, executives are able to determine quickly that the Northeast region was facing significantly greater discounting challenges than all other regions, thus deserving greater managerial attention.

Similar to the plots of net price to volume or net price to market regions, executives can examine other potential sources of price variances and market heterogeneity. For instance, if shipping is a typical negotiation point or cost issue, executives may find value in examining net prices against distance shipped, similar to that of net price to volume, to uncover the seriousness of the issue. Alternatively, if competitive presence, sales territory, channel type, or other categorical issues may be considered as a driver of price differences, plots similar to that of net price to market region can be used to identify categorical issues that drive price variances. Executives may find it necessary to examine several different variables prior to identifying the specific issues that correlate with net prices. Statistical analysis will aid this process.

PRICE WATERFALL

The third means of aggregating data concerning discounting for senior executive review is the price waterfall. As stated, the net price band identifies the size of the opportunity for improving discount practices. Once the opportunity has been identified, the more strategic area for improving discount practices is in identifying market segmentation variables that lead to different discounting phenomena. These segmentation variables can be used to direct market development investments and other efforts to capture more sales from the more profitable segments of the market. Net price by market variable analysis is typically useful in this endeavor. The third method, price waterfalls, takes a more intensive approach to improving net prices. Price waterfalls enable senior executives to uncover relationships between the form of the price discount and customer price sensitivity.

Price waterfalls identify the discounts provided and their effects on the differences between the internal reference price and the net price. The internal reference price may be the MSRP, the list price, or some other form of base price from which all discounts are granted. Price waterfalls plot the type of discount given, the timing of that discount, and the size of those discounts. They include both on-invoice and off-invoice discount types, and provide a holistic view into the impact and types of different discounts. See Exhibit 8-5 for an example using the SoftCo scenario.

Exhibit 8-5 Price Waterfall

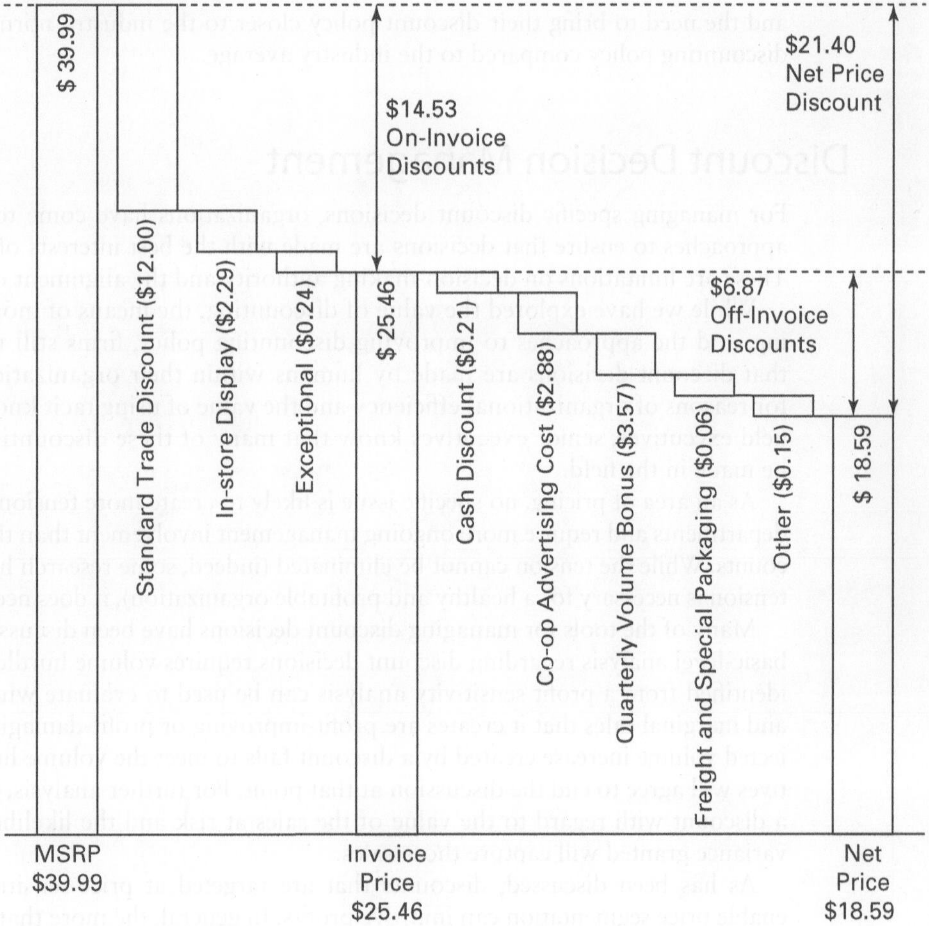

Price waterfalls are useful for two reasons. First, they highlight the types of discounts that the firm provides and their impact on actual net prices, and therefore profitability. Second, they create a model for exploring potential means of reducing discounts without affecting profits, and perhaps even of improving net volumes.

For instance, brand manufacturers operating in retail markets often give both trade allowances and promotional allowances, perhaps in the form of cooperative advertising or in-store displays. Branded manufacturers may find that sales at the retail level are more sensitive to the dollars spent on in-store displays than on cooperative advertising. As such, executives may determine that it is in their best interest to shift discount dollars out of the budget for cooperative advertising and increase discount allowances for in-store displays. The effect is of shaping the price waterfalls.

Shaping the price waterfalls is a technique designed to shift discounts into areas where they deliver greater improvements in volume and reduce discounts from the types that have little impact on sales. Firms often find that sales volumes to different customers or through channels are sensitive to different types of discounts. The price waterfall enables senior executives to review quickly the discounts provided and their effectiveness, and to test different hypotheses regarding discount structures to identify the most profitable discounting policy.

Each discount identified in a price waterfall represents an opportunity for potential improvement. The market may be more sensitive to some forms of discounts than others. As such, the firm profits by shifting discounts out of forms that the market is less sensitive, and into areas where they have a greater impact. Similarly, the firm may find that it is offering some forms of discount to a greater or lesser degree than its competitors. Again, when such an area is identified, executives can determine the impact of those discounts and the need to bring their discount policy closer to the industry norm or improve their discounting policy compared to the industry average.

Discount Decision Management

For managing specific discount decisions, organizations have come to rely on two key approaches to ensure that decisions are made with the best interests of the firm at heart. These are limitations on decision-making authority and the alignment of incentives.

While we have explored the value of discounting, the means of monitoring discounting, and the approaches to improving discounting policy, firms still must face the fact that discount decisions are made by humans within their organizations. Furthermore, for reasons of organizational efficiency and the value of using tacit knowledge gained by field executives, senior executives know that many of these discounting decisions must be made in the field.

As an area of pricing, no specific issue is likely to create more tension between different departments and require more ongoing management involvement than those related to discounts. While the tension cannot be eliminated (indeed, some research has shown that this tension is necessary for a healthy and profitable organization), it does need to be managed.[3]

Many of the tools for managing discount decisions have been discussed previously. The basic-level analysis regarding discount decisions requires volume hurdles. Volume hurdles identified from a profit sensitivity analysis can be used to evaluate whether the discount and marginal sales that it creates are profit-improving or profit-damaging. When the projected volume increase created by a discount fails to meet the volume hurdle, most executives will agree to end the discussion at that point. For further analysis, firms can examine a discount with regard to the value of the sales at risk and the likelihood that the price variance granted will capture those sales.

As has been discussed, discounts that are targeted at price-sensitive customers and enable price segmentation can improve profits. In general, the more that a discount affects a specific objective, and the higher the value of meeting that objective, the more valuable that discount becomes to the firm. Sometimes, this rule even overrides the restrictions on discounts uncovered through a profit sensitivity analysis.

These guidelines regarding discounts and other forms of price variances are useful for informing decisions, but these guidelines alone do not ensure that individual managers make good discounting decisions. Discount decisions, as discussed, are naturally dispersed within the organization. Many independent executives contribute to discount decisions every day. Organizations need more than guidelines to manage these independent decisions; they need decision management systems.

To improve independent decision-making regarding discounts, organizations use a management framework. Two key approaches have been pursued to improve the decision management framework. The first is to restrict decision-making rights within the organization, assigning the responsibility for decisions that might have the highest impact to executives with the greatest oversight. The second is to restructure incentives to encourage better alignment between the motivations that influence field management decisions and the organization's goals.

DECISION RIGHTS

As a first line of defense against abusive discounting, organizations will limit decision-making rights within the organization. Individual salespeople may be granted limited discretion over discounting. Discount requests greater than that which individual executives are allowed to grant are then referred to higher-level managers for their approval or rejection. In this manner, discount decisions are escalated up through the organization as their impact increases.

For instance, specific salespeople may be given authority to grant combined discounts up to 2.5 percent. Beyond 2.5 percent, salespeople must request authorization for the discount from their territory manager. Territory managers may also face some limitations on their decision-making authority, perhaps driving all discounts that result in a 5 percent or greater net price variance to be referred to sales executive managers for review. For discounts beyond 9 percent, sales executive managers must confer with their chief executive officer (CEO). The CEO retains authority for any discounts greater than 9 percent. In this manner, discount decisions are escalated up the organization as the depth of the discount increases. Actual cutoff points are specific to the firm and vary between industries.

Other forms of limiting discount decision-making authority and escalating discount decisions are common. Some firms find it more useful to include limitations on discounts based on dollar amounts. Small total dollar discounts are left up to the discretion of lower-level managers, while larger total dollar amount discounts require approval by senior executives. Discount decisions can also be restricted according to type, such as allowing larger discounts when related to market development funds and smaller discounts when related to cash payments, freight, and other accounting or operational functions. Alternatively, discount decision-making rights may be related to discount purposes where certain market segments are deemed of greater strategic importance to the firm than others and the organization seeks to fast-track decisions related to specific strategic initiatives.

DECISION INCENTIVES

A supplementary means of improving decision-making within the organization is through improving the alignment of the incentives facing decision makers and the goals of the organization. This implies that the financial incentive structure, or more specifically the compensation package offered to individuals with discount authority, is structured to address certain decision biases that those individuals may hold.

Organizations typically aim for long-term financial health, but field executives typically are rewarded for short-term financial performance. In the face of the short-term financial rewards for individual salespeople, they may be encouraged to grant discounts more freely than would be most beneficial to the firm so that they meet their short-term sales objectives. Many organizations have changed a portion of the financial incentives of salespeople to address the time-orientation differences between the salespeople and the organization as a whole.

Within the sales compensation package, there are often several factors. Salespeople often earn a base salary or draw against future earnings to ensure some financial stability throughout the natural volatility in closing sales opportunities. On top of this base earning potential, salespeople typically face highly leveraged earnings, where bonuses and commissions are set in proportion to performance. Some of these performance incentives may be set according to behavioral objectives, such as teamwork or compliance with broader corporate goals, but most performance incentives are based on sales.

The sales performance portion of the incentive package for salespeople has undergone many improvements over the years. The dominant orientations have been to provide performance incentives based on volume, revenue, or profits.

Volume-based performance objectives are used in some industries; however, they fail to provide any incentive to reduce discounts. If salespeople have no discounting authority, volume-based performance incentives are not necessarily bad. However, most industries grant salespeople some discretion over discounting. In these industries, volume-based performance incentives are misaligned with any corporate objectives in capturing higher prices and minimizing discounts.

Revenue-based performance incentives represent a better alignment between the desires of salespeople and those of the organization. With revenue-based incentives, a discount lowers the revenue earned and thus decreases the monetary compensation for the individual salesperson while also decreasing the revenue of the firm. However, we have seen that a 30 percent decrease in price affects the profitability of the firm far more than 30 percent, perhaps even making the sale totally unprofitable. Meanwhile, when performance incentives are based on revenue, a 30 percent decrease in price can decrease the salesperson's compensation by only 30 percent, and it will decrease the compensation by less than 30 percent if he or she also earns a base salary. Given the choice of angering a customer by saying "no" to a discount request or pestering the firm for a discount on behalf of the customer, salespeople whose income is based on revenue will often choose the latter. Even revenue-based performance incentives are insufficient to align the goals of individual salespeople properly with those of the firm.[4]

The third approach has been to tie performance incentives to profits.[5] Alternatively named profit- or kicker-based commissions, performance incentives tied to profits increase when net prices are above targets, and they decrease when they fall below targets. In their most aggressive forms, profit-based commissions actually increase and decrease sales compensation more than they do individual sales profitability. An example formula for calculating the profit-based commission is provided in Equation 8.1:

$$\text{Sales Credit} = [\text{Target Price} - k\,(\text{Target Price} - \text{Actual Price})] \cdot \text{Units Sold} \qquad \text{Eq. 8.1}$$

The kicker, k in Equation 8.1, is a factor greater than or equal to 1 divided by the percentage contribution margin at the target price. For instance, if the contribution margin at the target price is 25 percent, the kicker should be 4 or higher. With a kicker of 4, a 10 percent discount reduces the sales credit by 40 percent, rather than 10 percent. This is in line with the effect of a discount on the profitability of the firm. Because salespeople often take a shorter-term view of the firm than do management (they can always move on), some authors suggest raising the kicker even higher than 1 over the target contribution margin to bring their incentives more in line with the corporate goals.

Tying sales incentives to profits and using kicker-based commissions is not for the fainthearted. Even though the shift from revenue-based incentives to profit-based incentives can be structured such that the change in the sales commission structure leaves the average salesperson unaffected while further rewarding the best salespeople and strongly encouraging behavioral changes among the worst, firms that make this change face multiple disruptions. Many executives who have adapted profit-based commissions found that most salespeople embrace the change, stay, and thrive, some are more lukewarm and adjust with time, and a minority move on to new positions. Departure rates as high as 30 percent have been reported anecdotally.

On the positive side, executives that have changed to profit-based performance incentives have also reported a change in the behavior of their salespeople. Specifically, salespeople have been observed to shift their requests from discounts to requests for further marketing support. These newly rejuvenated salespeople are often found hunting for further evidence to justify a higher price or asking for and creating other value-based sales messages. This will shift the pressure point from being between salespeople and price managers to being between sales and marketing communications or sales and product management.

Summary

- Discount management consumes tremendous organizational resources due to the frequency and variety of discounting. Furthermore, the fundamental vagueness of figuring out how much discounting is too much makes discounting decisions challenging.
- Natural tension arises within an organization around discount management due to conflicting sources of organizational productivity. The value of increased productivity by pushing discounting questions further down into the organization conflicts with the value of closely managing price variances. The value of exploiting tacit knowledge held by field managers conflicts with general beliefs developed from explicit knowledge held by senior executives.
- Aggravating the challenges in discount management are conflicting incentives between short-term sales objectives and long-term strategic objectives, and conflicting risk profiles between field executives charged with specific sales opportunities and senior executives managing a wider portfolio of sales opportunities.
- While knee-jerk reactions to excessive price discounting that end up prohibiting all discounts may halt the increasing disparity between prices set at the strategic level and those tactically used in the market, they may also damage profitability due to the value of using price discounts in price segmentation and capturing marginal sales.
- The three key approaches to monitoring discount practices are net price bands, net price by market variable, and price waterfalls.
- Net price is the actual price paid by customers after all forms of discounts have been accounted for, including both on-invoice and off-invoice discounts. Net price bands highlight the heterogeneity in effective price paid and potentially identify unprofitable transactions for elimination. High levels of heterogeneity in net price paid indicate the possibility of improving profitability by decreasing the unit sales with lower profitability and increasing unit sales with higher profitability.
- Plots of net price against market variables enable senior executives to uncover drivers of net price heterogeneity. These drivers can be used to identify market segments or practices that are more profitable as opposed to those that are less profitable.

- Price waterfalls enable senior executives to uncover relationships between the form of the price discount and customer price sensitivity. They identify the size and type of discounts used and their effect on net price paid.
- From an organizational viewpoint, two key approaches for price discount management are limiting decision-making rights and altering decision incentives.
- In price discounting decisions, best practices assign different depths or types of discounts to different levels within the organization. Those seeking discounts beyond their decision-making rights must escalate the decision up the organization.
- Improvements to incentives regarding discount decisions have focused on shifting performance-based incentives from volume to revenue, and from revenue to profits. Shifting performance-based incentives to transactional profits has proved daunting for many organizations.

Exercises

1. Real-estate agents typically work on pure commission. A study found that agents tend to keep their own homes on the market for an average of ten additional days and sell it for more than 3 percent more than a client's home.[6]
   a. For whom does a discount have a larger negative effect, the homeowner or the real-estate agent?
   b. Is the financial incentive of a real estate agent aligned with a homeowner?
2. Discussion question: What is the difference between explicit knowledge and implicit knowledge? Should all discounting rules be strictly enforced? How should a firm manage exceptions?
3. How can heterogeneity in willingness to pay be revealed through a net price band?
4. A maker of silicones conducts a net price by market variable investigation and discovers that prices tend to be lower for customers who have little need for service and tend to buy in bulk. Executives consider two options: reducing marketing oriented towards low-service, bulk purchasers of silicone or creating a new offering targeting low-service, bulk purchasers at a lower price point. Which approach would you support and why?
5. A manufactured-good firm finds that its market share has been slipping in a geographic market. It chooses to conduct a benchmarking study of its price waterfall against the industry standard and discovers that the standard trade discount to retailers by competitors in that geographic market is somewhat higher than the firm's, while the cooperative advertising budget of competitors in that geographic market is somewhat lower than the firm's. What action would you suggest and why?
6. A plumbing fixture firm finds that its market share has been growing. It chooses to conduct a benchmarking study of its price waterfall against the industry standard and discover that its quarterly bonus is higher than the industry average, while its slotting allowance and in-store marketing support discounts are lower than the industry average. What action would you suggest and why?
7. Consider the following firms and the salesperson incentive structure: a firm selling knives door to door at a set customer price; a firm selling jet engines to airlines at a negotiated price that is reviewed by many executives; and a firm selling cake mix to bakers and grocers where deals are made by individual salespeople. Which firm might find volume-based incentives most appropriate? Which firm might find revenue-based incentives most appropriate? Which firm might find profit-based incentives most appropriate? Are profit-based incentives always the most efficient? Why might a firm choose not to use them?

Notes

[1] Michael Marn has written extensively on pocket price bands and price waterfalls. Michael V. Marn and Robert L. Rosiello, "Managing Price, Gaining Profit," *Harvard Business Review* 70, No. 5 (September–October 1992): 84–94. Michael V. Marn, Eric V. Roegner, Craig C. Zawada, "The Power of Pricing," *The McKinsey Quarterly*, 1 (2003): 26–39. Michael V. Marn, Eric V. Roegner, and Craig C. Zawada, "Transaction," in *The Price Advantage* (Hoboken, NJ: John Wiley & Sons, Inc., 2004): 23–42.

[2] Jim Geisman and John Maruskin, "A Case for Discount Discipline," *Harvard Business Review* 84, No. 11 (November 2006): 30–31. Donald V. Potter, "Discovering Hidden Pricing Power," *Business Horizons* (November–December 2000): 41–48.

[3] Christian Homburg and Ove Jensen, "The Thought Worlds of Marketing and Sales: Which Differences Make a Difference?" *Journal of Marketing* 71, No. 3 (July 2007): 124–42.

[4] Steven Levitt examined some of the decision-making biases inherent in revenue-based sales incentives in a highly familiar setting of housing sales. Steven D. Levitt and Stephen J. Dubner, "How Is the Ku Klux Klan like a Group of Real-Estate Agents?" in *Freakonomics* (New York: HarperCollins., 2005): 55–88.

[5] Sales incentives have been discussed in Thomas T. Nagle and Reed K. Holden, "Value-Based Sales and Negotiation," in *The Strategy and Tactics of Pricing: A Guide to Profitable Decision-Making*, 3d ed. (Upper Saddle River, NJ: Prentice Hall, 2002): 215–17.

[6] op cit Levitt/Dubner, 72.

PART
3

Establishing Price Structures

Chapter

9

Price Structures and Multipart Pricing

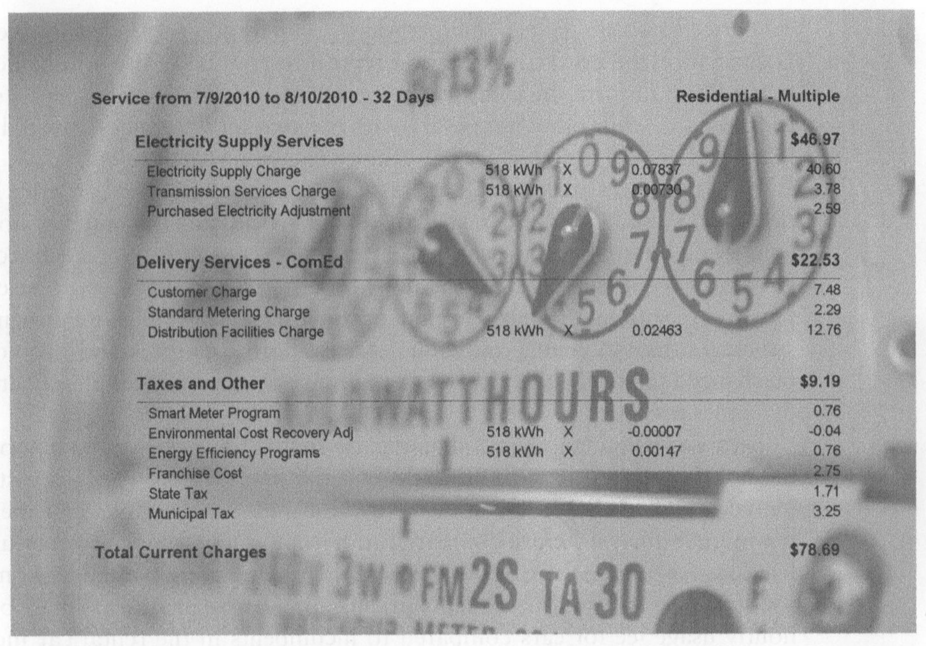

Service from 7/9/2010 to 8/10/2010 - 32 Days					Residential - Multiple
Electricity Supply Services					**$46.97**
Electricity Supply Charge	518 kWh	X	0.07837		40.60
Transmission Services Charge	518 kWh	X	0.00730		3.78
Purchased Electricity Adjustment					2.59
Delivery Services - ComEd					**$22.53**
Customer Charge					7.48
Standard Metering Charge					2.29
Distribution Facilities Charge	518 kWh	X	0.02463		12.76
Taxes and Other					**$9.19**
Smart Meter Program					0.76
Environmental Cost Recovery Adj	518 kWh	X	-0.00007		-0.04
Energy Efficiency Programs	518 kWh	X	0.00147		0.76
Franchise Cost					2.75
State Tax					1.71
Municipal Tax					3.25
Total Current Charges					**$78.69**

- What is a price structure?
- Do unit prices really reflect value?
- How do the drivers of value determine the pricing structure?
- What is a two-part tariff?
- What is a tying arrangement?
- How do two-part tariffs and tying arrangements differ? How are they the same?
- How are multipart price structures used in different industries?
- Stretch Question: When should an executive use two-part tariffs versus tying arrangements?

The price structure is the architecture around which the firm's pricing mix is designed.[1] It can be used to price-segment the market. Unlike price promotions and discounting, which change the price from the firm's reference price, the price structure adjusts the firm's reference price. In this and the coming chapters, we will explore some of the price structures that have the greatest impact in detail.[2]

As a tactical means to refine prices and improve price segmentation, executives turn to price promotions and discounts. Because discounts and price promotions adjust prices on a sale-by-sale basis, they are easy to implement but are not necessarily the easiest to optimize and manage. Price promotions and discounts, while very common, are only one method of price segmentation. The alternative method to price-segment the market is through the price structure itself.

By comparison, price structures are a strategic means to price-segment the market. The price structure defines the price extracted from different market segments. It will adjust automatically the invoice price of all transactions, not simply promotional or specific sales situations. Executives can structure prices such that the total price paid will be proportional to a customer segment's willingness to pay. Price structures are a strategic pricing policy choice.

Price Structures

The price structure defines the method by which total transaction prices are determined. For instance, the price structure of a typical residential utility bill includes multiple items that add up to form the total transaction charge. On a monthly basis, some of the items are constant, while other items vary with the amount of service delivered. Combined, these items in this utility bill form what is known as *multipart pricing*.

Price structures are a more steadfast component of pricing than price levels and promotions. Once established, price structures quickly become the industry norm against which competing alternatives are compared and market segments are defined. Changing price structures requires redefining the decision criteria for customers to select between products and redefining the market segments themselves. It is far more difficult to change price structures than to change individual prices. Both list prices and promotional prices can be changed relatively quickly, but changing price structures implies changing the industry dynamics itself.

Because changing industry dynamics is such a powerful strategic tool, price structures are a critical strategic weapon. New entrants will explore new price structures as a potential means of displacing industry incumbents. For example, consider Skype's prepaid per-minute price structure compared to telecom industry incumbents using postpaid, set fees for local phone calls; Southwest's initial pricing of individual legs on trips in comparison to airline industry incumbents pricing roundtrips; or Zipcar's membership fee plus an hourly usage fee for cars compared to incumbents in the rental car industry pricing for entire days only. Each of these firms sought to redefine the price point for customers to enter the market and did so by redefining the price structure.

RETHINKING THE UNIT

At first blush, the issue of what is priced appears mundane. Firms produce or distribute goods and services, and they price them. When executives take this approach to pricing, they are effectively establishing unit pricing as the price structure, and the metric that determines the total price paid is the units sold. With unit pricing, the interplay between the overall market demand curve and marginal costs determines the optimal price to charge. However, the issue of what should be priced is a bit more complex.

For examples of different price structures, consider how a bill is determined in different industries. Construction, consulting, and legal firms have each used billable-hour pricing and are venturing into completed-project pricing. Alternatively, consider the price structures at dining establishments, where some restaurants use buffet or all-you-can eat pricing, others use fixed prices for entire meals, and still others charge for specific items. Even butter can have an itemized price in some restaurants. When a firm considers a different way of calculating the transaction price, it is considering a different price structure.

We know that different customers have different willingness to pay. Willingness to pay is not necessarily derived from the unit that is being sold, but from the desired benefit of the product or service. The benefits of a product themselves depend upon the goal that the customer is seeking to accomplish and the importance of that product in contributing to goal accomplishment. Different customers have different goals and seek different benefits from a product, and therefore they will have different willingness to pay for that product. By uncovering drivers related to their heterogeneity in willingness to pay, executives can go beyond simple unit pricing. They can structure their pricing such that prices vary in proportion to the driver of the willingness to pay.

The identity of a price structure is defined by the basic metric that it uses to define the price. While it may be most natural to define the priced unit according to a number of goods sold or hours worked, other arrangements that are less internal-accounting in origin and more customer-centric in viewpoint are possible. Moreover, customer-centric pricing is more profitable in most markets. In a customer-focused price structure, prices are associated with the benefits that customers derive from the product rather than units of consumption. When the basis for pricing is shifted from units sold to goals accomplished, the firm has restructured its prices to focus on the customer.

In defining the price structure, two key questions to address are (1) What drives the value that customers place on the offering? (2) How can the firm capture prices in proportion to the value that customers perceive? By raising these questions, executives can uncover a metric for pricing beyond the units sold and toward the value delivered.

USING DEMAND HETEROGENEITY

Each of the fundamental approaches to setting prices focused on pricing in proportion to the value that customers place on the product. Often, customers don't value the product as much as they value what the product enables them to do. For some customers, the product is the focal instrument for enabling the accomplishment of a valuable goal. For others, the product is one of many options that enable a marginally important goal. Pricing in proportion to the value that customers place on the outcomes they can achieve with a product can enable the firm to capture much higher value. Yet the challenge that a firm faces is in finding a means to capture a price in proportion to the utility that the product enables. Properly identifying the unit of measurement with which to associate a price enables firms to align their price capture to the driver of value from the customer's perspective.

Demand heterogeneity refers to the manner in which different customers are willing to pay different amounts in different purchasing situations. Demand heterogeneity can derive from differences between customers, or differences within a single customer's willingness to pay depending upon the situation, timing, urgency, or a host of other factors. Pricing structures that match demand heterogeneity will improve profits.

In designing the price structure to price-segment the market, the overarching goal is to set the price that different customers pay for the product equal to their specific willingness to pay (so long as it is above marginal costs). Hence, demand heterogeneity informs price heterogeneity. Demand heterogeneity is both a driver of price structure selection and a limitation of the effectiveness of different price structures.

For instance, a tradesperson will place a higher value on a cordless drill than a homemaker, and neither values the drill as much as they value the ability to make holes and fasten screws. While a firm may like to price in proportion to the value of drilling holes, the competitive and substitute forces make pricing-by-the-hole untenable. As such, toolmakers must sell tools instead of holes; but they do not have to sell just one type of tool, nor do they have to use just one price. The tool manufacturer can sell trade tools at a different price than they sell homemaker tools, and at least partially capture prices in proportion to the driver of value from each customer's perspective. Redefining the unit, as in creating different products for different market segments by the tool manufacturer, is a method of addressing the disparity in variation in utility that customers derive from the product.

Redefining the unit to align with demand heterogeneity can come in many forms. One method is to change the unit from that of the sale of a product to that of the ability to use a product. Rental agreements and subscription-based services redefine the unit away from the units of product sold to units of agreement sold that enable customers to use a product. From housing to insurance, and even software as a service, redefining the unit into a leased or subscription-based offering has been observed.

Another method of redefining the unit can come in the form of multipart pricing. Multipart pricing is a powerful approach for increasing the profitability of a firm. In it, the transaction price is calculated from using two or more metrics rather than just one. For instance, Zipcar sells drivers a contract that grants the right to use its cars and charges a per-hour fee for actually driving their cars. In this way, the Zipcar is both pricing the value that customers have on having access to cars and on using cars.

Other methods of redefining the unit may focus more on actually changing the product sold. Add-ons, versions, and bundles are all means of redefining the product sold to deliver value in closer proportion to the value sought, and also of enabling the firm to capture greater value in the process. From software to home appliances and even automobiles, add-on sales, product versioning, and bundling have each found a role in improving profits. Returning to our example of cordless drills, tool manufacturers make models specifically designed for the professional market separate from those for household use. There are still other means to redefine the unit that improve profits. In yield management, the metric changes from the simple product to a combination of the product and the timing of the product purchase. Airlines and hotels have found yield management to be a powerful profit tool.

Price structures that mirror the perception of value tend to be more profitable than those that mirror variable costs. They do so by simultaneously extracting higher prices from customers who value the product more, while charging lower prices to a larger market segment that values the product less. Because the price structure and market segmentation are connected so closely, executives must make careful tradeoffs when selecting a price structure. Different price structures segment the market differently. Some are more effective in certain situations, while in other situations a different price structure is required. In the coming chapters, we will look at a variety of price structures, provide some insight into the power and pitfalls of these methods, and demonstrate their value through economic models.

Multipart Price Structures

TWO-PART TARIFFS

The most common economic example of a price structure beyond unit pricing is called a *two-part tariff.* Two-part tariffs have two elements in the pricing. The first element can be likened to an entrance fee. The entrance fee is a fixed sum charged to all customers regardless of their level of consumption. The second element is a per-use level of consumption or some other form of a metered fee. The metered fee is determined through some measurement of the units consumed. In one description of a two-part tariff, one would state that the entrance fee provides the privilege of purchasing the metered component.

In an idealized profit-maximization format, the first element is priced to extract all value from customers, while the second element is priced to recapture marginal costs. Such a format is possible if the market is homogeneous. When all customers have similar demand, the optimal structure in a two-part tariff is to set the entrance equal to the value that customers gain from consuming the product while setting the metered fee equal to marginal costs. The optimal entrance fee in homogeneous markets will transfer all the value created and delivered to customers to the firm in the form of profits.[3]

In more realistic implementations, both elements extract value from customers in proportion to their willingness to pay. In fact, the metered fee provides the dominant source of profits for the firm in many implementations of two-part tariffs. If the market is heterogeneous, the optimal structure of a two-part tariff will require both parts of the price structure to generate profits. In a heterogeneous market, the two-part tariff can transfer the value derived by customers to the firm only from the customers with the least demand. For all other customers, the value created and delivered by the firm is shared by both the customers and the firm. Because most every realistic market is heterogeneous, two-part tariffs will generally rely on earning profits from both the entrance and metered portions.

From a customer perspective, two-part tariffs charge different prices to customers in proportion to consumption. For low-consuming customers, the total price calculated from a two-part tariff is small; for a high-consuming customer, the total price is large.

Two-part tariffs require products that cannot be easily resold or stored for later use. This requirement stems from the need to prevent aftermarket transfer. In general, the ability of a firm to implement a two-part tariff decreases with competition. As competition increases, firms find their ability to charge an entrance fee decreases, and they must raise the price of the metered component within their price structure.

TYING ARRANGEMENTS

Very similar in structure to a two-part tariff is a tying arrangement. Like a two-part tariff, tying arrangements use two prices for selling multiple products that function together to deliver value to customers. Unlike two-part tariffs, the price structure in a tying arrangement is designed to create profits primarily through the sale of the second good, not the first good.

In a tying arrangement, the firm will sell two related products that function together to deliver value to a customer. Customers may be able to derive some value from the products independently, but most of the value that a customer derives is from the joint use of the two products.

In a classic deployment of a tying arrangement, the first product is a durable good and the second product is a consumable good that is used in conjunction with the durable good. For example, consider razor handles and razor blades. Razors are commonly sold with an introductory package that includes both the handle and the blades. Once the customer consumes the initial set of blades, further blades are purchased that are designed to be used with specific handles. If customers want to use a competitor's blades with their initial handle, they will find that the competitor's blades do not fit. By designing the razor handle and blades to fit each other specifically and not fit a competitor's handle or blade, the firm has tied the initial sale of the handle to all future sales of blades.

From a profit-capturing perspective, tying arrangements are the polar opposite of two-part tariffs. In a two-part tariff, firms will price the entrance fee relatively high to contribute a majority of the profits while pricing the metered unit relatively low to contribute only a fraction of the firm's profits. In a tying arrangement, the first product, which is also the durable portion of the sale, is priced relatively low, if not below marginal costs, and will deliver only a small fraction of the firm's profits, if any. Meanwhile, the second product, or the consumable portion of the sale, is priced relatively high, and its sales will deliver a majority of the firm's profits, if not all of them. In many tying arrangments, the profits from the consumable portion of the sale are used to subsidize the losses from the durable portion of the sale.

Firms are driven from two-part tariffs towards tying arrangements through the forces of competition.[4] Two-part tariff price structures are common in industries where firms have a monopoly position over their product, if not at least limited competition. In markets where tying arrangements are common, firms compete with one another to bring customers into a long-term relationship in which profits are made through repeat purchases. By pricing the durable product low in a tying arrangement to solidify a lasting customer-firm relationship, the firm can capture more customers. Once customers are captured, they tend to continue their relationship with their chosen supplier because of the durable good. As such, the firm profits by selling the subsequent consumable products at a relatively high margin.

For tying arrangements to be profitable, customers must maintain their relationship with the firm. Profits are created through the sale of the consumable portion of the tying arrangement, not the sale of the durable portion. Repeat customers who return to the firm to purchase the consumable portion of the tying arrangement are those who contribute the highest portion of the firm's profits in the long run. One-time customers who purchase only the durable portion of a tying arrangement may actually be unprofitable for the firm to serve.

Because the frequency of purchases and the duration of the relationship between the customer and the firm are the key drivers of profit in a tying arrangement, firms operating in these markets often examine customer lifetime values. The customer lifetime value is the profit that a firm can anticipate earning from a customer during the span of the relationship. Customer lifetime value calculations, as we will see in Chapter 13, highlight the importance of retaining customers in tying arrangements to generate profits.

In other words, once the sale of the durable good is made at a low or perhaps even negative profit margin, the firm must expect that it will retain that customer and generate profits in the future through the sale of the consumable goods. Customer defections, or the creation of aftermarkets where customers can purchase the consumable goods though an alternative supplier, destroy the ability of tying arrangements to generate profits.

To reduce customer defection and restrict the ability of customers to seek the consumable part of the tied goods from another source, firms often use some form of switching barrier within the market for the consumable good. The switching barrier may be a patented interface between the consumable and durable good. For instance, gaming consoles require gaming media that has been generated through patent-protected and licensed software. Alternatively, firms have attempted to use a simple contractual arrangement wherein the sale of the durable good binds customers to purchasing the consumable good from that manufacturer. For instance, mobile telephone network operators often provide free handsets in exchange for a long-term service contract.[5] In a few cases, firms will have little other influence over future purchases than customer inertia. For instance, Apple has given away music management software (iTunes) in an attempt to capture revenue through the sale of music at the iTunes store, but customers can use iTunes with any digital music format. For whichever format used, executives will seek to create a proprietary aftermarket to lock customers into purchasing the consumable product specifically from that firm.

Competition drives the price of the durable good down in markets that use tying arrangements. For instance, markets for razor handles and blades, two tied goods, are highly competitive. Producers of blades and handles compete strongly for customers. In these markets, customers have a tendency to select products based on the price of the first sale and routinely underestimate the future costs of further sales. In a tying arrangement, the first item sold will be a durable item that forms the basis for the future firm-customer relationship. The consumable goods required to derive value from the durable good are purchased only in the future. Hence, the initial price that customers pay for the durable good may have more influence over their product selection than the potential future prices they have to pay for the tied consumable good. When the basis of product selection is the price of the durable good, firms are encouraged to lower the price of the durable good and capture profits through higher-priced tied goods.

In contrast, firms in two-part tariff markets often face limited competition for customers. For instance, consider some firms that use two-part tariffs. Utilities have often been described as natural monopolies, even though modern deregulation has attempted to introduce competition. Likewise, amusement parks like those run by Disney have a monopoly on their branded character, Mickey Mouse in Disney's case, eliminating competition for customers who seek to have their photo taken with the profit-generating character (or rodent in Disney's case).

While tying arrangements are common, they have also been subject to numerous legal restrictions.[6] In a famous case involving Xerox, U.S. courts ruled that tying arrangements can violate certain antitrust laws. Similar decisions have been made in many other judicial territories. In the Xerox case, copier machines were sold with contractual obligations for customers to purchase all future supplies, including paper, from Xerox. The courts ruled this arrangement illegal. Specifically, court cases have been interpreted to suggest that tying arrangements are subject to legal action when (1) two separate products or services are involved; (2) the purchase of the tying product is conditioned on the additional purchase of the tied product; (3) the seller has sufficient power in the market for the tying product; (4) a not-insubstantial amount of interstate commerce in the tied product market is affected.

As with other pricing strategies and tactics, executives should not simply choose to avoid any consideration of tying arrangements due to legal concerns, nor should they blithely pursue them. Rather, they should choose a pricing structure that maximizes profits without crossing the line into legal restrictions and ethical challenges. From the numerous examples, we can see that tying arrangements are often legal.

JAZZ CLUBS AND MULTIPART PRICING—AN ILLUSTRATIVE EXAMPLE

To elucidate how a multipart price structure works, we have chosen jazz clubs. Consider a jazz club that charges a $25 entrance fee at the door and $7 per beverage. The entrance fee grants customers the right to come into the club and consume beverages. Without paying the entrance fee, customers would not be able to visit the bar and enjoy a drink. All customers must pay the entrance fee to enter the jazz club and purchase drinks if they want. The number of beverages consumed is the metric that determines the total price paid by customers. The $7 per beverage is the metered price. Customers do not have to purchase a beverage; hence, they can determine their total price paid for an evening's entertainment as they wish.

To see the effect of a multipart price structure at a jazz club, we can calculate the total price paid and the average price per beverage as customers increase their consumption. Exhibit 9-1 presents a schedule of the total expenditures as a customer consumes more beverages. After entering the jazz club and having only one beverage, the total price paid is $32. After six beverages, the total expenditures will reach $67.

Exhibit 9-1 Jazz Club Price Structure

Beverages	Total Expenditure	Effective Time of Enjoyment	Effective Average Price per Half Hour
0	$25.00	0 hr and 0 min	N/A
1	$32.00	0 hr and 30 min	$32.00
2	$39.00	1 hr and 0 min	$19.50
3	$46.00	1 hr and 30 min	$15.33
4	$53.00	2 hr and 0 min	$13.25
5	$60.00	2 hr and 30 min	$12.00
6	$67.00	3 hr and 0 min	$11.17

The tastiness and thirst-quenching characteristics of a beverage are not the only drivers to encourage customers to purchase beverages at the jazz club. If the price of a beverage at a jazz club was set only by the thirst-quenching properties of the beverage, then surely the price per beverage would be much lower. Customers have alternatives such as visiting a convenience store or staying at home and drinking tap water. Rather, the main driver of value to the customer at a jazz club is the jazz and the environment.

As customers spend more time in the jazz club, they derive more value from the experience. Part of the purpose of the beverages is to provide customers with something to keep their hands busy as they while away their time in the jazz club. To some degree, beverages are a proxy metric for the time spent in the jazz club. As customers buy more beverages, they are also spending more time in the jazz club. With each beverage consumed, they derive more benefits from the experience, and therefore they have a higher willingness to pay for the overall experience. The sale of beverages enables the jazz club to capture a price that is somewhat proportionate to the overall time spent by a customer at the jazz club or the value it delivers to individual customers.

To make this relationship clear, suppose that on average a customer drinks one beverage every 30 minutes. We can make a schedule of the price paid in proportion to both this person's beverage consumption and time spent at the jazz club. See Exhibit 9-1. From this perspective, we see that the total price paid over the course of a three-hour visit to the jazz club increases every half hour.

Why is time itself not the metric? As with many markets, the actual metric that drives value for the customer may be difficult to measure or difficult to use to extract payment from the customer. In creating a proxy metric for value, firms will identify a portion of the offer that is related to the true value that customers gain from the product, even though that proxy metric may have little in common with the cost structure of the firm.

For instance, referring back to our example of the jazz club, the cost of a beverage is a very small portion of the price per beverage at most jazz clubs. The real costs are mostly fixed with respect to hiring jazz musicians and staff and paying rent. However, charging customers directly for the jazz club's fixed costs would be unpalatable for many customers.

Which part of the multipart price structure delivers greater profits for firms operating in competitive markets but enjoying limited customer switching between competitors? Consider the price structure from the perspective of attracting and capturing customers. If customers are more sensitive to the price of the metered good than the entrance fee, then the entrance fee will tend to be priced relatively high while the metered good may be priced relatively low. For instance, amusement park users tend to be more sensitive to the price per ride than the price to enter the amusement park, hence the more successful amusement parks tend to price rides low (if not free), while park entrance fees are set relatively high. However, if customers are more sensitive to the entrance fee than the price of the metered good, then the entrance fee will tend to be priced relatively low while the metered fee is priced relatively high. For instance, gamers tend to be more sensitive to the price of the gaming console than they are to the price per game, hence the dominant gaming platform makers tend to price gaming consoles low (if not at a loss), while individual games are priced relatively high.

Returning to our example of the jazz club, $7 per beverage is relatively in line with the price paid for beverages at comparable high-end establishments; hence, customers are likely to find it acceptable. Similarly, a $25 charge to enter the jazz club is somewhat low for a live concert; hence, many customers would find it acceptable as well. In terms of profits, the jazz club is likely to make most of its profits on beverages because it is customary for the musicians to take a substantial cut of the entrance fees.

Also calculated in Exhibit 9-1 is the average price paid per half hour. Notice that the average price per half hour decreases as a customer spends more time at the jazz club. If we plot the average price paid per half hour against time, we find a curve that resembles

Exhibit 9-2 Average Price Per Half Hour Against Time Spent

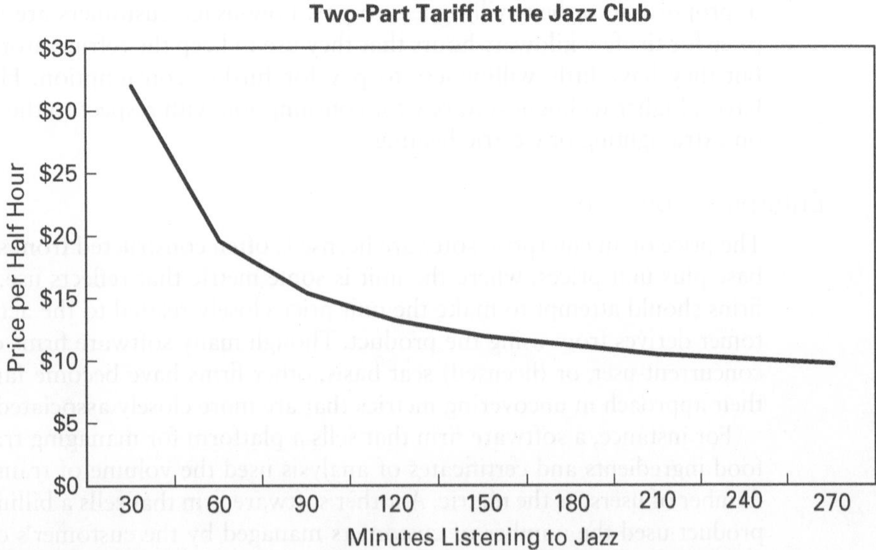

a demand curve. In this way, a multipart price structure can be said to mirror demand heterogeneity in the market. See Exhibit 9-2.

MULTIPART PRICE STRUCTURES IN INDUSTRY

As we have seen, the multipart price structure can enable a firm to better capture profits from their customers. Combined, the entrance fee plus the metered fee, or durable plus consumable good sales, enable the firm to shift profits between different parts of the pricing structure. Furthermore, the unit being priced can be closely related to the true driver of customer benefits while not actually reflecting any metric of costs or delivering significant benefits in and of itself.

Other firms also take advantage of the ability of multipart price structures to enhance profits. We find multipart price structures in the utility, enterprise software, publishing, partial ownership industries, and health care industries, among others. In each case, customers will gain some utility simply by having access to the product provided, and then they gain further utility from actually using and interacting with the product. The choice of the unit being metered and priced in a two-part tariff will depend on factors relating to both the cost and the value that customers place on the product.

Utilities

Utilities use one of the purest forms of a two-part tariff. They regularly charge a metering fee or connection fee plus a price per quantity of utility delivered. For electricity, the unit metered is typically the kilowatt-hours of power delivered. In natural gas, the gas delivered is typically metered and priced per therm or cubic meter. For water, a utility might measure cubic feet of water, liters, or some other volumetric measure. For telecommunications, minutes used or gigabytes transferred can be measured and priced.

All customers benefit from having access to the utility services; hence, all customers have some willingness to pay simply because they are connecting to the utility. Even a "green home" would benefit from having backup electricity provided by the local utility. The value that customers place on using the output of the utility varies in proportion to the quantity being used. For instance, residential customers may value keeping the refrigerator cold much higher than adding a fifteenth light to their home. When it comes to heating, they may face alternatives between using electricity and using natural gas. Two-part tariffs charge low-usage customers a higher average price than high-usage customers in proportion to their willingness to pay. Low-usage customers are willing to pay a high price for the few kilowatt-hours that they use to keep the refrigerator on plus a few lights, but they have little willingness to pay for further consumption. High-usage customers have a higher willingness to pay for consumption with respect to the value that they place on extra lighting or electric heating.

Enterprise Software

The price of an enterprise software license is often constructed from some combination of base plus unit prices, where the unit is some metric that reflects use. Enterprise software firms should attempt to make the unit price closely related to the actual value that a customer derives from using the product. Though many software firms charge on a per-user, concurrent-user, or (licensed) seat basis, other firms have become far more creative with their approach in uncovering metrics that are more closely associated with value.

For instance, a software firm that sells a platform for managing transactions related to food ingredients and certificates of analysis used the volume of transactions, rather than number of users, as the metric. Another software firm that sells a billing and customer-care product used the number of customers managed by the customer's company as a means for determining the price. Inventory management software can be priced in proportion to the average number of units inventoried, educational software may be priced according to the number of students at the school, hospital software according to the number of beds in the hospital, and industrial design management software can be priced according to the number of designs under management.

Some enterprise software firms will even set the metric proportional to the complexity of the problem managed. In this case, it is assumed that some customers may use only a portion of the potential functionality of the software even though the entire software is available, while other customers will exploit the full functionality of the software, thus deriving greater value and having a higher willingness to pay.

When pricing enterprise software, the goal should not be simply to price according to the number of users, but rather to uncover a metric that is closely associated with the value that enterprises derive from using that software. Users may be poorly correlated with value. Similar claims may be made when pricing information goods, such as access to stock prices, law journals, or auto care and damage history.

Partial Ownership

Multipart price structures are also common in partial ownership industries, such as time-share vacation homes, leased-time yachting, or car sharing. An annual membership fee may be associated with the cost of customer management, while also granting members access to the shared asset. Usage fees have been observed to be determined on a per-week, per weekend, per-day, or per-hour basis. Heavy users pay a lower average price per use, while light users pay a higher average price per use. As with other multipart price structures, the average price paid will somewhat match the consumers' willingness to pay for marginal consumption.

Healthcare

One may say that even healthcare pricing functions effectively as a multipart price structure. Healthcare customers may purchase insurance that ensures access to health care and then pay a second fee per doctor's visit or medical service. As with other products and services, customers derive value from having access to the service separate from the value that they derive from actually using the service, making multipart pricing palatable as a pricing mechanism for the market. All customers derive value from knowing that healthcare is available when needed. Also, by pricing for the use of health care, even if it is only a nominal fee, the structure can discourage abusive practices such as patients taking up doctors' time on issues not medically significant.

Ink

Computer printer manufacturers like Hewlett-Packard (HP) have one of the purest forms of tying arrangements. Typically, the price of printers is low to capture customers while the price of ink is high to capture profits. The printer is the durable portion of the sale, while the ink is the consumable. HP ties the sale of ink to its sale of printers through proprietary technology that governs the interface between an HP ink cartridge and an HP printer. To solidify the tie between printer and ink sales further, HP requires customers to accept an agreement that mandates the exclusive use of HP ink in exchange for a product warranty.

REFINING THE ENTRANCE FEE AND METERED PRICE

Executives often find that they can improve revenues further and capture a greater share of the value that they deliver to customers by altering the entrance fee or metered price.[7] For instance, consider the decision tradeoffs of very-high-volume customers. High-volume applications often face different, perhaps wider alternatives than low-volume usages. The greater number of alternatives may depress the willingness to pay of these customers on a per-use basis. Alternatively, a high-usage customer may be willing to pay significantly more for access to the service than a low-usage customer, and thus, the two-part tariff still fails to capture value in proportion to usage.

One approach to managing the disparity in willingness to pay of low-volume customers over high-volume customers has been to use a block tariff. The block tariff refers to changing the price of the metered service at different levels of consumption. The first block of consumption will be priced somewhat higher than subsequent blocks. After a customer has consumed that much or more of a service, the metered price will decrease until the next block of consumption has been breached. The last block of service is priced at or above the long-run average marginal cost to produce.

For instance, the metered part of electric power is often priced through a block tariff. See Exhibit 9-3. As consumption increases, the price per unit of consumption decreases at specific points. The utilities profit from this approach both by capturing higher prices from light users who require electricity for lighting, and by capturing profitable marginal revenue from heavy users who require electricity for heating as well.

Exhibit 9-3 Block Tariff

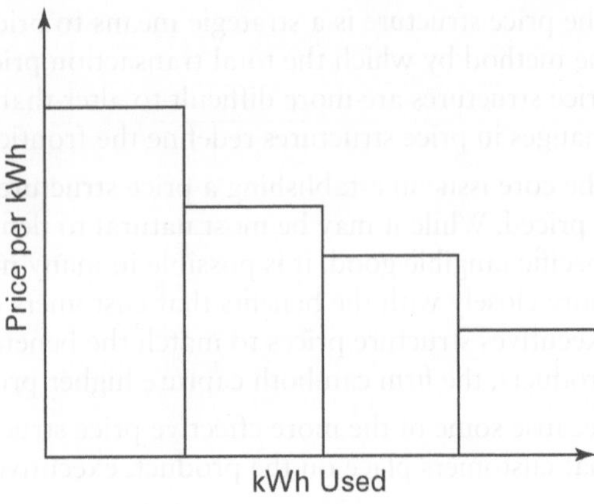

Exhibit 9-4 Inclined Tariff

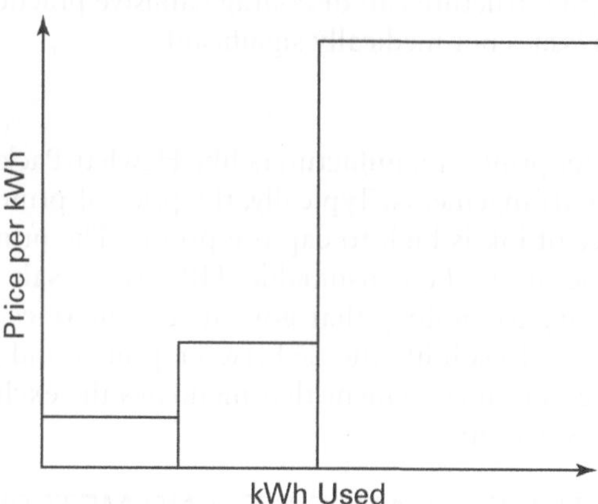

Recently, utilities have come under pressure from regulators to discourage consumption of their product rather than encourage it. Realizing that certain resources are limited, such as water, or that negative externalities, such as global warming and carbon production from fossil-fueled electric plants, are factored poorly into the costs of production, regulators have sought to use pricing as a means of changing consumer behavior and discourage excessive use. In both residential water and electricity markets, market regulators are considering price structures such that the initial consumption is priced low and the price per consumption increases as consumption increases. This pricing mechanism is not one designed to maximize profits, but rather to ensure that all residential customers have access to a basic level of service and to charge higher prices from customers who have a much higher consumption level to discourage this behavior. The result has been named an inclined tariff. See Exhibit 9-4.

Alternatively, Zipcar, a car-sharing firm, structures its rate plans at two different levels, each with a distinct entrance fee and per-hour fee.[8] The "occasional driving plan" charges an annual fee of $50 and has hourly rates starting at $9.25. (Specific hourly rates depend upon the type of car used.) The "extra value" plan requires a monthly fee of $50, making the annual equivalent $600, but the hourly rates are lower, starting at $8.33. As block tariffs demonstrated with electricity prices, this price structure allows Zipcar to segment customers according to their demand. Unlike block tariffs, this structure changes both the entrance fee and the metered fee simultaneously.

Summary

- The price structure is a strategic means to price-segment the market. It defines the method by which the total transaction price is determined. Once established, price structures are more difficult to alter than the other aspects of pricing, hence changes in price structures redefine the frontier of competition.
- The core issue in establishing a price structure is identifying the basic unit that is priced. While it may be most natural to define the priced unit according to a specific tangible good, it is possible in many markets to associate the priced unit more closely with the benefits that customers derive from the product. When executives structure prices to match the benefits that customers derive from its products, the firm can both capture higher profits and serve more customers.
- Because some of the more effective price structures are those that reflect the value that customers place on the product, executives should seek to understand demand

heterogeneity, or the differences in willingness to pay associated with different purchasing situations, customer segments, and markets, in defining the pricing structure.

- In a two-part tariff price structure, the total price for using the product is deconstructed into two elements. The first element is an entrance fee charged to all customers regardless of their level of consumption. The second element is a metered fee that tracks the units consumed. In an extreme form, the entrance fee is priced to extract all value from customers, while the metered fee is priced to recapture marginal costs.
- Similarly, in a tying arrangement, there are two prices for selling a set of products that function together to deliver value to customers. In a classic deployment of a tying arrangement, the first product is a durable good and the second product is a consumable good that is used in conjunction with the durable good. From a profit-capturing perspective, tying arrangements are the polar opposite of two-part tariffs. In a tying arrangement, the durable product is priced with a relatively low margin while the consumable product is priced with a relatively high margin. In many cases, the profits from the consumable portion of the sale are used to subsidize the losses from the durable portion of the sale.
- Both two-part tariffs and tying arrangements are subject to regulatory intervention and legal restrictions in some situations, but they are permitted in numerous situations.

Exercises

1. A rental car firm's executive is considering two different price structures: price per day versus price per mile. Identify a situation in which a price-per-day structure would most match the value that customers are willing to pay. Alternatively, identify a situation in which a price-per-mile structure would most match the value that customers are willing to pay.
2. Congestion road pricing has often been suggested by economists as a means of reducing traffic during rush hour. Under congestion road pricing, high tolls are extracted from drivers during high-traffic periods, while low or no tolls are extracted from drivers during low-traffic periods. In what way would congestion road price structures match demand heterogeneity?
3. Costco and Sam's Club both offer annual memberships in exchange for discounted prices. Customers tend to purchase items in bulk at Costco and Sam's Club. How are shopping clubs like Costco or Sam's Club priced like a two-part tariff? Do two-part tariffs simply offer "bulk discounts"? What other sources of value might the annual membership confer to patrons of Costco or Sam's Club?
4. Both HP and Kodak offer printers and ink to the market. HP tends to price their printers low and their ink high. Kodak tends to price their printers high and their ink low. What is the price structure used by HP? By Kodak? If customers are more sensitive to the upfront price of a printer, which price structure is likely to prove more profitable?
5. A plastic injection molding company sells both molds and plastic pieces from the mold. The executives are uncertain whether they should price their molds and plastic pieces in a manner that resembles a two-part tariff or a tying arrangement. If customers tend to be concerned with long-run manufacturing costs, which price structure is likely to capture the larger number of customers? If customers tend to be concerned with upfront design costs, which price structure is likely to capture the larger number of customers?

6. Prague has a strong mass transit system that can be used by both commuters and tourists. Transit executives offer single-trip passes for 26 CZK (Czech Koruna), 1-day passes for 100 CZK, and 30-day passes for 550 CZK.
   a. Which segment is most likely to purchase a 1-day pass? A 30-day pass?
   b. How many trips must a tourist make to make a 1-day pass a better value than using single-trip passes?
   c. If a tourist is unsure of his or her transit needs and unsure of the availability of single-trip passes, but wants to make sure he or she has sufficient transit, which is he or she more likely to purchase? Single-trip tickets or a 1-day pass?
   d. Why might someone claim that the price of a 1-day pass is set according to the value of peace of mind?
7. After reading Appendix 9, consider a firm serving a homogeneous market with a downward-sloping demand curve as described in Equation 9.1. Suppose that there are 1,000 customers, each with a maximum demand of 10 units, and the maximum utility that any customer can derive from the product is $100. Furthermore, assume that the variable costs for a product are $20 and the firm's fixed costs are zero. If the firm uses a two-part tariff, answer the following questions.
   a. What is the optimal metered price P_M?
   b. What is the optimal entrance fee P_E?
   c. What is the profit earned from any single customer?
   d. How many units does an individual customer consume?
   e. What are the profits earned from the market?
   f. How many units are sold to the market?
8. After reading Appendixes 6 and 9 and completing Exercise 9.7, consider a firm serving a homogeneous market with a downward-sloping demand curve as described in Equation 9.1. Suppose that there are 1,000 customers, each with a maximum demand of 10 units, and the maximum utility that any customer can derive from the product is $100. Furthermore, assume that the variable costs for a product are $20 and the firm's fixed costs are zero. If the firm uses unit pricing, answer the following questions.
   a. What is the optimal unit price?
   b. What are the profits earned from the market?
   c. How many units are sold to the market?
   d. How much lower are the profits earned from pure unit pricing than those earned from a two-part tariff?
   e. How many fewer units are sold from pure unit pricing than those earned from a two-part tariff?
9. After reading Appendix 9, consider a firm serving a heterogeneous market consisting of two equal-sized market segments ($\chi = .5$), each with a downward-sloping demand curve as described in Equation 9.10. Suppose that there is a total of 1,000 customers, each with a q_{max} of 10 units. Let the more demanding customers gain a maximum utility from the product of $120 and the less demanding customers gain a maximum utility from the product of $80. Furthermore, assume that the variable costs for a product are $20 and the firm's fixed costs are zero. If the firm uses a two-part tariff, answer the following questions.
   a. What is the optimal metered price P_M?
   b. What is the optimal entrance fee P_E?

c. How many units are sold to a customer in the more-demanding segment?
d. How many units are sold to a customer in the less-demanding segment?
e. How many units are sold in total?
f. What are the total profits earned from the market?
g. After completing Exercise 9.7, how much lower are profits in the case of a heterogeneous market than a homogeneous market?

Appendix 9 An Economic Model of a Two-Part Tariff

HOMOGENEOUS MARKET

One of the earliest price structures examined after the development of economics as a study of the relationship between prices, demand, and supply was the two-part tariff.[9] In the simplest models, the market was defined to be completely homogeneous in that all customers were assumed to have the same willingness to pay for additional units and derive the exact same consumer surplus for participating in the market. With completely homogeneous demand, two-part tariffs can extract all the value that consumers derive from the product into the form of profits for the firm. While this model is useful for demonstrating the value to the firm of two-part tariffs, it is highly questionable in actually setting prices due to the numerous gross approximations of demand homogeneity.

To demonstrate, let us evaluate the optimal pricing and maximum profit that a firm can earn when using a two-part tariff. The two-part tariff requires two prices. Let P_E be the entrance fee paid by all customers. Let P_M be the metered price, or price per unit purchased. Paying the entrance price grants permission to consumers to pay the metered price per item in a two-part tariff pricing structure.

Furthermore, let us use a linearly downward-sloping demand curve for each individual customer:

$$q = q_{\max} \cdot \left(1 - \frac{P_M}{S}\right) \qquad \text{Eq. 9.1}$$

S is the maximum utility that any customer can derive from the product, and therefore that is the highest price that can be charged. When the metered price equals the maximum utility ($P_M = S$), no units are sold. Similarly, $q_{\max}$ is the maximum units that a customer would purchase. When the metered price is zero ($P_M = 0$), the demand is maximized ($q = q_{\max}$). See Exhibit 9-5. Equation 9.1 is highly similar to Equation 6.1, used in Appendix 6, with the exception of using an individual's demand, q, rather than the overall market's demand, Q, and the incorporation of the new metered price, P_M. Because the market is considered to be completely homogeneous, the overall market's demand is equal to the individual's demand multiplied by the number of individuals within the market. If we let N be the number of individuals in the market, we find

$$Q = N \cdot q \qquad \text{Eq. 9.2}$$

The maximum possible entrance price that the firm can extract from customers would be the potential value that customers would gain by consuming whatever amount of product they purchase. Graphically, in the absence of an entrance fee, the value that a customer gains is defined by the area of the triangle bounded along the diagonal by the demand and along the base by the metered price paid. This area is represented as the shaded area in Exhibit 9-6. The height of this triangle is simply the difference between the utility gained by entering the market (S) and the metered price (P_M). The base of the triangle is the number

Exhibit 9-5 Two-part Tariff with a Homogeneous Market

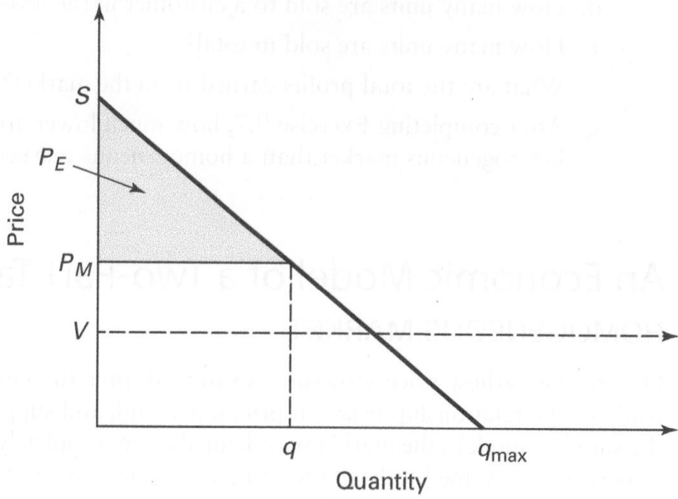

of units consumed calculated from Equation 9.1. Because the area of this triangle is simply one-half the base multiplied by the height, we find the optimal entrance fee to be

$$\hat{P}_E = \frac{q_{max}}{2S} \cdot (S - P_M)^2 \qquad \text{Eq. 9.3}$$

With a fixed entrance fee charged to each customer, we find the profit earned from individual customers to be

$$\pi_i = P_E + q \cdot (P_M - V) \qquad \text{Eq. 9.4}$$

where π_i is the profit earned from an individual customer and V is the variable costs. We have set the fixed costs to zero to keep this example simple without losing generality.

To find the optimal metered price, we maximize the firm's profits with respect to the metered price. Recalling that the entry fee (P_E) and the units sold (q) are also functions of the metered price, while variable costs are not, we find the first derivative of profits with respect to the metered price to be

$$\frac{\partial \pi_i}{\partial P_M} = \frac{\partial P_E}{\partial P_M} + \frac{\partial q}{\partial P_M} \cdot (P_M - V) + q \qquad \text{Eq. 9.5.a}$$

where, from Equation 9.1, we find

$$\frac{\partial q}{\partial P_M} = \frac{-q_{max}}{S} \qquad \text{Eq. 9.5.b}$$

and, from Equation 9.3, we find

$$\frac{\partial P_E}{\partial P_M} = \frac{-q_{max}}{S} \cdot (S - P_M) \qquad \text{Eq. 9.5.c}$$

Setting the derivative of the firm's profit equation with respect to the metered price equal to zero to find the optimal price, and inserting Equations 9.5.b and 9.5.c into Equation 9.5.a, we find that

$$0 = \frac{-q_{max}}{S} \cdot (S - \hat{P}_M) - \frac{q_{max}}{S} \cdot (\hat{P}_M - V) + \frac{q_{max}}{S} \cdot (S - \hat{P}_M) \qquad \text{Eq. 9.6}$$

Simplifying Equation 9.6, we find that the optimal metered price reduces to the marginal cost to produce:

$$\hat{P}_M = V \qquad \text{Eq. 9.7}$$

At this price, the profit earned from any individual customer is simply the revenue earned from the entry fee.

$$\hat{\pi}_i = \hat{P}_E \qquad \text{Eq. 9.8}$$

Overall, the market has N identical customers; hence the firm's overall profit is simply

$$\hat{\pi} = N \cdot \hat{\pi}_i = \frac{N \cdot q_{\max}}{2S} \cdot (S - V)^2 \qquad \text{Eq. 9.9}$$

after substituting Equation 9.7 for the optimal metered price into Equation 9.3 for the optimal entrance fee and simplification.

We can contrast the optimal prices within a two-part tariff to that found in a per-unit fee price structure. In Appendix 6, we derived both the optimal unit prices and the profit when the firm had only one unit price that it offered to the entire market. We see that the optimal metered price in a two-part price structure (Eq. 9.7) is below the optimal unit price in a per-unit price structure (Eq. 6.5.) Hence, customers can be expected to consume more of a product when the firm uses a two-part price structure than they would if the firm offered only per-unit pricing. (Compare Equation 6.6 to Equation 9.1.) In an optimized two-part price structure with a homogeneous market, the firm earns all its profits from the entrance fee. These profits are significantly greater than what the firm could have earned with per-unit pricing only. In fact, by comparing Equation 6.7 to Equation 9.9, we see that the profit contribution doubles when the firm uses a two-part tariff rather than per-unit pricing alone.

The simplicity of the two-part tariff in increasing profits from an economic perspective is compelling for many executives. In essence, the two-part tariff enables the firm to optimize its profits by setting its metered price equal to the marginal cost to produce, thus encouraging customers to purchase as much of the product as they possibly could demand. Meanwhile, the firm captures profits by extracting all the value that consumers gain from the product through the entrance fee. Because the two-part tariff is one of the cleanest forms of perfect price discrimination in homogeneous markets, government regulations often limit the ability of firms to maximize their profits through two-part tariffs in markets that have a tendency to behave in monopolistic manners.

However, as we alluded to earlier, this model made a number of simplifying assumptions. One of the most damaging assumptions was that the market was perfectly homogeneous; in other words, all customers had the exact same willingness to pay for each unit consumed.

HETEROGENEOUS MARKET

By incorporating market heterogeneity into our models, we immediately find that the power of a two-part tariff to increase profits is limited. To demonstrate the effect of market heterogeneity on optimal prices and profits in a two-part tariff, let us consider a market with two segments. Let segment A have a higher demand for the product than segment B ($S_A > S_B$). Using a similar model for consumer demand as before but adjusting for the distinction in demand between segment A and B, we can state

$$q_A = q_{\max} \cdot \frac{S_A}{S_B} \cdot \left(1 - \frac{P_M}{S_A}\right) \qquad \text{Eq. 9.10.a}$$

$$q_B = q_{\max} \cdot \left(1 - \frac{P_M}{S_B}\right) \qquad \text{Eq. 9.10.b}$$

Exhibit 9-6 Two-part Tariff with a Heterogeneous Market

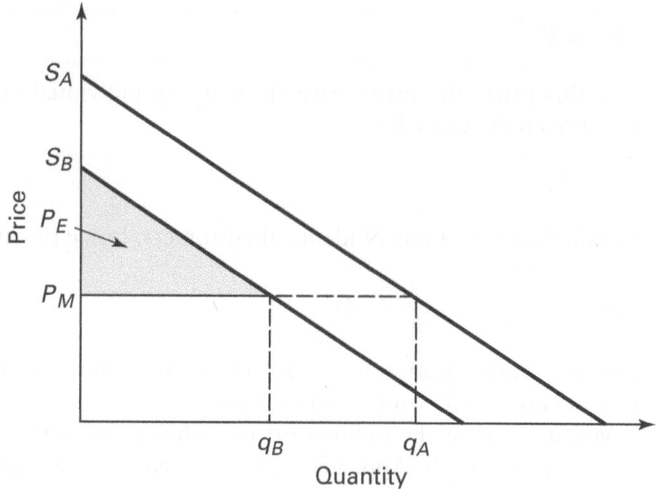

In effect, Equation 9.10 states that both market segments A and B have the same willingness to pay per unit, but overall, segment A is willing to purchase more units than segment B. A plot of these demand curves, shown in Exhibit 9-6, shows two parallel demand curves, each having the same slope but one positioned above the other.

Furthermore, let us once again assume that the market consists of N customers, but this time, we know a fraction of them are in segment A and the rest are in segment B. If χ (pronounced "chi") is the fraction of the market in segment A, then $1 - \chi$ is the fraction of the market in segment B. Hence, the number of units sold becomes

$$Q = N \cdot [\chi \cdot q_A + (1 - \chi) \cdot q_B] \qquad \text{Eq. 9.11}$$

With two market segments, each facing the same offer for the entrance fee and metered price, the firm cannot set the entrance fee at a level that extracts all the consumer surplus. Instead, the maximum entrance fee that it can extract from the market is simply the value gained by those customers with the least demand. This value is represented by the shaded area in Exhibit 9-6. Once again, the area of this triangle is half of the difference between the maximum utility that the least-demanding segment gains from the product and the metered price $(S_B - P_M)$ multiplied by the quantity that this segment will purchase at this metered price q_B. After simplification, we find the optimal entrance fee to be

$$\hat{P}_E = \frac{q_{\max}}{2S_B} \cdot (S_B - P_M)^2 \qquad \text{Eq. 9.12}$$

Any higher price would drive the segment B customers out of the market. A price that was any lower would fail to capture the maximum profits for the firm.

On an average-customer basis, the firm's profit equation consists of the fixed entry fee charged to every customer plus the average units sold per customer multiplied by the profit margin between the metered price and the variable costs. From Equation 9.11, we know that the average number of units sold to a customer is simply $\chi \cdot q_A + (1 - \chi) \cdot q_B$; hence the average profit earned per customer is

$$\pi_i = P_E + [\chi \cdot q_A + (1 - \chi) \cdot q_B] \cdot (P_M - V) \qquad \text{Eq. 9.13}$$

We have once again assumed that fixed costs are zero to simplify the math without losing generality.

To find the optimal metered price, we once again maximize the firm's profits with respect to the metered price. Recalling that the entry fee (P_E) and the units sold (q_A and q_B) are functions of the metered price while the fraction of customers in a specific market segment and the variable costs are not, we find the first derivative of profits with respect to the metered price to be

$$\frac{\partial \pi_i}{\partial P_M} = \frac{\partial \hat{P}_E}{\partial P_M} + \left[\chi \cdot \frac{\partial q_A}{\partial P_M} + (1-\chi) \cdot \frac{\partial q_B}{\partial P_M}\right] \cdot (P_M - V) + \chi \cdot q_A + (1-\chi) \cdot q_B \quad \text{Eq. 9.14.a}$$

where, from Equation 9.12, we find

$$\frac{\partial \hat{P}_E}{\partial P_M} = \frac{-q_{\max}}{S_B} \cdot (S_B - P_M) \quad \text{Eq. 9.14.b}$$

and, from Equation 9.10, we find

$$\frac{\partial q_A}{\partial P_M} = \frac{\partial q_B}{\partial P_M} = \frac{-q_{\max}}{S_B} \quad \text{Eq. 9.14.c}$$

Setting the derivative of the firm's profit equation with respect to the metered price equal to zero to find the optimal price, and inserting Equations 9.14.b and 9.14.c into Equation 9.14.a, we find that

$$0 = \frac{-q_{\max}}{S_B} \cdot (S_B - \hat{P}_M) + \left[\chi \cdot \frac{-q_{\max}}{S_B} + (1-\chi) \cdot \frac{-q_{\max}}{S_B}\right] \cdot (\hat{P}_M - V) + \chi \cdot q_{\max} \cdot \frac{S_A}{S_B} \cdot \left(1 - \frac{\hat{P}_M}{S_A}\right) + (1-\chi) \cdot q_{\max} \cdot \left(1 - \frac{\hat{P}_M}{S_B}\right) \quad \text{Eq. 9.15}$$

With algebra, one can show that Equation 9.15 reduces to state that the optimal metered price is simply

$$\hat{P}_M = V + \chi \cdot (S_A - S_B) \quad \text{Eq. 9.16}$$

Therefore, the optimal entrance fee becomes, from Equations 9.12 and 9.16,

$$\hat{P}_E = \frac{q_{\max}}{2S_B} \cdot [S_B - V - \chi \cdot (S_A - S_B)]^2 \quad \text{Eq. 9.17}$$

At these prices, we can show the firm's profit for all N customers to be (from Eq. 9.13)

$$\pi = \frac{Nq_{\max}}{2S_B} \cdot \left[(S_B - V)^2 + \chi^2 \cdot (S_A - S_B)^2\right] \quad \text{Eq. 9.18}$$

Market heterogeneity has two significant effects on a two-part tariff. The first is that it reduces the optimal entry fee to participate in the market by a factor related to the fraction of customers who have a higher demand for the product and the differences in demand between the two segments. The second is that it increases the optimal metered price by an amount dependent on the size of the two segments and, again, the differences in demand between the two segments. In total, the effect of increasing the metered price, thus selling fewer units and decreasing the entry fee, and thus capturing less of the value that customers derive from the product, both lead to a lower profitability of two-part tariffs as markets become increasingly heterogeneous.

This leads to a generalization that executives should move toward using a higher entry fee and setting the metered price closer to the variable costs as customers become more homogeneous. As the market becomes more heterogeneous, executives should set a higher metered price and a lower entry fee. Eventually, the two-part tariff structurally devolves into a tying arrangement as market heterogeneity increases.

Notes

[1] Minet Schindehutte and Michael H. Morris, "Pricing as Entrepreneurial Behavior," *Business Horizons* 44, No. 4 (July–August 2001): 41–48.

[2] Price structures for segmenting the market, and in particular two-part tariffs, are a popular subject in pricing. For an entertaining source of examples, see Richard B. McKenzie, "Free Printers and Pricey Ink Cartridges," in *Why Popcorn Costs So Much at the Movies and Other Pricing Puzzles* (New York: Springer Science and Business, 2008): 143–58. Thomas T. Nagle and Reed K. Holden, "Segmented Pricing: Tactics for Separating Markets," in *The Strategy and Tactics of Pricing: A Guide to Profitable Decision Making*, 3d ed. (Upper Saddle River, NJ: Prentice Hall, 2002): 227–51.

[3] An extreme form of two-part tariffs can be found with buffet pricing, or so-called all you can eat pricing, where in the metered item is not priced at all, and all revenue is derived from the entrance fee. See Babu Nahata, Krzysztof Ostaszewski, and Prasanna Sahoo, "Buffet Pricing," *Journal of Business* 72, No. 2 (April 1999): 215–28.

[4] Beth Hayes, "Competition and Two-Part Tariffs," *The Journal of Business* 60, No. 1 (January 1987): 41–54.

[5] Dipak C. Jain, Eitan Muller, and Naufel J. Vilcassim, "Pricing Patterns of Cellular Phones and Phonecalls: A Segment-Level Analysis" *Management Science* 45, No. 2 (February 1999): 131–41.

[6] An examination of antitrust cases involving durable equipment makers and proprietary aftermarkets is presented in Severin Borenstein, Jeffrey K. MacKie-Mason, and Janet S. Netz, "Exercising Market Power in Proprietary Aftermarkets," *Journal of Economics and Management Strategy* 9, No. 2 (Summer 2000): 157–88. Benjamin Klein, "Market Power in Aftermarkets," *Managerial & Decision Economics* 17, No. 2 (March–April 1996): 143–164.

[7] An economic review of two-part tariffs and similar pricing mechanisms can be found in Joseph S. DeSalvo and Mobinul Huq, "Introducing Nonlinear Pricing into Consumer Choice Theory," *Journal of Economic Education* 33, No. 2 (Spring 2002): 166–79.

[8] Zipcar website. http://www.zipcar.com/chicago/check-rates (Accessed on May 7, 2009).

[9] The model of consumer choice and profit maximization with two-part tariffs presented here is a highly simplified extraction of the one presented by Walter Y. Oi, "A Disneyland Dilemma: Two-Part Tariffs for a Mickey Mouse Monopoly," *The Quarterly Journal of Economics* 85, No. 1 (February 1971): 77–96.

Chapter 10

Add-ons, Accessories, and Complementary Products

Arvind Balaraman, 2010/Used under license from Shutterstock.com

- What are complementary products?
- What should be included in the base product, and what should be offered as an add-on product?
- How should base products be priced compared to add-on products?
- How does heterogeneity in demand lead to add-on price structures?
- How is the pricing of signpost items and optional equipment influenced by consumer behavior?
- How do network effects drive price structures?
- How can complementary products be used to drive lock-in?
- Stretch Question: When should add-on products be priced relatively low, and when should they be priced relatively high?

In examining price structures, we quickly realize that products are rarely sold in isolation. Rather, customers will purchase multiple items to use in conjunction with each other to achieve their goals. When the purchase of one product leads to an increased likelihood of purchase for another product, we can call these two products *complementary products.* Add-on and accessory pricing concerns complementary product pricing.

Many products are the gateway to additional add-on modules or optional accessories. Add-ons and accessories are found in tangible and intangible goods, durables and consumables, and business and consumer products. For instance, Apple iPods and iPhones can be accessorized with a Bose iPod docking station and speakers. Likewise, General Electric (GE) washing machines can be purchased in isolation or in conjunction with a GE dryer; and enterprise software can be purchased to manage a single business function or multiple business functions with add-on modules.

When we identify a particular product as the gateway to the purchase of other products, we have identified an add-on or accessory pricing structure. Within an add-on pricing structure, there are subtle effects arising from consumer behavior that can drive changes to the pricing structure away from that which would be predicted from pure economic tradeoffs alone. For instance, economic tradeoffs derived either from conjoint analysis or exchange value calculators might imply that an accessory adds $5 to the value of a product. However, some consumer behavioral effects and more subtle economic effects may enable the firm to capture more than $5 from the sale of an accessory, and other effects may drive the value differential between the base product and the accessory to less than $5. Understanding these effects enables executives to improve add-on and accessory pricing beyond that which direct price-level measurements would imply, and target promotional pricing towards the part of the offer that will lead to the largest improvement in profit.

Add-on Price Structure

Add-on pricing is the default approach for most products, and the approach is relatively unlimited in its application. We see add-on price structures in pizza and pizza toppings, automobiles and optional features, mobile handsets and related accessories, even tennis rackets and balls. In industrial markets, firms will sell tens of thousands of units, each priced individually, where the total invoice price is the sum of each unit price multiplied by the number of units ordered, and therefore the purchase price of one item is added to the purchase price of the others to form the total invoice price.

At a high level, any product that is used in conjunction with other products can be examined through the lens of an add-on pricing structure. Also, any product in which the benefits and parts can be deconstructed to be additive and customers will use or value the product in different ways can be considered from the perspective of an add-on strategy.[1]

In an add-on price structure, distinct products are priced and sold individually. The products may be independent complements, wherein the purchase of any one product increases the likelihood of the purchase of any other complementary product, but each product can provide benefits independently. For instance, vanilla ice cream and Reese's peanut butter cups each provide value independently, but they can also be consumed jointly. Alternatively, the products may be tied complements, wherein the base product defines the product category and complementary products can be purchased to enhance the benefits of the base product, yet the complementary products provide little benefit without the base product. For example, customers may want cheese pizza and enhance it with pepperoni topping, but they rarely purchase pepperoni without the base pizza product.

Within an add-on or accessory pricing structure, the total price paid is a sum of the constituent parts of the purchase. If product A is priced at price P_A, and product B is priced at price P_B, then the price paid for both product A and B is $P_{Total} = P_A + P_B$. A simple economic model of add-on pricing is provided in Appendix 10.

The margin structure within an add-on pricing strategy is not as straightforward as it is with stand-alone products. As discussed, pricing stand-alone products is largely influenced by competitive issues and the differential value of that product with respect to similar products. Add-on pricing structures may appear at first glance to be an extension of unit pricing; however, further factors can skew the prices within an add-on strategy. With add-on products, the price structure is also influenced by the potential to use add-on products as a price segmentation hedge and the impact of complementary product sales on the sale of the base product.

From a pure price segmentation perspective, one might expect the price of a base product to yield a lower contribution margin than the price of the complementary product. Add-on pricing structures can be a form of price discrimination wherein customers who seek higher utility pay for that increased utility by purchasing additional features, and customers who have a lower willingness to pay purchase only the core product and forego utility-enhancing optional features. In this way, the base product represents the entry point into the product category. A pure price segmentation argument with perfect segmentation hedges would suggest that the base product should be designed to yield the minimal benefits required to satisfy customers with the lowest willingness to pay and be priced at a level that would attract the largest market. Further add-ons, or complementary products, would enhance the benefits of the base product and could serve as a means to capture higher profits from customers with a higher willingness to pay.

However, price segmentation is not the only factor that influences an add-on pricing structure. With complementary products, sales of the base product affect the sales of add-on products, and vice versa. Furthermore, network, signpost, and competitive effects all influence the price structure within an add-on strategy. Hence, there are many different influences on setting the price and determining contribution margins of the base product and complementary products.

The base product could yield small margins and the complementary products could yield high margins, such as with computer printers and ink, or razor handles and blades, as discussed in Chapter 9. Alternatively, the base product could yield high margins and the complementary products could yield low margins, such as with tennis rackets and tennis balls. Likewise, both the base and complementary products could yield somewhat equal margins, such as with desks and chairs.

We can quantify the margin challenge mathematically. Let $\%CM_A$ and $\%CM_B$ be the percentage of the contribution margin on products A and B respectively, where A is the base product and B is the add-on product. In constructing an add-on price structure, executives must determine if the contribution margins will be similar to that of a tying arrangement, in which $\%CM_A < \%CM_B$, or similar to that of a two-part tariff in which $\%CM_A > \%CM_B$, or relatively constant in which $\%CM_A = \%CM_B$.

Along with the challenge of defining the price and margin structure in an add-on strategy, marketers face the challenge of defining which attributes and features should be included in the base product and which should be developed as complementary or optional features. The desire to penetrate a new market or respond to an economic downturn with a lower price point may encourage firms to reduce the features in the base product and offer them as options instead. In other situations, competitive pressures, market evolution, and network effects may encourage the firm to take previously optional features and combine them into the base product.

Determining which part of a set of complementary goods delivers higher margins, or whether all complements yield similar margins, is a highly strategic issue subject to many influences. We will examine how add-on price structures enable price segmentation before turning to the influences on an optimal add-on pricing and margin structure.

Left out of this consideration is the possibility that complementary products will cannibalize sales of the base product. Such a situation would be considered as substitutes, not complements, and the sales of substitutes tend to be negatively correlated while the sales of complements tend to be positively correlated. Complementary products encourage the sale of one another. As such, the price for one affects the volume sold of that item as well as the volume sold of its complement, and therefore the optimal price for the complementary product. From a formal economic point of view, we would state that the cross-product elasticity of demand, or the percent change in quantity sold of one unit with respect to the percent change in price of another unit, is negative for complements.

Price Segmentation in Add-on Price Structures

To demonstrate an add-on price structure, let us examine the options associated with a Nokia 6103 mobile phone handset in 2007. The Nokia 6103 could be purchased with many additional accessories. There was a car kit for enabling hands-free conversations while driving; a connectivity cable to enable the handset to work in conjunction with a computer for updating contacts, synchronizing the calendar, downloading photos, or uploading ringtones and music; a travel charger for various countries with different plug receptor styles; an automobile charger; and an audio adapter for listening to music or having conversations without holding the phone against the ear. See Exhibit 10-1.

An individual customer may seek a specific set of features. In an add-on price structure, each customer can select the specific features that he or she desires. Moreover, different customers may have different levels of demand for a specific accessory. Demand for one feature may be high for some customers and low for others. Plotting the demand for a feature along each of the features, and connecting these demands for customer segments, creates a spider diagram of the demand profile for that customer. Different customers will have different demand profiles.

For instance, Exhibit 10-2 shows the demand profiles for two different customer segments for Nokia 6103 accessories. A customer in the traveling segment may want to have several travel chargers and mobile chargers but have little demand for other features. For example, a heavy business traveler may demand multiple travel chargers—one for work, one for home, one for the briefcase, and one for traveling in a foreign country where plug receptacles are different. Meanwhile, a returning Nokia customer who is upgrading to a new handset may already own the desired number and variety of chargers. This upgrading customer may instead want the added pleasure of a connectivity adapter to transfer numbers between handsets or the charger adapter to enable his or her old travel charger to work with the new handset plug-in interface. In both cases, the base Nokia 6103 handset will satisfy many of this person's core functional needs, but the specific demand profile for accessories will be different.

As can be seen in the customer segment demand profile, the add-on price structure allows for a high degree of customization of the product and benefits delivered. This also enables the total price paid for the base product plus accessories to better match the willingness to pay of highly heterogeneous customers.

If all the accessories were included in a single package along with the base product, many customers would be asked to purchase a number of features from which they gain no benefit, and the price for the single package would likely be higher than their willingness to pay. The

Exhibit 10-1 Potential Accessories for Nokia 6103 Handset (2007)[2]

Car Kit CK-10	€139
Connectivity Adapter CA-42	€ 49
Wireless Headset BH-200	€ 59
Travel Charger AC-4	€ 19
Mobile Charger DC-4	€ 19
Audio Adapter AD-46	€ 25

Exhibit 10-2 Customer Segment Demand Profile

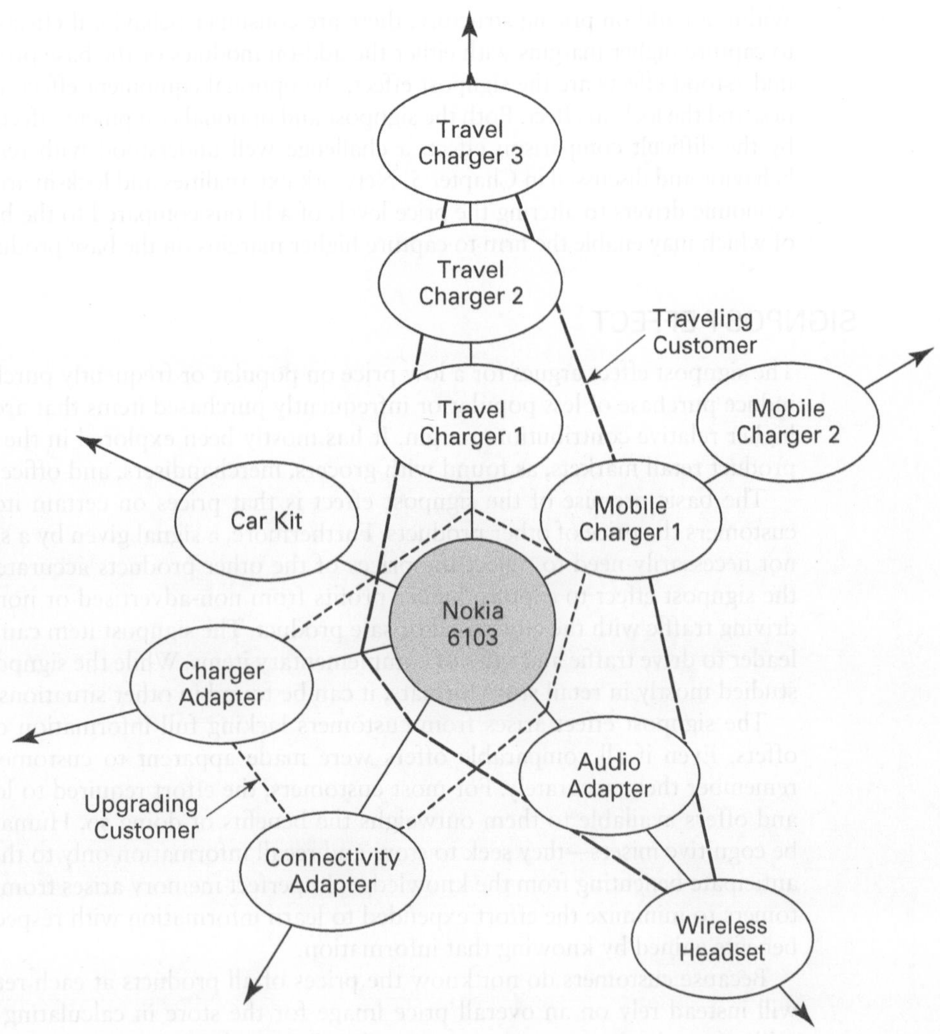

result would be what many customers refer to as a "gold-plated solution": lots of features that no one wants, at a price that no one is willing to pay. Not only would the profits be dampened, but the firm would be left vulnerable to a lower-priced and lower-featured competitor.

With an add-on strategy, the base product handset can be sold to many users with heterogeneous demand for additional features, and that heterogeneous demand for additional features can be satisfied through the purchase of add-on products and accessories at the customers' discretion. Each accessory, or multiple units of an accessory, act as a segmentation hedge, separating those customers with a higher willingness to pay for additional benefits from those without.

Add-on price structures are highly flexible. As can be seen from the demand profiles, they work well when the demand for features and benefits is highly heterogeneous between customers. Each customer can configure the product or set of products to his or her liking, and few customers are stuck paying for features that they do not value. When customer demand for features cannot be aggregated meaningfully into specific segments, add-on price structures are often found to be the easiest to manage and the most effective in capturing and satisfying customer demand.

Influences to Price Levels in Add-on Price Structures

Within an add-on pricing structure, there are consumer behavioral effects that enable firms to capture higher margins with either the add-on modules or the base product. Some better-understood effects are the signpost effect, the optional equipment effect, network externalities, and the lock-in effect. Both the signpost and optional equipment effects are highly driven by the difficult comparison effect, a challenge well understood with respect to consumer behavior and discussed in Chapter 5. Network externalities and lock-in are more measurable economic drivers to altering the price levels of add-ons compared to the base product, some of which may enable the firm to capture higher margins on the base product.

SIGNPOST EFFECT

The signpost effect argues for a low price on popular or frequently purchased products to induce purchase of less popular or infrequently purchased items that are priced to yield a higher relative contribution margin. It has mostly been explored in the context of multi-product retail markets, as found with grocers, merchandisers, and office suppliers.[3]

The basic premise of the signpost effect is that prices on certain items can signal to customers the price of other products. Furthermore, a signal given by a signpost item does not necessarily need to reflect the prices of the other products accurately. Firms can use the signpost effect to capture higher profits from non-advertised or non-sale items while driving traffic with the advertised or sale product. The signpost item can even act as a loss leader to drive traffic and sales of complementary items. While the signpost effect has been studied mostly in retail store formats, it can be found in other situations as well.

The signpost effect arises from customers lacking full information of all comparable offers. Even if all comparable offers were made apparent to customers, they may not remember them accurately. For most customers, the effort required to learn all the prices and offers available to them outweighs the benefits of doing so. Humans can be said to be cognitive misers—they seek to store and recall information only to the extent that they anticipate benefiting from the knowledge. Imperfect memory arises from the desire of customers to minimize the effort expended to learn information with respect to the expected benefits gained by knowing that information.

Because customers do not know the prices of all products at each retail location, they will instead rely on an overall price image for the store in calculating their anticipated utility for selecting one store over another. Prices of certain items can signal to customers the price image of other products within a store. Pricing these items low acts as a signpost to customers that the overall price image of the store is that of a low-priced outlet. Firms can profit from the signpost effect when they signal a low-price image while maintaining high prices on other items.

For instance, a customer looking to purchase a new tennis racket might first check the store's price on a can of tennis balls. If the balls seem low-priced, the customer may assume that the tennis rackets will also be priced low. If tennis balls seem to be priced high, the customer may walk out and seek bargains elsewhere.

With signpost items, retailers should select items for which customers are likely to have accurate expectation of prices and are complementary to the main item(s) they seek to sell. The signpost effect relies on the ability of customers to identify and interpret the signpost item accurately as priced favorably to induce customer interaction. Using popular and frequently purchased items for signpost pricing increases the likelihood that customers will have accurate price expectations. To drive sales to the main item, these signpost items should be complementary products.

The price signal communicated through the signpost effect does not necessarily have to be accurate to be effective. Customers are unlikely to have accurate price information on products that are purchased infrequently, such as furniture, stereo equipment, or computers. Firms can use low prices on popular or frequently purchased products to signal an overall low-price image; meanwhile, less popular or less frequently purchased products can be priced to yield a relatively higher margin. For instance, low prices on advertised items can signal an overall low-price image, while margins on unadvertised items can be maintained at a relatively higher level. The signpost effect will encourage the sale of both the advertised item and complementary products.

Effective strategic signpost pricing has been observed under the following circumstances: (1) Competing stores are heterogeneous in their format, some having a higher cost structure and others having a lower cost structure. (2) Customers are heterogeneous in their store preference, perhaps due to location or product availability, cleanliness and decor, customer service, or length of lines. (3) Customers select which retailer to purchase from based upon the expected utility that they will derive from patronizing a specific store. (4) Retailers signal their overall price image through advertised prices.

In these situations, stores can advertise the price of a select few products to increase the anticipated utility that a customer will capture by selecting a specific store. Meanwhile, they can sell other products at unadvertised prices that customers will discover only once they enter the store. Such circumstances can even encourage higher-cost retailers to price-match lower-cost retailers on advertised products to encourage store traffic, and yet capture profits through the sale of unadvertised products at higher prices.

OPTIONAL EQUIPMENT EFFECT

Manufacturers can couple lower-margin base models with higher-margin optional equipment. If the baseline product is compared with competing offers and the add-on products are rarely compared, the difficult comparison effect allows manufacturers to capture higher margins on add-on optional equipment. Moreover, manufacturers have something of a monopoly over factory-installed optional equipment, and as such, they can use these add-on items to effectively price-segment the market to some degree. The optional equipment effect with manufacturers is similar to signpost items in retail, in that a low-price offer that customers compare is used to drive customer traffic that can lead to offers of higher-margin items.

We can show this with an example from the auto industry. The 2007 BMW Z4 2.5 si Sports Roadster, equipped to manage E85 fuel, can be configured with a number of optional factory-installed features. See Exhibit 10-3. Factory options on the BMW Z4

Exhibit 10-3 BMW Z4 Base Price plus Optional Additional Features (2007)[4]

Base Suggested Retail Price for BMW Z4 2.5 si Sport Roadster, E85	**€61,330**
Options	
Ruby Black Metallic Exterior	€ 2,180
Individual Imola Red/Anthracite Bi-color Interior	€ 1,530
Composite Star Spoke Wheels	€ 565
Comfort Package	€ 810
Hi-fi Sys Prof DSP	€ 1,455
Navigation-system Professional	€ 2,690
Electric Fold Exterior Mirrors	€ 320
Wind Deflector	€ 335
Cruise Control	€ 365
Dark Poplar Wood Trim	€ 320
Total	**€71,900**

include exterior paint and surface, interior seat covering, interior trim, special wheel types, air conditioning, navigation system, folding exterior mirrors, and cruise control. The full price of the BMW Z4 changes substantially depending on the options selected.

Factory-installed optional equipment, unlike tying arrangements, does not require customers to make purchases after the initial transaction, and therefore it is unlikely to fall foul of antitrust concerns.

NETWORK EXTERNALITIES

Products are said to benefit from network externalities when the value of the product increases with the number of people who use it.[5] For instance, the value of Adobe Portable Document Format (PDF) files increases with the number of people who are able to read a PDF file. Similarly, email, mobile text messages, and online networking platforms benefit from network externalities in that the value any one user gains depends on the number of other users in the network. Network effects are a core strategic element behind Google's Adwords and Adsense offerings, Apple's iPhone and iPhone Apps offerings, Facebook, and even Twitter.

The network effect was first codified by George Gilder with fax machines in the 1980s, but it took Robert Metcalfe, co-inventor of the Ethernet, to popularize its consideration. According to Metcalfe's law, the value of a network under positive network externalities increases with the square of the number of people in the network. This claim is rather straightforward. Consider a network that includes n people. The value created by having other people in the network for any given customer is proportional to the number of other people in the network, or $(n - 1)$. Altogether, the total value of the network is proportional to the value of the number of people in the network, n, multiplied by the value that each person derives from the network $(n - 1)$, or $n \cdot (n - 1) = n^2 - n$. Thus, the value of the network increases with the square of the number of members within the network.

Firms that are launching products that are expected to benefit from positive network effects have a high motivation to increase the number of customers on their network quickly. This may encourage the launch price of the product to be greatly reduced from what it would be priced at in the absence of network effects to drive adoption. However, firms cannot indefinitely deliver products without capturing profits. They must profit from the network in some manner if they are to be expected to continue supporting it.

Network effects have led to the development of "freeware," or freely provided popular software offered in the hopes of developing a valuable network. With information goods, the cost of creation is high, but the cost of reproduction is low, if not zero. As such, adding more users to a network costs the firm very little, if anything. However, extracting value for creating and maintaining the network can remain a challenge. Hence, many firms offering freeware eventually seek revenue either from the users themselves or from others who seek access to that network.

Network externalities can lead to aggressive pricing behavior wherein the base product is offered at a low price, if not free, and profits are captured through the sale of complementary products. For instance, the pricing strategy of Adobe was to give the Adobe Reader for free to any user, but charge for the potential to create PDF files. Similarly, Apple priced access to its iTunes music file management system at zero, but it charged customers for downloading music through its online store. In these and similar cases, firms seek to earn profits from the users themselves by selling upgraded versions of the product or add-on products that enhance the product's functionality.

Similar to capturing profits from users themselves through the sale of complementary products, firms may also be encouraged to sell access to the network to third parties as a means of monetizing the network. The result is commonly referred to as a *two-sided market,* where one side of the market creates the network and the other side purchases access to that network. Using network effects to create two-sided markets is a classic strategy of newspapers and magazines. Periodicals provide subscriptions at a price lower than the marginal cost to produce those periodicals to create a reader base that advertisers will pay dearly to access. Similarly, LinkedIn and Facebook, two popular online social networking platforms, enable users to interact with other users freely, but LinkedIn sells access to its database of users to recruiters and Facebook sells advertising space.

LOCK-IN WITH COMPLEMENTARY PRODUCTS

Complementary products that increase switching costs of base products can encourage firms to price the base product high while pricing complementary products low, if not altogether abdicating any monopoly power over add-on products.[6] This occurs in cases where the base product is frequently purchased or is semidurable and purchased on the time scale of a year or two. To encourage customers to replace an expired item with a product from the same manufacturer, the firm can encourage customers to invest in complementary products. When they do, the complementary products act as a barrier to switching manufacturers at the time of replacement, thus locking in the customer.

Mobile handset makers accomplish this to some degree through encouraging customers to purchase power chargers, headsets, and car kits that contain proprietary protocols over connections for interactivity. For instance, Nokia offers branded accessories and encourages third parties to make compatible accessories simultaneously. When Nokia releases its latest handset, it sometimes takes care to ensure that it has some backward compatibility with earlier complementary products.

Similarly, users who purchase Microsoft Windows will invest significantly in complementary software that works only on the Windows platform. When the opportunity arises to switch platforms, perhaps to Linux or Apple OS X Leopard, customers may be reluctant to reinvest in new software that works on the new platform.

The lock-in effect can lead to a pricing strategy wherein complementary products are priced aggressively to encourage their dissemination into the market, while the core product is priced to capture profits as customers replace an expired product or extend their purchases within that category. In such a case, the firm may take a non-monopoly position in the market for complementary products because their dissemination drives the value of the core product.

Summary

- When the purchase of one product leads to an increased likelihood of purchasing another product, we can call these two products complementary products. Add-on and accessory pricing concerns complementary product pricing. In an add-on or accessory pricing structure, the price paid for a collection of individual products is the sum of the prices of each of those individual products.
- Add-on price structures enable price segmentation by providing the base product to a larger market and the add-on or accessory products to the subset of that market with a higher willingness to pay for greater functionality.
- The signpost effect argues for low pricing of popular or frequently purchased products in retail outlets to induce purchase of less popular or infrequently purchased items that are priced to yield a higher relative contribution margin.
- The optional equipment effect argues for a low price of the base-level product produced by a manufacturer and a relatively higher price for additional equipment at a higher relative contribution margin.
- Network externalities can influence the add-on price structure. If the value of the core product increases with the number of customers of that core product,

manufacturers have significant incentives to increase the customer base for that product. However, they must capture profits. To do so, they may either use add-on products to improve the margins captured from their customer base or create a two-sided market wherein other customers pay for access to the network.

- Complementary products can lock customers into a specific base product. If this lock-in is significant, firms can increase the margins on their base products relative to the margins that they capture with add-on or accessory products.

Exercises

1. Lou Malnati's offers a 12" cheese pizza for $13. Optional extra ingredients include mushrooms, onions, green peppers, black olives, sliced tomatoes, garlic, hot giardinera, anchovies, or fresh spinach. Each additional ingredient is priced at $1.70.
   a. Consider the demands of a vegetable lover. How much would Lou Malnati's ask for a cheese pizza with spinach, mushrooms, and sliced tomatoes.
   b. Consider the demands of a Mediterranean cuisine lover. How much would Lou Malnati's ask for a cheese pizza with black olives, onions, and anchovies?
   c. Draw a customer segment demand profile for different optional extra ingredients and identify the aforementioned vegetable and Mediterranean cuisine lovers.
   d. Discussion question: Why are add-on price structures commonly used?
2. A sporting equipment store offers a wide selection of soccer cleats, balls, jerseys, and gloves. Research indicated that customers have more accurate expectations of the prices of soccer cleats and jerseys than they have of the prices of gloves and balls.
   a. Which products might be suggested for use as a signpost item?
   b. Where might the price of the signpost items be compared to competing stores'—higher or lower?
   c. Where might the price of the non-signpost items be compared to competing stores'—higher or lower?
   d. What metric might you suggest that the store managers use to evaluate the effectiveness of a signpost-item price structure?
3. Triton Submarines LLC offers small submersibles that can take up to three individuals 1,000 m deep to explore the ocean. Triton recommends the following optional equipment as a part of the purchase of a Triton or Discovery submarine. Each item is priced to include an "integration fee," a fee directly charged by Triton for integrating the optional equipment with the submersible.

USBL Tracking System with Acoustic Modem	$52,812
Manipulator System	$45,800
Doppler Velocity Log	$17,250
High-Intensity Discharge External Lights X2	$13,645
Color Imaging Sonar System	$15,000

   a. How well can a customer price-compare submersibles?
   b. How well can a customer price-compare the optional equipment for a submersible?

   c. How well can a customer price-compare the integration fees for adding optional equipment to submersibles?
   d. In which part of the offer is Triton Submarine most likely to seek an above-average profit margin? The submarine, the optional equipment, or the integration fee?

4. Twitter is said to benefit from positive network externalities. Suppose that each user of Twitter values the ability to reach another person via Twitter at $0.0001 per user.
   a. Plot the value of Twitter to an individual user as the number of users already using Twitter increases from 1,000 to 1,000,000.
   b. Suppose that Twitter extracted value from its platform in proportion to the value that users place on the platform. What would be the value of the Twitter platform with 1,001 users, 10,001 users, and 1,000,001 users? Plot the value of the Twitter platform as the number of users increases from 1,001 to 1,000,001.
   c. Consider two different price structures for Twitter: (1) charging all users a flat fee of $10 per month versus (2) charging only heavy users (those with more than 1,000 followers) in proportion to the number of followers they have. Which of these two price structures is most likely to be accepted by customers? Which would be more profitable?

5. The Apple iPhone experience can be enhanced through the use of numerous additional applications, or apps, most of which are modestly priced. Apps can be developed by any firm, but are sold only through the Apple App Store. Similarly, the Google Android Smart Phone experience can also be enhanced through numerous apps that are also generally modestly priced. Unlike the iPhone Apps, however, Android Apps can be purchased from any vendor.
   a. Which approach gives the operating system vendor more control over the apps provided for its smart phones?
   b. Which approach is most likely to encourage wide dissemination of applications for a given smart phone operating system?
   c. Which approach is most likely to lead to lock-in effects with respect to the operating system?
   d. Given your answers to these questions, which strategy appears to be stronger, that for the Apple iPhone or the Google Android operating system? What other factors might drive Apple and Google to select the strategy that each did? Which of these firms would find it easier to change its strategy in the future?

6. After completing Appendix 10, consider a market whose heterogeneity in demand can be described with a uniformly distributed taste parameter varying from 0 to 1. The firm produces two products: the base product A, at a variable cost of $V_A = \$50$, and the add-on product *B*, at a variable cost of $V_B = \$10$. Assume zero fixed costs. Let the base product be valued by the most-demanding customers at $S_A = \$100$ and the add-on product be valued by the most-demanding customers at $S_B = \$500$.
   a. What is the optimal price of product A and product B?
   b. What fraction of the market would purchase product A under these assumptions?
   c. What fraction of the market would purchase product B under these assumptions?
   d. What would be the firm's profitability if the market had 10 million members?
   e. What portion of the profit would come from the base product, and what portion would come from the add-on product?

Appendix 10 Economic Model of Add-on Pricing[7]

Add-on price structures segment the market according to different customers' willingness to pay for different levels of benefits. To construct an economic model of prices and margins in an add-on price structure, we must incorporate market heterogeneity into our model for demand before turning to the challenge of optimizing prices and maximizing profits.

The simplest approach to modeling market heterogeneity in relationship to benefits derived and willingness to pay is to define a "taste" parameter that varies from zero to 1. Every individual customer has a specific taste parameter. The market overall has customers whose taste parameter can be any number between zero and 1. Customers with a low taste parameter (near zero) are those who value the product little and are not willing to pay much for the additional benefits that are provided through an add-on product. Customers with a high taste parameter (near 1) are those who value the product highly and have some willingness to pay for an add-on product. This approach to defining market heterogeneity with a taste parameter is completely general and not specific to any specific market.

The taste parameter can be thought of as a measure of how well a customer can convert a quality improvement into utility. Some do it well (a high taste parameter), others do it poorly (a low taste parameter). Alternatively, the taste parameter can be considered as a metric of price sensitivity versus utility sensitivity. Customers with a low taste parameter are significantly more price-sensitive, while customers with a high taste parameter are significantly more utility-sensitive.

To demonstrate, we model customer preferences with a customer net utility function. With two products, products A and B, where B is the add-on to A, consumers have a utility function for A alone and another utility function for A and B. Let us assume that the utility customers gain from B is in addition to that gained in A, and that B provides zero utility in the absence of A. This would be the case of a pure add-on product. The net utility function is simply the difference between the utility that customers derive from a product and the price that they paid. Under these assumptions, the net utility function is given by the pair of equations

$$U(t) = (S_A \cdot t - P_A) \text{ if purchasing A alone} \quad \text{Eq. 10.1.a}$$

$$U(t) = (S_A \cdot t - P_A) + (S_B \cdot t - P_B) \text{ if purchasing A and B} \quad \text{Eq. 10.1.b}$$

where P_A and P_B are the prices of products A and B, respectively, S_A and S_B are the maximum utilities that any customer can gain from products A and B, respectively, and t is our taste parameter, which varies between zero and 1. If no purchase is made, we assume that the customer neither gains nor loses utility—that is, that the utility function for not purchasing is zero. See Exhibit 10-4.

The taste parameter, t, accounts for the dispersion in willingness to pay between customers, or the market heterogeneity. As a model parameter, t is bound between zero and 1 ($t \in [0,1]$) For customers with a taste parameter of zero, ($t = 0$), they have no perceived utility from either the product or its add-on. For customers with a taste parameter of 1, ($t = 1$), they perceive that product A has a utility of S_A and would in fact be willing to pay S_A for the product. The fact that they have to pay only a price of P_A implies that they gain net utility of $S_A - P_A$ by consuming the product. Similarly, for customers with a taste parameter of 1, ($t = 1$), they perceive that the add-on product B has a utility of S_B and would in fact be willing to pay S_B for the add-on. The fact that they have to pay only a price of P_B implies that they gain net utility of $S_B - P_B$ by consuming the add-on. Intermediate values of the taste parameter indicate the value that specific customers place on quality differences. For instance, customers with a taste parameter of two-tenths ($t = 0.2$) value quality differences 20 percent as well as customers with a taste parameter of 1. Likewise, customers with a taste parameter of eight-tenths ($t = 0.8$) are able to value quality differences 80 percent as well as customers with a taste parameter of 1.

Exhibit 10-4 Consumer Utility Function for Add-on Structure

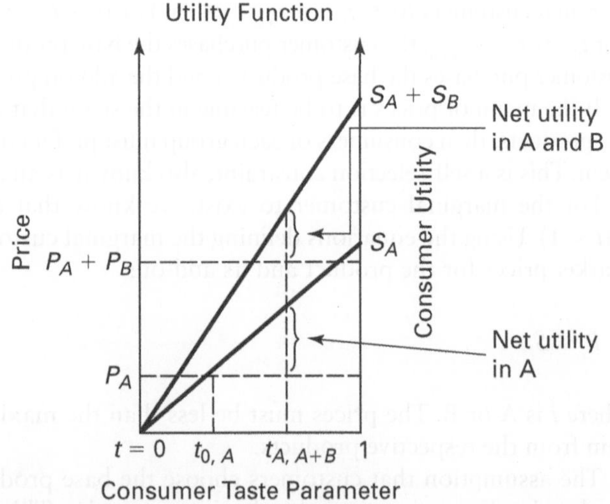

There are economically special types of customers who are indifferent between making a purchase and not making a purchase. These marginal customers can be identified by their taste parameters. With two products, the base product plus its add-on product, we have two types of marginal customers.

The first type of marginal customers is indifferent between making no purchase and purchasing product A alone, which is defined by the taste parameter $t_{0,A}$. For these customers, their net utility for purchasing the base product is exactly zero. Any customer with a taste parameter greater than $t_{0,A}$ will receive net consumer surplus from purchasing product A and thus will purchase. Any customer with a taste parameter less than $t_{0,A}$ would have negative net consumer surplus after purchasing and thus will not purchase. Thus, $t_{0,A}$ customers are marginal base-product customers. We assume that marginal customers with a taste parameter equal to $t_{0,A}$ purchase the base product without losing generality. By setting the net utility function for purchasing product A alone (Eq. 10.1a) equal to zero, we find the taste parameters of these marginal customers to be

$$t_{0,A} = \frac{P_A}{S_A} \qquad \text{Eq. 10.2}$$

The second type of marginal customers, $t_{A,A+B}$, is indifferent between purchasing product A alone and purchasing both products A and B. For these customers, the difference in net utility for purchasing the base product compared to purchasing the base plus and add-on product is zero. Any customer with a taste parameter greater than $t_{A,A+B}$ will receive more net utility from purchasing the add-on B with the base product A than from purchasing the base product A alone, and thus this person will purchase the add-on as well. Any customer with a taste parameter less than $t_{A,A+B}$ would have less net utility after purchasing the add-on B than from just purchasing the base product A, and thus this person will not purchase the add-on. Thus, $t_{A,A+B}$ customers are marginal add-on customers. We assume that marginal customers with a taste parameter equal to $t_{A,A+B}$ purchase the add-on without losing generality. By setting the net utility function for purchasing product A alone (Eq. 10.1a) equal to that for purchasing product A plus the base product (Eq. 10.1b), we find the taste parameters of the marginal add-on customers to be

$$t_{A,A+B} = \frac{P_B}{S_B} \qquad \text{Eq. 10.3}$$

Because the marginal customer between buying only one product and buying both products has at least bought the first product, we have restrictions on the taste parameters of these marginal customers ($0 \leq t_{0,A} \leq t_{A,A+B} \leq 1$). For $0 \leq t < t_{0,A}$, the customer doesn't purchase. For $t_{0,A} \leq t < t_{A,A+B}$, the customer purchases the base product A alone. For ($t_{A,A+B} \leq t \leq 1$), the customer purchases the base product A and the add-on product B.

If the menu of prices is to be feasible in the sense that customers will voluntarily choose the products, then consumers of each group must prefer consuming the package intended for them. This is a self-selection constraint, also known as an *incentive compatibility constraint.*

For the marginal customer to exist, we know that $t_{0,A}$ and $t_{A,A+B}$ must be less than 1 ($t < 1$). Using the equations defining the marginal customers, we uncover the limit of the market prices for the product and its add-on:

$$P_i < S_i \quad \text{Eq. 10.4}$$

where i is A or B. The prices must be less than the maximum utility that a customer can gain from the respective products.

The assumption that customers choose the base product prior to choosing an add-on product implies an interior self-selection constraint. This interior constraint yields a more interesting relationship regarding prices. For these customers, we know that $t_{0,A} \leq t_{A,A+B}$. Using the equations defining the marginal customers, we uncover a relationship between the market prices of the product and its add-on:

$$\frac{S_A}{P_A} \geq \frac{S_B}{P_B} \quad \text{Eq. 10.5}$$

That is, the base product A must deliver a better quality-to-price ratio than the add-on product B does.

If we assume a form of the distribution of taste parameter, we can furthermore derive optimal prices for the base and add-on products. For simplicity, let us assume that customers are uniformly distributed in their taste parameter. Thus, 10 percent of customers have a "taste preference" of less than 0.1, 50 percent of customers have a "taste preference" of less than 0.5, 90 percent of customers have a "taste preference" of less than 0.9. While a uniform distribution is unlikely to be an accurate description of the way in which customers value quality differences, it makes the analysis mathematically much simpler than assuming a Gaussian or beta distribution of the taste parameter.

If there are Q total customers in the market, then the total demand for product A is $Q \cdot (t_{A,A+B} - t_{0,A})$, and the total demand for products A and B is $Q \cdot (1 - t_{A,A+B})$.

Having described the market and how customers make choices, we can turn to the challenge of maximizing the firm's profits. The firm's profit equation is given by

$$\begin{aligned}\pi(P_A, P_B) = {} & Q \cdot (t_{A,A+B} - t_{0,A}) \cdot (P_A - V_A) \\ & + Q \cdot (1 - t_{A,A+B}) \cdot (P_A + P_B - V_A - V_B)\end{aligned} \quad \text{Eq. 10.6}$$

where we have set fixed costs equal to zero without losing generality; and V_A and V_B are the variable costs of the base product A and the add-on product B, respectively. The first term yields the profit earned by selling the base product A alone. The second term yields the profit earned from selling both the base product A and the add-on product B.

We can find the optimal prices of products A and B at the point where the first derivative of the firm's profit equation with respect to either independently varying price, P_A or P_B, is zero. Recalling that our marginal taste parameters are functions of prices, we find

$$\frac{\partial \pi}{\partial P_A} = 0 \Rightarrow 0 = -\frac{\partial t_{0,A}}{\partial P_A}(P_A - V_A) + (1 - t_{0,A}) \qquad \text{Eq. 10.7a}$$

$$\frac{\partial \pi}{\partial P_B} = 0 \Rightarrow 0 = -\frac{\partial t_{A,A+B}}{\partial P_B}(P_B - V_B) + (1 - t_{A,A+B}) \qquad \text{Eq. 10.7b}$$

where, from Equations 10.2 and 10.3, we know that

$$\frac{\partial t_{0,A}}{\partial P_A} = \frac{1}{S_A} \qquad \text{Eq. 10.8a}$$

$$\frac{\partial t_{A,A+B}}{\partial P_B} = \frac{1}{S_B} \qquad \text{Eq. 10.8b}$$

Using the expression for the marginal base product customer and its first derivative (Eqs. 10.2 and 10.8a) in the expression for identifying the optimal base price (Eq. 10.7a), we can find the optimal base price. Similarly, using the expression for the marginal add-on customer and its first derivative (Eqs. 10.3 and 10.8b) in the expression for identifying the optimal add-on price (Eq. 10.7b), we can find the optimal add-on price. After simplification, we find

$$P_i = \frac{S_i + V_i}{2} \qquad \text{Eq. 10.9}$$

where i is A or B. The optimal prices for the base and add-on products lie at the average of the maximum consumers' utility and the variable cost to produce.

Checking to ensure that the prices fit the requirement of creating a customer ($t < 1$), we find a variable cost condition given by

$$V_i < S_i \qquad \text{Eq. 10.10}$$

Moreover, because we know that the firm will not produce a product unless it can capture a price greater than its variable costs, we also find

$$V_i < P_i \qquad \text{Eq. 10.11}$$

Thus, the customer self-selection constraint and the firm's profit constraint yield the following relationship between variable costs, price, and potential utility:

$$0 \le t_i \le 1 \Rightarrow 0 \le V_i \le P_i \le S_i \qquad \text{Eq. 10.12}$$

The interior consumer self-selection constraint, which requires customers to make a tradeoff between buying either just product A or both A and B, yields a relationship between the marginal cost of the base product and its add-on. From constraining $t_{0,A} \le t_{A,A+B}$, we find

$$\frac{S_A}{V_A} \ge \frac{S_B}{V_B} \qquad \text{Eq. 10.13}$$

The base product A must also have a better quality-to-variable-cost ratio than the add-on product B.

At these prices, we find the total producer's profit is

$$\pi(add\text{-}ons) = \frac{Q}{4}\left\{\frac{(S_A - V_A)^2}{S_A} + \frac{(S_B - V_B)^2}{S_B}\right\} \qquad \text{Eq. 10.14}$$

The optimal prices of the base product A and the add-on product B are identical to those that would have been derived if they were separate products. (Compare Equation 10.9 with Equation 6.5 in Appendix 6.) Moreover, the profit is the same as if the products had been sold independently. (Compare Equation 10.14 with Equation 6.7 in Appendix 6.) In other words, to arrive at the price effects of the complementary nature of two products, such as a mobile phone and a phone charger or tennis balls and a tennis racket, we have to move beyond a simple economic model and toward a model that better incorporates consumer behavior. One such adjustment might be to assume that the demand for one of the products increases when it is sold as an add-on rather than as an isolated product. If either S_A or S_B increases due to the add-on nature of the products, then the prices and the firm's profits would increase as well. Otherwise, add-on pricing is exactly the same as standard unit pricing.

Notes

[1] Rafi Mohammed has written widely about the need to provide customers with a menu of prices. Rafi Mohammed, "Differential Pricing," *The Art of Pricing* (New York: Crown Business, 2005): 123–43.

[2] Nokia accessories prices observed online. http://www.nokia-accessories.ie/acatalog/#top (accessed on September 9, 2007). These are not the official Nokia prices, but they do provide insight into accessory pricing in an add-on pricing structure.

[3] An approachable review of signpost pricing can be found in Eric Anderson and Duncan Simester, "Mind Your Pricing Cues," *Harvard Business Review* 81, No. 9 (September 2008): 96–103. More academic discussion can be found in Duncan Simester, "Signalling Price Image Using Advertised Prices," *Marketing Science* 14, No. 2 (Spring 1995): 166–88. Eric T. Anderson and Duncan I. Simester, "The Role of Sale Signs," *Marketing Science* 17, No. 2 (January 1998): 139–55.

[4] Prices observed on the BMW website http://www.bmw.ie/ie/en/index_narrowband.html (accessed on September 9, 2007).

[5] Carl Shapiro and Hal R. Varian, "Networks and Positive Feedback," *Information Rules: A Strategic Guide to the Network Economy* (Boston: Harvard Business School Press, 1999): 183–84.

[6] Carl Shapiro and Hal R. Varian, "Recognizing Lock-in," *Information Rules: A Strategic Guide to the Network Economy* (Boston: Harvard Business School Press, 1999): 103–34.

[7] In this section, we demonstrate an economic model of add-on pricing. While this model will elucidate limited information with respect to pricing add-on products, it is necessary for the purpose of bridging the economic model used for single-item pricing with those that will be revealed in versioning and bundling.

Chapter

11

Versioning

Courtesy Symantec Corporation

Courtesy Symantec Corporation

Courtesy Symantec Corporation

- What is versioning? How is versioning different from bundling or add-on pricing?
- Why might versioning be superior to pure per-unit pricing of complementary products? Why might it be inferior?
- How does market heterogeneity inform the choice of versioning over complementary product pricing?
- Are production cost savings the only reason to offer versions rather than individual products?
- How do different psychological effects influence prices within a versioning structure?
- How should discounts be managed when a firm is versioning?
- Stretch Question: Should higher-featured versions always be sold at a discount compared to the sum price of the individual product features?

Versioning is an alternative approach to price segmentation from add-ons and other individual unit price structures. Like add-ons and unit pricing, versioning attempts to price-segment customers according to their willingness to pay for marginal improvements in attributes, features, and benefits. Unlike unit pricing, versioning constrains the route to customers for gaining additional benefits to the purchase of the next, higher value product in a product lineup.

In versioning, different variations of a similar product are sold simultaneously. Some versions offer more features or benefits, while others offer fewer features and benefits. As products span from feature-deprived to feature-enhanced, the price likewise increases.[1]

Versioning can be found in tangible goods markets at the retailer, manufacturer, and industrial levels. Retailers offer different versions of consumer products, such as store-brand laundry detergent, Gain, and Tide. Manufacturers offer various versions of similar products, such as Black & Decker coffeemakers that vary according to brewing capacity, exterior finish, programmability, thermal carafe, and the ability to brew espresso along with regular coffee. Even industrial suppliers will offer different versions of their products; for instance, polyethylene is sold in varying grades of purity for different uses.

A more prevalent use of versioning is with information goods. Software suppliers routinely version their products similarly to Intuit's Quickbooks line of business accounting software or Norton's line of computer security and maintenance software. Likewise, financial services can be sold in different versions; for instance, American Express offers the Green, Gold, and Platinum cards.

Even infrastructure can be marketed through versioning strategies. For instance, U.S. auto travelers have a choice between paying tolls with an EZPass or cash, and simply avoiding toll highways altogether.

If we examine the American Express offers more closely, we find a simple example of how versioning can be used to increase customer benefits and prices simultaneously.[2] Each of the Green, Gold, and Platinum cards will enable the cashless purchase of goods and include the Membership Rewards loyalty program; but customers seeking a higher level of service or access to special events must upgrade to the Gold or Platinum version of the card. In addition, only the Platinum card includes travel privileges, such as giving customers instant access to airlines' airport clubs. See Exhibit 11-1.

Likewise, we find a similar theme of increasing benefits delivered while simultaneously increasing the price demanded for Norton Security.[3] Norton AntiVirus, Internet Security, and 360 each protect users from computer viruses. However, added features such as download protection, shopping protection, and wireless protection are available only through Internet Security and 360. If customers want to allow Norton to manage computing performance automatically, they must upgrade all the way to Norton 360. See Exhibit 11-2.

Exhibit 11-1 American Express Card Features and Prices (2007)

Card	Features	Price
Green	Membership Rewards	\$95 annual fee
Gold	Membership Rewards Gold Events Purchase Protection Global Assist Hotline	\$125 annual fee
Platinum	Membership Rewards By Invitation Only Events Purchase Protection Global Assist Hotline Travel Privileges	\$450 annual fee

Exhibit 11-2 Norton Security Features and Prices (2008)

Product	Features	Price
Norton AntiVirus	Antivirus	39.99 £
Norton Internet Security	Antivirus Download Protection Shopping Protection Wireless Protection	49.99 £
Norton 360	Antivirus Download Protection Shopping Protection Wireless Protection PCTuneup Data Backup	59.99 £

Because versioning restricts choice over unit pricing mechanisms, it might be predicted that this strategy is less profitable than a comparable add-on price structure. With choice restricted, it is more difficult for the offers to match the customers' desired benefits and willingness to pay. With suboptimal matching between products demanded and products offered, sales may be depressed as customers look for alternative offers. A competitor that avoided a versioning strategy might be able to match demand and products better through a more typical unit pricing offer. As such, firms offering versions might be perceived as being at a competitive disadvantage to firms that focus on unit pricing.

However, in many industries, firms find that versioning is more profitable than a per-unit pricing structure. Moreover, customers may prefer versioning over pure unit pricing. If customers prefer versioning and firms improve profits through versioning, then the effects of versioning must be beyond that of combining individual items and prices to create specific versions.

There are multiple reasons that versions are often preferred over pure individual item structures, both by firms and customers. Versioning may deliver cost savings for the firm, which enables it to lower its prices below that which it would have used if it had marketed the items individually. The firm also may reduce challenges for customers by preassembling all the necessary parts of a full product into a single package rather than requiring customers to identify their specific needs, search for the multiple items that satisfy their needs, and assemble them into a working whole. Beyond these purely economic reasons, versioning also taps into psychological effects that further improve the product's receptivity by the market and therefore the profit improvement capability of a versioning pricing structure for the firm.

In this chapter, we will examine the versioning price structure prior to exploring the many effects that can lead to its competitive advantage or improve its deployment. In this exploration, we will uncover relationships between the prices of different versions, and contrast these prices with those that would have been used in a unit pricing structure. Of specific interest are effects that may drive the price of the version higher, lower, or equal to that of its equivalent compilation of unit-priced goods. That is, when would the price of a versioned good be different from the sum price of its additive parts?

Price Segmentation with Versioning

Strategies using versioning often rely on a good-better-best progression of products. The good product is priced lowest and has the fewest features and benefits; it is an entry-level product. The good product is feature-deprived, providing the minimal functionality to satisfy customers. In an extreme form, it is a stripped-down version of a higher-value product, with the bare-bones features required to compete within the product category. The best product is priced the highest and has the most features and benefits; it is a top-level offering. The best product is the most feature-enhanced, providing further functionality to meet the demands of a more discriminating clientele. In an extreme form, it is loaded with fancy features to satisfy even the most-demanding customer of the product category. Between good and best lies the better product, which is priced in the middle of the spectrum and loaded with a medium level of features and benefits.

Good-better-best strategies can easily be understood with a price-to-benefits map. As products progress from good to better to best, the price and benefits provided increase. Some customers are willing to pay more than others. When the willingness to pay and the benefits demanded follow a normal bell curve, we can map out the expected sales

Exhibit 11-3 Versioning Price-to-Benefits Strategy

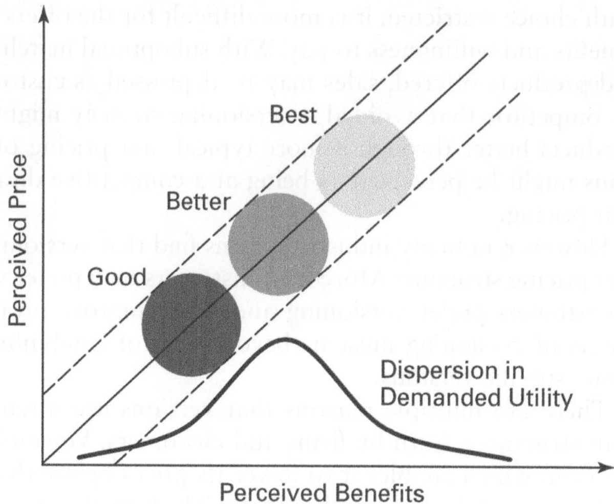

of the different versions. If the average customer seeks the benefits of the better product and derives greater utility after paying the demanded price, we would expect the middle, better product to be the most popular or frequently sold. The good and best products would attract lower levels of interest. See Exhibit 11-3.

Implementing a good-better-best strategy requires an understanding of the heterogeneity in benefits demanded. Marketers must determine which features should be used to enhance a product and which can be omitted to deprive a product of certain benefits but still remain within the category. The entry-level version must deliver sufficient functionality to satisfy a portion of the market's needs, but not all. The feature-enhanced versions must satisfy the demands of more utility-sensitive segments. The key is determining the feature distinction between the feature-enhanced and feature-deprived versions. Different versions must deliver meaningfully different benefits. The feature and benefit differentiations between the products act as segmentation hedges between the utility-sensitive customers and price-sensitive segments.

With information goods, a common approach is to design and develop the full-featured product and then remove features to create the other lesser-valued versions within the product lineup. In fact, for software, it is argued that firms should make the full product and disable certain forms of functionality to produce the feature-deprived versions. Features can be stripped out from the full product to serve those with a lower willingness to pay. Stripping out these features may cause the firm to suffer additional development costs in making the feature-deprived version; however, these costs are usually fixed. Like other fixed costs, they have no direct economic relationship to the pricing of the versions, but they retain an influence over the economic decision to develop and market these versions.

The price-to-benefits map also indicates a key limitation of pure good-better-best version strategies. Good-better-best approaches assume that benefits can be added in a monotonically increasing manner, such that the highest-priced version has significantly more features than the lower-priced version. More significantly, good-better-best strategies also assume that customers' heterogeneity in benefits sought is one-dimensional. That is, if the better version is created by adding enhancement E1 to a good product, and the best version is created by adding enhancement E2 to the better product, most customers that desire enhancement E2 also desire enhancement E1.

In some markets, customer heterogeneity in benefits demanded will correlate with willingness to pay. For instance, some customers are satisfied with a simple charge card, while others desire greater customer service and are willing to pay for enhanced benefits. In other markets, customer heterogeneity in benefits demanded does not correlate with willingness to pay. For instance, some customers like vanilla ice cream while others like chocolate, but both have the same willingness to pay. Market-specific customer insight must inform the pricing strategy of the correlation between benefits sought and willingness to pay. In markets where benefits desired does not correlate with willingness to pay, the versioning strategy cannot take a good-better-best approach and instead must devolve towards a more general multi-product strategy.

From a profitability perspective, a firm should not add $1 in marginal cost to a product unless it can increase the price by more than $1, holding all else constant. For this reason, most firms will earn larger margins on their feature-enhanced versions. Indeed, for infrastructure- or intellectual property–based goods, the marginal cost to reproduce is constant between the versions and hence the contribution margins are directly proportional to the price that a firm can capture with a product.

It is often tempting for executives to try to shift all customers to the highest-priced and highest-featured version. However, executives must balance this desire to shift customers towards higher price points with the potential negative consequences. Firms should be wary of leaving room at the bottom of the market for a competitor to introduce a low-feature, low-margin product that would give that competitor a foothold in the industry. Furthermore, shifting all the customers out of the lower-priced versions and into the highest-price version may imply that the price of the highest-value version is too low. In these cases, the firm is likely leaving money on the table.

Influences on a Versioning Strategy

To understand the value of versioning, we must look at the influences that give rise to a versioning strategy. These include marginal cost issues. However, in all markets, there are some interesting neuroeconomic and consumer behavioral issues that inform a versioning strategy or enable it to deliver higher profits than would be gained through an additive per-unit pricing strategy.

MARGINAL COSTS

Versioning strategies have often been defended from a marginal cost standpoint. If the marginal cost of producing an enhanced version is less than that of producing individual products that can be added to each other to deliver the same benefits as the enhanced version, then versioning will be more profitable than producing individual items. Sub-additive marginal costs contribute to the profitability of versioning in two ways: (1) They lower the costs for the firm to deliver the same level of benefits and thus enable the firm to capture higher profits. Moreover, a pure profit optimization argument based on downward-sloping demand curves indicates that the optimal price of the enhanced version will be less than the sum of the optimal prices of individual products if they were produced and sold individually. Thus, (2) sub-additive marginal costs allow the price to decrease slightly while delivering the same level of benefits, thus increasing the demand for the product.

Sub-additive marginal costs are the primary driver behind versioning in information markets. For example, hard disk drive manufacturers find it less expensive to produce a single hard disk drive with twice the storage capacity than to produce two individual hard disk drives. Likewise, software manufacturers face near-zero reproduction costs, but non-zero marginal packaging and selling costs, and therefore they would often reap higher profits through versioning over add-on price strategies.

PROSPECT THEORY

Of the psychological effects that influence price structures, prospect theory looms large. As explored in an earlier chapter, prospect theory indicates that it is better to unbundle gains and bundle pains. In terms of versioning, the gains that customers receive are the many benefits delivered through the product. Higher-level versions deliver more benefits; lower-level versions deliver fewer benefits. While all the benefits are bundled in a single product, the individual benefits can be isolated and highlighted during purchase decisions to encourage customers to select a higher-value product. With respect to the dictate of bundling pains, versioning bundles the pain of payment by asking customers to pay a single price for the litany of benefits rather than a separate price for each benefit. In this way, prospect theory predicts that versioning strategies encourage customers to purchase a higher level of benefits than they would under itemized pricing, and therefore the firm can earn higher profits from versioning.

Three common techniques are used to highlight the gains and benefits in different versions. First, marketing communications often delineate the value points of the enhanced version compared to the base product to highlight the added benefits. Second, packaging often varies between the base product and the enhanced version to highlight the value differential. Third, the product form factor can be differentiated between the base product and the enhanced version to clarify the value differential between the products visually. Combined, these and other techniques can effectively enable a firm to psychologically unbundle the gains in a versioning strategy to a similar level to the one they would have in an itemized pricing structure. Thus, when managed properly, both itemized and versioning structures unbundle gains equally well.

Versioning strategies dominate itemized price structures when it comes to bundling pain. With itemized pricing, each additional source of gain is clearly associated with an additional pain in the form of an additional price. The price increment in itemized pricing is explicit in the form of effectively asking customers if they want to pay price P_A or price $P_A + P_B$. In contrast, a versioning strategy provides additional gain in an enhanced version while subsuming the pain in a new price. The price tradeoff in a versioning strategy comes in the form of asking customers if they would prefer to pay price P_A or P_{Total}, where $P_{\text{Total}} > P_A$. In a sense, the versioning strategy asks if customers would prefer one pain or another larger pain, while the add-ons strategy asks if they would prefer one pain or two. Prospect theory indicates that they would generally prefer one larger pain over two smaller pains that add up to the same total larger pain; hence, versioning strategies dominate over itemized pricing in bundling pains.

Because of the implications of prospect theory, it is possible that a versioning strategy could yield a higher total price on an enhanced version than that delivered by add-on pricing from the sum of individual products. That is, if product Total delivers the sum benefits of products A and B, then prospect theory would predict that it is possible for P_{Total} to be greater than the sum of P_A and P_B. Research has yet to demonstrate that this conjecture is true, however.

EXTREME AVERSION

A well-understood effect in versioning is extreme aversion, an effect that arises from prospect theory but has been specifically identified with respect to the choices that customers make between competing versions. Given a good-better-best product lineup, customers tend to select the better version. While it may appear that the middle option offers the best price-to-benefits tradeoff for the most customers, research indicates that the price-to-benefits tradeoff is not the only driver. Instead, the tendency to choose the middle option rather than either the lowest or highest option is partially due to the aversion of customers to buying either the lowest- or highest-quality product.

Extreme aversion arises from loss aversion. Compared to a reference point, consumers are more averse to losses away from that reference point than they are gain-seeking to improvements to that reference point, as discussed with respect to prospect theory.[4] The losses in benefits in moving from a middle version towards a lower-quality version will loom larger than the gains in savings by purchasing at a lower price; hence, humans may be averse to the lowest product within a lineup. At the other end of the product lineup, the losses in price paid in moving from a middle version towards a higher version may loom larger than the gains in benefits; hence, humans may also be averse to the highest-value product. The result is a tendency of customers to select a middle version or, alternatively stated, an aversion to extremes.

An early study that revealed extreme aversion was conducted with VCR sales. Since that early study, extreme aversion has become a standard vantage point for managing a versioning strategy. For instance, given that customers are averse to extremes, firms have an incentive to produce or market an extreme version at the top of a product lineup, even if they expect very few customers to purchase this product, if only to decrease the aversion and increase the purchases of an otherwise high-end product.

Another method in which extreme aversion has informed versioning strategies is in the number of versions that a firm should produce. Generally, firms should make products at three or more different levels of benefits, rather than two or less, because of extreme aversion. With two or fewer versions, both versions are extremes, forcing customers to make careful tradeoffs between the two offers. With three or more, customers may feel safer knowing that they are choosing a middle version; thus, three or more versions may accelerate purchase decisions and increase sales.

VERSION RANGE, ORDER, AND NUMBER EFFECTS

While cost savings may encourage firms to execute versioning, and extreme aversion may explain why many versioning strategies with three or more products might be superior to ones with two or fewer, these results only generate more questions. For instance, how many versions are too many? What is the proper range of versions? In what order should the versions be presented?

From a profit maximization point of view, we have to acknowledge that each version comes with its own costs. Even if the marginal costs to produce different versions were zero, the marketing costs of defining, developing, and promoting an infinite number of separate versions would soon become prohibitive. Hence, one limit to the proliferation of versions is simply cost.

The number of versions is also limited by the need to enable customers to make quick and easy, yet meaningful, decisions. With too many versions, customers have difficulty making tradeoffs to identify the product that is most likely to satisfy their desire for utility and a low price. Customer confusion can lead to delayed purchases, depressing overall demand. In online environments, marketers have noticed significant improvements in sales when the number of versions offered at a time is reduced, rather than increased, even when the number offered is as little as two versus three at a time. When markets necessitate many different versions, firms must increase their expenditures on consultative selling and market communications to help customers through the decision-making process and identify the product that will deliver the best price-to-benefits for that customer.

Some studies have led to conclusions regarding the range of versions that a firm should offer as well.[5] If the range of products available varies too widely, some research indicates that customers may find the offers hard to believe. Customers may believe that it is not possible for the firm to deliver sufficient benefits in a single product at the top of the range to justify its price and simultaneously deliver anything of value at the bottom of the price range. These customers may be discouraged from all offers made and simply choose not to purchase.

These range effect observations have led to a general prescription among restaurateurs to ensure that the highest-priced item within a section be no more than twice the price of the lowest-priced item in that section. While this prescription may be accurate for restaurants, it is also observed that many firms routinely offer products at a much wider range of prices. For instance, a first-class cabin on an international flight might cost ten to twenty times the price of a coach flight. As such, any guideline to the maximum price range is likely to be industry- and market-specific.

Rather than providing a prescription on the maximum allowable range, the range effect can indicate a needed action by executives when they believe it is depressing sales. If a firm notices that sales are depressed after releasing a new version at the top or bottom of the price range, executives could conclude that the range effect has been uncovered. To reverse this negative outcome, they may either drop a product at the extreme or change the brand names of the products at one or the other extreme to distance the products further. Dow Corning executed this latter strategy with great results when launching the Xiameter brand in 2009 to reach a more price-sensitive segment while retaining the Dow Corning name for more utility- and service-sensitive customers in the silicone industry.

With respect to order, the experience of many salespeople and marketing executives has been supported by research that indicates that firms are usually better off when they present offers starting with the highest-priced product first. Presenting products in descending order—that is, from the highest- to the lowest-priced product—tends to encourage customers to select a higher-priced product on average than presenting the same products in ascending order. There are situations where the order may be changed, such as a sudden decline in the economy and a need to demonstrate low-cost options to the market, but generally, firms should highlight the most-expensive item within the lineup.

DISCOUNTING AND CONSTANT, DIVERGENT, OR CONVERGENT PRICE DIFFERENTIALS

When individual products within a versioning lineup are discounted, the price differences between the products will change. Changing price differentials between versions can influence customer choices regarding their desired version. Because the list prices of versions are usually optimized in relationship to each other, mismanaged discounts on one version can run amok with the profits earned on all versions within the product lineup. One approach to managing this potential challenge is to consider how a price discount affects the price differential between the versions. Specifically, executives can consider whether the discounting policy results in a constant, divergent, or convergent price differential.

The challenge can be illustrated with a price waterfall with a simple two-version strategy, a base product and an enhanced product, under the extreme consideration of zero marginal costs. Exhibit 11-4 shows simplified price waterfalls within a versioning strategy under constant, divergent, and convergent price differentials. With constant price differentials after discounting, both the base and enhanced versions receive the exact same monetary value of discounting and thus the difference in the net price paid is the same as the list price differences. With divergent price differentials after discounting, the base product will be discounted more than the enhanced version, and thus the price differential between the

Exhibit 11-4 Constant, Divergent, and Convergent Price Differentials

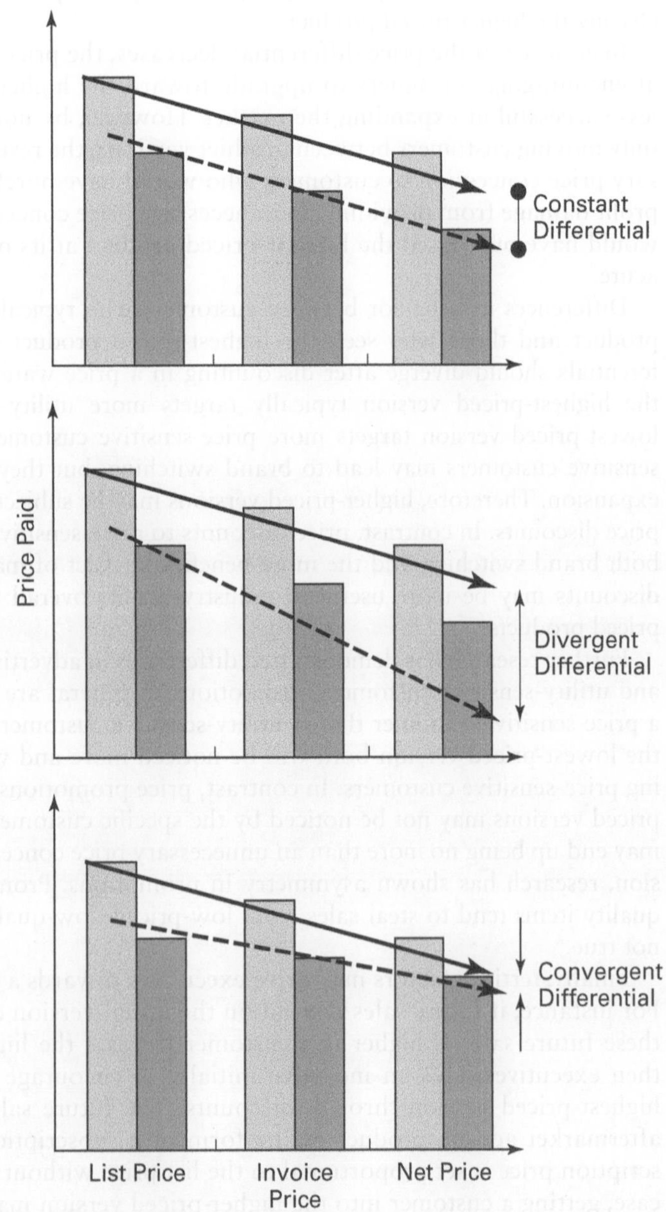

versions increases. With convergent price differentials after discounting, the base product will be discounted less than the enhanced version, and thus the price differential between the versions decreases.

From the viewpoint that list prices were optimized with respect to customer tradeoffs initially, any discounts should leave price differentials constant. The price differential defined by consumer utility while setting initial prices is a measure of the tradeoffs that customers make between price and benefits. Any divergence from these differentials will cause one product to cannibalize the sales of another product.

If the price differential increases, the low price of the lower-value version will encourage new customers into the market while also taking sales from the higher-priced versions.

This cross-product cannibalization results from customers perceiving that they will gain a higher net utility after purchasing the lower-priced product than they would from purchasing the higher-priced product.

In contrast, if the price differential decreases, the price promotion will be successful at encouraging consumers to upgrade toward the higher-priced version, and yet it is less successful at expanding the market. However, by not increasing sales overall and only moving customers between product versions, the result may simply be an unnecessary price concession to customers who would have purchased a product anyway. The profit damage from providing an unnecessary price concession to those customers who would have purchased the highest-priced product at its original list price is especially acute.

Differences in behavior between customers who typically purchase the lowest-priced product and those who seek the highest-priced product might suggest that price differentials should diverge after discounting in a price waterfall. In a versioning strategy, the highest-priced version typically targets more utility-sensitive customers, and the lowest-priced version targets more price-sensitive customers. Price discounts to utility-sensitive customers may lead to brand switching, but they are unlikely to yield market expansion. Therefore, higher-priced versions may be subject to a policy of having smaller price discounts. In contrast, price discounts to price-sensitive customers are likely to yield both brand switching and the more-beneficial aspect of market expansion. Hence, price discounts may be more useful to industry profits overall when focused on the lowest-priced products.

Further research has demonstrated differences in advertising sensitivity between price- and utility-sensitive customers. Promotions in general are more likely to be noticed by a price-sensitive customer than a utility-sensitive customer. Hence, price promotions on the lowest-priced version both will be noticed more and will be more useful in capturing price-sensitive customers. In contrast, price promotions on intermediate- and higher-priced versions may not be noticed by the specific customers that they are targeting and may end up being no more than an unnecessary price concession. Supporting this conclusion, research has shown asymmetry in promotions. Promotions on high-priced, high-quality items tend to steal sales from low-priced, low-quality items, but the converse is not true.[6]

Finally, tertiary factors may drive executives towards a convergent price differential. For instance, if future sales depend on the initial version chosen and the revenue from these future sales is higher if a customer chooses the highest-priced version initially, then executives have an incentive initially to encourage most customers toward the highest-priced version through discounts. The future sales may take the form of an aftermarket add-on product or the form of a subscription service in which the subscription price is set proportional to the list price without the initial discount. In either case, getting a customer into the higher-priced version may bring significant economic benefits to the firm beyond the profits gained in the initial sale. To encourage customers to purchase the highest-priced version initially, executives may decide to discount the highest-priced version more than the lowest-priced version. The result would be a convergent price-to-benefits. In a convergent price-to-benefits discounting policy, customers that are marginally considering upgrading will be further encouraged towards a higher-priced version, while the firm will be seeking to recapture lost revenue through future sales.

Selecting the optimal price discounting pattern between a constant, divergent, or convergent price differential clearly requires careful analysis. Consumer utility valuations imply that the price differentials optimized in setting the prices of the individual versions should be held constant. An analysis of consumer behavior in light of the market segments attracted to different versions would suggest a divergent price differential. In addition, other factors, such as future sales tied to the initial version selection, could suggest a convergent price differential. Which of these effects should dominate a price discounting policy is subject to the specifics of the market challenge.

Mixed Versioning and Add-on Price Structures

Versioning can be used profitably in conjunction with an add-on pricing structure. For instance, let us reconsider the previously discussed examples of an add-on pricing structure. Nokia does not sell only one version of mobile handsets. Different handsets include different features, and customers can still add accessories to all the models. Likewise, BMW makes other models beyond the Z4, and the Z4 comes in different versions, such as the coupe.

Because feature-enhanced versions are targeted to utility-sensitive customers, and the profit motive encourages the use of feature deprivation and enhancement as a segmentation hedge between the utility- and price-sensitive segments, firms should offer more accessories at the top of the product lineup rather than the bottom. Feature-enhanced versions include many of the optional features available with feature-deprived versions, while also granting access to a wider variety of further enhancements. The number and type of features available increase as one moves towards the more-feature-enhanced version. This strategy has been well executed by Apple with its iPod, iPhone, and iPad product lines. Higher-valued versions of the iPod, iPhone, and iPad allow customers to purchase more media, more types of media such as movies and games, and even greater functionality.

Selling accessories to different versions can be conceptualized as spider diagrams along the zone of indifference. See Exhibit 11-5. Moving up the zone of indifference, the versions improve from the feature-deprived version to the feature-enhanced version as one moves from good to better to best. Concurrently, the number of add-ons increases as one moves from good to better to best. In the case shown in Exhibit 11-5, the good version cannot be customized with any optional features, the better version allows customization with additional options of A and B, and the best version subsumes the option B into its product structure while allowing customization with options A, C, and D.

Exhibit 11-5 Versioning with an Add-on Price Structure

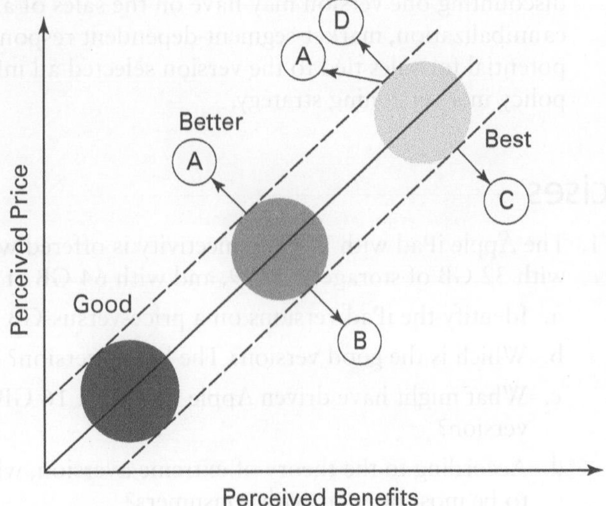

Summary

- In versioning, different variations of a similar product are sold simultaneously. Some versions offer more features or benefits, while others offer fewer features and benefits. As the product spectrum moves from feature-deprived to feature-enhanced, the price likewise increases.
- Versioning strategies often follow a good-better-best progression. The good product is priced lowest and has the fewest features and benefits. The best product is priced the highest and has the most features and benefits. In between lies the better product, which is priced in the middle and loaded with a modicum of features and benefits.
- Versioning strategies have often been defended from a marginal cost standpoint. If the sum marginal cost of producing independent products is greater than the marginal cost of producing a product that delivers the same benefits, then the manufacturer will achieve greater profit with a versioning strategy over an add-on strategy.
- According to prospect theory, it is better to unbundle gains and bundle pains. The many benefits delivered through the product are sources of gains. Each of these gains can be highlighted and isolated during a purchase decision to encourage customers to select a higher-value version. As to the dictate of bundling pains, versioning bundles the pain of payment by asking customers to pay a single price for the litany of benefits, rather than a separate price for each benefit. In this way, versioning strategies encourage customers to purchase a higher level of benefits than they would under itemized pricing; therefore, the firm can earn higher profits from versioning.
- Extreme a version has been used to explain the tendency of customers to select the middle option within a versioning offering, and not necessarily because it delivers them the best utility for the price paid, but because consumers are simply averse to buying either the lowest-quality or highest-priced product.
- In managing a number of versions, executives must consider cost and psychological limitations to the number and range of products that they will offer. In general, firms should highlight the highest-priced version and present products in descending order.
- The discounting policy in a version price structure should consider the effects that discounting one version may have on the sales of all other versions. Cross-product cannibalization, market-segment-dependent responses to discounts, and the potential for sales tied to the version selected all influence the optimal discounting policy in a versioning strategy.

Exercises

1. The Apple iPad with WiFi connectivity is offered with 16 GB of storage at $499, with 32 GB of storage at $599, and with 64 GB of storage at $699.
   a. Identify the iPad versions on a price-versus-GB plot.
   b. Which is the good version? The better version? The best version?
   c. What might have driven Apple to offer a 16 GB version of the iPad? A 64 GB version?
   d. According to the theory of extreme aversion, which version of the iPad is likely to be most popular with consumers?

2. General Electric (GE) offers front-loading washers in varying sizes and having various levels of programmability. The GE Profile Energy Star 4.2 cu ft washer, which offers more than 26 cycles, is priced at $1,299. The GE Energy Star 4.0 cu ft, 26-cycle washer is priced at $899. The GE Energy Star 4.0 cu ft, 10-cycle washer is priced at $699.
   a. Identify the GE washer versions on a price-versus-cycles plot.
   b. Which is the good version? The better version? The best version?
   c. According to the theory of extreme aversion, which version of washer is likely to be most popular with consumers if these were the only washers GE offered?
   d. If GE wanted to sell more Profile Energy Star washers, where should GE concentrate its product development—on a version more expensive than the Profile Energy Star version or one that is less expensive than the Energy Star 4.0 cu ft, 10-cycle washer?
   e. To block a competitor from taking share at the lower end of the market, where should GE concentrate its product development—on a version more expensive than the Profile Energy Star version or one that is less expensive than the Energy Star 4.0 cu ft, 10-cycle washer?
3. Lou Malnati's offers a 12" cheese pizza for $13, which can be customized with spinach, mushrooms, and sliced tomatoes for $1.70 for each additional ingredient. Alternatively, a customer can order a 12" "Lou" for $17.25, which comes with spinach, mushrooms, and sliced tomatoes covered with cheese.
   a. From an economic perspective, which should a customer order when desiring a cheese pizza with spinach, mushrooms, and sliced tomatoes? The Lou, or a cheese pizza with three different toppings?
   b. Identify a means in which prospect theory would predict that the Lou would have a higher demand than a cheese pizza with three extra toppings.
   c. Discussion question: Did the "Lou" have to be priced at a discount compared to the sum price of a cheese pizza with three extra toppings? Under what conditions might the "Lou" have been priced higher?
4. In the 2008–2009 Great Recession, Nordstrom added products at the lower end of its product categories, such as an exclusive line of Elie Tahari professional women's clothing priced 30 percent lower than Elie Tahari's main collection, and the Easy Money jean brand, priced at under $100. Most other competitors turned to discounts to attract customers.
   a. During a recession, should retailers anticipate that demand would increase for high-featured, high-priced versions or low-featured, low-priced versions?
   b. Which approach should be more profitable—discounting existing offers or adding new offers at the lower end of the product category? Why?
   c. What are some drawbacks of launching new products at the lower end of the product category in general? Specifically, what are some drawbacks of launching new products at the lower end of the product category during a recession?
5. Discussion: In response to the advent of music downloading, many analysts predicted the death of the CD. However, in 2009, consumers in Britain purchased 113 million physical albums but downloaded the equivalent of only 15 million albums' worth of music. CDs were not what they were in the prior decade. For instance, at HMV in London's Oxford Street, the CD of *Plastic Beach* by Gorillaz could be purchased for £7.99; the experience version, which

included a DVD and access to online content, could be purchased for £17.99; and the third version, which included a T-shirt, could be purchased for £19.99. Moreover, deluxe CDs accounted for 27 percent of Universal's sales from its biggest new releases in 2009.

a. What are some benefits that CDs offer compared to music downloads? How might the demands of listeners differ between downloaded songs and CD purchases? How do the deluxe versions of CDs increase these value differentials?

b. Newspapers and magazines fear that they will suffer from the same challenges as CDs when customers can view news articles for free online. What are some benefits to physical periodicals over digital news articles? What are some benefits to digital news articles over physical periodicals? How might the demands of readers differ between online news and periodical purchases? How might publishers enhance their physical products to increase the value differentials?

6. After completing Appendix 11, consider a market whose heterogeneity in demand can be described with a uniformly distributed taste parameter varying from 0 to 1. The firm produces two products: the base product A, at a variable cost of V_A = \$50, and an improved version with a variable cost of V_T = \$60. Assume zero fixed costs. Let the base product be valued by the most-demanding customers at S_A = \$100 and the improved version be valued by the most-demanding customers at S_B = \$600. Assume that the least-demanding customers within the market assign no value to the product, S_0 = \$0.

a. What is the optimal price of the base product A and the improved version T?

b. What fraction of the market would purchase the base product A under these assumptions?

c. What fraction of the market would purchase the improved product T under these assumptions?

d. What would be the firm's profitability if the market had 10 million members?

e. How are these results similar to those found in Exercise 10.6?

f. If versioning the total product increased demand for that product by \$5, such that the improved version was valued by the most-demanding customers at S_B = \$605, how would the results differ from these questions?

Appendix 11 Economic Model of Versioning

Similar to add-on price structures, versioning price structures segment the market according to different customers' willingness to pay for different levels of benefits. As such, the economic model for versioning will be highly similar to that for add-on price structures.[7] (See Appendix 10.) While the model that we demonstrate does not provide a general approach to pricing competing versions, nor does it indicate all the limitations of versioning, the number of versions a firm should offer, or how one version should be defined compared to another, it does provide insight into the drivers behind a successful versioning strategy. In particular, we uncover that the customer heterogeneity in their willingness to pay for enhanced benefits drives the profit tradeoffs of expanding the market to lower price points while minimizing cannibalization of sales from the higher-quality version.

As in Appendix 10, we will incorporate market heterogeneity in relationship to benefits derived and willingness to pay with a taste parameter that varies from zero to 1

($t \in [0, 1]$). Customers with a low taste parameter (near zero) are those who value the product little and are not willing to pay much for the additional benefits that are provided through an upgraded version. Customers with a high taste parameter (near 1) are those who value quality improvements highly and have some willingness to pay for an upgraded version.

We model customer preferences with a customer net utility function. As a minimal requirement for versioning, assume that the product can be made of two qualities at two different marginal costs. With two products, A and T, where T is the upgraded version of A, consumers have a utility function for A and another utility function for T. The net utility function is simply the difference between the utility that a customer derives from a product and the price they paid. Under these assumptions, the net utility function is given by the following pair of equations:

$$U(t) = S_0 + S_A \cdot t - P_A \quad \text{if purchasing version A} \qquad \text{Eq. 11.1.a}$$

$$U(t) = S_0 + S_T \cdot t - P_T \quad \text{if purchasing version T} \qquad \text{Eq. 11.1.b}$$

where P_A and P_T are the price of products A and T, respectively; S_A and S_T are the maximum utility any customer can gain from products A and T, respectively; and t is our taste parameter, which varies between zero and 1. In this model, we have assumed a zero-point utility of S_0, with S_0 being the value that all customers place on the product versions regardless of their taste parameter.[8] If no purchase is made, we assume that customers neither gain nor lose utility—that is, that their utility function for not purchasing is zero. See Exhibit 11-6.

In a similar manner, as in Appendix 10, we will find the taste parameters of the marginal customers. At the bottom end of the market, there are marginal customers who are indifferent between making no purchase and purchasing product A defined by the taste parameter $t_{0,A}$. By setting Equation 11.1.a equal to zero, we find

$$t_{0,A} = \frac{P_A - S_0}{S_A} \qquad \text{Eq. 11.2}$$

Exhibit 11-6 Customer Utility Function for Versioning

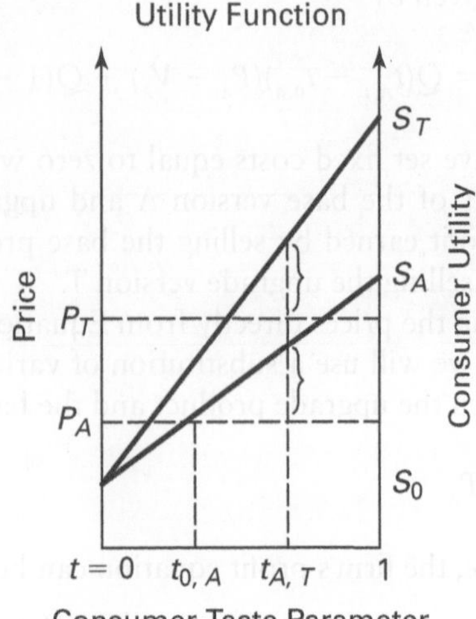

At the upper end of the market, there are marginal customers who are indifferent between purchasing the base version A and the upgrade version T defined by the taste parameter $t_{A,T}$. By setting Equation 11.1.a equal to Equation 11.1.b, we find

$$t_{A,T} = \frac{P_T - P_A}{S_T - S_A} \quad \text{Eq. 11.3}$$

If we assume that the marginal customer between buying the base version A and the upgrade version T will at least purchase the base product, we have the restriction of increasing marginal taste parameters. $0 < t_{0,A} < t_{A,T} < 1$. For $0 \le t < t_{0,A}$, customers do not purchase. For $t_{0,A} \le t < t_{A,T}$, customers purchase the base version A. For $t_{A,T} \le t \le 1$, customers purchase the upgrade version T. As before, we will also assume a uniform distribution of taste parameter and a total market demand of Q.

For customers that purchase the upgrade version to exist, we know that their taste parameter must be less than 1. Using the equation defining the marginal upgrade customer, we find

$$P_T < P_A + (S_T - S_A) \quad \text{Eq. 11.4}$$

Equation 11.4 indicates that the price of the upgraded version must be less than the price of the base version after adjusting for the quality gap (as valued by the most-eager customers, those with a taste parameter of 1.) By offering the upgrade version at a price lower than the quality-adjusted price of the base version, utility-sensitive customers will gain a higher net utility from the upgrade version than they would from the base version.

For customers that purchase the basic version to exist, we know that their taste parameter must be less than that of those who select the upgrade version. By comparing the taste parameters of the marginal base and upgrade customers, we find

$$\frac{S_A}{P_A - S_0} > \frac{S_T}{P_T - S_0} \quad \text{Eq. 11.5}$$

Equation 11.5 indicates that the basic version must offer a better quality-to-price ratio than the high-quality version. This second requirement comes from the need for the basic version to attract the more-price-sensitive customers.

Having described the market and how customers make choices, we can turn to the challenge of maximizing the firm's profits. The firm's profit equation in a versioning price structure is given by

$$\pi(P_A, P_T) = Q(t_{A,T} - t_{0,A})(P_A - V_A) + Q(1 - t_{A,T})(P_T - V_T) \quad \text{Eq. 11.6}$$

where we have set fixed costs equal to zero without losing generality. V_A and V_T are the variable costs of the base version A and upgrade version T, respectively. The first term yields the profit earned by selling the base product A. The second term yields the profit earned from selling the upgrade version T.

Optimizing the prices directly from Equation 10.6 is a little difficult. To make the process simpler, we will use a substitution of variables. Let us define Δ to be the price differential between the upgrade product and the base product:

$$\Delta \equiv P_T - P_A \quad \text{Eq. 11.7}$$

In which case, the firm's profit equation can be written as

$$\pi(P_A, \Delta) = Q(t_{A,T} - t_{0,A})(P_A - V_A) + Q(1 - t_{A,T})(P_A + \Delta - V_T) \quad \text{Eq. 11.8}$$

where the marginal customers become

$$t_{0,A} = \frac{P_A - S_0}{S_A} \quad \text{Eq. 11.9.a}$$

$$t_{A,T} = \frac{\Delta}{S_T - S_A} \quad \text{Eq. 11.9.b}$$

Notice that $t_{0,A}$ is independent of Δ and $t_{A,T}$ is independent of P_A.

To optimize the firm's profits with respect to the price of the base version or the price differential of the upgraded version, we set the first derivative of Equation 11.8 with respect to P_A or Δ equal to zero and find

$$\frac{\partial \pi}{\partial P_A} = 0 \Rightarrow 0 = -\frac{\partial t_{0,A}}{\partial P_A}(\hat{P}_A - V_A) + (1 - t_{0,A}) \quad \text{Eq. 11.10.a}$$

$$\frac{\partial \pi}{\partial \Delta} = 0 \Rightarrow 0 = -\frac{\partial t_{A,T}}{\partial \Delta}(\hat{\Delta} - (V_T - V_A)) + (1 - t_{A,T}) \quad \text{Eq. 11.10.b}$$

where, from Equation 11.9, we find

$$\frac{\partial t_{0,A}}{\partial P_A} = \frac{1}{S_A} \quad \text{Eq. 11.11.a}$$

$$\frac{\partial t_{A,T}}{\partial \Delta} = \frac{1}{S_T - S_A} \quad \text{Eq. 11.11.b}$$

Using the results found in Equations 11.9 and 11.11 in Equation 11.10 and solving for the optimal price of the base version and price differential for the upgrade version, we find

$$\hat{P}_A = \frac{S_0 + S_A + V_A}{2} \quad \text{Eq. 11.12.a}$$

$$\hat{\Delta} = \frac{(S_T + V_T) - (S_A + V_A)}{2} \quad \text{Eq. 11.12.b}$$

Alternatively, after reverting to our original variable P_T,

$$\hat{P}_T = \frac{S_0 + S_T + V_T}{2} \quad \text{Eq. 11.12.c}$$

The optimal prices (Eq. 11.12) are the average of the marginal cost to produce and the total utility as perceived by the most-discriminating customers—those with a taste parameter of 1. (Similar constraints on the prices and costs, as found with an add-on price structure in Appendix 10, can be found in the versioning price structure. We leave this exercise to the reader.)

At these prices, we find the firm's total profit of

$$\hat{\pi} = \frac{Q}{4}\left\{\frac{(S_0 + S_A - V_A)^2}{S_A} + \frac{[(S_T - V_T) - (S_A - V_A)]^2}{S_T - S_A}\right\} \quad \text{Eq. 11.13}$$

In the first part of the firm's optimal profit equation (Eq. 11.13), we see that the basic version increases the firm's profits by serving a broader market with a lower-priced product (market expansion). From the second part of the firm's profit equation, we also see that the profits earned from the upgraded version are reduced by the existence of the basic version. This is the result of the cannibalization of sales from the upgraded version by the basic version. Hence, the price of the basic version represents a compromise between the profit-destructive cannibalization of sales from the upgraded version and the profit-creating market expansion by offering the core benefits at a lower price point.

The prices and profits earned in versioning are highly similar to those earned from an add-on price strategy. See Appendix 10 and Equations 10.9 and 10.14 for more detail. A notable exception is the inclusion of a zero point utility. Let us compare our price of the upgraded version T to that of the base product A plus the add-on product B in Appendix 10, as well as the profits earned under versioning to that under an add-on strategy. To enable an equal comparison, let us assume that the zero point utility is zero ($S_0 = 0$).

From a cost perspective, an upgraded version might have a lower variable cost of production than that of producing and marketing two different products, the base product plus the add-on product. Let us define δV as the potential cost savings generated by packaging A and B into a single product versus selling them independently. In this case, the relationship between V_T for the upgraded version and V_A and V_B in the add-on price strategy will be

$$V_T = V_A + V_B - \delta V \qquad \text{Eq. 11.14}$$

Furthermore, consumer behavior and neuroeconomic effects, like those discussed with respect to prospect theory, indicate that an upgraded version might deliver a higher perceived utility than the sale of two independent products, the base product and the add-on product. Let us define δS as the perceived gain in utility that customers receive from buying a single upgraded version over the utility that they receive from buying two products, the base plus its add-on. In this case, the relationship between the maximum potential utility of the upgraded version and that of the base product plus its add-on will be

$$S_T = S_A + S_B + \delta S \qquad \text{Eq. 11.15}$$

With the marginal cost savings of δV and improved utility of δS, we find that the optimal price of the upgraded version compared to selling a base product plus its add-on module will be

$$\hat{P}_T = \hat{P}_A + \hat{P}_B + \frac{\delta S - \delta V}{2} \qquad \text{Eq. 11.16}$$

where we have used Equations 10.9, 11.12.c, 11.14, and 11.15 with $S_0 = 0$ to uncover Equation 11.16.

If there are no marginal cost savings ($\delta V = 0$), then the optimal price of the upgraded version can be higher than the sum price of the base product and its add-on. The increase in the optimal price of the upgraded version would be equal to half of the perceived increase in utility by bundling the two products into one rather than purchasing two separate products. Prospect theory predicts that the upgraded version may actually be perceived as having a higher utility (or at least less disutility in the form of the pain of payment) than the sale of two individual products, the base plus its add-on. Other effects may also indicate that customers have a higher utility from a packaged upgrade version compared to the sale of independent products. For instance, consider the willingness to pay for a table that must be assembled versus one that comes fully assembled. When combining the parts into a single package does increase the utility, it is possible for versioning to result in a higher price for the upgraded version than the sum price of the base product and its add-on. That is, that $P_T > P_A + P_B$. This is an intriguing result, especially in the situation where the utility increase derives solely from the effects discussed with respect to prospect theory.

If there is no change in utility ($\delta S = 0$), then the optimal price of the upgraded version can be lower than the sum price of the base product plus its add-on. That is, that $P_T < P_A + P_B$.

The decrease in the optimal price of the upgraded version would be equal to half of the marginal cost savings by bundling the two products into one rather than producing and marketing two separate products. When versioning reduces costs, as it would in producing a single hard drive at twice the capacity compared to selling two hard drives, optimal pricing would predict that a portion of these cost savings would be passed on to customers.

If there are neither increases in utility nor savings in marginal costs in a versioning strategy over an add-on strategy, or if these two effects exactly counterbalance one another, then the optimal price of the upgraded version will equal the sum price of the base product and its add-on. $P_T = P_A + P_B$. Thus, versioning can result in optimal prices that are greater than, less than, or equal to those generated by an add-on price structure.

Comparing the firm's profits earned under a versioning structure to those earned under an add-on structure, we find that versioning can indeed be more profitable than itemized pricing. Writing the profit equation under versioning in terms of the utility and marginal costs under an add-on structure, we find

$$\hat{\pi}\,(versions) = \frac{Q}{4}\left\{\frac{(S_A - V_A)^2}{S_A} + \frac{[(S_B + \delta S) - (V_B - \delta V)]^2}{(S_B + \delta S)}\right\} \qquad \text{Eq. 11.17}$$

(We have assumed that S_0 is zero to make the comparison between equations simpler.) The profits earned under versioning are greater than those earned in an add-on strategy. Compare Equations 11.17 to 10.14. Versioning improves the profits captured on the upgraded product over those earned on the add-on product by an amount dependent on the increase in utility and decrease in marginal costs that result from producing and marketing a single upgraded version rather than having customers buy both the base product and add-on to deliver the same set of features.

Notes

[1] Carl Shapiro and Hal R. Varian, "Versioning Information," in *Information Rules: A Strategic Guide to the Network Economy* (Boston: Harvard Business School Press, 1999): 53–82. Carl Shapiro and Hal R. Varian, "Versioning: The Smart Way to Sell Information," *Harvard Business Review* 76, No. 6 (November–December 1998):106–14.

[2] Prices observed on the American Express Personal Cards website, https://home.americanexpress.com/home/mt_personal.shtml?us_nu=globalbar (accessed on September 9, 2007).

[3] Prices observed on the Symantec UK website, http://www.symantec.com/en/uk/index.jsp (accessed on September 9, 2007).

[4] Itamar Simonson and Amos Tversky, "Choice in Context: Tradeoff Contrast and Extremeness Aversion," *Journal of Marketing Research* 29, No. 3 (August 1992): 281–95.

[5] Paula Bennett, Mike Brennan, and Zane Kearns, "Psychological Aspects of Price: An Empirical Test of Order and Range Effects," *Marketing Bulletin* 14 (January 2003): 1–8.

[6] Robert C. Blattberg and Kenneth J. Wisniewski, "Price-Induced Patterns of Competition," *Marketing Science* 8, No. 4 (Autumn 1989): 291–309.

[7] The model presented here is adapted from Paul Belleflamme, "Versioning in the Information Economy: Theory and Applications," *CESifo Economic Studies*, Munich 51, No. 2/3 (January 2005): 329–58. An alternative model can be found in Hemant K. Bhargava and Vidyanand Choudhary, "Information Goods and Vertical Differentiation," *Journal of Management Information Systems* 18, No. 2 (October 2001): 89–106.

[8] The assumption of a zero-point utility is necessary to show that versioning is optimal over selling only one quality of a good under the conditions of zero marginal cost. Zero marginal costs are a common assumption in information markets. The zero-point utility might better be thought of as a secondary dimension of utility that all customers value equally, while the taste parameter defines the valuation difference that customers place on the key dimension of differentiation.

Chapter

12

Bundling

Jbcn/Alamy

- What is price bundling?
- How does the nature of the desires of different market segments determine the success of a bundling strategy?
- How should a bundle be priced relative to stand-alone products?
- What conditions favor price bundling over other pricing strategies?
- What should influence the design of a bundle?
- How should bundles be positioned for customers?
- Are promotional bundles more effective than discounts?
- When is bundling likely to be illegal?
- Stretch Question: What distinguishes bundling from versioning?

In general, bundling is a loosely applied term. However, in pricing, this term refers to a very specific situation. Price bundling, as discussed here and defined by many authors, specifically deals with the sale of two or more distinct products at a single, bundled price. By considering distinct products, bundling differs slightly from the prior discussions of add-on strategies and version pricing in that the distinct products themselves can be used in isolation or in combination. That is, each distinct product delivers value without the use of the other products; and each of the distinct products within the bundle has its own individual market. In price bundling, the bundle price is below the sum of the individual product prices but above that of any individual product alone. While this definition of bundling can be relaxed to address other situations, bundling as a pricing strategy has been best explored and is perhaps best applied under these conditions.

Price bundling is found in many contexts. Restaurants may offer a price-fixed meal which includes appetizer, entree, and dessert. Any single item in the price-fixed meal could be purchased in isolation, or all three could be purchased in a single sitting. The price-fixed meal is priced below the sum price of the individual appetizer, entree, and dessert. Perhaps the best-known example of a variation on this theme is the McDonald's Value Meal. Telecoms may offer a bundle of fixed-line telephone service, high-speed Internet connection, television subscriber service, and mobile telephone service at a discount compared to the price of buying each of the services independently. Similar bundles have been offered by Vodafone, AT&T, O2, and several other firms around the world. Software firms may bundle various office productivity tools such as a word processor, spreadsheet, email manager, and presentation tool, with the most-famous example being Microsoft Office. Similarly, sporting events and concert and dance series will offer bundles called season passes, which allows season-pass holders to attend multiple events rather than just one-off events.

Price bundling is not the same as feature bundling (sometimes also referred to as product bundling). In feature bundling, disparate features of and benefits of different products are combined into a single multifunctional product. Feature bundling delivers additional value over pure price bundling by combining multiple features of distinct products into a single bundled product. That is, the integral architecture of a feature bundle is itself a source of value. As such, customers would receive a higher value and firms can capture a higher price with a feature bundle than with a customer buying separate products.

One example of feature bundling is Apple's iPhone, which includes the features of a portable music device, mobile phone, and web browser in a single device. Customers could purchase each of these items separately, but by purchasing them in a single, combined product, they gain additional value. Moreover, a feature bundle may have lower marginal costs than separate item sales. With the iPhone, for instance, the production costs of separate mobile handsets, mobile web browsers, and mobile music devices would be greater than that for a single product.

Other factors also influence the pricing and product strategy when creating a feature bundle, such as the effect of a feature bundle on competitive dynamics. When pricing a feature bundle, the price can be set according to the perceived value that consumers have for the collection of benefits plus the value of integrating these benefits into a single product. As we will discover, the optimal price of a price bundle is determined through a slightly different mechanism.

Price Segmentation with Bundling

Price bundling is a strategy that benefits from heterogeneity in demand—specifically, demand that is contrasting between products. Heterogeneity in demand implies that different customers value different items differently. Contrasting demand heterogeneity implies that different customer segments will hold contrasting viewpoints on the value of specific items within the bundle. For example, consider a price bundle created from two different products. One segment of customers might value the first product highly and the second product very little, while another segment will hold the polar opposite view, valuing the first product little and the second product highly. In this case, we would state that the customer segments hold contrasting demand.

The McDonald's Value Meal is a familiar price bundle that can illustrate how price bundling works. To simplify this example, consider a McDonald's Value Meal that contains a burger and fries (ignore the drink for the purpose of this discussion) being offered to a market with two hypothetical market segments. The Burger Lover segment might be satisfied with just a burger. The Fries Lover segment might be satisfied with just fries. In this example, the Burger Lovers and Fries Lovers have contrasting demand for burgers and fries. By selling both the burger and fries at a bundle discount, Burger Lovers are encouraged to enjoy fries, while Fries Lovers are encouraged to partake of a burger.

Contrasting demand between segments can be associated with many of the examples of price bundling. In the telecom industry, a savvy technology-oriented person might value mobiles and high-speed Internet service highly, while having little value for a fixed-line telephone service or subscription television. In contrast, a more conservative customer may value fixed-line telephony and subscription television highly, but have little value for mobiles and the Internet. Similarly, in the office productivity software market, a finance customer may value spreadsheets highly, while a salesperson may value word-processing and presentation tools highly.

Bundling exploits contrasting demand within the market for the different products by driving multiple segments to purchase more products than they would if the products were only available separately. If each product was priced individually to optimize its own independent profitability, then the optimal price of the individual products would be set to capture the independent segments that value that product the most. In this case, the segment that doesn't value one of the products very highly purchases only the specific products that it values and ignores the others. In a sense, bundling is a selective discount given preferentially to customers who value one item less than the other.

The price of the bundle should be lower than the sum price of the independently priced optimized products to encourage disparate customers with disparate independent product valuations to purchase all products in a single bundle, and it should be higher than the price of any specific product within the bundle to discourage cannibalization.

Price bundling improves profitability by reducing the dispersion in the willingness to pay between the multiple customer segments. For instance, consider products A and B and customer segments Blue and Red. If the Blue segment desires product A at $5 and product B at $2, and the Red segment desires product B at $5 and product A at $2, then optimizing the prices of the individual products for their specific market segments might lead to pricing products A and B each at $5. However, a price bundle set at $7 would capture both segments. Moreover, it will do so by giving a selective discount to the specific segments proportionate to their willingness to pay. At $7, Blue customers will get a $3 discount on product B to encourage their purchase, but Red customers will not get a discount on B. However, that same price of $7 will give a $3 discount to Red customers on product A, but not to Blue customers. The price bundle reduces the dispersion in willingness to pay by acting as a selective price segmentation hedge between the different market segments, giving each a discount on the specific product that it values less.

In general, the larger the number of goods bundled, the greater the reduction in disparity in willingness to pay. Because uncertainty about the value that customers place on a product is an enemy of effective pricing, the predictive power of bundling can be highly profitable.

Bundling also benefits from the psychological effects discussed in prospect theory. Because the bundle price is lower than the sum price of the individual goods, the bundle price will be perceived as a discount in comparison. Discounts are an extra source of gain for customers. Hence, the bundle may improve sales even further than that predicted on a purely customer utility basis.

The bundle price appears as a discount on the sum price of the two individual products. However, it should not be treated as merely a discount when considering the analysis of the profitability of bundling. That is, a standard analysis of volume hurdles in which the bundle discount is applied to one or the other product would fail to demonstrate the profit-creating power of price bundles. With price bundling, we must create a different bundle volume hurdle. Before we construct the bundle volume hurdle, let us demonstrate the strategic value of bundling. (The bundle volume hurdle can be found in Appendix 12.A.)

Strategic Bundling

An example will best illustrate the effect of bundling on volumes, prices, and profits and can form the basis of a template for analyzing bundling in different situations. While price bundling can be found in many industries, we have chosen to use an opera house selling tickets to Wolfgang Amadeus Mozart's *Don Giovanni* and Antonin Dvorak's *Rusalka*. Both of these pieces premièred in Prague, Czech Republic, and are performed periodically at the Estates Theater in the Old Town Square section of the city.

We will assume that the marginal cost of filling a seat at a theatre is negligible. Seating one more patron requires no further staff, and burdens the performers no further as well. Furthermore, once a theater is built, the number of seats is set; seating one more customer is virtually without cost so long as the performance is not sold out. Perhaps the only marginal costs faced by the theater are those associated with wear and tear on the facility or washroom usage, both of which should be minimal. This condition can easily be relaxed and marginal costs can be included in the model, but as a first foray into bundling, we are striving to keep the scenario simple.

As mentioned, price bundling exploits contrasting demand. For our opera house, let us assume that one segment of the market highly values the tragic opera *Rusalka* while the other segment highly values the comedic opera *Don Giovanni*. Let us furthermore assume the opera house could easily entertain both segments simultaneously. We will assign valuations for these operas for the disparate market segments and state that comedic opera seekers are willing to pay 1,500 CZK (Czech koruna) for *Don Giovanni*, but only 700 CZK for *Rusalka*. Meanwhile, tragic opera seekers are willing to pay 1,500 CZK for *Rusalka* but only 700 CZK for *Don Giovanni*. See Exhibit 12-1 for a summary of the market segments and their willingness to pay.

In this two-segment case with ample seats for all potential customers, revenue is maximized, regardless of the size of individual segments, by offering the bundle at 2,200 CZK rather than offering either opera at its individual profit-maximizing price. The 2,200 CZK bundle price tag arises from considering the minimum cross-segment willingness to pay for both operas. At 2,200 CZK, both segments will attend both operas. If the individual operas were offered at 1,500 CZK apiece and no bundle existed, patrons would attend one and only one of the two operas, and the opera house would forgo potential volume. Alternatively, pricing at a level of 700 CZK that would attract both segments, patrons would attend both operas, but at a lower overall price, and the opera house would forgo potential profit.

The bundle price of 2,200 CZK is a discount from the sum of the higher individual prices at 3,000 CZK, but is at a premium compared to the sum of the lower individual prices at 1,400 CZK. Moreover, the bundle price at 2,200 CZK is attractive to both segments; thus, it captures the volume that would be lost if priced at the higher price and would be gained at the lower price. Hence, the bundled price improves volume sales compared to the higher total price but captures a higher overall price compared to the lower total price.

This simple example of a two-segment market with contrasting demand demonstrates the value of optimizing the price of the bundled offering compared to optimizing the price of the individual offerings. With only two segments, no marginal costs, and equally

Exhibit 12-1 Willingness to Pay for Opera of Two Market Segments

Market Segment	*Don Giovanni*	*Rusalka*
Comedy Lovers	1,500 CZK	700 CZK
Tragedy Lovers	700 CZK	1,500 CZK

opposing reservation prices, pure bundling is always more profitable than mixed bundling. In pure bundling, the individual products are not offered and only the bundled offering is made available. Effectively, pure bundling redefines the product. The individual products are subsumed into a new, larger bundled product and all price optimization issues shift towards managing the bundled price as the individual products cease to exist.

Markets with more than two segments or otherwise failing to meet the prior assumptions may benefit from mixed bundling, rather than pure bundling. In mixed bundling, both the bundled offering and the independent offerings are made available to customers. We can build from our prior example to demonstrate the profit impact of mixed bundling.

Let us expand our example to include two additional segments to demonstrate the value of mixed bundling compared to either pure bundling or an unbundled-only offering. In this example, we assume that the Tragedy Lover and Comedy Lover segments still exist. We will further assume that we have two additional segments, one devoted to Mozart and the other devoted to Dvorak. Furthermore, let us assume that each segment is of relatively equal size. (Though the assumption of relatively equal-sized market segments is not strictly required, we use it to overcome trivial cases of highly skewed markets.) Let the Mozart Devotees be willing to pay 1,600 CZK for *Don Giovanni* but only 100 CZK for *Rusalka*. Meanwhile, let the Dvorak Devotees be willing to pay 1,600 CZK for *Rusalka* but only 100 CZK for *Don Giovanni*. Again, these segments have contrasting demand for the products. See Exhibit 12-2 for a summary of the market segments and their willingness to pay.

In this four-segment case with ample seats for all potential customers, revenue is maximized by offering the bundle of both *Don Giovanni* and *Rusalka* at 2,200 CZK while offering the individual operas at 1,600 CZK each. At 2,200 CZK for the bundle, both Comedy Lovers and Tragedy Lovers will be enticed to attend both *Don Giovanni* and *Rusalka* because this bundle price is at their sum individual reservation prices. Meanwhile, 2,200 CZK is above the sum reservation price of both Mozart Devotees and Dvorak Devotees to entice them to attend both operas. However, the individual price of 1,600 CZK for a single opera is sufficiently low to entice them to attend the specific opera that they desire.

The case for mixed bundling can easily be shown graphically in a plot of willingness to pay for differing products for the four-segment market. In Exhibit 12-3, we have plotted along the vertical axis the reservation prices that different segments have for *Don Giovanni*. On the horizontal axis, we have plotted the reservation prices that different segments have for *Rusalka*. The arc of prices that heterogeneous segments are willing to pay extends farther from the origin for the bundled offering than it does for either of the independent products. As such, including the bundle in the menu of offerings improves profitability compared to offering the independent products alone.

Even in a two-segment market, where the willingness to pay is not evenly contrasting and market shares are unequal, a pure bundle can fail to be more profitable than either an unbundled or mixed-bundle pricing structure. For instance, consider a two-segment market with a small Tragedy Lover segment willing to pay 300 CZK for *Don Giovanni* but 1,700 CZK for *Rusalka* and a large Comedy Lover segment as described above. It can

Exhibit 12-2 Willingness to Pay for Opera of Four Market Segments

Market Segment	*Don Giovanni*	*Rusalka*
Comedy Lovers	1,500 CZK	700 CZK
Tragedy Lovers	700 CZK	1,500 CZK
Mozart Devotees	1,600 CZK	100 CZK
Dvorak Devotees	100 CZK	1,600 CZK

Exhibit 12-3 Contrasting Demand for Opera in a Four-Segment Market

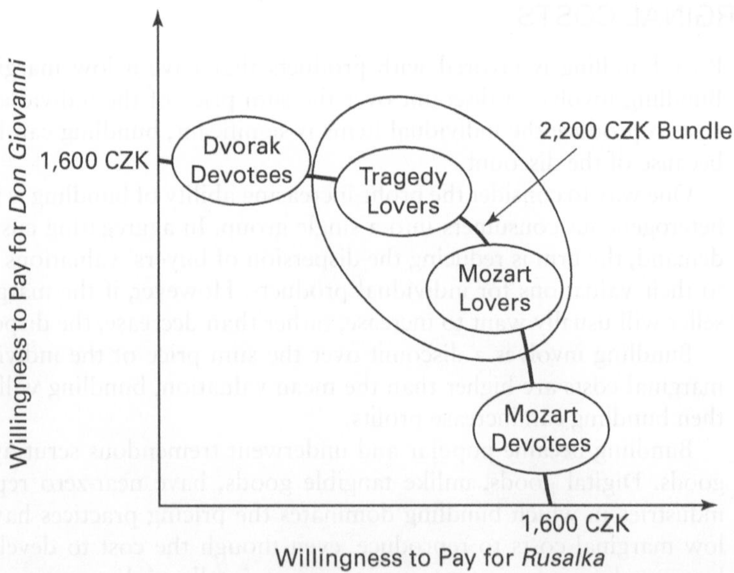

be shown that the most-profitable pricing structure is to offer both *Don Giovanni* and *Rusalka* bundled at 2,200 CZK for the Comedy Lover segment, and *Rusalka* stand-alone tickets at 1,700 CZK for the Tragedy Lover segment. This instance effectively reverts to a versioning strategy.

In practice, mixed bundling is favored over versioning or add-on strategies under the following conditions:

- Each product in the bundle has an independent market.
- The markets for each product overlap.
- The consumption of one product does not subtract from the value in consuming the other product.
- The distribution of reservation prices between customers is broad and contrasting with respect to their desire for specific products.
- The marginal costs to produce the products are low.

Various economists and marketers have devised different models to demonstrate the value of bundling.[1] The specific models that they use vary in their generality and applicability. In general, to demonstrate that mixed bundling is more profitable than versioning or add-on pricing strategies, one must show that three or more customer types with contrasting demand exist.

A direct method to find the optimal prices in bundling is through trial and error, as follows: (1) For inputs, executives must uncover the size of the various market segments and their willingness to pay for different products within the bundle. These may be discovered through conjoint analysis or other market research techniques. (2) Various price menus are created for the different individual products and the bundles. (3) With each price menu, researchers can calculate the anticipated consumer surplus for each market segment assuming that each segment self-selects the offer that delivers the highest surplus. (4) The revenues and profits are predicted against the specific price menu under consideration from the segment size and choices as well as estimates of marginal costs. (5) The price menu selected will be the one that optimizes profits. A robustness test can be conducted to account for variations in segment sizes and reservation prices.

Bundle Design

MARGINAL COSTS

Price bundling is favored with products that have a low marginal cost of production. Bundling involves a discount over the sum price of the individual items. If the marginal cost to produce the individual items is significant, bundling can be detrimental to profits because of the discount.

One way to consider the profit-increasing ability of bundling is in its ability to aggregate heterogeneous consumers into a single group. In aggregating customers with contrasting demand, the firm is reducing the dispersion of buyers' valuations in the bundle compared to their valuations for individual products. However, if the marginal costs are large, the seller will usually want to increase, rather than decrease, the dispersion of valuations.

Bundling involves a discount over the sum price of the individual items. If the mean marginal costs are higher than the mean valuation, bundling will decrease profits. If not, then bundling can increase profits.

Bundling became popular and underwent tremendous scrutiny with respect to digital goods. Digital goods, unlike tangible goods, have near-zero reproduction costs. Other industries in which bundling dominates the pricing practices have a similar property of low marginal costs to reproduce, even though the cost to develop the product may be large, such as information, entertainment, intellectual property, and infrastructure-based products.[2] Even high-fixed-cost manufactured goods, such as silicon chips, may benefit from bundling due to their very low marginal costs.

Reviewing the examples of bundles that we have discussed so far, we see that the marginal cost condition holds. In each case, we can easily imagine that some customers would prefer certain products within the bundle while others would prefer other parts of the bundle; hence, the market would have contrasting demand heterogeneity. Moreover, they also meet the challenge of having low marginal costs; hence, the sales of more items, even at a lower bundled price, is likely to improve profitability.

The price of food ingredients at a restaurant represents a small fraction of the overall cost structure. Rather, many of the costs in running a restaurant are somewhat fixed in the form of space leases and staff pay, neither of which changes significantly with the addition of one more customer.

Telecoms have large infrastructure costs but very low marginal costs. The cost of adding one more service once the infrastructure has been established is often, though not always, zero or close to zero.

Likewise, marginal costs in software have long been considered to be negligibly small. As a digital good, the costs are highly skewed towards the development of the product, not in its reproduction. A similar claim can often be made with respect to pharmaceutical offerings where the cost of manufacturing a dose is very low compared to the cost of developing new pharmaceutical regimens.

Similarly, entertainment venues face high fixed costs and low marginal costs. Once an entertainment event has been booked and the seats have been installed, the venue's cost structure is highly fixed and profitability depends on the portion of the seats booked. If a seat if not booked, then adding a single further customer increases marginal costs negligibly, while the sale of that seat improves profitability directly.

PROMOTIONAL BUNDLING AND BRAND SWITCHING

Accepting that bundling can improve profits by encouraging customers to purchase more items than they would have in absence of the bundle, the natural next question is the origin of these purchases. That is, does bundling encourage customers to purchase more from the category of items or to switch brands or retail outlets within the category? Put another way, bundling can influence both consumer choice (what to buy) and consumer incidence (how much to buy). For established market categories, retail sales data and academic experiments have been somewhat conclusive about this issue, and it appears that the additional sales that occur due to bundle promotions arise from brand switching (influencing what to buy) more than category expansion (how much to buy).[3]

For instance, retailer promotional bundling often comes in the form of "buy one, get one free" or "buy two and get $0.50 off." It has been found that these types of bundles are strong at encouraging consumers to switch brands or retail outlets, but they are very limited at either encouraging consumers to accelerate buying (buying earlier and stocking up) or increasing category-level spending (buying more than what would usually be purchased). Even when customers fail to purchase the necessary quantity to qualify for the bundle discount, the bundle promotion is effective at encouraging sales, perhaps by creating the perception of being a low-priced outlet.

Likewise, manufacturers face decision tradeoffs between price-promoting a single item or price-promoting a broader line of items with a promotional bundle. In examining the effectiveness of single-item versus bundling promotions, it has been found that promotional bundles tend to be more effective than per-unit promotions if the goal is to increase item or brand-line sales. As with retailer promotional bundling, the increase in sales comes primarily from encouraging customers to switch brands within the category, not from increasing category sales to new customers. In other words, bundle promotions attract already heavy users from other brands, rather than covert nonusers or light users to heavy users.

This ability of bundling to appeal selectively to heavy users over light users can have dramatic effect on profitability if heavy users are disproportionately responsible for purchases, such as is found in beer sales. Attracting heavy users to select a manufacturer's brand preferentially and converting these users into loyal customers can be a strong long-term profit driver.

Further investigation into the effect of bundling on driving brand or retail-outlet switching has shown a leverage effect. According to the leverage effect, the savings that customers gain in a bundle for their preferred item is partially allocated to an increase in willingness to buy the other items in the bundle. Thus, the most-desired item in the bundle increases the preference of all items in the bundle compared to competing brands or outlets not in the bundle. If the aim is to increase sales of one specific item, it suffices to select only a few attractive items that can increase sales of the focal item through the leverage effect. The leverage effect partially explains the ability of bundling to induce brand switching between less-desired items within the bundle.

Brand betrayal limits the optimal size of a bundle. Brand betrayal implies that customers reject the brand that they would normally choose and switch to another brand instead. In bundling, brand betrayal can arise when customers perceive the quantity requirement on a bundle as being set too high so as to exclude most customers from the benefits of the bundle. Thus, the size of the potential bundle cannot be set too high, but it should be set high enough to influence heavy category users.

DISAGGREGATED SAVINGS IMPROVE BUNDLE SELECTION

Another area of investigation into the consumer response to bundling has indicated that bundling is more likely to engender a greater consumer response, or lift in sales, when the savings in a bundle are disaggregated. It's a given that customers like savings. If the savings in a bundle are created in multiple parts, first a savings on the individual items within the bundle and second by a savings on the bundle itself, customers are likely to perceive the savings as greater than if the savings were incorporated as a single lump sum.[4]

An investigation into luggage offerings led to this conclusion. Consider the sale of two pieces of luggage, a garment bag and a Pullman, with the price schedule as shown in

Exhibit 12-4 Luggage Bundle Offers

	Price if Items Bought Separately	
Item	**Regular Price**	**Sale Price**
Garment Bag	$99	$89
Pullman	$99	$89
	$198	$178

OR
Buy the Garment Bag and Pullman as a Set for $158

Exhibit 12-4. There are three frames through which consumers could perceive savings if they bought both the garment bag and the Pullman:

- **Frame 1** The perceived savings are those of the bundle only ($178 − $158 = $20)
- **Frame 2** The perceived savings on the items if purchased separately and additional savings on the bundle are perceived as two separate savings ($20 + $20 = $40)
- **Frame 3** Savings on the items and the bundle are not perceived separately, but jointly ($198 − $158 = $40)

Research indicates that Frame 2 dominates. Separating the savings induces a higher likelihood to purchase than providing a single large-bundle discount.

This result fits with the notion from prospect theory that sellers should unbundle gains and bundle pains. Discounts are a form of gain in the sense that they provide a customer savings compared to the reference price. Offering two discounts, one on the individual items and a second on the total bundle, appeared to be more effective in encouraging purchases than offering one single large-bundle discount.

Further research into manipulating the prices of the individual items compared to the bundle indicates that the additional savings offered directly on the bundle have a greater relative impact on buyers' perceptions of transaction value than savings offered on the bundle's individual items.

BUYERS' MENTAL ARITHMETIC OF BUNDLES

Bundling has also been examined with respect to buyers' mental arithmetic. Mental arithmetic concerns how customers evaluate the savings of a bundle—specifically, whether buyers associate the savings with the more-desired item within the bundle, or alternatively, associate the savings with the least-desired items within the bundle.

According to the reference-dependent model, customers will first evaluate each item within the bundle and determine their willingness to pay, or reference price, for each specific item within the bundle, and then add up these reference prices to determine their willingness to pay for the bundle.[5] In this approach, customers will associate most of the savings in a bundle with the least-desired item.

For instance, assume that a bundle offer consists of two products, each having a market price of $8, and that the consumer integrates the attributes of each product to establish a reference price of $8 for product A and $4 for product B. In this case, the offer to sell product A at $8 would have a net utility of zero, whereas the offer to sell product B at $8 would have a negative utility of −$4. If the two products are bundled at a price of $12, the reference-dependent model predicts that the valuation of the bundle will be higher when the discount is assigned to the product with a price reference below the market price. Thus, consumers will assign the discount to the less-valued product in the bundle.

The reference-dependent model was examined by asking which offer customers perceived as more attractive: (1) Buy a large 1-topping Papa John's pizza for $7.99 and get an order of 10 chicken wings for $3.99; or (2) Buy an order of 10 chicken wings for $7.99 and get a large 1-topping Papa John's pizza for $3.99. It was found that consumers who valued pizza more than chicken wings would find the first offer more attractive than the second, even though the economic effect is the same.

The reference-dependent model has positive implications with respect to bundling and marketing. It implies that most of the savings from the bundle are incorporated into a perceived savings on the least-preferred item within the bundle and thus would have little effect on resetting the expectation price of the most-desired item. This implication would be desirable from a price expectation management viewpoint.

Unfortunately, early in the examination of consumer behavior with respect to bundling, it became apparent that the purely economic model of bundling gave an incomplete picture into how customers view a bundle.[6] From an economic viewpoint, we would expect that a customer's willingness to pay for a bundle would be the sum of their willingness to pay for the individual items, similar to the reference-dependent model. However, several studies demonstrated that customers often failed to value the bundle at the sum price of the individual products, as they would according to the reference-dependent model.

A competing model of mental arithmetic with respect to bundling is the weighted-additive model. According to the weighted-additive model, consumers evaluate a bundle starting at the most-preferred item within the bundle and work their way down to the least-preferred items. Moreover, the bundle savings would be perceived as savings on the most-preferred item.

Customers may evaluate a bundle by first anchoring their valuation of the bundle on the value that they place on the most-desired item within a bundle, and then adjust their valuation of the bundle to incorporate the other items within the bundle.[7] Under the weighted-additive rule, it is believed that one of the items in the bundle will be more important to a consumer than the other items in the bundle. A consumer will scan a bundle to identify the most-important or focal product, evaluate this product at its offer price, and then evaluate additional products within the bundle and update the bundle valuation as he or she proceeds. The product that is most valued will receive the most-weight by consumers when evaluating the bundle. In other words, the overall bundle evaluation is determined by examining the items in decreasing order of their perceived importance and adjusting the bundle evaluation in the direction of the succeeding item evaluations.

For instance, consumers prefer to receive a discount on a liked magazine as opposed to a disliked magazine in a bundle of liked and disliked magazines. The liked magazine has more weight in the overall valuation of the bundle and, consequently, the discount of this liked magazine has more weight in the valuation of the bundle than the discount on the less-liked magazines. Consequently, most of the discount on the bundle will be perceived as a discount on the most-liked item within the bundle and will not be perceived as a discount on the overall bundle or on the less-desired items within the bundle.

Furthermore, consumers seem to fail to adjust their initial valuation of the bundle away from their initial anchor. That is, if the additional items in the bundle increased the value of the bundle compared to the preferred item, consumers would not increase their valuation of the bundle appropriately to reflect their value of these additional items. The result would be that the bundle would routinely be undervalued by consumers compared to their willingness to pay for individual items within the bundle, even if their willingness to pay for the individual items was less than the asking price for these items. Moreover, the bundle savings would be incorporated into a perceived savings on the most-preferred item, thus resetting the expectation price of the most-desired item in the bundle. Neither of these implications would be desirable from a price expectation management viewpoint.

Which model is a more generally accurate description of mental arithmetic, the weighted-additive or the reference-dependent model, is an area of active investigation. However, even without knowing which dominates, executives can use these insights to proactively manage the frame through which customers perceive an offer and achieve better results.

For instance, in business markets, it is common for a purchasing agent to request a discount on a bundle of multiple items in one quarter and then expect that same discount to be applied to only the most-desired item in the next quarter. When purchasing agents execute this maneuver, one could claim that they are practicing a weighted-additive rule in evaluating the bundle by placing the majority of the savings on the most-desired item within the bundle. Sellers in this situation are advised to avoid this trap by explicitly identifying the savings in one quarter as coming from the less-desired items within the purchasing order so as to not be cornered into providing a deep discount on the more-valued items in subsequent quarters.

LEGAL ISSUES

While bundling is generally a legally accepted practice, there are rare but notable instances in which bundling can have negative legal ramifications.[8] The most notable cases in recent history are those brought against Microsoft with respect to its choice of bundling various products with its Windows operating system and Internet browser. Bundling cases have also been brought forth in other industries, such as steel, rail, and even salt. Careful analysis has led to a rough understanding of the legality of bundling, but case law is under constant revision and can be modified with each new case.

The relevant law has been divided into the per se rule and the rule of reason. The spirit of both rules is that a bundling strategy should not harm consumers by limiting competition. Under the per se rule, bundling has been ruled illegal when it is (1) pure bundling (2) of separate products (3) by a firm with market power and (4) when a substantial amount of commerce is at stake. Under the more-stringent rule of reason, bundling has been ruled illegal under the same conditions as the per se rule if two further conditions exist: (5) the bundle poses a threat that the bundling firm will acquire additional market power over at least one of the products that is bundled with the tying product, and (6) no plausible consumer benefits offset the potential damage to competition.

As reflected in these understandings, market power is one of the key issues with respect to price bundling. In competitive markets, almost all competitors are free to bundle. In markets with a high concentration of market share with any single firm, bundling is more likely to be legally suspect, even if that firm does not hold a complete monopoly.

The second key issue is whether the bundle adds value to consumers or simply is used to block competitors. Strategic product bundling that effectively raises the barriers to entry into the market will tend to increase the market power of incumbents and thwart new entrants. If it can be shown that the bundle provides significant customer advantages, courts may allow it. If not, executives should evaluate actions to mitigate the legal risks of bundling.

The specific examples of bundling that have been discussed in this chapter are unlikely to raise any legal challenges because they focus on mixed bundling rather than pure bundling and assume highly competitive industries.

Tradeoffs in Add-on, Version, and Bundle Pricing

Each of the three pricing structures, add-ons, versions, and bundles, takes advantage of heterogeneity in customer willingness to pay to define price segments and improve profitability. However, each pricing strategy is favored under a different set of conditions. Executives should consider their market, specifically the demand drivers of their market, before selecting one approach over the other.

However, the primary driver to determining whether a firm should select an add-on, versioning, or bundling strategy is customer heterogeneity. Markets with high heterogeneity in demand and multiple dimensions of demand heterogeneity tend to favor add-on pricing strategies, wherein customers can select a base product and customize their product with various complementary add-on products. Markets in which the heterogeneity in demand can be modeled along a single dimension, wherein a base product is increasingly enhanced to produce higher-benefit and higher-priced versions, favor versioning. Markets in which the heterogeneity in demand can be modeled as contrasting, wherein some customers prefer the first set of products, other customers prefer the second set of products, and all product benefits are additive for all customers, favor bundling strategies.

The second key driver to selecting an add-on, versioning, or bundling strategy is the cost structure. In an add-on pricing strategy, each individual complementary product is priced independently, and no specific product would be marketed unless some customers were willing to pay a price higher than the marginal cost to produce. Likewise, versioning strategies can manage increases in marginal costs as the product is enhanced in features up to the point that some customers are willing to pay significantly more for the enhanced features than the marginal costs to produce the product with those features. In this way, marginal costs affect the profitability of versioning strategies in something of the same proportion as they affect the profitability of add-on strategies. In contrast, high marginal costs significantly discourage a bundling strategy because the bundled price is often much lower than the sum price of the individual products. With high marginal costs, firms usually desire to disaggregate market segments according to their willingness to pay for specific products rather than aggregate them into a single bundled segment.

There are other, more nuanced factors that influence the selection between an add-on, version, or bundling price structure. For instance, consider the interplay between prospect theory and price structure. Add-on price structures require customers to pay a separate price for each additional product; yet prospect theory encourages marketers to bundle pain and unbundle gain. As such, prospect theory would predict that the demand for additional products would be dampened compared to their underlying economic trading capacity because each additional product brings additional pain, in the form of price, along with the additional benefits. In contrast, versioning strategies bundle the pain into a single, albeit higher, price for customers to capture additional benefits. Finally, bundling strategies are highly favored by prospect theory because they not only deliver more benefits to customers, but are structured so as to bring a new additional benefit in the form of a discount compared to the sum of the individual product prices.

We have summarized the effects of market heterogeneity, cost structures, and prospect theory on the selection of add-on, versioning, or bundling price structures in Exhibit 12-5.

Exhibit 12-5 Tradeoffs in Add-on, Versioning, and Bundling Price Structures

	Customer Heterogeneity	Marginal Cost	Prospect Theory
Add-ons	Wide heterogeneity in preference	Applicable with both high and low marginal costs	Discourages add-ons
Versioning	Heterogeneous preference along a dominant dimension of benefit enhancement	Applicable with both high and low marginal costs	Encourages versioning
Bundling	Contrasting preference for different products between customers	Not applicable with high marginal costs. Favored with low marginal costs	Encourages bundling

Summary

- In bundling, two or more distinct products are sold at a single, bundled price. The bundled price is lower than the sum price of the individual products, but higher than the price of any individual product within the bundle.
- Bundling exploits contrasting demand within the market, wherein some customers prefer one item within the bundle more than the second, while others prefer the second item in the bundle more than the first. The bundle aggregates these two customers into a single segment, one that would prefer to pay the bundle price for receiving both products rather than a single lower price for only one item in the bundle.
- Bundling is favored by products with low marginal costs.
- In mixed bundling, both the individual products and the bundle of the products are marketed. In pure bundling, the individual products are not marketed, only the bundle. Pure bundling represents the equivalent of redefining the product category.
- Bundling is more effective at encouraging brand or retail outlet switching than at encouraging increased consumption or accelerated purchasing.
- Bundling strategies benefit from the leverage effect, wherein the most-desired item in the bundle increases the preference for all items in the bundle compared to competing brands.
- Promotional bundling is more effective at creating consumer interest if the savings are disaggregated; that is, the savings of the bundle are identified as both a savings on the individual items and an additional savings on the purchase of the entire bundle.
- Consumers' mental arithmetic regarding bundling varies between different frames. In some cases, it is believed that customers associate the bundle savings with the least-preferred item (reference-dependent rule) in the bundle. In other cases, it is believed that customers associate the bundle savings with the most-preferred item (weighted-additive rule).
- Bundling has come under legal restrictions when used primarily as a competitive tactic by dominant firms.

Exercises

1. AT&T offers Internet, mobile telephone services, landline telephone services, and digital TV. Consider two different segments, the Millennial and Traditional, with willingness to pay for different products and market share shown here. Assume a market size of 50 million homes.

Market Segment	Mobile + Internet Willingness to Pay	Phone + TV Willingness to Pay	Market Share
Millennial	$95	$25	30%
Traditional	$30	$115	70%

   a. Scenario A: Consider an AT&T price menu of two packages, one of Mobile + Internet for $95 and the other of Phone + TV for $115, and complete the chart by answering the following questions.

      i. Calculate the consumer surplus for each segment with each offering (Consumer Surplus = Price − Willingness to Pay).

ii. Calculate the revenue earned from each offering and market segment in millions of dollars. (Assume that if the consumer surplus is zero or positive for a given segment and offering, the segment purchases. Calculate revenue as the product of price, market share, and overall market size if the segment purchases.)

iii. What is the total revenue earned under this scenario?

	Consumer Surplus	
	Mobile + Internet	Phone + TV
Millennial		
Traditional		

	Revenue	
	Mobile + Internet	Phone + TV
Millennial		
Traditional		

b. Scenario B: Consider an AT&T price menu of three packages: Mobile + Internet for $95, Phone + TV for $115, and Mobile + Internet + Phone + TV for $145. Complete the chart by answering the following questions.

i. Calculate the consumer surplus for each segment with each offering.

ii. Calculate the revenue earned from each offering and market segment in millions of dollars.

iii. What is the total revenue earned under this scenario?

	Consumer Surplus		
	Mobile + Internet	Phone + TV	Mobile + Internet + Phone + TV
Millennial			
Traditional			

	Revenue		
	Mobile + Internet	Phone + TV	Mobile + Internet + Phone + TV
Millennial			
Traditional			

c. How much larger, in millions of dollars, is the revenue earned under scenario B than scenario A?

d. What is the percentage increase in revenue under scenario B over scenario A?

e. How were the above price points identified? Were there other price points that would increase revenue for AT&T above that calculated?

2. Disney offers both hotel rooms and entrance to their theme parks at their resorts. Consider four different market segments with willingness to pay for rooms and market shares shown below. Assume a market size of 5,000 individuals per day.

Segment	Room	Theme Park	Market Share
Amusement Park Lover	$200	$150	20%
Luxury Lover	$300	$50	10%
Conference Devotee	$325	$5	20%
Disney Devotee	$50	$200	50%

a. Plot the willingness to pay for the different market segments. (Use a bubble plot to designate the size of the different market segments on the plot.)

b. Scenario A: Consider a Disney price menu of Hotel Room at $300 and Theme Park Entrance at $150. Complete the chart by answering the following questions.
   i. Calculate the consumer surplus for each segment with each offering.
   ii. Which segments purchase which offering?
   iii. Calculate the revenue earned from each offering and market segment in millions of dollars.
   iv. What is the total revenue earned under this scenario?

	Consumer Surplus	
	Room	Theme Park
Amusement Park Lover		
Luxury Lover		
Conference Devotee		
Disney Devotee		

	Revenue	
	Room	Theme Park
Amusement Park Lover		
Luxury Lover		
Conference Devotee		
Disney Devotee		

c. Scenario B: Consider a Disney price menu of Hotel Room for $200 and Theme Park Entrance for $150. Complete the chart by answering the following questions.
   i. Calculate the consumer surplus for each segment with each offering.
   ii. Which segments purchase which offering?
   iii. Calculate the revenue earned from each offering and market segment in millions of dollars.
   iv. What is the total revenue earned under this scenario?

	Consumer Surplus	
	Room	Theme Park
Amusement Park Lover		
Luxury Lover		
Conference Devotee		
Disney Devotee		

	Revenue	
	Room	Theme Park
Amusement Park Lover		
Luxury Lover		
Conference Devotee		
Disney Devotee		

d. Scenario C: Consider a Disney price menu of Hotel Room for $325, Theme Park Entrance for $200, and Hotel + Theme Park Bundle for $350. Complete the chart by answering the following questions.
   i. Calculate the consumer surplus for each segment with each offering.
   ii. Which segments purchase which offering? Assume customers will maximize their consumer surplus.
   iii. Calculate the revenue earned from each offering and market segment in millions of dollars.
   iv. What is the total revenue earned under this scenario?

	Consumer Surplus		
	Room	Theme Park	Room + Theme Park
Amusement Park Lover			
Luxury Lover			
Conference Devotee			
Disney Devotee			

	Revenue		
	Room	Theme Park	Room + Theme Park
Amusement Park Lover			
Luxury Lover			
Conference Devotee			
Disney Devotee			

e. What are the optimal prices of the Hotel Rooms and Theme Park Entrance in the absence of bundling?

f. How much larger, in millions of dollars, is the revenue earned with bundling than without?

g. What is the percentage increase in revenue earned with bundling than without?

h. How did bundling increase the overall revenue earned?

3. The *Chicago Sun Times* offers political, business, sports, and entertainment news. For the sake of this exercise, let us consider the market as consisting of four different market segments with willingness to pay and market shares shown below. Assume a market size of 400,000 subscribers.

Segment	Politics + Business	Sports + Entertainment	Market Share
Politico	$90	$5	20%
Executive	$75	$25	30%
Soccer Mom	$25	$75	30%
Weekend Warrior	$5	$90	20%

a. Plot the willingness to pay for the different market segments.

b. Find the optimal prices for the *Chicago Sun Times* Politics + Business Edition and Sports + Entertainment Edition in the absence of further bundling. What is the revenue earned if the *Chicago Sun Times* offered only these products?

c. Find the optimal price for the complete *Chicago Sun Times* under the condition of pure bundling. The complete *Chicago Sun Times* includes Politics, Business,

Sports, and Entertainment. What is the revenue earned for the *Chicago Sun Times* when it offers pure bundling only?

d. Find the optimal prices for the *Chicago Sun Times* under mixed bundling. In mixed bundling, there are three products: the Complete Edition, which includes Politics, Business, Sports, and Entertainment; the Politics + Business Edition; and the Sports + Entertainment Edition. What is the revenue earned for the *Chicago Sun Times* when it offers mixed bundling?

e. How much greater revenue is earned under pure bundling for the *Chicago Sun Times* than by offering only stand-alone editions (Complete Edition vs. Politics + Business Edition and Sports + Entertainment Edition)?

f. How much greater revenue is earned under mixed bundling for the *Chicago Sun Times* than by offering only stand-alone products and pure bundling (Complete Edition, Politics + Business Edition, and Sports + Entertainment Edition vs. Complete Edition)?

g. What factors may drive the *Chicago Sun Times* not to offer mixed bundling?

4. Adobe Creative Suite 5 is offered in several different versions. Consider the following three offers: Web Premium at $1,799, Production Premium at $1,899, and Master Collection at $2,599. The features of these products are listed below.

Adobe CS5 Component		Web Premium $1,799	Production Premium $1,899	Master Collection $2,599
Image Editing	Photoshop Extended	X	X	X
	Illustrator	X	X	X
	InDesign			X
	Acrobat Pro	X		X
Web Editing	Flash Catalyst	X	X	X
	Flash Professional	X	X	X
	Flash Builder Standard	X		X
	Dreamweaver	X		X
	Fireworks	X		X
	Contribute	X		X
Video Editing	Premier Pro		X	X
	After Effects		X	X
	Soundbooth		X	X
	OnLocation		X	X
	Encore		X	X

a. Identify and describe at least three different market segments that Adobe is attempting to attract with these offers and their willingness to pay.

b. Are Adobe software products good candidates for bundling? Why or why not?

5. Bauhaus, a German home improvement store, is considering a June promotional bundle consisting of a patio set plus patio sun umbrella for 425€. Normally, the patio set of four chairs and a table sells for 300€, and the patio sun umbrella sells for 200€. Both products have a 50 percent contribution margin. If the promotional bundle is anticipated to reduce the sales of patio sets by 75 units and the sales of patio umbrellas by 25 units, how many promotional bundles must be sold for the promotion to improve profits?

Appendix 12.A Promotional Bundle Volume Hurdle

In Chapter 2, we investigated the sensitivity to profits earned from a single product with respect to a change in its price and developed a volume hurdle. The volume hurdle identified the level of sales required for price discount to increase profitability. In this appendix, we will develop a different volume hurdle—the volume hurdle for promotional bundling.

With promotional bundling, we are no longer selling a single item, but rather two items. If we attempted to apply the same rules created for discounting a single item to discounting a bundle of items, we would quickly find challenges. One of the larger of these would be identifying the portion of the discount that should be ascribed to each individual product. Rather than trying to resolve this challenge, we will derive a different bundling volume hurdle.

The bundle volume hurdle can be derived through identifying the required increase in sales generated from selling a bundle at a discount compared to selling individual items. This is a quantifiable question that can be derived directly from the firm's profit equation.

First, let us look at the firm's profit equation in the absence of bundling. Assume that the firm is selling two products, product A and product B. We find the firm's profits to be

$$\pi\,(individual) = Q_A \cdot (P_A - V_A) + Q_B \cdot (P_B - V_B) \qquad \text{Eq. 12.1}$$

where we have assumed no fixed costs without losing generality to make the derivation simpler. Q_A and Q_B are the volume of sales of products A and B, respectively, in the absence of bundling. P_A and P_B are the prices of products A and B, respectively, and V_A and V_B are the variable costs of products A and B, respectively.

In bundling, the sales volumes of the individual items within the bundle and the sales of the bundle itself will be different than in the absence of bundling. There can be four different ways in which the bundle affects sales:

1. The bundle can take sales away from customers that would have bought A but not B. These are customers that are upgrading their purchase from that of A alone to that of the bundle. Let the change of volume from these customers be denoted by $\Delta Q_{A\to T}$. $\Delta Q_{A\to T}$ takes sales from A but adds them to the bundle.
2. The bundle can take sales away from customers that would have bought B but not A. These are customers that are upgrading their purchase from that of B alone to that of the bundle. Let the change of volume from these customers be denoted by $\Delta Q_{B\to T}$. $\Delta Q_{B\to T}$ takes sales from B but adds them to the bundle.
3. The bundle can take sales away from customers that would have bought both A and B. In this case, the bundle is a pure price concession to this customer segment. Let the change of volume from these customers be denoted by $\Delta Q_{AB\to T}$. $\Delta Q_{AB\to T}$ takes sales from A and B but adds them to the bundle.
4. The bundle can create some new customers that would not have purchased either A or B. Let the change of volume from these customers be denoted by ΔQ_{new}. ΔQ_{new} adds sales to the bundle but has no effect on the sales of A or B.

In the presence of a promotional bundle, the firm's profit equation becomes

$$\begin{aligned}\pi\,(bundle) = {} & (Q_A - \Delta Q_{A\to T} - \Delta Q_{AB\to T}) \cdot (P_A - V_A) \\ & + (Q_B - \Delta Q_{B\to T} - \Delta Q_{AB\to T}) \cdot (P_B - V_B) \\ & + (\Delta Q_{A\to T} + \Delta Q_{B\to T} + \Delta Q_{AB\to T} + \Delta Q_{\text{new}}) \\ & \cdot (P_A + P_B - \delta P_T - V_A - V_B)\end{aligned} \qquad \text{Eq. 12.2}$$

In Equation 12.2, the first term represents the profits earned from product A, the second term represents the profits earned from product B, and the third term represents the profits earned from the bundle, under the condition of a promotional bundle. We have assumed that there are no changes in variable costs associated with promotional bundling because the promotional bundle simply takes two individual items that were on the market and sells them at a new, bundled price. We have also introduced a new term, δP_T, which is the price discount of the bundle compared to the sum price of the individual items.

The bundle volume hurdle is identified by requiring the profits earned under the bundle promotion to be greater than what would be earned compared to individual product sales alone. Alternatively stated, we desire the change in profits to be higher:

$$\Delta\pi = \pi(bundle) - \pi(individual) > 0 \qquad \text{Eq. 12.3}$$

We can define the contribution margins CM_A and CM_B for products A and B, respectively, to be

$$CM_A = P_A - V_A \qquad \text{Eq. 12.4.a}$$

$$CM_B = P_B - V_B \qquad \text{Eq. 12.4.b}$$

Then, using Equations 12.1 and 12.2 for the profits earned under individual sales and a bundle promotion into the condition for improved profitability in Equation 12.3 along with the substitutions of 12.4, we find

$$\begin{aligned}(\Delta Q_{A\to T} + \Delta Q_{B\to T} + \Delta Q_{AB\to T} + \Delta Q_{\text{new}}) \cdot (CM_A + CM_B - \delta P_T)\\ - (\Delta Q_{A\to T} + \Delta Q_{AB\to T}) \cdot CM_A - (\Delta Q_{B\to T} + \Delta Q_{AB\to T}) \cdot CM_B > 0\end{aligned} \qquad \text{Eq. 12.5}$$

Equation 12.5 contains the quantities that define the anticipated sales from the bundle and the loss of sales from the individual products. To make these changes explicit, let us define the change in volumes ΔQ_A and ΔQ_B of products A and B, respectively, as

$$\Delta Q_A = \Delta Q_{A\to T} + \Delta Q_{AB\to T} \qquad \text{Eq. 12.6.a}$$

$$\Delta Q_B = \Delta Q_{B\to T} + \Delta Q_{AB\to T} \qquad \text{Eq. 12.6.b}$$

and also define the sales of the product bundle, ΔQ_T, as

$$\Delta Q_T = \Delta Q_{A\to T} + \Delta Q_{B\to T} + \Delta Q_{AB\to T} + \Delta Q_{\text{new}} \qquad \text{Eq. 12.6.c}$$

Using the definitions in Equation 12.6 and our condition in Equation 12.5 and solving for the required sales from the bundle, we find the promotional bundle volume hurdle of

$$\Delta Q_T > \frac{CM_A \cdot \Delta Q_A + CM_B \cdot \Delta Q_B}{CM_A + CM_B - \delta P_T} \qquad \text{Eq. 12.7}$$

Each term on the left side of Equation 12.7 can be estimated prior to executing a promotional bundle. The contribution margins CM_A and CM_B can be calculated for the individual products and this does not change the presence of a promotional bundle. Similarly, the discount of the promotional bundle compared to the prices of the individual products, δP_T, will be determined in the design of the promotion. Prior to the promotional bundle, the change in sales of A and B, expressed as ΔQ_A and ΔQ_B, can be estimated to develop an understanding of the required bundle volume hurdle. After the promotional bundle has been executed, the cannibalization of sales can be measured and the sales of the bundle, ΔQ_T can be compared to the hurdle in Equation 12.7 to determine whether the bundle improved profits or damaged them.

Just as with standard volume hurdles for single-item discounts, executives can use the bundle volume hurdle to determine whether a bundle discount improved or harmed profits, and to forecast whether a bundle will add or subtract to profitability.

Appendix 12.B Economic Model of Bundling

Economic research into bundling has focused on creating abstract models to demonstrate the conditions under which bundling is more profitable than the absence of bundling.[9] While the model does not provide a general approach to pricing a bundle, it can be used to define the requirements of bundling and explains how bundling improves profits under certain circumstances. The model will be highly similar to that used in exploring the economics of add-on and versioning price structures to enable easy comparison. One driver in particular is important: some customers must have contrasting demand between the items in the bundle.

We will assume that the optimal prices of the independent products are unchanged under bundling. While this is an overly restrictive assumption, we can still demonstrate the power of bundling under this restriction. This assumption is true in many cases. For instance, consider a firm that has optimized the prices of independent products for independent markets and is considering launching a new bundled product containing many of the individual products. In this case, it may be unlikely that the firm will change the prices of the individual products simply by launching a new bundled offer.

For the few customers Q_T, with contrasting demand for products A and B, the net utility function is given by the following set of equations:

$$U(t) = S_A \cdot t - P_A \quad \text{if purchasing product A} \qquad \text{Eq. 12.8a}$$

$$U(t) = S_B \cdot (1 - t) - P_B \quad \text{if purchasing product B} \qquad \text{Eq. 12.8b}$$

$$U(t) = S_A \cdot t + S_B \cdot (1 - t) - P_T \quad \text{if purchasing bundle T of A and B} \qquad \text{Eq. 12.8c}$$

where we have defined S_A and S_B as the maximum value that any of these customers will place on products A and B, respectively; and P_A, P_B, and P_T are the prices of the individual products A and B and the price of the bundle T.

We have once again used a taste parameter (t) to account for the heterogeneity in demand between different market segments. (See Appendix 6 for more about this.) The taste parameter varies between zero and 1 ($t \in [0, 1]$). Customers with a low taste parameter (near zero) are those who value the product A little but value product B highly. Customers with a high taste parameter (near 1) are those who value the product A highly but value product B very little. In this way, the taste parameter accounts for the contrasting demand for these Q_T customers. For simplicity, we will assume a uniform distribution in the customer taste parameters within this segment. As the value for product A increases, the value for product B decreases. See Exhibit 12-6.

In a similar manner as before, we find marginal customers with contrasting demands. In this case, we have two marginal customers: One is indifferent between purchasing product A alone and purchasing the bundle ($t_{A,T}$); the other is indifferent between purchasing product B alone and purchasing the bundle ($t_{B,T}$). We assume that customers of all types exist, thus $0 \le t_{B,T} \le t_{A,T} \le 1$. When $0 \le t < t_{B,T}$, the customer purchases only B. When $t_{B,T} \le t \le t_{A,T}$, the customer purchases the bundle T, which includes both products A and B. When $t_{A,T} < t \le 1$, the customer purchases only A.

From our utility function 12.8a and 12.8c, the customers indifferent between buying A alone and the bundle T will have equal utility for purchasing either A or the bundle T:

$$S_A \cdot t_{A,T} - P_A = S_A \cdot t_{A,T} + S_B \cdot (1 - t_{A,T}) - P_T \qquad \text{Eq. 12.9}$$

Solving for $t_{A,T}$, we find

$$t_{A,T} = 1 - \frac{P_T - P_A}{S_B} \qquad \text{Eq. 12.10}$$

Exhibit 12-6 Customer Utility Function with Contrasting Demand for Bundling

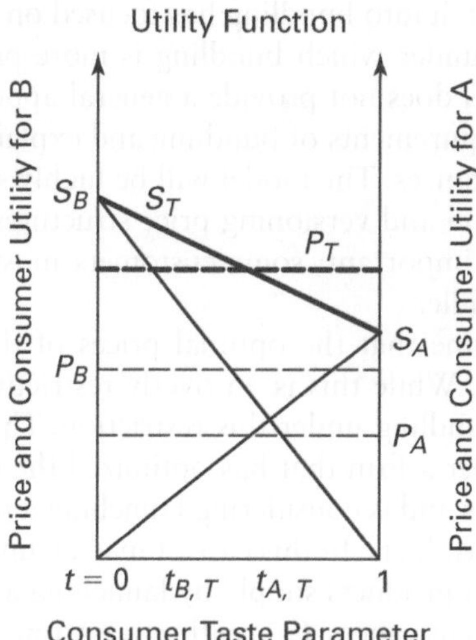

Similarly, from our utility function 12.8b and 12.8c, the customers indifferent between buying B alone and the bundle T will have equal utility for purchasing either B or the bundle T:

$$S_B \cdot (1 - t_{B,T}) - P_B = S_A \cdot t_{B,T} + S_B \cdot (1 - t_{B,T}) - P_T \qquad \text{Eq. 12.11}$$

Solving for $t_{B,T}$, we find

$$t_{B,T} = \frac{P_T - P_B}{S_A} \qquad \text{Eq. 12.12}$$

For customers to make a tradeoff between the bundled products and the independent product A, we know that $t_{A,T}$ must be less than 1. Similarly, for customers to make a tradeoff between the bundled products and the independent product B, we know that $t_{B,T}$ must be greater than zero. These conditions imply that

$$t_{A,T} \leq 1 \Rightarrow P_T \geq P_A \qquad \text{Eq. 12.13.a}$$

$$t_{B,T} \geq 0 \Rightarrow P_T \geq P_B \qquad \text{Eq. 12.13.b}$$

Equation 12.13 indicates that the price of the bundle must be greater than the price of either product if some customers are to purchase an independent product while others choose the bundle.

We also know that some customers will choose the bundle. For these customers to exist, the taste parameter of those choosing between product B and the bundle must be less than that of the customers choosing between product A and the bundle. This implies

$$t_{B,T} \leq t_{A,T} \Rightarrow P_T \leq \frac{S_A \cdot P_A + S_B \cdot P_B}{S_A + S_B} + \frac{S_A \cdot S_B}{S_A + S_B} \qquad \text{Eq. 12.14}$$

The bundle price has to be less than the utility-weighted average price of the individual parts, plus the product of the utilities over the sum of the utilities.

We now turn to the challenge of maximizing the firm's profit. The firm's profit equation for these customers with contrasting demand is given by

$$\begin{aligned}\pi(P_T) = {} & Q_T (1 - t_{A,T})(P_A - V_A) + Q_T \cdot t_{B,T} (P_B - V_B) \\ & + Q_T (t_{A,T} - t_{B,T})(P_T - V_T)\end{aligned} \qquad \text{Eq. 12.15}$$

where we have defined V_A and V_B be the marginal cost of products A and B, respectively, and V_T as the variable costs of the bundle. We have set fixed costs equal to zero without losing generality.

To find the optimal price of the bundle, we set the first derivative of the firm's profit equation with respect to P_T equal to zero under the assumption that P_A and P_B do not change in the presence of bundling:

$$\frac{\partial \pi}{\partial P_T} = 0 \Rightarrow 0 = -\frac{\partial t_{A,T}}{\partial P_T}(P_A - V_A) + \frac{\partial t_{B,T}}{\partial P_T}(P_B - V_B)$$
$$+\left\{\frac{\partial t_{A,T}}{\partial P_T} - \frac{\partial t_{B,T}}{\partial P_T}\right\} \cdot (\hat{P}_T - V_T) + (t_{A,T} - t_{B,T}) \qquad \text{Eq. 12.16}$$

with

$$\frac{\partial t_{A,T}}{\partial P_T} = \frac{-1}{S_B} \qquad \text{Eq. 12.17a}$$

$$\frac{\partial t_{B,T}}{\partial P_T} = \frac{1}{S_A} \qquad \text{Eq. 12.17b}$$

Using the results of Equations 12.10, 12.12, and 12.17 in Equation 12.16 and simplifying for P_T, we find the optimal bundled price as a function of the prices of the individual products as follows:

$$\hat{P}_T = \frac{V_T}{2} + \frac{S_A \cdot S_B}{2 \cdot (S_A + S_B)} + \frac{S_A \cdot (2P_A - V_A) + S_B \cdot (2P_B - V_B)}{2 \cdot (S_A + S_B)} \qquad \text{Eq. 12.18}$$

We can simplify Equation 12.18 by using the optimal prices of the individual products found in Equation 6.5 in Appendix 6. If $P_A = 1/2\ (S_A + V_A)$ and $P_B = 1/2\ (S_B + V_B)$, the optimal prices of products A and B in independent markets, then P_T becomes

$$\hat{P}_T = \frac{S_A + S_B + V_T}{2} - \frac{1}{2} \cdot \frac{S_A \cdot S_B}{(S_A + S_B)} \qquad \text{Eq. 12.19}$$

The optimal bundle price represents the individual product prices, adjusted for the marginal cost savings in bundling, minus the product of the utilities divided by the sum of the utilities. This optimal bundle price is less than what it would be in the absence of selling the individual products.

At this price, we in turn look at the restriction on costs. We find the bundle cost has to be less than the utility-weighted average costs of the individual parts plus the product of the utilities divided by the sum of the utilities:

$$t_{B,T} \leq t_{A,T} \Rightarrow V_T \leq \frac{S_A \cdot V_A + S_B \cdot V_B}{S_A + S_B} + \frac{S_A \cdot S_B}{S_A + S_B} \qquad \text{Eq. 12.20}$$

The cost of bundling will often meet the condition set in Equation 12.20. As such, bundling is likely to improve the profitability of the firm. We leave it to the reader to identify the profit increment resulting from this economic model. As noted in this chapter, we suggest finding the optimal price of a bundle and its profit impact through simpler models that simply consider segment sizes and their willingness to pay for different products.

Notes

[1] One of the more-complete analysis of bundling can be found in Stefan Stremersch and Gerard J. Tellis, "Strategic Bundling of Products and Prices: A New Synthesis for Marketing," *Journal of Marketing* 66, No. 1 (January 2002): 55–72. See also Yannis Bakos and Erik Brynjolfsson, "Bundling Information Goods: Pricing, Profits, and Efficiency," *Management Science* 45, No. 12 (December 1999): 1613–30; and Ward Hanson and R. Kipp Martin, "Optimal Bundle Pricing," *Management Science* 36, No. 2 (February 1990): 155–74.

[2] Infrastructure-based industries are industries with high sunk costs and low marginal costs, such as telecoms, utilities, cellular phone providers, and highways.

[3] For retail-level promotional bundling, see Bram Foubert and Els Gijsbrechts, "Shopper Response to Bundle Promotions for Packaged Goods," *Journal of Marketing Research 44*, No. 4 (November 2007): 647–62. Francis J. Mulhern and Robert P. Leone, "Implicit Price Bundling of Retail Products: A Multiproduct Approach to Maximizing Store Profitability," *Journal of Marketing* 55, No. 4 (October 1991): 63–76.

[4] For a study of how consumers view bundling, see Manjit S. Yadav and Kent B. Monroe, "How Buyers Perceive Savings in a Bundle Price: An Examination of a Bundle's Transaction Value," *Journal of Marketing Research* 30, No. 3 (August 1993): 350–58.

[5] Chris Janiszewski and Marcus Cunha, Jr., "The Influence of Price Discount Framing on the Evaluation of a Product Bundle," *Journal of Consumer Research* 30, No. 4 (March 2004): 534–46.

[6] Stephen M. Goldberg, Paul E. Green, and Yoram Wind, "Conjoint Analysis of Price Premiums for Hotel Amenities," *Journal of Business* 57, No. 1, Part 2: Pricing Strategy (January 1984): S111–32.

[7] Manjit S. Yadav, "How Buyers Evaluate Product Bundles: A Model of Anchoring and Adjustment," *Journal of Consumer Research* 21, No. 2 (September 1994): 342–53. Manjit S. Yadav, "Bundle Evaluation in Different Market Segments: The Effects of Discount Framing on Buyers' Preference Heterogeneity," *Journal of the Academy of Marketing Science* 23, No. 3 (July 1995): 206–15.

[8] Stefan Stremersch and Gerard J. Tellis, "Strategic Bundling of Products and Prices: A New Synthesis for Marketing," *Journal of Marketing* 66, No. 1 (January 2002): 55–72.

[9] The model presented here is adapted from Paul Belleflamme, "Versioning in the Information Economy: Theory and Applications," *CESifo Economic Studies, Munich* 51, No. 2/3 (January 2005): 329–58.

Chapter 13

Subscriptions and Customer Lifetime Value

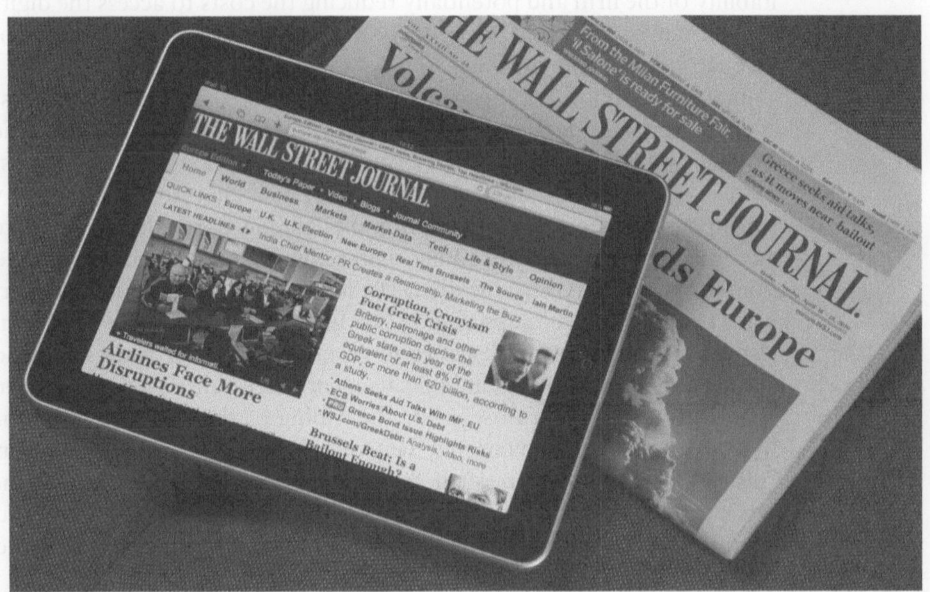

Lourens Smak/Alamy

- How should subscriptions be priced?
- What determines the value to the firm of creating and capturing a customer?
- How do subscribers differ from customers who purchase products on the spot market?
- How does the inability of customers to anticipate their future actions influence subscription prices?
- What are informational asymmetries, and how do subscriptions help address barriers to purchase?
- What is Software as a Service (SaaS), and how should it be priced?
- Stretch Question: How do subscription offerings price-discriminate between heavy users and light users?

Subscription price structures may have been pioneered with magazines and newspapers, but from this humble origin, they have become standard pricing practices in many industries. As early as the seventeenth century, subscriptions to publications and books had become common practice in England.[1] Today, many information providers apply subscription pricing for access to their data, such as stock quotes, legal rulings, business profiles, and other research-oriented journals. Book clubs, music clubs, gyms, and other organizations have also long used subscription pricing. The list of industries in which someone can find subscription-based pricing is continually growing.

More recently, there has been a proliferation of Application Service Provider (ASP) and Software as a Service (SaaS) price structures for enterprise applications.[2] These pricing models have not only made significant inroads into the market, but they have also expanded the market for enterprise software to include small and medium-sized businesses. In these pricing models, software firms sell access to their software using subscription pricing rather than one-off sales followed by periodic update and upgrade sales, or maintenance and service contracts.

Many firms profit from subscription arrangements due to their ability to reduce the transaction costs. With digital goods delivered electronically, the costs of reproduction may be negligible; but the administrative costs of managing transactions can be significant. Through subscription offerings, transaction costs can be reduced, thus improving the profitability of the firm and potentially reducing the costs to access the digital good. As a result, the market is expanded. Even in non-digital markets, transaction costs can be reduced through subscription arrangements.

In a subscription arrangement, a series of related individual purchases is converted into a single purchase decision. For instance, rather than purchasing individual issues of a periodical or individual visits to a gym, the subscription enables the customers to receive a number of issues or multiple visits through a single transaction. Even when payments are spread out over time, the subscription model reduces the decision to enter into the purchase agreement to a single point rather than requiring the customers to decide to purchase each time they want to receive the item. The items in the subscription can vary as well; with software, for example, the subscription will include not only the license to use the software, but also access to updates and service to ensure that the software is functioning. Sometimes it also includes data hosting and management when sold as a complete service.

Subscriptions also can separate the timing of the payment from that of consumption. In some cases, the payment may be made through a periodic lump sum that covers many episodes of consumption, such as yearly newspaper subscriptions and daily delivery. In other cases, the payment may be concurrent to the time of usage, such as membership contracts that cover a year and require monthly payments and allow customers access to the product continually during that year.

In pricing the subscription relative to the sale of the individual items, there are two key metrics. The first is the total period price or the sum price that customers would pay if they purchased all the items within the subscription. This is the maximum price that can be charged for the subscription in absence of a significant change in the value proposition. The second is the customer period value, or the sum price that the customer would pay during the period given average customer purchasing patterns. The customer period value sets the minimum price for the subscription that the firm should offer. Any price below this level would leave the firm worse off than if it had simply offered all its products for sale through individual purchases.

Moderating the price between these two levels set by the total period price and customer period value are issues related to consumer behavior and changes in the value proposition. For numerous reasons, firms find it relatively impossible to charge subscription prices equal to the total period price. However, this should not imply that subscription prices should equal the lower, expected customer period value. Subscription prices typically are significantly higher than the expected period value due to increases in the total benefits that customers gain through the subscription arrangement relative to individual item purchases. Further complicating subscription price structures are changes to the value proposition. For instance, with many software subscription services, firms not only offer customers access to the software, maintenance, and support, but they also assume responsibility for hosting and managing the data. This represents an increase in the economic value delivered to customers, thus further enabling higher prices.

Pricing the Subscription

When considering adding subscription sales to individual product sales, the firm should ensure that it will be more profitable with subscriptions than it is with individual product sales at a minimum. To ensure this, we would expect the price of the subscription to lie between two boundaries. See Exhibit 13-1. The upper bound is defined by the total period price, or the price that customers would pay if they purchased every item in the subscription. The lower bound is defined through the expected customer period value.

The method of calculating the customer period value is extremely similar to that of the customer lifetime value. While relatively simple to execute, an analysis of the customer period or lifetime value requires careful identification of a number of factors. Let us examine a common practice in calculating these two price boundaries before we turn to influences in determining the appropriate price between these boundaries.[3]

TOTAL PERIOD PRICE

The total period price is simply the price that customers would pay if they purchased every item within the subscription. It is the maximum price that customers would consider paying.

For instance, a monthly magazine with a newsstand price of $3.95 would have a total period price for one year of $47.40. See Exhibit 13-1. Likewise, gym visitors paying $10 per visit to use the gym three times a week for 52 weeks might expect a total period price for annual gym use of $1,560.

Even when the individual items within the subscription are different, the total period price is the sum of the individual unit prices. For instance, a basic enterprise software subscription might include the license to use the software coupled with maintenance and support to provide access to critical software updates and disaster recovery support. Other services may also be added to a software subscription, such as data hosting and management. In this case, the total period price is the sum of the price of the software license, maintenance and support, and data hosting and management.

Exhibit 13-1 Boundaries on the Subscription Price

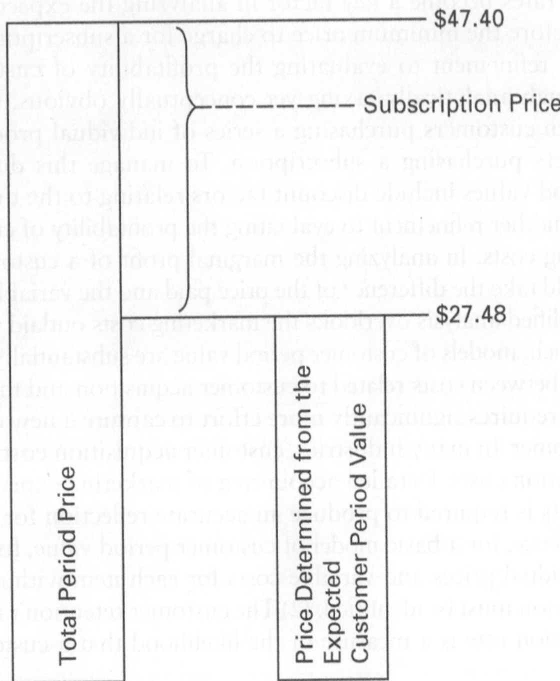

To build a model of the total period price for enterprise software, suppose that the initial software license fee is $325,000, and that maintenance and support is priced at 18 percent of the initial license fee. Then, a five-year subscription to the software would have a total period price of $617,500, which includes both the price of the initial license and ongoing maintenance and support. On a monthly basis, the total period price of the subscription would be $10,292, neglecting any effects from the timing of payments.

Firms rarely price subscriptions at the total period price, however. While the potential exchange value is the total period price, subscription prices much lower than this total period price are often more profitable than selling the units individually. In calculating the total period price, we have assumed that customers would buy every unit during the period and furthermore, that they would remain customers throughout the period under consideration. Customers rarely behave this way. Even dedicated customers of a product cannot be expected to purchase every unit. The total period price leaves the most-demanding customer indifferent between purchasing the individual products on the spot market and purchasing the subscription. Given the drawbacks of subscriptions, such as the pre-commitment to the future consumption of a good that may or may not be demanded in the future, customers lack any incentive to purchase the product on a subscription basis if the subscription price equals the total period price. As such, firms usually find it more profitable to price subscriptions below the potential total period price in the absence of a change in the value proposition.

CUSTOMER PERIOD VALUE

The customer period value calculates the expected profits earned from a customer during the period, given a customer's actual purchase behavior. By calculating the customer period value, we can identify the minimum price that the firm should consider charging for a subscription.

The largest conceptual differences between the customer period value and the total period price are the inclusion of factors that reflect actual customer behavior. For instance, it is not uncommon for customers to purchase a few issues of a magazine or visit the gym a few times prior to ending their relationship with the product. As such, customer retention rates become a key factor in analyzing the expected profitability of a customer and therefore the minimum price to charge for a subscription.

A refinement to evaluating the profitability of customers is the timing of payments. Though analytically taxing yet conceptually obvious, the timing of payments differs between customers purchasing a series of individual products on the spot market and customers purchasing a subscription. To manage this difference, calculations of customer period values include discount factors relating to the time value of money to the firm.

Another refinement to evaluating the profitability of customers reflects differences in marketing costs. In analyzing the marginal profit of a customer transaction, at first glance one would take the difference of the price paid and the variable costs to produce. However, such a simplified analysis overlooks the marketing costs outlaid to capture and retain that customer. As such, models of customer period value are substantially more accurate when they discriminate between costs related to customer acquisition and those related to customer retention.

It requires significantly more effort to capture a new customer than to retain an existing customer. In many industries, customer acquisition costs are five to ten times the customer retention costs. Detailed accounting of marketing expenditures allocated between the two efforts is required to produce an accurate reflection for specific firms.

Hence, for a basic model of customer period value, four issues must be resolved: (1) The individual prices and variable costs for each item within the series of products in the subscription must be identified. (2) The customer retention rate must be identified. The customer retention rate is a measure of the likelihood that a customer who purchases an individual item will also purchase the next item within a series of products in the subscription. (3) The timing of the payments and the applicable discount rate are required to put the subscription payments and series of individual payments on an equal financial footing. (4) The marketing costs must be allocated between customer acquisition and customer retention.

To demonstrate the calculation of a customer period value, we can return to the challenge of pricing a twelve-month magazine subscription. The minimum subscription price that the firm should accept would be that which leaves the firm equally well off between customers who choose the subscription and those who purchase at the newsstand. Hence, we need to calculate the customer period value for a customer who purchases individual items at the newsstand, and uncover the subscription price that leaves the customer period value unchanged when a customer enters into a subscription relationship with the firm versus purchasing the products at the newsstand.

Let us first evaluate the profitability of a customer who purchases the magazine at the newsstand. Let the price of each issue made available at the newsstand be \$3.95 and let the costs to produce and distribute be \$1.45 to both newsstand customers and subscribers. Let the customer retention rate (r) be 80 percent, meaning that 80 percent of the customers who purchase the first issue decide to purchase the second issue, and 80 percent of those choose to purchase the third issue, leaving us with only 64 percent of the original customer base (80 percent · 80 percent = 64 percent). We can repeat this calculation for subsequent periods. Let the discount rate be 11 percent, corresponding to a monthly discount rate (d) of 0.873 percent.[4] Finally, let the marketing expenses be allocated such that, on average per customer, \$1.25 is spent on acquiring new readers and \$0.125 is spent on retaining existing readers. (In many industries, it is not uncommon for initial customer acquisition costs to exceed the initial customer contribution margin.) In this case, the customer period value for the twelve months following the acquisition of a new reader can be calculated to be \$9.64. See Exhibit 13-2 for details of the calculation.

Exhibit 13-2 Customer Period Value for Newsstand Magazine Sales

Month	Price	Variable Cost	Customer Acquisition and Retention Costs	Customer Profitability	Retention Probability	Discount Factor	Customer Period Value
n	P	V	MKT	$P - V - MKT$	$r^{(n-1)}$	$\frac{1}{(1+d)^{(n-1)}}$	$\frac{(P - V - MKT) \cdot r^{(n-1)}}{(1+d)^{(n-1)}}$
1	\$3.95	\$1.45	\$1.250	\$1.25	1.000	1.000	\$1.25
2	\$3.95	\$1.45	\$0.125	\$2.38	0.800	0.991	\$1.88
3	\$3.95	\$1.45	\$0.125	\$2.38	0.640	0.983	\$1.49
4	\$3.95	\$1.45	\$0.125	\$2.38	0.512	0.974	\$1.18
5	\$3.95	\$1.45	\$0.125	\$2.38	0.410	0.966	\$0.94
6	\$3.95	\$1.45	\$0.125	\$2.38	0.328	0.957	\$0.75
7	\$3.95	\$1.45	\$0.125	\$2.38	0.262	0.949	\$0.59
8	\$3.95	\$1.45	\$0.125	\$2.38	0.210	0.941	\$0.47
9	\$3.95	\$1.45	\$0.125	\$2.38	0.168	0.933	\$0.37
10	\$3.95	\$1.45	\$0.125	\$2.38	0.134	0.925	\$0.29
11	\$3.95	\$1.45	\$0.125	\$2.38	0.107	0.917	\$0.23
12	\$3.95	\$1.45	\$0.125	\$2.38	0.086	0.909	\$0.19
Total	\$47.40	\$17.40	\$2.625	\$ 27.38			\$9.64

In setting the minimum acceptable subscription price, we seek to ensure that an average customer is at least as profitable when he or she enters into a subscription as when purchasing the magazine at the newsstand. If we assume that the subscription is paid with the first issue, we can find the minimum subscription price by taking the difference between the customer period value of purchasing at the newsstand and the customer period value of a subscription provided for free.

As before, for the subscription the costs to produce and distribute are $1.45, the customer acquisition costs are $1.25, and the annual discount rate is 11 percent. In the case of a subscriber, the customer retention rate during the period of the subscription can be set at 100 percent if cancellations are not allowed. In this case, the customer period value of a subscription provided for free is a loss of $17.84. See Exhibit 13-3 for details of the calculation. Hence, any subscription price greater than $27.48 = $9.64 + $17.84 would leave the firm better off than it would be on average by selling the magazines solely through the newsstand. This is the price determined from the customer period value used in Exhibit 13-1.

We can adjust the model of customer period value to include further refinements in assumptions. Common refinements include allowing for changes in cost structures between selling a series of individual items and selling a single subscription. If we want to include customers who pick and choose which items they purchase within the series or customers who stop and restart a subscription, the overall approach to the calculation is not terribly dissimilar but does require more complex modeling. Doing so would not change the overall conceptual approach to evaluating the customer period value, but it would add a layer of complexity. We leave this exercise to readers, applied to the specific business that they are managing.

Exhibit 13-3 Customer Period Value for Subscription Sales

Month	Price	Variable Cost	Customer Acquisition and Retention Costs	Customer Profitability	Retention Probability	Discount Factor	Customer Period Value
n	P	V	MKT	$P - V - MKT$	$r^{(n-1)}$	$\frac{1}{(1+d)^{(n-1)}}$	$\frac{(P - V - MKT) \cdot r^{(n-1)}}{(1+d)^{(n-1)}}$
1	P	$1.45	$1.25	P + ($2.70)	1	1.000	P + ($2.70)
2		$1.45		($1.45)	1	0.991	($1.44)
3		$1.45		($1.45)	1	0.983	($1.42)
4		$1.45		($1.45)	1	0.974	($1.41)
5		$1.45		($1.45)	1	0.966	($1.40)
6		$1.45		($1.45)	1	0.957	($1.39)
7		$1.45		($1.45)	1	0.949	($1.38)
8		$1.45		($1.45)	1	0.941	($1.36)
9		$1.45		($1.45)	1	0.933	($1.35)
10		$1.45		($1.45)	1	0.925	($1.34)
11		$1.45		($1.45)	1	0.917	($1.33)
12		$1.45		($1.45)	1	0.909	($1.32)
Total	P	$17.40	$1.25	P + ($18.65)			P + ($17.84)

Customer Lifetime Value

The magazine subscription example demonstrated the value of understanding the customer period value. If we expand this analysis to include further periods, such as the entire lifetime of the customer interaction with the firm, we would be calculating the customer lifetime value.[5] The spreadsheet method used previously for calculating the customer period value for magazines is straightforward, but simpler methods can be derived using a few tools from some more-advanced mathematics.

Customer lifetime values influence pricing decisions in many areas outside of subscriptions. Many times, firms make an initial sale at a loss in the hopes of earning profits on the sale of subsequent items. For instance, consider tying arrangements. The sale of razor handles may be subsidized by the expected profits on the sale of future razors; the sale of printers may be subsidized by the profits earned on the future sale of ink; and the sale of game consoles may be subsidized by the profits earned on the future sales of gaming titles.

We have seen that a number of factors influence an analysis of the lifetime profitability of a customer, and that financial issues such as the price paid, costs to produce, timing of payments, and discount rate all directly affect the profitability of a customer. Furthermore, we have observed that customer behavior factors and marketing efforts to influence customer behavior also affect the profitability of a customer, such as the customer retention rate and customer acquisition and retention costs.

The expected customer period value is a sum of the profits earned from that customer during each purchase after discounted back to the present value and including the probability that a customer will make a future purchase. Mathematically, we can write this as

$$CPV = (P_i - V_i - A) + \sum_{n=2}^{N} \frac{(P_s - V_s - R)r^{n-1}}{(1+d)^{n-1}} \qquad \text{Eq. 13.1}$$

The first term, $P_i - V_i - A$, is the profitability of the first sale, where P_i is the price paid, V_i is the variable costs of the initial item purchased, and A is the allocated customer acquisition marketing cost. The second term is a sum over the period of future sales of the profits earned discounted back to the present value, where Σ means to take the sum of the term to the left as the period variable n goes from 2, the first period of purchasing a subsequent item, to N, the last period in the subscription. (For example, a twelve-month subscription would use an N of 12.) $P_s - V_s - R$ is the profits earned of the subsequent sales when all subsequent sales are of the same product, where P_s is the price paid, V_s is the variable cost of the subsequent items purchased, and R is the allocated customer retention marketing costs. In the numerator of the second term, the term of r^{n-1} is included to account for the probability that a customer will actually purchase in the future, where r is the period customer retention rate. The term $(1 + d)^{n-1}$ in the denominator of the second term is the familiar discount factor using the period discount rate d.

When the future purchases of a customer are relatively similar and the marketing expenses on customer retention are expected to be somewhat constant, we can create a generalized algebraic formula for calculating the customer lifetime value that includes all these factors. Using a property of converging sums, we can rewrite Equation 13.1 for the customer period value to

$$CPV = (P_i - V_i - A) + (P_s - V_s - R) \cdot \left[\frac{r}{(1+d-r)} \cdot \left(1 - \left(\frac{r}{1+d}\right)^{N-1}\right)\right] \qquad \text{Eq. 13.2}$$

Equation 13.2 has the advantage over Equation 13.1 of being a completely algebraic formula that can be easily calculated.

If we are not considering a simple period of customer purchases but rather the entire customer lifetime, Equation 13.2 can be further simplified to

$$CLV = (P_i - V_i - A) + (P_s - V_s - R) \cdot \left[\frac{r}{1 + d - r} \right] \quad \text{Eq. 13.3}$$

where we have used *CLV* rather than *CPV* to highlight the inclusion of the overall customer lifetime, rather than simply a period of purchases.

Behavioral Effects with Subscriptions

The previous quantitative analysis of the total period price and customer period value price has narrowed the uncertainty in pricing a subscription. The subscription price should be less than the total period price if it is to attract customers into the subscription arrangement; hence, it would be less than $47.40 in the magazine example. Also, the subscription price should be higher than that which would leave the customer period value unchanged if it is to improve the profitability of the firm; hence, it should be above $27.48 in the magazine example. Within this range, subscription prices are influenced by a number of qualitative behavioral effects.

MARKET SEGMENTATION

Within the market for a series of products, there will be natural market heterogeneity or differences in the preferences of customers. Some customers would prefer to consume all products within series, while others would prefer to choose the products that they purchase.[6]

If customers can predict their future demand, those who suspect that their total period purchases will be above the subscription price would rationally choose the subscription. Meanwhile, variety seekers who suspect that their total period purchases will be below the subscription price would choose to purchase the individual items that they want. In this case, the subscription price represents a discount to more-loyal customers.

Differences in market segments regarding the desire of customers to purchase the entire series of products should encourage firms to price the subscription at a price higher than that which would be predicted by considerations of the average customer loyalty alone. Effectively, those who would purchase the subscription are also signaling their product loyalty and can be anticipated to have a higher retention rate. Customers with a higher retention rate also have a higher customer period value. As the customer period value increases, so too does the minimum subscription price, which improves the profitability of the firm.

Because the retention rate of customers who purchase the subscription is higher than that of customers who select individual products, a firm can charge subscribers a higher price than it would for the average customer in the market. Hence, subscription prices are usually higher than that determined by equilibrating the customer period values alone.

LOCK-IN

When customers subscribe to a series of products, they become locked into an arrangement with the supplier. Many customers are aware of the value of pre-committing their purchases to suppliers. However, customers suffer from uncertainty about their ability to predict their future demand. They also value the ability to abandon a supplier relationship in the future if that supplier fails to deliver the expected set of benefits. Because of the negative impact that lock-in presents to customers, the subscription price must be below the total period price to induce customers to purchase.

INCREASED CONSUMPTION PATTERNS

With some subscription offerings, customers tend to consume more of the product than they otherwise would. One reason for this increased consumption is that once the customer has entered into the subscription arrangement, future consumption of the product comes with a zero or otherwise low marginal price. For instance, research has shown that magazine subscribers typically read more articles than customers who buy the magazines at the newsstand. Another factor that increases consumption is the ability of subscription offerings to address a market failure arising from information asymmetries.

Many products sold through a subscription suffer from information asymmetries between buyer and seller. Information goods are notoriously experience goods. Prior to the consumption of an information good, such as reading a magazine, listening to song, or accessing a database, buyers have little knowledge of the value of consuming the information. Meanwhile, sellers of information goods have better knowledge of the value of their information, and as such will rationally seek to capture a higher price. This leaves an informational asymmetry for many subscription goods between sellers, who know the value of their offerings, and buyers, who do not.

The subscription offering helps reduce market failures in the face of informational asymmetry by reducing risks faced by the customer. When customers subscribe to a magazine, they do not know the future contents of all the magazines that they will receive, and therefore they cannot *a priori* know the value of any individual issue. While customers may be unable to determine the value that they will derive from any individual item within the subscription, they can anticipate that their overall utility from the series of offerings will be greater than the overall subscription price. Hence, the subscription reduces the risk that buyers will stop reading the magazine because they purchase a specific issue that they find unsatisfactory.

The effect of reducing information asymmetry through subscriptions is one of increasing overall demand for the subscription in relation to the sale of individual units. Thus, the volume of issues sold should be higher for a firm that sells units both individually and through subscriptions, than for a firm that offers the product only through individual unit sales. Moreover, the price of the subscription can be somewhat higher than that determined by considerations of the customer period value alone.

Overestimation Bias

When customers are choosing between a subscription membership and a pay-for-use offer, they sometimes fall subject to an overestimation bias of their positive future behavior.[7] For example, people join gyms in the hope that they will exercise more, an activity that contributes positively to their quantity and quality of life. Unfortunately, customers are poor predictors of their own future behavior. Many times, customers will join the gym, attend a few times, and then fail to return to the gym even though their gym membership is still active. This is an example of an overestimation bias: Humans tend to overestimate their own future positive behavior.

In studies of actual purchases and behaviors, it was found that customers of gyms that purchase a monthly membership paid on average 70 percent more than they would under a pay-as-you-go arrangement, and moreover 80 percent of the monthly subscribers would have been better off had they paid per visit for the same number of visits. These observations lead to the understanding that customers overestimate their future efficiency; that is, they overestimate their ability to perform desirable tasks such as health club attendance or, alternatively, to consciously switch contracts to the type of arrangement that would provide the greatest economic benefit.

As an extension of the overestimation bias, researchers have also examined different subscription payment arrangements and the likelihood that a customer will renew the membership. It was found that the timing of payments affects consumer behavior when monthly or frequent payments encourage use, and they may also encourage higher customer retention. Gym customers selected between a monthly contract with monthly payments and an annual contract with annual payments. While all customers were likely to overestimate their usage of the gym facility regardless of the contract they selected, those who selected the monthly contract were more likely to use the gym more frequently and renew their membership.

This has led to the understanding that, in subscription offerings in which customers are subject to an overestimation bias of their future positive behavior, concurrence of usage and subscription payment leads to longer memberships and therefore a potentially higher profitability.

Value Proposition Changes and SaaS

In many cases, the benefits delivered through a subscription arrangement are greater than those delivered on a pay-per-item basis. For instance, magazine subscriptions often include other items positioned as gifts, such as a book, reference guide, or other token of appreciation. Similarly, gyms will often provide a "free" T-shirt or other gift to new members. These gifts are usually provided without increasing the price of the subscription due to their inconsequential nature. However, other subscription offerings do include specific items and benefits that are substantially consequential to the customers and are not offered directly by the supplier for separate purchase. When the value proposition changes significantly between the subscription offering and that of the sale of individual products, firms have the opportunity to increase the subscription price to that of a premium offer as well.

SAAS

With Software as a Service (SaaS) offerings in enterprise software, the benefits delivered through the subscription are substantially more valuable, and the variable costs to serve are also higher. SaaS offerings include not only the license to use the software, but also the management of the software and the customer's data itself. The inclusion of managing a customer's data not only increases the benefits to the customer but also increases the costs to the provider. As such, firms marketing SaaS have sought to increase the price of their offering over that of the total period price of the software alone.

These firms have found that selling SaaS at a premium over that of the software alone met stiff customer resistance. Some of the reasons that customers would eschew paying a premium for a subscription service have already been mentioned, such as the lock-in effect and natural market segmentation based on expected future demand. Yet perhaps one of the larger reasons is that SaaS may not convincingly deliver greater value than the software alone.

The benefits of SaaS are significantly higher than those of a straight software license, but it is uncertain that these benefits necessarily accrue to the customer's balance sheet. Companies purchasing SaaS avoid costs related to increased computing power and data storage, increased manpower for managing the data, and increased technical training to manage the enterprise software. Unfortunately, many of these cost savings are incremental and may be inconsequential from the customer's frame of reference.

For instance, an enterprise customer that purchases software may perceive that its information technology (IT) staff can manage the product without any change in staffing requirements. If the SaaS arrangement does not actually reduce the customer's staff, it is difficult to state convincingly that it delivers labor cost savings. Only in the aggregate of several SaaS contracts may an enterprise customer realize any tangible labor cost savings. Similar arguments are often made with respect to the costs of managing the software and computing requirements.

Despite the added benefits of providing SaaS, the uncertainty in the realization of these benefits, coupled with the overall behavioral effects that suppress subscription prices, makes it difficult for enterprise software firms to realize a significant premium on their SaaS offerings. Even when firms are unable to fully realize higher prices on SaaS, they may benefit from other behavioral effects of subscription services such as higher customer retention rates that improve the customer overall lifetime value.

As more enterprise software providers adapt SaaS offerings, it can be expected that enterprise customers will come to accept higher premiums for SaaS over that of the sale of software licenses and maintenance and service contracts due to the ability of customers to begin realizing the potential costs savings generated through SaaS offerings.

EXAMPLE: QUICKBOOKS

We can see some of the challenges of SaaS through examining a well-known firm that is using this arrangement. In 2009, Intuit offered both QuickBooks Simple Start and QuickBooks Online Basic.[8] Simple Start is a product sale, designed to have customer renewals at the end of each year. Online Basic is sold through an SaaS model and is positioned by Intuit as comparable to QuickBooks Simple Start but with a few added benefits.

As with other SaaS models, Online Basic provided customers with secure online data management accessible through any Internet browser, freeing them from the responsibility of installing the software, storing data, and managing data backup and recovery plans. Online Basic also granted customers the right to expanded email support services. Similar support services were provided to Simple Start users only at a premium. Online Basic also allowed customers to cancel their contract at any time.

In terms of pricing, Simple Start had a list price of $99.95 for new customers, while renewing customers received a $20 discount. Meanwhile, Online Basic was sold for a flat rate of $9.95 per month. From a total period pricing perspective, Online Basic was priced at a small premium compared to Simple Start. Over a twelve-month period, a Simple Start customer would pay a total price of $119.40. Such a small premium can be justified on the basis that Online Basic does provide a few added benefits. However, the small size of the premium also highlights the challenges in capturing the value of providing the added benefits of SaaS.

On a customer period value basis, an Online Basic subscriber may have been less profitable than a Simple Start customer in the first year. To compare the customer period value of a Simple Start customer to that of an Online Basic subscriber, we need to quantify business factors related to the customer period value.

First, the revenue from an Online Basic subscriber is spread out over time and future payments should be discounted back to the present time. We will use an annual discount rate of 6 percent to incorporate the costs associated with spreading out payments over time. This corresponds to a monthly discount rate of 0.487 percent.

Second, the variable cost structures for Online Basic subscribers may be higher than that for Simple Start customers. Simple Start is available through a digital download; hence it would have negligible costs of reproduction. Let us use a value of $0 for the variable costs in delivering Simple Start. In contrast, the added features of Online Basic over Simple Start increase the costs to serve. Let us use a value of $1.50 per month for the variable costs associated with the increased customer service coupled with the provision of data storage, management, and online access for Online Basic.

Third, let us assume that the marketing costs are similar across both products. Moreover, it is strongly suspected that most of Intuit's marketing efforts are focused on capturing new customers rather than retaining existing customers. Hence, let us use a value of $20 per customer to represent the customer acquisition costs, and $2 per customer per year ($0.167 = $2/12 per month) to represent the customer retention costs.

Finally, Intuit faces unique challenges in retaining small business customers. Even if Intuit has highly dedicated customers, the churn in business establishments is significant as companies get started and go out of business. Let us use a customer retention rate of 75 percent per year, which corresponds to a monthly retention rate of 97.6 percent.[9]

Under these assumptions, the first-year value of a Simple Start customer is $79.95, or the difference between the price paid and the customer acquisition costs. See Exhibit 13-4. For the overall customer lifetime, the value of a Simple Start customer increases to the more-significant value of $268.54.

Using the values listed above and Equation 13-2, we find the customer period value of an Online Basic customer for the first year is only $65.41. Hence, Simple Start customers are potentially more profitable than Online Basic customers in the first year, despite the fact that Online Basic customers pay a higher total period price. The higher profitability of Simple Start customers found in this analysis is a result of incorporating the higher costs to serve Online Basic customers.

When we examine the overall customer lifetime, we find that under these assumptions, the total value of an Online Basic subscriber is $271.65. The increase in value of an Online Basic customer relative to a Simple Start customer found in considering the overall customer lifetime is largely due to the lower renewal price offered to Simple Start customers.

From this analysis, we see that over the customer's overall lifetime, an Online Basic customer appears to be as valuable as a Simple Start customer. However, we have not taken into account other factors related to consumer behavior. Online customers may be more likely to stay with Intuit and thus have a higher retention rate, which improves their profitability.

We have also seen the challenges presented in profitably offering SaaS are non-negligible. The fact that SaaS subscribers may be able to cancel their subscription at any

Exhibit 13-4 QuickBooks Simple Start and Online Basic Plus Summary Values

Variable		Simple Start	Online Basic	
		(annual)	(annual)	(monthly)
Price of Initial Product	P_i	$99.95	N/A	$9.95
Price of Subsequent Products	P_S	$79.95	N/A	$9.95
Variable Cost of Initial Product	V_i	$0.00	N/A	$1.50
Variable Cost of Subsequent Products	V_S	$0.00	N/A	$1.50
Customer Acquisition Cost	A	$20.00	N/A	$20.00
Customer Retention Cost	R	$2.00	$2.00	$0.167
Discount Rate (Annual)	d	6%	6%	0.487%
Retention Rate (Annual)	r	75%	75%	97.6%
Customer Period Value (Yr 1)	CPV	$79.95		$65.41
Customer Lifetime Value	CLV	$268.54		$ 271.65

time, coupled with the higher costs to serve, drives firms to raise SaaS prices above that of the equivalent total period price when they seek to make SaaS subscribers equally profitable to other customers.

Summary

- Subscriptions convert the sale of a series of related individual purchases into a single purchase decision. The timing of payments in a subscription can be separated from the timing of consumption. Although subscriptions are often paid at the time of entering into the contract, payments can be spread out over the course of the subscription period.
- Two key quantitative metrics can guide subscription pricing decisions. Subscriptions should be priced below the total period price paid, or the price that customers would pay if they purchased every item in the subscription. Subscriptions should be priced higher than that price that leaves the firm equally profitable with respect to customer period value.
- The customer period value is quantitatively determined by the net contribution that a customer makes with each purchase during the period of time under consideration, the marketing costs associated with customer acquisition and retention, the discount value to incorporate the time value of cash, and the retention rate.
- The customer lifetime value is simply the customer period value over the lifetime of the customer relationship.
- Subscription offerings are influenced by numerous consumer behavioral effects. Most notably, subscriptions can act to segment the market between those who anticipate consuming all the individual products and those who anticipate consuming only a small portion of the overall offerings.
- The lock-in effect can suppress the potential price of a subscription in relation to the total period price.
- Customers who subscribe to a series of offerings usually increase their consumption compared to what they would have consumed if they purchased the items individually. For instance, magazine subscribers typically read more articles than customers who buy magazines at the newsstand.
- In information markets, subscriptions address a market failure created by information asymmetries. Information goods are, by nature, experience goods. Sellers of information goods have better knowledge of the value of the information that they hold than buyers do. As such, buyers have a difficult time evaluating the value of, and therefore their willingness to pay for, information goods. By selling information through a subscription rather than individually, the risk to buyers is reduced, so their demand increases.
- In some markets, customers are subject to an overestimation bias of their own future behavior. For instance, in fitness markets, many annual subscribers fail to utilize their gym subscription and would actually be better off purchasing access on a per-visit basis.
- With SaaS, the value proposition is significantly enhanced over that of the outright sale of the software license and maintenance and service agreements. The provider both manages the software and its updates and hosts the customer's data. It is possible to charge a premium price of SaaS based on economic arguments alone; however, customers have shown resistance to this, which may be due to an inability to capture the full benefits of SaaS offerings.

Exercises

1. Allstate sells auto insurance to many customer segments. Consider a segment of customers whose semiannual insurance bill is $345.
   a. If the average variable cost of providing auto insurance coverage is 75 percent of the price, what is the variable cost of insurance?
   b. If the customer acquisition costs are $50 per customer and the customer retention costs are 20 percent of the customer acquisition costs, what are the customer retention costs per customer?
   c. If the annual retention rate is 90 percent, what is the semiannual retention rate?
   d. If the applied annual discount rate is 8 percent, what is the semiannual discount rate?
   e. Assume that the price and average variable cost don't change over time. What is the customer lifetime value of a customer in this market segment?
   f. If Allstate failed to satisfy this segment and retention rates dropped to 85 percent, what would be the new customer lifetime value of a customer in this market segment?
   g. If Allstate took steps to improve customer retention rates to 95 percent, what would be the new customer lifetime value of a customer in this market segment?
   h. How much should Allstate be willing to pay, on a per-customer basis, for improving retention rates for this segment from 90 percent to 91 percent?
2. Symantec sells computer antivirus and Internet security products to consumers. Consider the Norton Internet Security product, with a list price of $69.99 sold through the retail channel. Assume that packaging and delivering Norton Internet Security to the retail channel costs $7 per unit. Furthermore, assume that annual renewals of Norton Internet Security are sold directly by Symantec through its online store as a digital download at no cost to Symantec. Outside of retail channel costs, assume that Symantec spends on average $6 per customer on sales and marketing for acquiring new customers and $1.20 per customer on sales and marketing for retaining existing customers. Let the annual discount rate used by Symantec be 12 percent and assume that a customer acquired through the retail channel must be reacquired every four years as he or she get a new computer.
   a. From this information, what is the variable cost for Norton Internet Security for the first sale? For subsequent sales?
   b. If the retail channel requires 50 percent of the retail list price to stock Norton Internet Security, what are Symantec's total customer acquisition costs for a retail Norton Internet Security customer?
   c. What is the profitability of a new Norton Internet Security retail customer for Symantec?
   d. If direct digital downloads of annual upgrades are discounted by $20 from the retail list price, what is the effective annual renewal price of Norton Internet Security?
   e. What is the profitability of a renewing Norton Internet Security customer for Symantec?
   f. If the retention rate is 90 percent, what is the four-year value of a Norton Internet Security customer acquired through the retail channel?
   g. If the retention rate is 75 percent, what is the four-year value of a Norton Internet Security customer acquired through the retail channel?
   h. If the retention rate is 50 percent, what is the four-year value of a Norton Internet Security customer acquired through the retail channel?

3. WebEx, an online meeting and teleconference service, is sold on a per-use basis or through an annual subscription. For small online meetings of three people or less, WebEx charges $95.40 for a one-hour online meeting including teleconferencing. Consider a WebEx customer segment interested in holding a small online meeting once per month. Assume that the cost borne by WebEx for teleconferencing for a small meeting is $36 per meeting. Let the monthly discount rate be 0.7974 percent.
   a. What is the total period price of purchasing a one-hour online meeting with WebEx if a customer purchases it twelve times per year?
   b. For a non-subscribing customer, assume the marketing expenses are allocated such that, on average per customer, $5 is allocated for acquiring new customers and $0.50 is allocated for retaining existing customers. Furthermore, let the effective retention rate be 75 percent between meetings. What is the one-year customer period value of a non-subscribing user?
   c. For subscribers, assume the marketing expenses are allocated such that, on average per customer, $5 is allocated to acquiring new customers and nothing is spent on retaining existing customers. Furthermore, let the effective retention rate be 100 percent between meetings for subscribers. What subscription price would leave the customer period value for a subscriber equal to that of a non-subscriber?
   d. From this analysis alone, what range of prices would you expect to see for an annual subscription to WebEx?
   e. WebEx advertises an annual subscription at $708. Does this price lie within the range predicted from this analysis?
   f. Repeat this analysis considering a customer segment that typically has a low retention rate, only 20 percent. How much more profitable is it for WebEx to convert a low-retention customer into a subscribing customer than to let that customer simply purchase WebEx as needed?
4. The *Financial Times (FT)* is sold at the newsstand for $2 per issue. For 52 weeks per year, the *FT* prints 6 issues per week. Assume the cost to produce and distribute the *FT* is $0.75 to both newsstand customers and subscribers. Let the applied discount rate be 0.03055 percent for the inter-issue period.
   a. How many issues per year does the *FT* produce?
   b. What is the total period price of purchasing every issue of the *FT* published that year at the newsstand?
   c. For newsstand readers, assume that the marketing expenses be allocated such that, on average per customer, $0.10 is allocated for both acquiring new readers and retaining existing readers. Furthermore, let the effective reader retention rate be 99 percent between issues. What is the one-year customer period value of a newsstand reader?
   d. For subscribers, assume that the marketing expenses be allocated such that, on average per customer, $20 is allocated to acquiring new readers and nothing is spent on retaining existing readers. Furthermore, assume that the retention rate of subscribers is 100 percent over the course of one year. What subscription price would leave the customer period value for a subscriber equal to that of a newsstand reader?
   e. From this analysis alone, what range of prices would you expect to see for an annual subscription to the *FT*?
   f. The *FT* offers an annual subscription at $99. Does this price lie within the range predicted from this analysis? If not, how would you account for the difference? Hint: Consider the effect of two-sided markets on subscription prices.

5. Discussion question: SalesForce.com provides SaaS for sales-force automation and customer relationship management applications to enterprise customers. How should SalesForce.com position itself against other sales-force automation and customer relationship management applications? Would large- or small-enterprise customers be more attracted to the SaaS offer from SalesForce.com? Should SalesForce.com bill customers monthly or annually? Explain your reasoning.

Notes

[1] Sarah L. C. Clapp, "The Beginnings of Subscription Publications in the Seventeenth Century," *Modern Philology* 29, No. 2 (November 1931): 199–224.

[2] Arun Sundararajan, "Nonlinear Pricing of Information Goods," *Management Science* 50, No. 12 (December 2004): 1660–73. Peter C. Fishburn and Andrew M. Odlyzko, "Competitive Pricing of Information Goods: Subscription Pricing versus Pay-per-Use," *Economic Theory* 13, No. 2 (March 1999): 447–70.

[3] Most academic research has treated subscription-based offerings as a bundle of individual products or as one part of a two-part tariff; yet it fails to undertake the task of guiding an executive in pricing a subscription. The approach presented here differs for the following reasons: (1) offers made in a subscription include products that are not purchased and consumed at the same time, unlike most product bundles; (2) decisions in pricing subscriptions may have access to information not available to those of bundling, such as customer retention rates; and (3) many products sold through subscriptions are subject to specific behavioral effects, such as information asymmetry, that change the nature of the purchasing decision. For a discussion of the failure of the use of quantitative methods in pricing subscriptions, see Underwood Dudley, "Two-Year Magazine Subscription Rates," *American Mathematical Monthly* 100, No. 1 (January 1993): 34–37.

[4] To convert annual percentage rates (d_{yr}) to monthly percentage rates(d_{mn}), we can use the following equation:

$$d_{mn} = \left[(1 + d_{yr})^{\frac{1}{12}}\right] - 1.$$

[5] Robert C. Blattberg and John Deighton, "Manage Marketing by the Customer Equity Test," *Harvard Business Review* 74, No. 4 (July–August 1996): 136–44.

[6] Amihai Glazer and Refael Hassin, "On the Economics of Subscriptions," *European Economic Review* 19, No. 23 (October 1982) 343–56. Peter C. Coyte and David L. Ryan, "Subscribe, Cancel, or Renew: The Economics of Reading by Subscription," *Canadian Journal of Economics* 24, No. 1 (February 1991): 101–23.

[7] John Gourville and Dilip Soman, "Pricing and the Psychology of Consumption," *Harvard Business Review* 80, No. 9 (September 2002): 90–97. Stefano Della Vigna and Ulrike Malmendier, "Paying Not to Go to the Gym," *American Economic Review* 96, No. 3 (June 2006): 694–719.

[8] Prices for Intuit QuickBooks Pro and Online Plus retrieved from the Intuits website, www.intuit.com (accessed on June 6, 2009).

[9] To convert retention rates from an annual to a monthly basis, simply take the twelfth root. Thus, a 75 percent annual retention rate is equivalent to a 97.6 percent monthly rate (97.6 percent = $75\%^{1/12}$).

Chapter

14

Yield Management

Stuart McCall/Photographer's Choice/Getty Images

- How do airlines and hotels use yield management to set prices?
- How do airlines and hotels control the number of seats or rooms available within a fare class?
- What is dynamic nesting, and how does it improve booking control?
- How should capacity be allocated among different fare classes?
- Should low-fare demand influence the number of seats reserved for high-fare customers?
- Stretch Question: What other firms and markets can benefit from yield management techniques?

Almost all consumers who have purchased an airline ticket in the past twenty years will have noticed that they can expect to pay a lower price if they purchase the ticket earlier rather than later. Yield management, also known as revenue management, is a pricing structure that drives prices higher as the time of use of the product approaches. In yield management, the seller attempts to maximize the profits it earns on selling a resource by changing the price of the product over time.

Yield management is one of many dynamic pricing techniques.[1] In yield management, the price offered to customers increases as capacity approaches exhaustion. It is a technique for maximizing the expected revenue earned on a fixed-capacity resource by selling units of that capacity at different prices. It uses timing and expectations of demand as a means to price-segment the market. It is a probabilistic pricing technique that relies on probability-weighted demand expectations to determine the availability of fare classes, each of which has a different price.

The practice of yield management expands beyond the airline industry and can be used in a number of industries. From an internal operations perspective, there are four key determinants for using yield management: (1) Capacity is limited and perishable. (2) Customers will reserve units of capacity ahead of time. (3) The firm can sell that resource at a variety of prices, also known as fare classes, each of which has a fixed price. (4) The firm can change the availability of the predefined fare classes over time.

We can see each of these issues with respect to the airline industry. The capacity on a specific flight is inherently limited. Adding more seats on a specific flight either requires changing the plane used or adding a further flight. Furthermore, once the flight departs, a seat unsold on that flight cannot be filled in the future. The potential revenue from that seat is forever lost, and the value of that seat on that plane on that flight perishes forever. Because both customers and the airline are well aware that capacity on any given flight is limited, customers regularly will book a seat on a plane ahead of time to assure its availability. Outside of versioning, wherein airlines sell first-, business-, and coach-class travel, airlines are also able to create a variety of fare classes within each section. Each of these fare classes offers an otherwise identical seat at a different price, some highly discounted and others at full fare. In addition, once the airline has sold a predetermined number of discounted seats, it can decide to stop selling those seats and revert to selling only full-fare seats.

Similarly, hotels face the same set of constraints and opportunity for using yield management. The number of rooms available is fixed, the potential to sell a hotel room (and therefore its value) perishes every morning, and customers will book a hotel room ahead of time. As such, hoteliers will often use yield management techniques as well, setting room-rate classes to offer otherwise identical rooms at different prices and restricting the availability of discounted rooms over time. Other consumer products can be priced using yield management, such as rental cars, passenger rail tickets, sporting and theatrical events, and even restaurant bookings.

Yield pricing has also found its place within industrial markets. Freight transport firms, including air freight, container ships, and even trucking, face the same constraints in capacity flexibility and perishability. Like passenger air travel, customers of these industries are likely to reserve transport capacity ahead of time. Similarly, media firms selling broadcast advertising benefit from yield management techniques due to the same set of constraints and opportunities. Given the drivers of yield management techniques, other industries, such as contract manufacturing, might also benefit from this price structure.

Moving beyond an operational perspective of the constraints faced by the firm, we can also find some similarities in the structure of the markets served in these industries. Although some of the markets where yield pricing is practiced are consumer-oriented and others are industrial, all the markets where yield pricing has been deployed enjoy a large number of potential customers. Moreover, not only are different customers willing to pay a different price for an otherwise similar good, but their willingness to pay will change over time depending on the specific drivers of their demand and their own behavior as customers. Furthermore, many of the customers of these industries transact with firms on a "one-off" basis. While firms in these industries may nurture and value customer loyalty, they are also aware that the demand for their service is contingent on specific factors that will draw a number of customers into the market on a sporadic basis, rather than a continual flow where predictability in pricing would be valued higher. Alternatively stated, the market heterogeneity in willingness to pay extends beyond the customer-segment level and is expressed in the timing of the purchase and the occasion that drove the purchase. As such, customers in these industries accept a high degree of price variance, and the firms serving in these industries enjoy a wide degree of pricing latitude.

In this chapter, we will explore some of the basic concepts and analytical foundation to yield management. While we will use the airline and hotel industries as examples, the exact same issues and techniques are used by both other consumer and industrial firms that practice yield management.[2]

Fare Classes and Booking Control

Yield management is a technique to maximize revenue by dynamically controlling the number of units sold within any given fare class. For example, consider airline fare classes and booking processes. The airline will market a number of fare classes on a given flight. Just as the total number of seats available on a given flight is fundamentally limited, the airline will limit the number of seats available in any given fare class on that flight. The booking limit is the number of available seats within a given fare class on a specific flight.

When a customer attempts to make a reservation, the firm will review the booking limit on the available fare classes. If there is sufficient availability within the fare class, the reservation is booked. If the reservation for a fare class would exceed the booking limit, that reservation is denied; and the firm may instead offer a different fare class or alternative reservation to capture that customer. For example, consider a family booking four seats on a flight. If the booking limit is currently three seats for the lower-priced fare class but there are ample seats at the higher-priced fare class, then the offer is made to book the seats at the higher-priced fare and denied at the lower-priced fare. This process is known as *booking control*.

FIXED ALLOTMENT

One of the first approaches to controlling bookings was through fixed allotment. In the fixed allotment approach, available capacity is divided into discrete chunks (fare classes), and each fare class is allocated a fixed number of seats. Customers can book seats in any fare class until the fixed allotment of seats in that fare class has been filled. Once that fixed allotment has been reached, seats on that flight will be offered only in other fare classes.

So long as customers book the allotted seats in the lowest-priced fare class prior to filling up higher-priced fare classes, the fixed allotment approach works to maximize revenue. However, if customers fill up the allotted seats in the higher-fare class prior to filling up those in a lower-fare class, then the fixed allotment approach would direct the firm to force customers into lower-priced seats even if these customers might be willing to pay the higher fare. Clearly, such a result would not maximize the potential revenue.

For an example of the fixed allotment approach, consider a 120-seat aircraft with three fare classes on a specified flight. Let 24 seats be allocated to business class at $550 a seat, 60 seats be allocated to full-fare coach at $300, and 36 seats be allocated to discounted coach at $200. Furthermore, assume that the airline provides increasing amenities with each fare class, such as allowing for seat choice and the free transport of two pieces of baggage for full-fare-coach and business-class customers, but not to discounted-coach customers. In this price structure, it is possible for the airline to sell all 60 full-fare coach seats prior to selling all the allocated 36 discounted coach seats. When the full-fare coach seats fill up prior to the discounted coach seats, the fixed allotment approach to yield management would encourage the airline to deny any further full-fare coach customers as it holds seats open for discounted customers. Clearly, denying seats for higher-priced customers while holding seats for lower-priced customers fails to maximize revenue.

Exhibit 14-1 Dynamics of Booking Limits, Protection Levels, and Seats Sold

	Reservation Request	Booking Limit			Protection Level			Action	Seats Sold			
	Fare	\$550	\$300	\$200								
	Fare Class	1	2	3	1	2	3		1	2	3	T
		b_1	b_2	b_3	y_1	y_2	y_3					
1	2 seats in Class 2	120	96	36	24	84	120	Accept	0	2	0	2
2	1 seat in Class 1	118	94	34	24	84	118	Accept	1	2	0	3
3	30 seats in Class 3	117	93	33	24	84	117	Accept	1	2	30	33
4	5 seats in Class 3	87	63	3	24	84	87	Reject	1	2	30	33
5	5 seats in Class 2	87	63	3	24	84	87	Accept	1	7	30	38
6	1 seat in Class 3	82	58	0	24	82	82	Reject	1	7	30	38
7	4 seats in Class 1	82	58	0	24	82	82	Accept	5	7	30	42
8	54 seats in Class 2	78	54	0	24	78	78	Accept	5	61	30	96
9	2 seats in Class 2	24	0	0	24	24	24	Reject	5	61	30	96
10	2 seats in Class 1	24	0	0	24	24	24	Accept	7	61	30	98
11	1 seat in Class 3	22	0	0	22	22	22	Reject	7	61	30	98

DYNAMIC NESTING

Dynamic nesting is the approach taken to controlling bookings that improves on the limitations of the fixed allotment approach. As with the fixed allotment method, dynamic nesting assigns each fare class a booking limit. Unlike a fixed allotment method, the booking limits on all fare classes are reduced as seats are reserved in any individual fare class in dynamic nesting to prevent the possibility of rejecting high-fare bookings while reserving seats for low-fare bookings.

In this section, we will first describe the mechanics of dynamic nesting, then provide an example in Exhibit 14-1. Readers may wish to look ahead to the exhibit while reading the description.

To describe dynamic nesting, let us define b_i as the booking limit for class i, where i goes from 1 to n, and n is the number of fare classes under management. The first fare class, $i = 1$, will have the highest fare, and the last fare class, $i = n$, will have the lowest fare. In dynamic nesting, the booking limits decrease as one goes from the most expensive to the least expensive fare class. That is, for n fare classes, dynamic nesting requires

$$b_1 \geq b_2 \geq b_3 \geq \cdots b_n \qquad \text{Eq. 14.1}$$

The booking limit for the highest fare class will equal the total number of seats available on the aircraft. By setting b_1 equal to the number of seats on the plane, the airline can book all seats at full fare if customer demand warrants it. That is, if the airline receives reservations for nothing but the highest fare class, the airline will book the entire plane at that fare class. (The dynamic nesting approach that we describe can be refined to include issues regarding fixed differences between different fare classes, such as seat sizes and configurations. Such refinements would still incorporate the conceptual approach described herein, and therefore they are ignored for the current discussion to keep it simple for educational purposes.)

In dynamic nesting, the booking limits on all fare classes are reduced as seats are reserved in any individual fare class. That is, if a customer books a seat in the first fare class, the first-fare-class booking limit, as well as all lower-fare-class booking limits, is reduced by 1. Likewise, if a customer books a seat in the third fare class, the booking limit on the first, second, third and all other fare classes is reduced by 1 as well.

So long as customers request fewer seats than the booking limit on that fare class, the reservation is accepted and the ticket is sold. If a customer requests more tickets than are available within a fare class, that request is denied and the customer is allowed to book only within the next higher available fare class.

In dynamic nesting, booking limits are also described in terms of protection levels. The protection level for a fare class is the number of seats held available for that fare class and all higher fare classes. In a sense, protection levels are the mirror image of booking limits. If we define y_i as the protection level for class i, then the protection level for class i is equal to the difference between the total booking limit and the $i + 1$ booking limit:

$$y_i = b_1 - b_{i+1} \quad \text{Eq. 14.2}$$

Under this definition of the protection levels, the nesting condition of decreasing booking limits becomes one of increasing protection levels:

$$y_1 \leq y_2 \leq y_3 \leq \cdots y_{n-1} \quad \text{Eq. 14.3}$$

The protection level on any given fare class is held constant until all seats in the next-lower-priced fare class are reserved in dynamic nesting. Once all available seats in lower-priced fare classes are reserved, further reservations reduce the protection on that fare class. In this way, the higher-priced fare classes are the most protected and are kept available for last-minute customers.

We can show how dynamic nesting of booking limits and protection levels works by returning to our example of a 120-seat aircraft with three fare classes. Again, the airline might expect 24 seats to be reserved in business class at \$550, 60 seats to be reserved in full-fare coach at \$300, and 36 seats to be reserved in discounted coach at \$200. With this price structure, n equals 3. The first fare class is business class, the second fare class is full-fare coach, and the third fare class is discounted coach.

To manage the expected reservation requests with dynamic nesting, the airline should set the booking limit for business class at $b_1 = 120$, that for full-fare coach at $b_2 = 96$, and finally for discounted coach at $b_3 = 36$. With a booking limit of 36 for the discounted coach seats, the airline will allow only 36 seats to be booked at a discounted coach fare. It will also allow a full 96 (60 + 36) seats to be booked at full-fare coach if all full-fare coach reservations are made before any discounted-fare reservations. Likewise, it will allow 120 (24 + 60 + 36) seats to be booked at the business class fare if all business class customers made reservations before any full-fare or discounted-fare customers. In this manner, dynamic nesting overcomes the shortcomings of a fixed allotment method. No customer who would otherwise pay a higher fare is forced into a lower fare class.

Following from the definition of the protection level for any given fare class, the airline will initially set the protection level for business class at $y_1 = 24$ ($b_1 - b_2 = 120 - 96 = 24$), that for full-fare coach at $y_2 = 84$ ($b_1 - b_3 = 120 - 36 = 84$), and that for discounted coach at $y_3 = 120$ ($b_1 - b_4 = 120 - \varnothing$). As customers reserve seats in a given fare class, the airline will reduce the booking limits for that fare class and all lower fare classes until a fare class is exhausted. Consequently, protection levels for specific fare classes will be reduced sequentially starting from the lowest protected class and moving up to the highest protected fare class.

In Exhibit 14-1, we show an example of how booking limits and protection levels would be updated dynamically as customers make a hypothetical series of reservations. Each line in the table represents a reservation request, the booking limits and protection levels at the time of the request, the decision to accept or reject the reservation request, and the resulting number of seats sold in each class.

In dynamic nesting, a class can be closed as a result of accepting bookings for a higher class. We see this in the fifth request for five seats in Class 2. Once the request has been accepted, the booking limit for Class 3 fares has reached zero while those for Class 1 and 2 are still above zero, implying that no further bookings would be accepted in Class 3 even though the last reservation was for Class 2. Even though the airline will not have sold the full booking limit on the lowest-fare seats, the airline would refuse to sell further seats within that fare class to protect seats for higher-paying customers. When used in this manner, the booking limit on a fare class closes once the aircraft has that many seats booked, regardless of the combination of fare classes booked.

Furthermore, dynamic nesting ensures that fare classes are closed in order, from the lowest-priced fare class to the highest-priced fare class. We see this in the fact that the fifth booking closes the discounted coach fare class, while the eighth booking closes the full-fare coach class. In this manner, higher fare classes are consistently more protected than lower fare classes.

CANCELLATIONS, NO-SHOWS, AND OVERBOOKING

It is common for customers to make reservations and subsequently cancel them before departure or fail to appear at the time of departure. To manage cancellations and no-shows, two techniques are commonly used in yield management. First, to account for no-shows, booking limits can be initially adjusted upward above available capacity according to the expected number of no-shows. If all customers show up for an overbooked flight, the airline may make an offer to encourage customers to accept a later flight. Second, to manage cancellations, seats can be added back to the booking limits of the appropriate fare classes once a reservation is canceled. Other approaches are used and are profit-effective, yet these two are the simplest.

Capacity Allocation and Revenue Optimization

Dynamic nesting ensures that fare classes are closed off from the bottom up and that customers can always purchase from more expensive fare classes until capacity is exhausted. A prerequisite for dynamic nesting is setting the booking limits and subsequent protection levels for the different fare classes. Capacity allocation refers to the method by which booking limits are defined for the relevant fare classes.

We can explore the capacity allocation problem by analyzing a simple two-class problem. Capacity allocations with multiple classes can be managed conceptually with the same approach as that presented in this section. More commonly, however, capacity allocation decisions with multiple fare classes are made using managerial decision heuristics that develop as an approximation of the two-class solution presented here and which can be found in more advanced texts on revenue management.

CAPACITY ALLOCATION WITH CERTAIN DEMAND

If the demand is known ahead of time (that is, if demand is perfectly forecasted), then the capacity allocation challenge is trivial. Giving the highest priority to the most expensive fare class and the lowest priority to the least expensive, capacity would be allocated according to forecasted demand.

For example, suppose a hotel operator was managing 30 rooms, each with equal amenities. At this hotel, the standard room rate is \$250 per night and the discount rate is \$150. To improve revenue, the hotel may have a yield management policy to hold some full-fare rooms available for last-minute customers arriving on the night of the stay, while selling discounted rooms to customers who make early reservations.

If the hotel operator strongly suspects that on a particular night, it will have exactly 10 people showing up to request a room, that operator should hold 10 rooms available for full-fare customers arriving on that night. This would imply that the protection level for full-fare customers for the hotel would be set at 10 ($y_1 = 10$), while allowing the remaining rooms to be reserved at the discounted rate ($y_2 = 30$). In comparison to selling all the rooms at the discounted price on a first-come, first-served basis, a yield management policy to protect 10 rooms for full-fare customers would increase nightly revenue by $1,000.

CAPACITY ALLOCATION WITH UNCERTAIN DEMAND

Yield management can be extended to include uncertainties in demand. Even when demand is uncertain, past experience can be used to forecast that demand will lie within some range. To optimize capacity allocation decisions in the face of uncertain demand, yield management techniques can rely on the quantification of the probability that demand will lie at different levels.

The normal distribution function, also known as the Gaussian or bell curve, is commonly used to describe demand in the face of uncertainty. To define the normal distribution function of demand, forecasters only need to quantify two aspects, the expected average and the range in demand. See Appendix 14 for a mathematical description of the normal distribution function.

Probability Function

Returning to our 30-room hotel, the hotel operator may expect that on average, 10 rooms will be demanded at full fare on a given night, but it is uncertain as to whether full-price demand will be for 6 rooms or 14 rooms (10 plus or minus 4). In this case, the average demand is 10. The standard deviation is a measure of the uncertainty in the demand. Higher standard deviations express higher uncertainty, while lower standard deviations express lower uncertainty. Demand for hotels varies considerably from night to night. The hotel operator may believe that 68 percent of the time, the full-price demand is between 6 and 14 rooms. That is, the operator is 68 percent confident that the true demand will be somewhere between 6 and 14 rooms, and accepts that 32 percent of the time, the demand is outside this range. In this case, the standard deviation in demand for rooms is 4. (In a normal distribution, 68 percent of the time, the expressed demand will lie within one standard deviation of the average expected demand.) The normal distribution in demand for the previously described case is shown in Exhibit 14-2. (We have approximated the distribution function in this graph using a discrete representation of the normal distribution function. See Appendix 14.)

Cumulative Probability Function

The normal distribution describes the probability that exactly 6, 10, 14, or any other number of customers would be willing to pay for a full-priced room on the evening in question. But the probability of selling 10 full-priced rooms isn't the probability that *exactly* 10 people will want a full-priced room—it is the probability that 10 *or more* people will want a full-priced room. Yield management optimizes revenue by setting protection levels on higher-priced rooms according to the probability of selling these rooms, not simply the probability that demand is exactly equal to the protection levels. To find the probability of selling 10 more rooms, we need to use the cumulative probability function, or more specifically, 1 minus the cumulative probability function when using a continuous function.

The cumulative probability function can be used to describe the probability that demand is at or below a given level. Thus, 1 minus the continuous cumulative probability function describes the probability that demand is at or above a given level.

We can show how the cumulative probability function helps define allocation rules by returning to our example hotel with average demand of 10 and standard deviation in demand of 4 for full-priced rooms. See Exhibit 14-3, which has been calculated using the discrete approximation of the normal distribution function. (See Appendix 14 for details on the discrete approximation of the normal distribution function.) The demand schedule shows that if 1 room is protected for full-price customers, there is a 99 percent probability for that room to be purchased at full price. Likewise, if 8 rooms are protected, there is a 73 percent probability that all 8 rooms would be demanded at full price, if 10 rooms are protected, there is a 55 percent

Exhibit 14-2 Normal Distribution for Full-Price Demand: *The Normal Distribution Function Representing the Demand for Full-Price Rooms is Shown for an Average Demand of 10 and Standard Deviation in Demand of 4.*

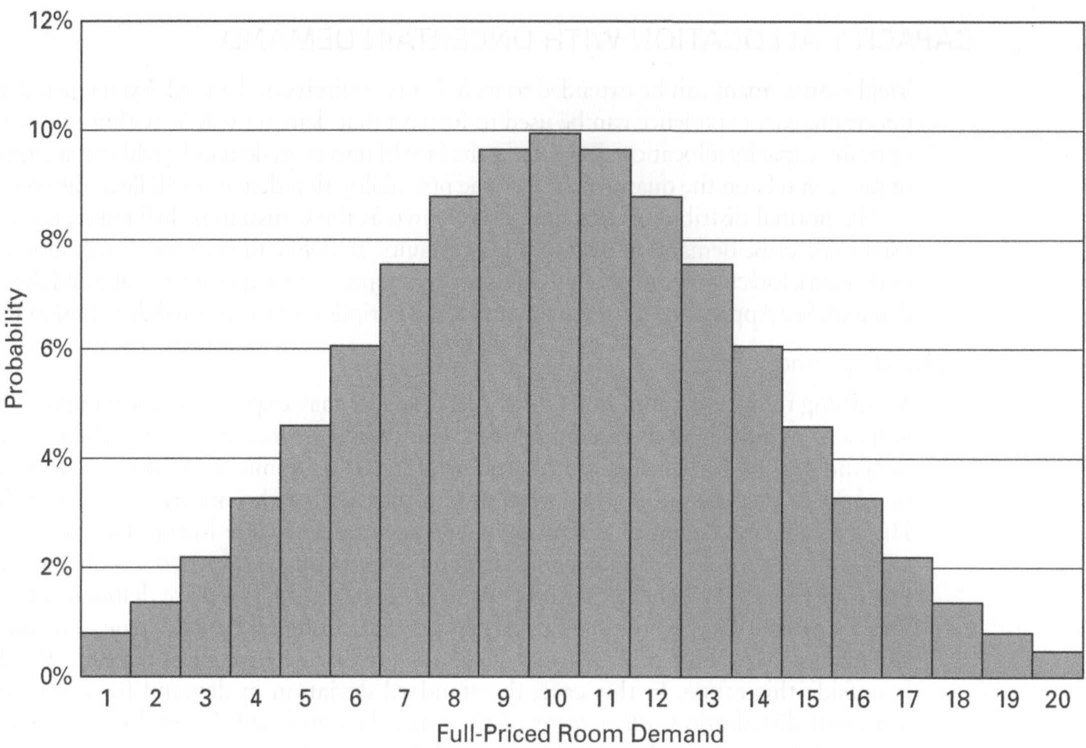

probability that all 10 rooms would be demanded at full price, and if 12 rooms are protected, there is a 35 percent probability that all 12 rooms would be demanded at full price.

The fact that the demand schedule predicts that only 55 percent of the time, the hotel would sell 10 protected rooms is the result of 10 being the median number of rooms expected to sell at full price. The definition of the median average is that it lies in the middle. In this case, 10 percent of the time exactly 10 rooms would be demanded, 45 percent of the time fewer than 10 rooms would be demanded and 45 percent of the time more than 10 rooms would be demanded.

Revenue Optimization

Cumulative distribution functions enable yield managers to forecast demand. Using the demand expectations associated with different protection levels along with the revenue impact, capacity can be allocated in a manner that is predicted to optimize revenue.

At the time of setting protection levels, it is not known whether the demand will be at, above, or below that predicted. However, the probability of selling that room at full price can be predicted from the normal distribution function. Hence, we can form an expectation value of the revenue earned from full-priced rooms at a given protection level.

One method to optimize revenue is to examine protection-level decisions in terms of their marginal impact on expected revenue. Protecting a room for a full-price customer comes at the cost of not allowing the sale of that room to a discount-price customer. If the discounted room can be predicted to sell with certainty, the room should be protected for full-price customers only if the expected revenue earned from the next full-price customer is in excess of the discounted fare.

Let us return to the example hotel with an expected full-price demand of 10 rooms and standard deviation in demand of 4. If 10 rooms were protected for full-price customers,

Exhibit 14-3 **Probability that All Protected Full-Priced Rooms Are Sold:** *The Cumulative Distribution Function Representing the Demand for Full-Priced Rooms is Shown for an Average Demand of 10 and Standard Deviation in Demand of 4.*

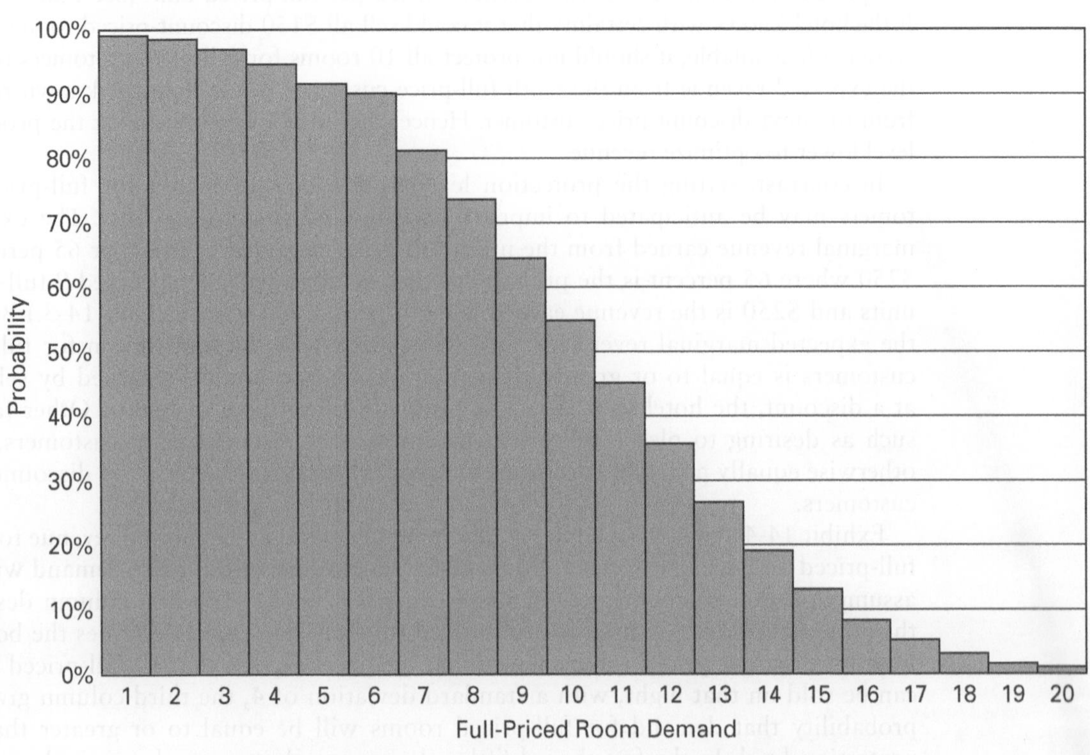

Protection Level for Full-Priced Rooms	Probability that Demand for Full-Priced Rooms Will Be Greater Than or Equal to the Protection Level
i	$1 - G(i - .5, \mu, \sigma)$
0	100%
1	99%
2	98%
3	97%
4	95%
5	92%
6	87%
7	81%
8	73%
9	65%
10	55%
11	45%
12	35%
13	27%
14	19%
15	13%
16	8%
17	5%
18	3%
19	2%
20	1%

the expected marginal revenue earned from the tenth full-price customer is only $138, or 55 percent of $250 where 55 percent is the probability that demand will be or exceed 10 full-priced units and $250 is the revenue earned per full-priced unit. (See Exhibit 14-3.) If the hotel knows with certainty that it could sell all $150 discount-priced rooms if they were made available, it should not protect all 10 rooms for full-price customers because the expected revenue from the tenth full-price customer is less than the known revenue from the next discount-price customer. Hence, the hotel may wish to set the protection level lower to optimize revenue.

In contrast, setting the protection level to 9 rooms or higher for full-price customers may be anticipated to improve revenue and therefore profits. The expected marginal revenue earned from the ninth full-price customer is $162, or 65 percent of $250 where 65 percent is the probability that demand will be or exceed 9 full-priced units and $250 is the revenue earned per full-priced unit. (See Exhibit 14-3.) Because the expected marginal revenue earned from protecting the ninth room for full-price customers is equal to or greater than the revenue that could be earned by selling it at a discount, the hotel should set the protection level here or higher. Other factors, such as desiring to please full-price customers over discount-price customers, drive otherwise equally profitable decisions to favor full-price customers over discount-price customers.

Exhibit 14-4 shows a schedule of anticipated demand and expected revenue for both full-priced and discount-priced rooms given uncertainty in full-price demand with the assumption that discount-price demand exceeds capacity. The first column describes the potential protection level for full-priced rooms. The second describes the booking limit for discount-priced rooms. Given that the hotel expects that 10 full-priced rooms can be sold on that night, with a standard deviation of 4, the third column gives the probability that demand for full-priced rooms will be equal to or greater than the protection level. In the fourth and fifth columns are the expected marginal and total revenue earned from protecting the last full-priced room. The remaining columns calculate the total revenue expected to be earned from the discount-price classes as well as the total overall expected revenue.

From Exhibit 14-4, it is found that the optimal protection level under these assumptions is 9. By protecting 9 rooms for full-price customers, the hotel will knowingly be protecting fewer full-price rooms than is demanded on average. In fact, it expects the full-price room demand to be 10 or higher 55 percent of the time. The hotel will also be protecting the ninth full-priced room that it would otherwise expect to sell at a discounted rate but will sell at full price only 65 percent of the time. However, with a full-price booking limit of 9, the probability adjusted expected revenue from the ninth full-price customer is greater than that of the twenty-first discount customer.

At all lower full-price booking limits, the probability adjusted expected revenue from the last full-price customer exceeds that of the last discount customer. At any higher full-price booking limit, the probability adjusted expected revenue from the last full-price customer is below that of the last discount customer. Hence, the hotel can expect on average to maximize its profits by protecting 9 rooms for full-price customers, rather than simply the average of 10 rooms or any other number of rooms as well.

The optimal allocation of protection levels at 9 rooms can also be found by looking at the column for total expected revenue. At 9 rooms protected, total revenue is maximized. The total expected revenue for different protection levels described in Exhibit 14-4 is plotted as in Exhibit 14-5. From either the schedule in Exhibit 14-4 or the plot in Exhibit 14-5, we can see that the overall revenue is maximized with a protection level of 9. We can also see in Exhibit 14-5 that if the protection level increases further, the expected revenue contribution from full-price customers begins to level off, making higher protection levels come at a direct cost of lost discount revenue.

Exhibit 14-4 Protection Level, Demand Forecast, and Expected Revenue: *The Protection Level, Demand Forecast, and Expected Revenue are Found for a Two-Class, 30-Room Hotel Given a Full-Price Average Demand of 10 and Standard Deviation of 4, and Discount-Price Demand that Exceeds Capacity.*

Protection Level for Full-Price Rooms	Booking Limit for Discount Rooms	Probability that Full-Price Demand Equals or Exceeds Its Protection Level	Expected Marginal Full-Price Revenue	Expected Total Full-Price Revenue	Expected Total Discount Price Revenue	Expected Total Revenue
		$1 - G_f(i-5, \mu, \sigma)$ $\mu = 10$ $\sigma = 4$	$\$250 \cdot [1 - G_f \cdot (i-5, \mu, \sigma)]$			
1	29	99%	$248	$248	$4,350	$4,598
2	28	98%	$246	$494	$4,200	$4,694
3	27	97%	$242	$736	$4,050	$4,786
4	26	95%	$237	$973	$3,900	$4,873
5	25	92%	$229	$1,202	$3,750	$4,952
6	24	87%	$218	$1,420	$3,600	$5,020
7	23	81%	$203	$1,622	$3,450	$5,072
8	22	74%	$184	$1,806	$3,300	$5,106
9	**21**	**65%**	**$162**	**$1,968**	**$3,150**	**$5,118**
10	20	55%	$138	$2,106	$3,000	$5,106
11	19	45%	$113	$2,219	$2,850	$5,069
12	18	36%	$89	$2,308	$2,700	$5,008
13	17	27%	$67	$2,374	$2,550	$4,924
14	16	19%	$48	$2,422	$2,400	$4,822
15	15	13%	$33	$2,455	$2,250	$4,705
16	14	9%	$21	$2,476	$2,100	$4,576
17	13	5%	$13	$2,490	$1,950	$4,440
18	12	3%	$8	$2,497	$1,800	$4,297
19	11	2%	$4	$2,501	$1,650	$4,151
20	10	1%	$2	$2,504	$1,500	$4,004
21	9	0%	$1	$2,505	$1,350	$3,855
22	8	0%	$1	$2,505	$1,200	$3,705
23	7	0%	$0	$2,506	$1,050	$3,556
24	6	0%	$0	$2,506	$900	$3,406
25	5	0%	$0	$2,506	$750	$3,256
26	4	0%	$0	$2,506	$600	$3,106
27	3	0%	$0	$2,506	$450	$2,956
28	2	0%	$0	$2,506	$300	$2,806
29	1	0%	$0	$2,506	$150	$2,656
30	0	0%	$0	$2,506	$–	$2,506

Exhibit 14-5 Revenue Optimization in Yield Management

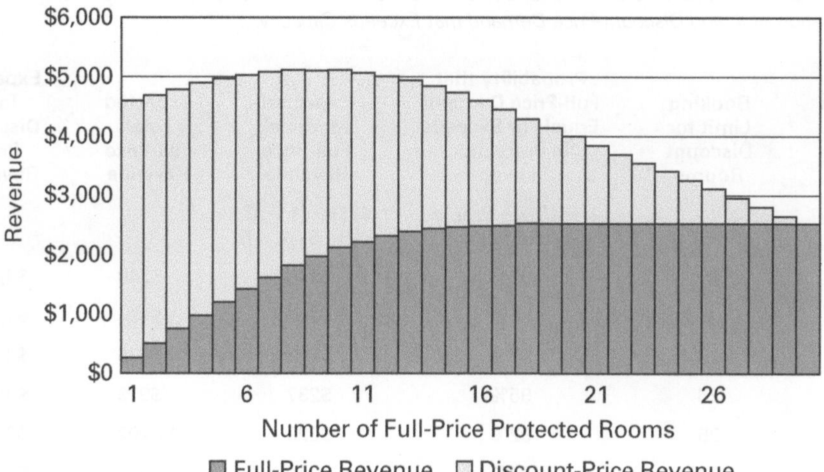

Decision Tree Approach

Yield management optimizes revenue by allocating capacity between different fare classes in a manner that maximizes the expected overall revenue earned on the resource. As seen in the hotel example, yield management includes a careful tradeoff between the expected revenue earned from lower-price customers versus that from higher-price customers. On one hand, if the firm turns away discount bookings in the hopes of earning a full-price customer that never materializes, the empty seat or room goes unsold. This is called *spoilage* because inventory becomes spoiled the moment the plane takes off or the evening comes to a close. On the other hand, if the firm accepts discounted sales that force it to turn away full-price customers, it runs the risk of selling seats at a less favorable price. This is called *dilution* because the potential revenue is diluted with excess low-price sales. The goal in capacity allocation decisions within yield management is to balance the lost revenue of spoilage with that of dilution to maximize expected revenue.

We can represent this tradeoff simply with a decision tree. See Exhibit 14-6. Let C be the capacity of the resource and B be the booking limit on the lower price class. The decision to be made is whether the firm should increase the lower-price booking limit by 1. Increasing the lower-price booking limit by 1 increases the risk of dilution. Holding the lower-price booking limit constant increases the risk of spoilage.

If the booking limit on the lower price class is increased by 1 but the discount price demand is less than the current booking limit, then the increase in the booking limit will have no impact on revenue. In dynamic nesting, capacity unsold in a lower price class remains available for sale to a higher fare class, hence increasing the discount-price-class booking limit by 1 when no discount customer will demand that capacity has no effect on revenue. The probability that the discount-price demand is less than the current booking limit is $G_d(B)$, where $G_d(B)$ is the cumulative probability function that discount-price demand is equal to or less than the current booking limit, B. (Readers may find it useful to consider the continuous form of the normal distribution function for this section.)

If the booking limit on the lower price class is increased by 1 and the discount-price demand is greater than the current booking limit, then the increase in the booking limit may affect revenue. The probability that discount-price demand is greater than the current booking limit is $1 - G_d(B)$. To determine if the potential impact is positive or negative, we have to examine the probability that a full-price customer will arrive.

Exhibit 14-6 Two-Class Capacity Allocation Decision Tree

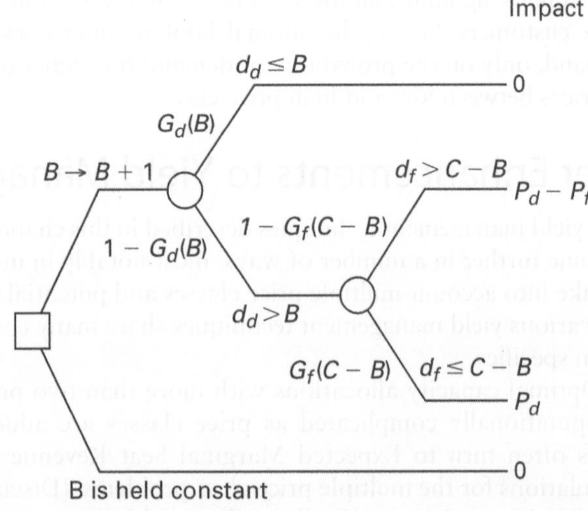

If the discount-price demand is greater than the current discount-price booking limit, an increase in this booking limit means that the firm is taking the chance of gaining revenue equal to the price of the discount price class (P_d) in the hope that the full-price demand is below the current protection level. The probability that the full-price demand is below its current protection level is $G_f(C - B)$, where $G_f(C - B)$ is the cumulative probability function that full-price demand is equal to or less than the current protection limit, $C - B$. The probability that the full-price demand is at or above its current protection level is $1 - G_f(C - B)$. Increasing the booking limit on the discount fare runs the risk of forfeiting potential full-fare revenue of P_f to gain discount revenue of P_d, at a cost of $P_d - P_f$.

Altogether, the expected impact on revenue from increasing the booking limit by 1 is equal to the probability-weighted sum of the possible outcomes. We can express this as

$$\begin{aligned} E[B \rightarrow B+1] &= G_d(B) \cdot 0 + [1 - G_d(B)] \cdot [(1 - G_f(C - B)) \cdot (P_d - P_f) \\ &\quad + G_f(C - B) \cdot P_d] \\ &= [1 - G_d(B)] \cdot [P_d - P_f \cdot (1 - G_f(C - B))] \end{aligned} \quad \text{Eq. 14.4}$$

If the expected impact on revenue from increasing the booking limit by 1 is equal to or greater than zero ($E[B \rightarrow B + 1]$), then increasing the booking is expected to improve revenue and decrease spoilage. If not, then it would harm revenue by increasing dilution.

Because the optimal discount fare booking limit is that in which further increases in the booking limit either have no effect or a negative effect on the expected revenue, we can find the discount price optimal booking limit by setting Equation 14.4 equal to zero. After some rearrangement, we find that

$$1 - G_f(C - \hat{B}) = \frac{P_d}{P_f} \quad \text{Eq. 14.5}$$

The resulting Equation 14.5 is Littlewood's rule, where $\hat{B}$ is the optimal booking limit. The left side of Equation 14.5 is the probability that full-price demand will exceed the protection level. The right side is the ratio of the price classes. Littlewood's rule is a simple means to finding the optimal booking limit for any two-class revenue optimization problem under a yield management price structure.

While it may appear counterintuitive that the optimal protection level does not depend on the forecasted discount-price demand, it is a result of the nesting of booking limits. With nested booking limits, all the seats not sold to discounted customers are available for full-price customers. Hence, the optimal booking limit does not depend on the discount fare demand, only on the probability of demand for higher-price customers and the dispersion in prices between low and high price classes.

Further Enhancements to Yield Management

The yield management techniques described in this chapter have been extended to improve revenue further in a number of ways, most notably in improving capacity allocation rules to take into account multiple price classes and potential dependent demand effects. While the various yield management techniques share many conceptual commonalities, they differ in specifics.

Optimal capacity allocations with more than two price classes quickly become more computationally complicated as price classes are added. To address these challenges, firms often turn to Expected Marginal Seat Revenue (EMSR) heuristics to accelerate calculations for the multiple price class problems. (Discussions on EMSR can be found in advanced texts that specifically explore yield management.)

Far more challenging have been the effects of dependent demand, especially in light of network effects. Customers often do not seek to purchase a single price class on a specific flight nor a single night at a hotel, but rather a series of connected purchases that might include multiple legs between airports or multiple nights at a hotel. The simple yield management technique presented herein fails to optimize revenue in the face of dependent demand challenges. Network management techniques have been introduced to improve the revenue earned on multiple resources with dependent demand.

Summary

- Yield management is a dynamic pricing technique used to optimize revenue earned from a fixed-capacity resource.
- From an internal perspective, the key requirements for using yield management include (1) limited and perishable capacity, (2) customers reserving a portion of the capacity ahead of time, (3) the firm selling a portion of the capacity at a variety of prices, also known as fare classes, and (4) the firm changing the availability of fare classes over time.
- Yield management is used in a variety of industries, most notably with airlines and hotels but also with freight transport and broadcast advertising.
- From a market perspective, yield management is favored by large markets, with multiple customers exhibiting different willingness to pay that is partially correlated with the time of purchase.
- Yield management uses booking control to manage the availability of price classes. The dominant approach to booking control in yield management is dynamic nesting, a technique that ensures that the highest price class has the highest availability regardless of the order in which customers request price classes.
- In dynamic nesting, the booking limit of all equal and lower price classes is reduced as seats in a given price class are reserved. Once a price class has reached its booking limit, no further reservations are allowed within that class.
- Yield management uses capacity allocation rules to determine booking limits of price classes. The goal in capacity allocation decisions is to maximize the probability-weighted expected revenue from a resource.

- Because future demand is uncertain, capacity allocation decisions must be made using probabilities. One method is to assume a normal distribution in demand to assign the probability that demand will exhaust capacity at a given capacity allocation.
- Capacity allocation decisions force tradeoffs between the costs of spoilage, where inventory goes unsold, and the cost of dilution, where inventory that could have been sold at a higher price is sold at a lower price.

Exercises

1. Consider a hotel operator offering rooms in two different price classes. The full-price class offers rooms at 250 € and the discount-price class offers rooms at 150 €. Assume that the hotel has 30 rooms and that the hotel operator has determined to reserve 9 rooms for full-price customers.
   a. What are the initial booking limits for full-price and discount-price rooms?
   b. What are the initial protection levels for full-price and discount-price rooms?
   c. If the following set of room requests is made, which reservations are accepted and which are rejected? How are the booking limits and protection levels changed over time? How many rooms are sold after each reservation request has been made? Complete the following chart.

		Booking Limit		Protection Level		Action	Rooms Sold		
	Price	250 €	100 €						
	Price Class	1	2	1	2		1	2	T
		b_1	b_2	y_1	y_2				
1	1 room @ Discount Price								
2	1 room @ Full Price								
3	17 rooms @ Discount Price								
4	1 room @ Full Price								
5	2 rooms @ Discount Price								
6	2 rooms @ Full Price								
7	1 room @ Discount Price								
8	1 room @ Full Price								
9	5 rooms @ Full Price								
10	1 room @ Discount Price								
11	1 room @ Full Price								

2. Southwest Airlines offers 11 flights between Chicago and Phoenix daily. A "Wanna Get Away" one-way fare is $182, while an "Anytime" one-way fare is $398. Assume that 137 seats are available on a Southwest Airlines 737–300 aircraft.
   a. What is the optimal booking limit on "Wanna Get Away" seats if Southwest Airlines expects 30 "Anytime" customers, plus or minus 15, at one standard deviation? How many seats would be protected for "Anytime" customers?
   b. What is the optimal booking limit on "Wanna Get Away" seats if Southwest Airlines expects 60 "Anytime" customers, plus or minus 30, at one standard deviation? How many seats would be protected for "Anytime" customers?
   c. Given this fare structure, is the optimal number of "Anytime" fare seats protected for Southwest greater than or less than the anticipated expected "Anytime" fare seats demanded?

3. Intercontinental Chicago Magnificent Mile offers numerous rooms. Suppose the Intercontinental Chicago offered rack-rate rooms at $400 and discounted rooms at $223. Assume that there are 792 rooms available at the Intercontinental Chicago Magnificent Mile.
   a. What is the optimal booking limit on discount fare rooms if the Intercontinental Chicago expected 75 rack-rate customers, plus or minus 37, at one standard deviation? How many rooms would be protected for full-price customers?
   b. What is the optimal booking limit on discount-price rooms if the Intercontinental Chicago expected 180 rack-rate customers, plus or minus 90, at one standard deviation? How many rooms would be protected for full-price customers?
   c. Given this fare structure, is the optimal number of rack-rate rooms protected for the Intercontinental Chicago greater than or less than the anticipated expected rack-rate rooms demanded?
4. Ryanair offers £10 one-way flights from London-Stansted, U.K., to Wroclaw, Poland.
   a. How many seats do you suspect Ryanair offers per flight at this fare? More or less than 10?
   b. If Ryanair believed it could sell all its seats at its regular fare of £89.99, how many seats would Ryanair sell at the £10 fare?
   c. Discussion question: Why does Ryanair sell seats at £10 fare?
5. KLM serves Chicago, U.S., to Prague, Czech Republic, with a single flight daily. In economy class, KLM offers one-way discounted fares at $450 and one-way full fares at $1,200. Assume that there are 295 economy-class seats on a KLM 747-400. Over a long history of observation, KLM estimates that full-fare economy-class demand is normally distributed, with a mean of 112 passengers and a standard deviation of 56, while discount demand is normally distributed, with a mean of 274 passengers and a standard deviation of 137.
   a. A consultant advises KLM that it can optimize expected revenue by optimizing the booking limit. What is the optimal booking limit?
   b. The airline has been setting a booking limit of 183 on discount demand, to preserve 112 seats for full-fare passengers. What is the expected revenue per flight under this policy? (Hint: use a spreadsheet to help you figure this out.)
   c. What is the expected gain from using the optimal booking limit over the original booking limit?
   d. Lufthansa determines to enter the market, and KLM anticipates its discount fare demand will drop to 186 passengers per flight with a standard deviation of 93. Full-fare demand is unchanged. What is the new optimal booking limit?

Appendix 14 The Normal Distribution Function

The normal distribution function has been explored for over three centuries and is commonly used to describe not only consumer behavior, such as demand, but a range of other phenomena in science, economics, and other disciplines. The probability distribution function for the normal distribution is given by

$$g(x, \mu, \sigma) = \frac{1}{\sqrt{2\pi}\sigma} \exp\left[\frac{-(x-\mu)^2}{2\sigma^2}\right] \qquad \text{Eq. 14.6}$$

where the average demand is denoted by the Greek letter μ (pronounced "mu"); the standard deviation is denoted by the Greek letter σ (pronounced "sigma"); and $g(x)$ is the probability of finding demand x given a normal distribution in demand.

The cumulative distribution function at some point is the sum of the probabilities that the demand is at that point or at any point up to that point. For continuous functions, sums are calculated using integrals. Thus, the cumulative distribution that demand will be at or below some point is simply

$$G(x, \mu, \sigma) = \int_{-\infty}^{x} g(x', \mu, \sigma)dx' \qquad \text{Eq. 14.7}$$

Cumulative distribution functions have the property of ranging from 0 at $G(-\infty)$ to 1 at $G(+\infty)$. That is, we know that the actual demand for a product has a value somewhere in the range between $-\infty$ and $+\infty$, be it at 0, 6, 10, or 14. Hence, the total probability that demand will express itself is 1.

To find the probability that demand is equal to or greater than some level—that is, that demand is at or exceeds some protection level—simply subtract the cumulative distribution function from 1. This property follows from the definition of the cumulative distribution function. If we know that $G(x)$ is the probability that demand is less than or equal to x units, then $1 - G(x)$ is the probability that demand will be x or higher.

$$\text{Probability Demand Exceeds } x = 1 - G(x) \qquad \text{Eq. 14.8}$$

Normal distribution functions and their cumulative distribution functions are standard functions found in most computational software.[3]

Because rooms cannot be sold in fractional or negative amounts, but only as positive whole units, we use the discrete normal distribution rather than the continuous normal distribution function. The discrete normal distribution can be approximated from the continuous normal distribution through the following equations. Let $G(i, \mu, \sigma)$ be the cumulative probability that the discrete demand is for i or fewer units as approximated from the continuous normal distribution function, then the discrete probability that the demand is for i units can be expressed as

$$\begin{aligned} g_D(0, \mu, \sigma) &= G(0.5, \mu, \sigma) && \text{for } i = 0 \\ g_D(i, \mu, \sigma) &= G(i + 0.5, \mu, \sigma) - G(i - 0.5, \mu, \sigma) && \text{for } i = 1, 2, 3, \ldots n \end{aligned} \qquad \text{Eq. 14.9}$$

Similarly, the cumulative probability function that demand is greater than i or equal to i, which is used to calculate if a room is sold given a booking limit, is approximated as

$$\text{Probability Demand Meets or Exceeds } i = 1 - G(i - 0.5, \mu, \sigma) \qquad \text{Eq. 14.10}$$

Because the discrete version of the normal distribution function requires approximations, certain small errors will arise. The significance of these errors will depend on the nature of the challenge being addressed. In this chapter, we have used the discrete normal distribution function as approximated through Equations 14.9 and 14.10.

Notes

[1] Avrind Sahay, "How to Reap Higher Profits With Dynamic Pricing" *MIT Sloan Management Review* 48, No. 4 (Summer 2007): 53–60.

[2] Much of the discussion on yield management provided in this chapter is also discussed in greater detail in Robert L. Phillips, "Revenue Management" and "Capacity Allocation," in *Pricing and Revenue Optimization* (Stanford: Stanford Business Press, 2005): 120–175.

[3] To get the cumulative distribution function of a normal distribution in Microsoft Excel, use normdist(*x*,*mean*,*standard_dev*,*cumulative*), where *x* is the point of interest, *mean* is the average (*mean* = μ), and *standard_dev* is the standard deviation (*standard_dev* = σ). Set *cumulative* equal to TRUE.

PART

4

Pricing Strategy

Chapter 15

Competition and Pricing

Jeff HAYNES/Newscom

- Do firms purposely enter into price wars?
- Why do price wars break out?
- Under what conditions are price wars more likely?
- How should a firm react to an aggressive price-based competition?
- When can a firm use low prices strategically?
- How can executives anticipate a competitor's price moves?
- How can executives limit the likelihood of a price war?
- Stretch Question: How should pricing strategy be related to a firm's competitive position?

While the focus of strategic pricing is to align the firm's prices with its market's willingness to pay, we cannot ignore that the willingness to pay of customers is affected by the actions of competitors. Pricing is not done in a vacuum. Competitors, as well as their pricing actions, clearly limit the latitude that a firm has in managing prices strategically.

The role of competition has been implied throughout this text. In using exchange value models and their ability to reveal a customer's willingness to pay, a key component is developing an understanding of the price and value of competing alternatives. Likewise, in developing prices based on consumer perceptions, the perceived value that customers give to a product is influenced by the perceived price points of the alternatives.

In much of strategic pricing, the goal is to drive the competitive frontier to another dimension. As explored in the discussion of the profit sensitivity to price changes in Chapter 2, it is only possible to lower prices and drive sufficient volume to improve profits in a limited number of situations. Tactically, price promotions can be effective in capturing marginal customers. Strategically, price competition usually leaves all firms impoverished. Rather than using price as a competitive weapon, most firms are better off using other levers of strategic marketing, such as market segmentation, product definition, promotional media selection, brand positioning, and distribution.

If we consider price structures, we find that the first firm to adopt a new price structure often reaps enormous rewards, while others must struggle to catch up. For instance, consider the effect that bundling office software in 1992 had on the fortunes of Microsoft compared to Lotus 123, WordPerfect, and Eudora. Unfortunately, a firm can only infrequently redefine the price structure in a way that strikes a strategic blow to its competitors.

These insights into strategic pricing are in line with a principle behind a concept regarding competitive advantage. All competitive advantage derives from being different from competitors, not copying them. Strategic resources are strategic precisely because they are rare and difficult to imitate. They deliver a competitive advantage because they enable a firm to be more profitable. When we search for sources of competitive advantage, we can find them in strategic resources that enable the firm to add value without adding as much cost, reduce cost without reducing as much value, or accelerating reaction time to seize new opportunities. None of these issues imply that price, in and of itself, is a strategic resource.

Moreover, simply selling a "me-too" product at a lower price is not the same as developing a strategic resource, and it is therefore unlikely to enable the firm to achieve greater profits than its competitors. Rather, selling products that deliver distinct value to distinct market segments, pricing the product according to the value that those segments are willing to pay, and communicating the value of that product to those segments, deliver superior returns.

Hence, we come to the conclusion that pricing below competitors does not constitute a competitive advantage. Even pricing to capture market share is a dubious argument because there is little value in having the largest share of the market without making profits. Yet we are also confronted with the obvious fact that competition affects pricing. So, how does competition influence pricing strategy? Should a firm ever price below its competition? There are cases where a firm should seek to undercut its competitors, just as there are cases where a firm should ignore a competitor that has lowered prices. In addition, there are situations where a firm must respond to a competitor's efforts to undercut it. In this chapter, we turn to the challenge of managing prices strategically in the face of competition.

The Origin of Price Wars

The purpose of all war is ultimately peace.
—Saint Augustine of Hippo

Rarely do companies enter a price war on purpose. Despite popular hearsay that a firm enters into price wars with the motive to drive competitors out of a market and then increase its price and gain higher profits, there has been scant economic evidence of success with this strategy. This is for good reason: It is hard to make this strategy work. The cost of a price war is inherently expensive, with the immediate loss of profits or, worse, mounting losses over time. Furthermore, the benefits of winning a price war are highly uncertain.

Rarely does a price war lead to an industry shakeout. Although a price war may weaken a competitor, it is hard to kill an established organization and permanently remove industry capacity. Decisive victories are rare.

Even if a competitor exits the market and the firm is able to raise its prices and enjoy monopoly profits, the nature of competitive markets implies that the higher profits earned by a firm in a market will only invite other competitors to enter or reenter that market. Hence, the monopoly position hard-won through a price war is highly unlikely to yield sufficient profits to cover the costs incurred in fighting the war.

Hence, the realistic purpose of a price war cannot be to kill the competition. Moreover, when executives find themselves in a price war, they should strive to achieve a future state of peace in which their firm can flourish.

Despite the fact that price wars are generally illogical, we know that they will break out at times. Their cause can be somewhat anticipated by considering the profit goals of most companies and their need to seize the opportunity to achieve these goals. Although companies will rarely initiate a purposeful price war, they will seek to seize opportunities in the market. Unfortunately, this orientation toward taking action to seize market share, coupled with an inability to either manage or anticipate actions with competitors, can lead to an unnecessary price war and reduction of overall industry profits.

We have already seen evidence that such results are common. In reviewing brand-versus industry-level elasticity of demand for a number of consumer products, we found that the brand-level elasticity of demand was typically in the elastic range while the industry-level elasticity of demand was typically in the inelastic range. From a profit maximization viewpoint, it never makes sense to price in the inelastic range. Hence, most of the industries considered would benefit from an overall price increase. However, that would imply that individual competitors within that industry, which individually face an elastic demand, would need to raise their prices collectively. If any one firm raises its prices without its competitors raising their prices simultaneously, customers will switch brands, and that one firm will lose market share and profits. Because it is unlikely that all competitors would be able to raise prices in a coordinated manner without illegal collusion, it is rare to see industry-level prices driven significantly high so as to maximize profits at the industry level.

PRISONER'S DILEMMA

We can see how the logic of competition and opportunity seeking can lead to an overall reduction of industrywide profits by considering the prisoner's dilemma. The prisoner's dilemma is so named because it describes the situation faced by two suspected criminals put into separate rooms for questioning. Law enforcement investigators then make offers to both suspects to confess and implicate the other in exchange for a lighter sentence. If no suspect confesses, the investigators don't have a case, and both suspects are set free. However, investigators usually choose not to reveal this fact. Because neither suspect can communicate his intention not to confess to the other, and because both of them are facing the offer of confessing in exchange for a lighter sentence, one of them is likely to yield to the pressure. Once that happens, both prisoners get a criminal sentence, although the one who confesses gets a lighter punishment than the holdout.

Competing firms considering a price reduction often face a payoff matrix that is similar to that faced by suspected criminals in the prisoner's dilemma. Consider two hypothetical competitors in the same industry, Alpha and Beta, and the payoff matrix that they face by taking a price action. See Exhibit 15-1. Four potential configurations can take place in this industry.

Exhibit 15-1 Prisoners Dilemma

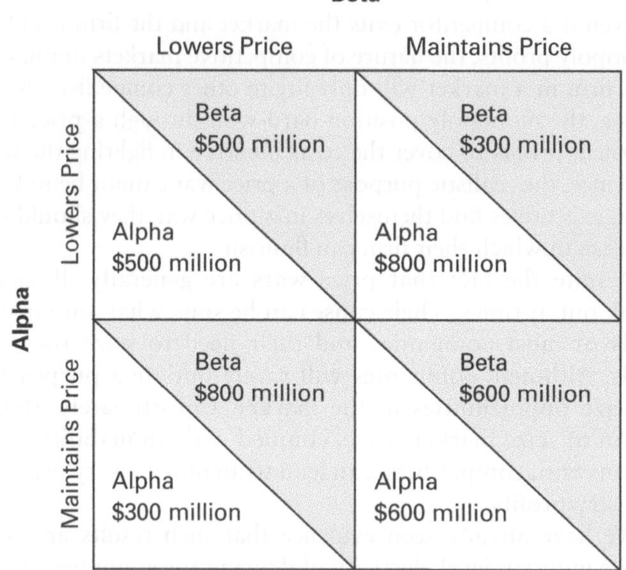

First, consider the case where neither party takes a price action, leaving the industry in a relatively stable condition. In our hypothetical payoff matrix, this is captured in the lower-right corner, where both Alpha and Beta enjoy $600 million in revenue. Note that in this position, the overall industry-level revenue is $1.2 billion.

In the next two scenarios, either competing firm can reduce its prices by itself, with the expectation of taking market share. Such a price action will leave that firm relatively better off, but at the expense of its competitor and with a small reduction overall in industrywide profitability. This is captured in the lower-left and upper-right corners of our hypothetical payoff matrix. In the example payoff matrix, such an action may raise the revenue of the competitor who uses price to gain market share to $800 million, while damaging the revenue of its competitor to $300 million. In this example, the overall industry-level revenue has been reduced to $1.1 billion.

Of course, if either firm alone took a price reduction to increase market share and revenue, it would only be in the competitor's best interest to react with a similar pricing action to recoup lost share. The result would be that both firms end up lowering price, represented in the upper-left corner of our payoff matrix. Such a position would raise the revenue of the damaged firm, but it would also lead to a continued erosion of industry-level profitability. In the example, both parties end up with $500 million in revenue, for overall industry-level revenue of $1 billion.

While the previous example was hypothetical, real competitors do face similar challenges in managing their prices. In our example, we assumed symmetrical effects between equally strong competitors. The approach to analyzing the dilemma facing competitors regarding price actions can be expanded to consider unequal competitors, multiple competitors, and differing payoff matrices. The point of this example isn't to analyze the specific situation of Alpha and Beta but to draw attention to the potential for opportunistic behavior from individual firms to lead to overall damage to all competitors within an industry.

The prisoner's dilemma indicates that all competitors in an industry are generally better off if none compete on price. If no competitor initiates a pricing action and maintains the current industry-level prices, all competitors are in a better position overall. However, incentives are such that most individual competitors have a short-term incentive to lower price to gain market share and increase revenues unless they consider the long-term reactions of their competitors. Once a firm considers the reaction of a competitor to a price action, it will discover that the damage such an action would inflict on the other competitors would likely encourage a similarly damaging reaction, thus leaving all firms weaker and removing revenue from the industry.

The goal in industry price management is to encourage competitors not to take mutually destructive pricing actions. If competitors could talk directly, mutually destructive pricing actions could be avoided. However, price collusion is highly illegal in all developed markets. However, the goal remains to encourage healthy pricing behavior throughout the industry.

STRUCTURAL DRIVERS

If all firms face short-term incentives to lower prices but long-term incentives not to lower prices, then any rational executive in any industry should understand that price reductions that encourage destructive retaliation should be avoided, and all price wars would cease. However, we know that somehow, price wars break out anyway.

Long-haul airlines have long been plagued with price wars, while branded food manufacturers appear to sustain a stable pricing environment. In looking at examples such as this and other industries as well, researchers have found five structural drivers to price competition. Although any single structural factor does not cause price competition in and of itself, companies in industries with that are weak in these structural factors are more likely to face pressure to compete on price.

Number of Competitors

Industries with fewer competitors tend to be able to monitor one another's pricing practices and respond appropriately. Therefore, a price action by any one competitor is likely to be observed and followed by a swift response from the other competitors, resulting in an overall destruction of industry-level profits, as previously discussed. Executives operating in industries with fewer competitors are also more likely to learn the costs of unnecessary price wars and the resulting negative-sum gains in initiating one.

In contrast, perfectly competitive markets imply numerous competitors. With many competitors, it becomes prohibitively costly to monitor the pricing actions of all competitors. Any single competitor may therefore be able to use price to gain market share in the short run without fearing immediate retaliation from all other industry competitors. Moreover, if competitors follow suit with a similar price action, it will be difficult for the initiating firm to discern whether competitors are reacting to its price action or some other force. Hence, it is difficult for companies operating in industries with many competitors to learn of the costs and overall industry-level results of their own pricing actions.

As such, companies in highly concentrated industries are more likely to refrain from excessive price pressures, while those operating in industries that lack concentration often unwittingly enter into them.

Competitors' Managerial Maturity

To understand the implications of using price to grab market share requires some level of maturity among the executives. Mature competitors are better positioned to both anticipate competitors' response to prices and be aware of competitors' pricing practices. New entrants or immature competitors may lack the ability to detect competitors' pricing actions or make grievous errors in anticipating the response to a price action. This kind of maturity may not just be a reflection of the executives at one particular firm, but the ability of the least reflective executive within that industry to avoid setting off an unnecessary price war. In highly competitive industries, executives are known to state: "I can price only as well as the stupidest competitor."

High Fixed Costs and Low Marginal Cost

Industries facing high fixed costs but low marginal costs often face extreme pressure to lower prices to capture marginal revenue. Because marginal costs are low (and in some cases zero), most marginal revenue can be added directly to the overall corporate bottom line. Software firms, which face extreme pressures to gain revenue that translates into profit, are operating in an environment that encourages an inordinate amount of price discounting. In software markets, discounting up to 90 percent from the list price is not unheard of, and many enterprise-class software firms consider discounts around 60 percent from the list price to be normal.

Industry Maturity and Economic Savings

The need for maturity extends beyond the executives and into the issue of the industry growth rate. With young, high-growth industries, executives face numerous incentives to grab market space in the hope of leveraging their operational demands into lower cost structures as the industry matures. These incentives may come from the expectation of future economies of scale, scope, or learning. If a firm can expect to gain future economies of scale, scope, or learning, it may have an incentive to use low prices to capture market share, penetrate new capabilities, or accelerate the learning curve in the expectation of long-term cost savings.

Economies of scale refers to the cost savings that a firm can gain that depend on the size of the firm as measured by its long-run, sustainable rate of output. As production volume increases, fixed incremental costs that arise from product development or capacity increases can be spread over a larger number of units, reducing the long-run average cost. Economies of scale first gained serious management attention after Henry Ford invented the modern assembly line for the automotive industry in 1913. Economies of scale can derive from multiple sources. For instance, as production volumes increase, workers can specialize, gaining proficiency and reducing time lost on task switching, leading to reduced production costs. Likewise, more efficient production technologies can be employed as the volume of production increases.

Economies of learning refers to reductions in cost that come from experience, as measured by accumulated output. Economies of learning result from learning by doing. They can arise from increases in labor efficiency, standardization, better utilization of equipment, more efficient use of resources, or product design improvements that enable fast manufacturing. Economies of learning gained serious management attention from the production of aircraft for World War II. The relationship was probably first quantified in 1936 at Wright-Patterson Air Force Base in the United States, where it was determined that every time cumulative aircraft production doubled, the required labor time decreased by 10 to 15 percent.[1]

Economies of scope refers to the production cost reductions as the breadth of a firm's activities increases. Like economies of scale, economies of scope depend on spreading shared costs over a larger number of units. Unlike economies of scale, economies of scope do not necessarily rely on savings from specialization. For an example of economies of scope, a gas station can use the same fixed assets to sell both fuel and food. Likewise, the same university classroom can be used to teach mathematics, business, and literature. In economies of scope, a single resource is used for multiple activities. By spreading the costs of maintaining that resource over multiple activities, the overall cost structure of the firm is reduced. Economies of scope became popular to discuss as a source of profitability as the modern conglomerate began to dominate industrial affairs during the middle of the twentieth century, and the term was coined in 1975.[2]

Industry Maturity and Network Externalities

Just as companies may be willing to price low in new industries in the hopes of gaining future cost savings from economies in scale, scope, or learning, they may also feel pressure to price low in the hopes of gaining an inordinate portion of the future revenue due to network externalities.

Products are said to benefit from network externalities when the value of the product increases with the number of people who use it. Network externalities can drive price wars in industries facing two-sided markets or highly profitable complementary goods markets. For instance, the format war between Toshiba's HD-DVD and Sony's Blu-ray was largely driven by the network externalities that could be gained by either Toshiba or Sony in the sales of patented technology for creating and using media. Nintendo's Wii, Microsoft's Xbox, and Sony's PS3 all face network externalities in the creation of game titles and the number of users with consoles. Similarly, Apple's iPhone and Research in Motion's BlackBerry face strong network externalities in the distribution of mobile handsets and applications for these handsets. Even user share can drive network externalities, as it does for social networking websites like Facebook, LinkedIn, and Skype.

Products that benefit from network effects are marketed by a firm under high motivation to increase the number of customers on its network. This may encourage the price of the products to be greatly reduced from what they would be priced at in absence of the network effects, to drive adaption. Once adaption is driven, the winner of the network may hope to gain an inordinate amount of the revenues from that industry because their network is more valuable than others.

Reacting to Price Reductions

It is often better to be a small competitor in a profitable industry than a large competitor in an unprofitable industry.

In calculating the response to a competitor's price reduction, executives must calibrate their actions carefully. The reaction must be limited so as not to create the conditions for a price war to break out, but the reaction must be strong enough to counter a competitor's price action and improve the firm's profits. If possible, the reaction should also communicate the message to a firm's competitors that price wars will be mutually destructive.

Three issues can be considered when calibrating a response to a competitor's price action. First, what are the direct costs and direct benefits of responding in tandem to a competitor's price move? Second, what are the likely secondary consequences from taking a price response? Third, does that competitor have a strategic cost advantage that enables it to profit at a lower industry price point?

DIRECT COSTS AND BENEFITS

When considering a response to a competitor's price reduction, executives should evaluate the costs and benefits of their response. To reduce the chance of the response tipping off a price war, executives can focus any price response on the direct revenue at risk and the direct profits threatened rather than the general malaise generated from a competitor's price reduction.

A competitor's price reduction will generally threaten some of the firm's revenue, but rarely all of it. In fact, sometimes it will threaten only a very small portion of the firm's revenue. By identifying the exact nature of the revenue at risk of loss, the firm can target any matching price reduction to recapture that specific marginal revenue.

One method to clarify the risk is to examine a series of questions similar to the following: Which market segment is at risk? Which customers are at risk of defecting to the competitor? How much of the revenue from those customers is placed at risk by the competitor's price reduction? Which specific products' sales are at risk? What business area is at risk? What is the probability that the specific revenue at risk will be lost? Are there other factors that may imply that the risks of losing revenue are still low after a competitor's price reduction?

Likewise, the benefits of responding can be examined through a series of questions similar to the following: What is the probability of retaining those sales after matching a competitor's price move? What profits would be gained by responding? What is the strategic importance of the specific revenue at risk? Does a foothold within the market threaten other revenue streams? Will blocking a competitor on the revenue at risk prevent that competitor from leveraging an entry point into other domains within the customer base?

SECONDARY CONSEQUENCES

When a firm responds to a price reduction by a competitor, two serious secondary consequences can arise. First, a price reduction in one situation may affect sales outside of the specific opportunity at risk. Second, the firm's response to a price reduction by a competitor by matching that price reduction may lead to further rounds of price reductions.

Price concessions in one opportunity may enable other customers to demand a similar price concession in other situations. In industrial markets, it is possible for customers to learn of price concessions granted to specific clients. Other customers may then use this information to demand similar price concessions during their next purchasing opportunity. As such, a price response to win a specific tactical sale can quickly become a strategic price reduction across the board. Likewise, in consumer markets, price concessions to some customers may be considered "unfair" if they are not provided to all customers. In the worst situation, highly profitable loyal customers discover price concessions granted to marginal customers but denied to themselves, and then go on to betray the brand. Firms can take steps to reduce these possibilities, but the threat should be assessed and mitigation strategies should be executed. The nature of this line of inquiry is to quantify the profits threatened if the price reduction spreads to other sales, and therefore determine if the price response will cost less than the expected sales loss.

The competitive nature of business and the desire to win every opportunity yields a managerial inclination to match or beat any competitor's price reduction. Left unchecked, this inclination can yield to developing an industry pricing atmosphere that is cutthroat, destroying the profits of all players within the industry and leaving all industry competitors weaker. Price responses to a competitor's price reduction may be followed by a further price cut by that competitor. The threat of a second round of price competition may lead to further profit erosion and loss of pricing credibility. Before responding, companies should calculate the potential of wandering aimlessly into a damaging price war that can spread throughout the industry. They may use a line of questions similar to this: If a price response is made, is it likely the competitor will further cut its price? Can the firm continue to match sequential price cuts?

STRATEGIC POSITION

Price reductions by a competitor may be driven by a difference in competitive advantage. When a competitor has a cost advantage, its ability to reduce prices and remain profitable is greater than the original firm's ability to follow suit. Firms at a cost disadvantage have a higher strategic interest in raising industry-level prices—or at least not lowering them—than those with a cost advantage. As such, a firm may be better off averting a price war and granting market share concessions rather than entering into a war that it cannot win.

An example of this kind of industry makeover occurred in the steel industry when Nucor launched the use of mini-mills in 1989 to produce specific products at a low cost that targeted specific segments of the market. In the face of the cost advantages of mini-mills for these specific products, larger integrated steel companies had to cede some market segments in the 1990s.

Another example can be found in the dynamic PC market. In the decades leading up to 2005, Hewlett-Packard (HP) and Dell slugged it out, with Dell typically winning the price challenges. Dell had historically held a cost advantage in making PCs due to its direct-to-the-customer channel strategy, made-to-order inventory and manufacturing process, and accelerated accounts-receivable-to-accounts-payable cash management. In contrast, companies like HP faced cost disadvantages in PC markets due to their retail-channel strategy, which was accompanied by higher inventory costs and slower payments from customers in comparison to the timing of payments to suppliers. This enabled Dell to price aggressively in the PC market and take market share. Between 2005 and 2009, however, the tides changed. HP had developed a consulting arm within its organization and acquired EDS, a systems integration firm, to enable it to couple software sales with PCs.[3] This granted HP more leeway than Dell to participate in bidding wars for big corporate PC contracts because HP could afford to reduce prices for PCs that it sells in combination with contracts for technical services and software, which have higher profit margins than PCs.

As these examples indicate, it is important for executives to examine the possibility that a competitor has a competitive advantage with respect to the pricing action. If they do, they may be wise to avoid a price response and make a market share concession. If they don't, it may signal the opportunity to attack.

Depending on a firm's strategic position, there are varying strategies that it can follow, including matching the price, pricing lower than the competitor's price, and accommodating the lost sales while maintaining its price. See Exhibit 15-2 for a summary of potential responses that a firm can take to a competitor's price reduction.[4]

Exhibit 15-2 Reacting to Price Reductions

Price Matching Is	Your Firm Is: Competitively Advantaged	Your Firm Is: Competitively Neutral or Disadvantaged
More Costly than Lost Sales or Allowing Market Entry	Ignore	Accommodate
Less Costly than Lost Sales or Allowing Market Entry	Attack	Defend

Initiating Price Reductions

The general who wins the battle makes many calculations in his temple before the battle is fought. The general who loses makes but few calculations beforehand.

—*Sun Tzu,* The Art of War

Measure twice, cut once.

—*Anonymous*

Outside of opportunism, there are strategic reasons for imitating a price reduction. Price may be a strategic focus of the firm, stripping out costs to serve a larger market at a lower price point and capture a significant market share. When a firm determines that it is in its best interest to resolve the price-to-value tradeoff in favor of its customers, it should gauge the likely competitive response prior to executing its strategy.

PRICE AS A STRATEGIC FOCUS

Southwest, IKEA, and Wal-Mart all share a common focus of reducing costs and prices simultaneously to profitably take market share and enter unserved and underserved markets. They are able to do this by carefully examining the points of value sought by the market and removing attributes and benefits that the market will forgo to achieve a lower price point. At times, they will also add new points of value that were previously unconsidered.

For example, IKEA, a furniture and home goods retailer, has in the past operated as a model firm for using price as a strategic focus. In designing a new product, IKEA would first determine the target price and market need, from which all further decisions would be made. Product attributes, such as the overall design, the use of specific wood laminate finishing on specific surfaces, and fastener selection, would then follow from the need to deliver the product at a cost below the target price. The result would be a set of functional products for home needs. Although IKEA's products were not known for longevity compared to products from high-end furniture stores, they were known for solving immediate furnishing needs effectively.

IKEA's cost containment flowed throughout the design of the retailer's operations as well. Suppliers would be selected through a competitive bidding process, parts of a specific dining set might be sourced from different suppliers, and even the fasteners might derive from Poland while the frame hails from Vietnam. Their focus on reducing costs, and hence profit at a lower price point, also drove IKEA to rely on customers for co-creating much of the value. Customers would be given the task of picking up their own furniture rather than having it delivered. They were also responsible for assembling the furniture at home. Even in marketing, IKEA placed a heavy reliance on customer word-of-mouth to drive traffic and subsequent sales.

Just as IKEA removed some attributes from the value proposition, it also created new ones. For instance, IKEA outlets were known for their well-lit retail space, large selection, and pleasant atmosphere, with complete room layouts to enable and encourage customer decision making. In contrast, other low-priced retailers were known for dank warehouses with a limited selection of items strewn about the floor in a seemingly random manner. While improving the shopping experience over its low-cost competitors did add some costs, it also greatly increased the attraction of IKEA to customers who otherwise would refrain from shopping altogether.

Competitors may try to copy a portion of the cost management techniques and price targeting, but they face a difficulty in creating a similar level of strategic fit between resources necessary to match IKEA's price point. This has enabled IKEA to enjoy a consistent cost advantage over competitors, leading to prices comparable to low-end furniture retailers while providing some points of differentiation that would attract some higher-end customers.

The use of price as a strategic focus can be an outcome from a highly customer-oriented strategy. In this strategy, price targets are set according to customer willingness to pay, rather than costs to produce. From price targets, firms like IKEA create cost targets. Most companies have operated from a manufacturing-and-cost orientation, from which prices are set. A customer-and-price orientation works in the exact opposite direction. Prices determine costs when price is a strategic focus, rather than letting costs determine price.

When using price as a strategic focus in a radical form of customer orientation, the need and willingness to pay of customers determine every attribute of the firm's operations and products. In such a focus, the firm manages its only value proposition by determining to enter a market only if the customer's willingness to pay can be met profitably with a product that it can make and distribute at a lower cost. If not, firms like IKEA walk away from that specific market opportunity rather than try to convince customers to pay a higher price for the product.

GAUGING COMPETITIVE RESPONSE

In reducing prices or increasing the price-to-value tradeoffs faced by customers, executives should gauge the response of their competitors.[5] That is, if a company reduces price, will competitors react at all? What options will the competitor actively consider? Which option will the competitor most likely choose?

Two facts make this process effective: (1) Surveys show that most companies use rudimentary analytical techniques in determining a competitive response and therefore their competitive responses will be somewhat predictable. (2) Most companies follow a predictable pattern in reacting to a competitor's move; and therefore, executives can anticipate a competitor's future reactions by studying its past reactions.

Will the Competitor React at All?

In many situations, competitors will not react to a pricing action. Four lines of inquiry will enable executives to gauge the likelihood of a competitor response: (1) Will your rivals see your pricing action? (2) Will competitors feel threatened? (3) Will mounting a response be a priority? (4) Can your rivals overcome organizational inertia?

(1) Will your rivals see your pricing actions? Most competitors rely on incomplete data to assess change in the marketplace. For example, Wal-Mart does not participate in the dominant market-tracking services in the United States, which is significant because Wal-Mart sells roughly 20 percent of grocery items purchased in the United States. Similarly, smaller stores or stores outside a defined category may take pricing actions that are not documented by major market-tracking services. Because of these gaps in data, many firms will fail to notice the pricing actions of their competitors. One survey of executives found that only 12 percent of the firms learned about a price change in time to prepare a preemptive response.

(2) Will competitors feel threatened? Even if a competitor sees a firm's pricing actions, it may not feel threatened. Accordingly, that competitor will not think that mounting a response is worth the expense. Most organizations assess performance strictly against annual budgets. If the financial goals in the budget can still be met despite a competitive pricing action, management will see the company as "on plan" and feel safe. Firms can use public statements, such as earning targets, security analysts' estimates, or financial returns, to gauge the competitor's targets. If a pricing action will not encroach on the competitor's financial goals, it may not react.

(3) Will mounting a response be a priority? Your competitors already have an agenda in place before you take a pricing action. A competitor may be planning product launches, marketing campaigns, reorganizations, major acquisitions, plant openings, or cost reduction efforts. If it were to respond to a pricing action, it might need to curtail some of these activities. The degree to which a competitor is already engaged in current strategic goals will limit its ability to respond to a pricing action.

(4) Can your rivals overcome organizational inertia? Even if a competitor's management wanted to react, its organization as a whole may resist. Executives must muster the will to react to known threats if the damage from the threat is not imminent. Also, whereas all competitors will notice a large move, companies overestimate the likelihood that a medium to small action will be noticed. Thus the likelihood of no response in the real world is quite high.

What Options Will the Competitor Actively Consider?

An overwhelming majority of firms consider a maximum of four responses to a price change or new product launch, so it is reasonable for executives to develop an expectation of the potential responses to a price action. The single most common counteraction is to introduce a "me-too" product or matching a price change, both of which are highly obvious responses. A large portion of managers will consider what their business unit did the last time that it faced a similar situation. To a smaller degree, managers might consider the actions by other business units, seek board or expert advice, or defer to the specific experience of the executive in charge.

Which Options Will the Competitor Most Likely Choose?

A large number of competitors will not participate in an examination of their response based on game theory. They will consider only their direct response to a pricing action and fail to consider subsequent responses. If they do consider subsequent responses, they are very likely to consider no more than one stage of counterresponses. Very few will consider more than one round of responses by more than one competitor. As such, it is possible for executives to anticipate a competitor's response to a price action.

When a competitor evaluates its options, it is likely to consider the financial effects of different outcomes—that is, the effects of a price action and price response on short- and long-term market share changes or short- and long-term earnings. Executives can apply their adversary's decision-making process by using their own analytical techniques, including the rounds of competition, to determine the options that they think a competitor will examine. In this process, executives can uncover the option that they can anticipate that competitors will perceive as the best, and therefore the one that competitors are most likely to choose.

Managing Price Actions

The best victory is when the opponent surrenders of its own accord before there are any actual hostilities. . . . It is best to win without fighting.

—*Sun Tzu,* The Art of War

Speak softly and carry a big stick.

—*Theodore Roosevelt*

Because price wars are potentially extremely destructive, it is often best to reduce the potential for them. Furthermore, if a war has been initiated, firms may be able to act to limit its spread. Two techniques in particular have been widely demonstrated to mitigate the potential of a pricing action to deliver negative repercussions. These are price signaling and tit-for-tat pricing. Both of these techniques are designed to communicate to competitors that it is in their best interest to compete on grounds other than just price.

PRICE SIGNALING

In price signaling, firms communicate a strategic pricing action to their competitors indirectly. Direct communication with competitors regarding prices is a form of illegal collusion;

therefore firms cannot talk directly to each other about pricing decisions. However, communicating price decisions to markets in general is often viewed as a necessary market function to let customers know of a future price change or investors know of a potential revenue impact. Hence, firms may communicate a price action in a public forum, such as to the press or investors, with the intention of informing the market of a price change. In the process, they will also be signaling to competitors their strategic pricing action.

Price signaling can be used both for managing price reductions while limiting the potential for the breakout of a war, and for encouraging prices to rise within an industry. It is used by both dominant and smaller industry players as a method to take price leadership and exhibit price followership.

There are two key requirements to signal price changes effectively: (1) The price change must be announced in a highly public forum; and (2) the reasons for the price action must be credible. To signal a price change to a competitor, the price actions should be announced in a highly public forum. Signaling price actions to one's competitors in the hopes that they will follow the lead or cede the battle requires competitors to hear the signal. As such, price signaling is mostly done in well-read periodicals, such as business newspapers like the *Wall Street Journal* or *Financial Times*, or magazines that dominate the relevant industry.

It is often best, although not required, to pre-announce price changes when price signaling. Courts generally accept the pre-announcements of price changes as a necessary means to inform shareholders and customers of future price levels. However, firms should be careful if they want to interpret this as carte-blanche permission to test different price actions and await competitor responses. "Testing the waters" announcements are far riskier from a legal perspective than announcing a plan and executing it. Even if the price action is subsequently revoked due to failure by competitors to follow, it is might be safer to follow through from a legal perspective.

In sending a price signal, firms should cite credible reasons for the price change. Industry-wide input cost increases apply pressure to all competitors. Citing these cost increases as the cause of a price increase enables competitors to take the same price increase because it is in their best interest to operate within a healthy industry. If the firm is reducing prices due to a change in market demands or a new cost capability, it should communicate this as well so as to discourage an attempt by competitors to match that new lower price.

TIT-FOR-TAT PRICING

Tit-for-tat pricing is an extreme form of price followership in which a firm matches its competitor's price actions at every stage of the game. If the competitor lowers its price, the firm lowers its own price as well. If the competitor raises its price, the firm follows suit. All price moves are done in response to the competitor's price actions.

Tit-for-tat pricing removes price as a strategic dimension of competition. Done repeatedly, competitors will discover that any price move will simply be matched. Therefore, they will discover that lowering prices just hurts themselves, not to mention the industry health overall.

In responding to a price reduction by a competitor, firms can couple their price reduction with an announcement of their reasons for lowering the price as related to industrywide pricing pressure and its damage to profitability. Once a competitor raises the price, firms can respond quickly with matching price increases to demonstrate their willingness to end the price war.

The point of tit-for-tat pricing isn't to destroy enemies but to convince them that the battle is not worth fighting. It is a means to fight for a peaceful resolution to a price war in which the firm can flourish in the future.

Summary

- Rarely do companies enter a price war on purpose. The cost of a price war is inherently expensive, with the immediate loss of profits or, worse, mounting losses over time. The long-term benefits are doubtful, with a likely resurgence of competitive pressures once the war is over.
- The prisoner's dilemma highlights the potential for an opportunistic pricing action to lead to an all-out price war that leaves all competitors within an industry worse off.
- Some industries are plagued by constant price pressures, while others compete in a relatively healthy pricing environment. The five key structural drivers that lead to excessive price competition are (1) a lack of industry concentration, (2) low levels of managerial maturity, (3) high fixed costs coupled with low marginal costs, (4) growth industries with the potential for economic savings to be generated as the industry matures, and (5) growth industries in which the potential exists for network externalities to drive customers to a handful of concentrated players as the industry matures.
- Competitive advantages can come from economies of scale, scope, or learning. Economies of scale refer to cost reductions that are derived from specialization or spreading the costs of fixed assets over more units as the volume of production increases. Economies of scope are derived from the breadth of a firm's activities, perhaps deriving from spreading the costs of fixed assets over a wider variety of units. Economies of learning are derived from experience as measured by accumulated output.
- In calculating the response to a competitor's price reduction, executives should calibrate their actions after considering three issues: (1) What are the direct costs and direct benefits of responding in tandem to a competitor's price move? (2) What are the likely secondary consequences from taking a price response? (3) Does that competitor have a strategic cost advantage that enables it to profit at a lower industry price point?
- Besides opportunism, there are strategic reasons for imitating a price reduction. For instance, price may be a strategic focus of the firm, stripping out costs to serve a larger market at a lower price point and capture a significant market share.
- When a company determines it is in its best interest to improve the price-to-value tradeoff in favor of its customers, it should gauge the likely competitive response prior to executing this strategy.
- Two techniques in particular have been widely demonstrated to mitigate the potential of a pricing action to deliver negative repercussions. These are price signaling and tit-for-tat pricing. Both of these techniques are designed to communicate to competitors that it is in their best interest to compete on dimensions other than price.

Sony vs. Microsoft Game Console Case Exercise

In 2007, Sony launched the PS3, the next-generation product to the PS2, into an already hotly contested gaming console market. Between 2007 and 2009, the Sony PS3 product line has been most comparable with the Microsoft Xbox product line. Within each of these product lines, different product versions differed chiefly in hard drive capacity. Between these product lines, the Sony PS3 differed from the Microsoft Xbox chiefly in offering HD Blu-ray video playing. Read the following reference articles concerning the gaming console market (listed under item 8) and address the following questions.

1. At what price did Sony launch the PS3, and how did its price and features compare to the most comparable Microsoft Xbox 360?
2. How did Microsoft react to Sony's entrance into the high-end gaming console market?
3. By September 2008, which gaming console was winning more market share, PS3 or Xbox, and how did the competitor with the lower market share react?
4. How did the prices of the Sony PS3 and Microsoft Xbox evolve between 2007 and 2009?
5. In August 2009, Sony announced a further price reduction on the PS3. What was Microsoft's reaction, and how quick was it?
6. If you were advising Sony executives, what strategic actions would you suggest to minimize the risk of an increase in price competition in the gaming console market? Would you give the same advice if the Microsoft Xbox began to outsell the Sony PS3?
7. If you were advising Microsoft executives, what strategic actions would you suggest to minimize the risk of an increase in price competition in the gaming console market? Would you give the same advice if the Microsoft Xbox had a cost advantage to the Sony PS3?
8. Sony vs. Microsoft Case References
   a. Nick Wingfield, "Sony Cuts PlayStation 3 Price to Lift Sales," *Wall Street Journal* (July 9, 2007): B-4.
   b. Roger Cheng, "Business Technology: Microsoft Sets Price Cuts in Bid to Boost Xbox Sales," *Wall Street Journal* (August 7, 2007): B-4.
   c. Nick Wingfield, "Microsoft Cuts Xbox to $199," *Wall Street Journal* (September 4, 2008): B-9.
   d. Se Young Lee, "Microsoft Lowers Price for Xbox 360," *Wall Street Journal* (August 28, 2009): B-6.

Notes

[1] Theodore Paul Wright, "Factors Affecting the Cost of Airplanes, Learning Curve," *Journal of the Aeronautical Sciences* 3, No. 4 (February 1936): 122–28.

[2] John C. Panzar and Robert D. Willig, "Economies of Scope," *American Economic Review* 71, No. 2 (May 1981): 268–72.

[3] Justin Scheck, "Corporate News: PC Makers to Show Their Mettle—Analysts Expect H-P Was Better Positioned Amid Downturn Than Dell," *Wall Street Journal Eastern Edition* (May 19, 2009): B-5.

[4] Thomas T. Nagle and Reed K. Holden, "Competition," in *The Strategy and Tactics of Pricing: A Guide to Profitable Decision Making*, 3d ed. (Upper Saddle River, NJ: Prentice Hall, 2002): 133.

[5] Kevin P. Coyne and John Horne, "Predicting Your Competitor's Reaction," *Harvard Business Review* 87, No. 4 (April 2009): 90–97.

Chapter

16

Product Life Cycle Pricing

Image copyright James Steidl, 2010. Used under copyright from Shutterstock.com

Grafissimo/iStockphoto.com

- How do unit sales and profits evolve over the product life cycle?
- How does customer behavior evolve over the course of the product life cycle?
- Can prices increase over the course of the product life cycle?
- How must the emphasis of pricing policy change over the course of the product life cycle?
- Stretch Question: How does the product life cycle inform pricing strategy?

The product life cycle is a useful concept for understanding industry market trajectories.[1] In its most strategic form (which is the form we will consider in this chapter), the product life cycle refers to entire product categories rather than individual products, brands, or firms within that product category. According to the product life cycle concept, product categories pass through phases of introduction, growth, maturity, and eventual decline, much like a biological ecosystem. In each phase of the product life cycle, specific characteristics of the market take form. Changes in market dynamics between the different product life cycle stages in turn drive a necessary change in marketing strategy, and more specifically pricing strategy, to capture the market profitably.

Product life cycles are understood as a measure of industry behavior with respect to time. The behavior under investigation may be measured in terms of revenue, market saturation, unit demand, or profits, and it is usually plotted on the vertical axis. Units of

Exhibit 16-1 Product Life Cycle

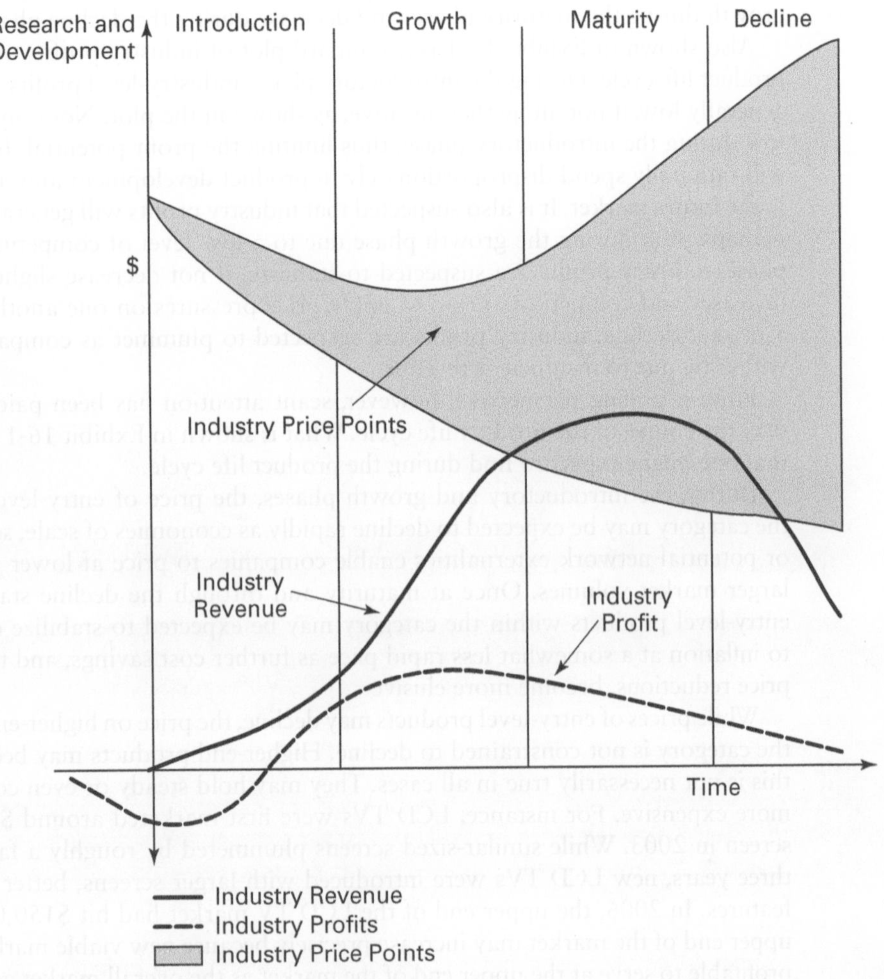

time, be it months, years, decades, or perhaps even centuries, are all on the horizontal axis. See Exhibit 16-1 for a purely qualitative, although conceptually representative, plot of the product life cycle.

Although Exhibit 16-1 represents each phase as having equal duration, most phases during the product life cycle are of differing durations. Moreover, before a product is launched and sales begin, a firm may spend years to decades in research and development. As such, the product category's profit at launch will be negative.

Once launched, the introduction of a new product may take months to years to find its market. Once a product has found its market, the growth phase is known to last as short as months and as long as decades. Maturity is usually, although not always, a prolonged state of affairs. For instance, synthetic laundry detergent like Tide, introduced in 1947, is currently still in the mature phase. Meanwhile, small stuffed animals such as Beanie Babies by Ty hit their heyday between 1995 and 1999 and then moved back into relative obscurity. The decline period can be as short as months, such as was seen in the market for standard metallic stents when they were displaced by drug-eluting stents, or decades followed by finding a niche use, such as in the case of coal locomotives, which are still used for amusement parks and specific applications.

As shown in Exhibit 16-1, industry revenues start low during the introductory phase, increase rapidly during the growth phase, stabilize or grow at the rate of population growth during the maturity phase, and decrease during the decline phase.

Also shown in Exhibit 16-1 is a standard plot of industry profits over the course of a product life cycle. During the introductory phase, industry-level profits are suspected to be generally low, if not altogether negative, as shown in the plot. Not only are sales volumes low during the introductory phase, thus limiting the profit potential, but also companies will rationally spend disproportionately in product development and marketing to invest in the future market. It is also suspected that industry profits will generally rise rapidly and perhaps peak during the growth phase due to a low level of competition. In the mature phase, industry profits are suspected to stabilize, if not decrease slightly, as competition increases and competitors begin to apply price pressures on one another. Finally, during a market decline, industry profits are suspected to plummet as companies are forced to withdraw due to insufficient revenue.

From a pricing perspective, however, scant attention has been paid to price changes over the course of the product life cycle. What is shown in Exhibit 16-1 is a band of prices that one might expect to find during the product life cycle.

During the introductory and growth phases, the price of entry-level products within the category may be expected to decline rapidly as economies of scale, scope, and learning or potential network externalities enable companies to price at lower points and attract larger market volumes. Once at maturity and through the decline stage, price levels of entry-level products within the category may be expected to stabilize or decline relative to inflation at a somewhat less rapid pace as further cost savings, and therefore potential price reductions, become more elusive.

While prices of entry-level products may decline, the price on higher-end products within the category is not constrained to decline. Higher-end products may become cheaper, but this is not necessarily true in all cases. They may hold steady or even continually become more expensive. For instance, LCD TVs were first marketed around $4,000 for a small screen in 2003. While similar-sized screens plummeted by roughly a factor of 10 within three years, new LCD TVs were introduced with larger screens, better sound, and other features. In 2006, the upper end of the LCD TV market had hit $150,000.[2] Prices at the upper end of the market may increase precisely because new viable market niches become profitable to serve at the upper end of the market as the overall market grows. Even during the decline of a product category, specific niches of the market may be willing to pay a high price for products while the market in general may have a low willingness to pay.

What follows is a description of the pricing challenge during each phase of the product life cycle. Changes in the pricing challenge result from changes in the market makeup or, more specifically, changes in the characteristics of customers that are associated with each phase in the product life cycle.

Introduction

During the introduction phase, a revolutionary product is launched, which creates an entirely new market. Although the term "revolutionary" is commonly applied to many products by marketers promoting their newest product formulations, truly revolutionary products are rare. Revolutionary products represent only a small fraction of the new products on the market at any given time, and many researchers with a more critical bent would argue that truly revolutionary products are launched sporadically on time scales of once per every few years, if not decades.

Examples of radically revolutionary products include locomotives and railways for transporting goods, information technology for managing records, and cellular phone systems for communication. Radically revolutionary products not only created a new market, but they also changed entire industries that were not directly related to the product launch, as well as customer behaviors as markets adapted these products. Less radical but no less revolutionary are products ranging from aluminum cans to hybrid corn seed and advanced metering infrastructure. The launch of these revolutionary products may have affected large swaths of the general public, but only a handful of industries were affected directly.

From a strategic sense, revolutionary products are products that satisfy a market need in a manner that hitherto had never been considered or was considered impossible. Revolutionary products may address an existing market need in an entirely different manner than other products on the market, or they may address a new market demand that had previously been considered unaddressable.

For instance, advanced metering infrastructure solutions were initially launched as a means to read residential electric meters without needing a human meter reader. In this application, the market need to read meters existed prior to the launch of advanced metering infrastructure solutions, yet the remote and automatic collection of meter data was not possible prior to the introduction of low-cost wireless communication solutions. As the market evolved over two decades, initial solutions in the advanced metering infrastructure market also evolved to address entirely new market needs, such as the speedy identification of power outages or demand-response market structures. Prior to the introduction of advanced metering infrastructure, power outages were identified primarily through customers notifying the power company of an outage. After the implementation of advanced metering infrastructure solutions, utilities were able to pinpoint the source of a power outage and remedy the situation quicker. Similarly, prior to the deployment of advanced metering infrastructure, utilities were limited in their ability to charge different rates depending on the time of day. Following their implementation, prices for electricity could be adjusted based on the time of day, overall demand level, or any other factor allowed by regulatory authorities.

Revolutionary products are disruptive in nature. The introduction of trains transformed the transportation industry, disrupting established industry structures focused on transport via canal or horse and wagon. Similarly, the introduction of broadcast television disrupted the previously established structure focused on radio broadcasts. More recently, the Internet has disrupted established business models of newspapers and other media, telephony and other communication technology, and postal services and other document delivery products.

Launching revolutionary products is a fundamentally different task from marketing existing products or launching products that are enhancements to existing products. They enter markets that did not exist before. As such, customers are unfamiliar with the new product category and their buying habits are nonexistent. Consequently, the analytical rigor for pricing the product is limited, while the freedom to establish the price structure is relatively wide.

Revolutionary products succeed by fulfilling a **latent demand**. Latent demand implies that the desire for the solution to a problem existed prior to the launch of the product, but that no viable solution existed. That is, the demand existed but could not express itself because no product existed that could fulfill the demand. Once the product is introduced, the latent demand becomes activated and is expressed in the form of purchases. In unleashing the latent demand, a new product category is created.

The concept of latent demand in relation to expressed demand can be considered as analogous to the physical concepts of potential energy and kinetic energy. A ball held at the top of the hill has potential energy that can be converted to kinetic energy once it is released and begins to roll down the hill. Similarly, a customer with a seemingly unattainable goal has latent demand for a means to reach that goal. Once that means becomes accessible by the introduction of a revolutionary product, the customer makes a purchase, converting this latent demand into an expressed demand.

For instance, the iPod and iTunes are solutions to the desire to access music electronically and portably. MP3 players, the Internet, and other technology existed prior to the introduction of iTunes and iPods, but never before were they assembled in such a seamless manner to enable easy customer purchase and enjoyment of music. In this sense, customers had a latent desire to purchase music by the song and carry it around conveniently, but previously they were unable to do so. With iTunes and iPods, the market expressed its desires, converting latent demand into expressed demand.

Similarly, Zipcar and other fractional car ownership services enable urbanites to access cars without actually owning them. Prior to Zipcar, urban dwellers in premier cities with functional mass transit would need to purchase a car for infrequent trips for large items or to travel beyond the urban core. Yet, a majority of the time, these urban dwellers would see their car sit idle in an expensive parking lot as they used mass transit, bicycles, or walking to commute to work or meet most daily transportation needs. With fractional car ownership, Zipcar customers have access to an automobile for the brief periods that they need them, and they do not have to assume the costs or responsibilities of full ownership such as gas and insurance. (Zipcar estimates that each single Zipcar serves the needs that would have otherwise required twenty individual cars.) Furthermore, individual Zipcars are made available at hundreds of sites at neighborhood parking lots within a single city on a per-hour basis, making them far more convenient to access, and at a lower overall cost, than traditional car rental services. Zipcar tapped into the latent demand for infrequent car mobility without the hassles of car ownership.

Another example can be found in the energy market. The market would like to find an economical means to tap into renewable energy sources, and thus there is a latent demand for green energy. In the absence of further advances in science and technology, we have maintained a global dependence on fossil fuels. In the coming years and decades, we can anticipate a new solution to be developed as the destructive impact of our reliance on fossil fuels becomes increasingly apparent and the global supplies of fossil fuels dwindle. Once it does, our latent demand for green energy will be expressed.

The focal marketing challenge during the introductory phase of the product life cycle is gaining critical mass. Companies launching a revolutionary product must identify which segment within the marketplace will benefit from its features and derive value from its use. They must understand the value proposition from that segment's specific viewpoint. In addition, they must educate that segment on the value that they will derive from the new product. All this must occur to capture the initial market.

CUSTOMERS OF INTRODUCTORY MARKETS

In the introduction phase of the product life cycle, customers have been characterized as Tinkerers and Visionaries, where Tinkerers constitute most of the early market and Visionaries constitute most the latter market during the introductory phase.[3] These two groups evaluate revolutionary products for entirely different properties. As such, they also exhibit different criteria when determining their willingness to pay, which in turn determines the company's price latitude.

Tinkerers

Tinkerers are people who appreciate a new product due to its revolutionary properties themselves. They are the very small segment of society that enthusiastically tracks technological and product developments. They primarily derive enjoyment out of watchfully participating in the evolution of technology and products overall. Tinkerers have a proclivity to "toy" with new products rather than solve business problems with the product. As such, tinkerers have been known by many names, such as "enthusiasts" and "hobbyists," as well.

When Tinkerers evaluate a new product, they seek to explore its properties, capabilities, and uses. They are often entranced by the architecture of the product, and compare products on the basis of their artful integration of technology with tangibility.

When they have an opportunity to interact with a new product, they are willing to play with it to make it do things that the originator may not have had in mind. In doing so, they are developing an expanded sense of value for the new product, and therefore they are co-creating the future market for the product. As such, Tinkerers are an important market segment to court, for they help entrepreneurial endeavors reach their goal.

In terms of behavior, Tinkerers are an interesting breed. They have been described as highly factually driven, eschewing lofty stories and instead seeking detailed evidence to evaluate the new product. When they have a difficulty with a new product, they will seek to bypass the firm's customer service, sales, and marketing people altogether and desire to work directly with technical departments to resolve a challenge.

Within organizations in business-to-business markets, Tinkerers are not typically key decision makers, and their influence over budgets is highly limited. Furthermore, they tend not to follow "value-added" arguments and instead seek to have access to technology "at cost."

From a pricing perspective, companies have an incentive to get new products to Tinkerers due to their willingness to co-create the future market for the product. Unfortunately, they also face the challenge of needing to price their product low to capture the Tinkerer segment, but in doing so, they will be artificially setting the reference price for the product too low for future sales. Doing this will drive the firm to forgo potential profits that may be earned in later product life cycle phases. To manage this divergent set of goals, some firms have attempted to distribute loaner kits and beta products—products specifically designed and priced for the Tinkerer segment but not quite appropriate for the general market. Usually, such Tinkerer-focused versions of revolutionary products are launched with stiff limitations on use or requirements for returning after a short examination period.

Visionaries

Visionaries are people who are seeking a quantum leap forward in addressing a challenge. They are constantly searching for revolutionary products that will help them achieve their desired goals. Unlike Tinkerers, Visionaries primarily derive enjoyment from revolutionary products by using them to solve a challenge or set of challenges in an entirely different manner than has hitherto been accomplished. In terms of market size, Visionaries constitute a small fraction of the potential market, but they are a much more significant segment than Tinkerers. Visionaries constitute the Early Adapters.

When Visionaries consider a revolutionary new product, they are not looking to make an incremental improvement but rather a strategic breakthrough in solving a problem. If they are a business customer, they are seeking an order-of-magnitude return on investment, not a standard small percentage of improvement with a long-term payback. They are driven by a dream, a goal to take a quantum leap forward in how things are done. Visionaries want to go where no human has gone before in terms of solving problems.

Visionaries are characterized as individuals with the insight to match an emerging solution to a strategic opportunity. They have the temperament to translate that insight into a high-visibility, high-risk project. Moreover, they have access to cash to pay for a revolutionary new product.

In business markets, Visionaries are necessarily senior executives. Visionaries require both charisma and the necessary power required to get the rest of the organization behind their decision to implement a risky but promising new technology. In approaching the purchase decision, they are willing to take the necessary risks with the revolutionary product but also will seek to identify routes to mitigate these risks. For instance, Visionaries in business markets have been described as highly project-oriented, implementing the revolutionary product in phases, where each phase is associated with a project milestone and potential exit. If a milestone is completed successfully, Visionaries may seek to productize that phase of the deliverable into a subproduct within the new product category.

Visionaries are known to be less price-sensitive than Tinkerers, but more results-sensitive. Their results sensitivity derives from their purchasing goals. Visionaries are looking for great improvements with overwhelmingly significant value to compensate them for the risks they are taking by purchasing a revolutionary, but untested and unproven, product. Upon success, they are willing to serve as a highly visible reference because the success of the product reflects not only on the revolutionary product's strengths but also the ability of the Visionary to recognize the strengths and exploit them. So long as the value is there, Visionaries are suspected to have the willingness to pay.

PRICING IN INTRODUCTORY MARKETS

Executives launching a revolutionary new product into the introductory market will have tremendous pricing latitude but will face two very difficult pricing challenges: (1) What should the price level be? (2) What should the price structure be?

In introductory markets, there may be no directly comparable products to serve as points of comparison. Moreover, the introductory market previously didn't exist prior to the product launch, and even after launch, the market will remain small for a while. Thus, it is unrealistic to use most econometric and customer-oriented research methods with any accuracy. Most importantly, the customers within the potential market have no experience with the product and, in general, will have a poor understanding of the potential value of the product. Thus, customer-reported willingness to pay is likely to yield a wide array of potential price points with little apparent logic and poor correlation with value.

To price a product within an introductory market, executives are usually best served by using exchange value models such as in the case of the Cordis drug eluting stent that was discussed in Chapter 1. The other dominant price-setting methodologies are fundamentally ill-suited for introductory markets. Customers are unfamiliar with the product category and uneducated regarding the benefits of specific features. Therefore, in general they will be ill-suited to make rational tradeoffs required for conjoint analysis techniques to yield meaningful results. As for economic price optimization techniques, these rely on a historic pattern of price changes and volume changes that does not exist for products that, prior to their launch, also did not exist.

Exchange value models rely on internal management's assessment of the value of a revolutionary product. One method for generating this model is to conduct an As Is/To Be analysis. In this type of analysis, management will develop an introspective understanding of the process in which customers solve a problem on the day before they purchased the revolutionary product, and then again on the day after. This enables them to develop a picture of the implications of their revolutionary product and hence the economic exchange value.

From the exchange value model, executives may be able to develop an understanding of optimal price structures as well. In this exercise, executives will be searching for metrics that enable the price to track to the value that it delivers to different customer segments.

Research into the habits of highly successful entrepreneurs indicates that companies launching revolutionary products are likely to be best served by pricing products at the upper end of the potential price spectrum generated from the exchange value calculator.[4] Part of the logic behind this approach to pricing high derives from the characteristics of the introductory market. The more temperamentally cautious market segments are unlikely to purchase a new revolutionary product regardless of its price. Visionaries, on the other hand, are the more realistic market segment to be captured, and they are not known for stinginess in spending; they are only demanding in terms of value delivered. Hence, highly successful entrepreneurs tend to price revolutionary products at the upper end of the potential price range. While entrepreneurs cannot succeed by overpricing the product in comparison to the value that it delivers, they also shouldn't be afraid to price a revolutionary product at a level that reflects its potential value to customers.

Growth

The growth phase of the product life cycle is marked with rapid changes in every dimension of the newly emerged market. New customers enter the market and adopt the products within the emergent category, leading to multiple market segments. Accompanying the entrance of more customers into the market are new competitors attracted by the profit potential of the new category. Competitors will explore different configurations and possibilities within the product category, leading to product proliferation, feature differentiation, and price-point variations. In addition, the product category will have passed the point of being revolutionary and begin a rapid evolutionary trajectory.

Evolutionary products are products in which specific features or benefits are added or subtracted from the core product. Product evolutions may come in the form of varying styles, designs, or types that satisfy different customer desires. They may also come in the form of feature differentiation, in which capabilities of the product are altered to satisfy specific needs of customer segments.

The rapid evolutionary nature of products in growth markets is supported by the concurrent entrance of both competitors and customers. As competitors develop new products for the market, they also expand the value points for different customers. By expanding the points of value delivered by products within the category, more customers are induced to purchase. When sufficient customers with differing tastes have entered, market segmentation becomes viable because it becomes profitable to serve specific market niches rather than the mass market as a whole. Also, the development of market niches encourages still more competitors to enter. It is a virtuous cycle of growth as both companies and customers derive value from the newly emerged product category.

In the growth phase of the product life cycle, firms may begin to realize cost savings as their business grows. These cost savings may derive from economies of scale, the reduction of production costs with increases in volume; scope, the reduction of production costs related to increases in the scope of business operations; or learning, the reduction of production costs related to improvements in manufacturing gleaned from experience. The cost savings not only enable firms to earn higher profits potentially, but also enable lower prices that further favor market growth.

In the growth phase, network externalities may emerge that enable firms to aggregate customers and rapidly improve their relative revenue standing. Network externalities may derive from peer-to-peer interactions with customers that are facilitated when all customers share a common technology, as happened with email communications, word processing, spreadsheets, and presentations during the 1990s. They may also derive from the participation of partners within the market, as has happened with software application developers that made products for specific computing, gaming, and mobile handset operating systems. These network externalities may enable specific competitors to succeed while others wither away.

The anticipation of realizing significant cost or revenue effects in the future maturity phase of the product life cycle can place excessive downward pressure on prices during the growth phase of the product life cycle. On the cost side, the anticipation of economies of scale, scope, or learning can encourage firms to use low prices as a means to generate the required economies. On the revenue side, the anticipation of network externalities that drive a disproportionate amount of the revenue to a single competitor or a small handful of industry competitors can also can encourage companies to use low prices as a means to generate the required customer mass.

CUSTOMERS OF GROWTH MARKETS

In the growth phase of the product life cycle, customers have been characterized as Early Majority, followed by the Late Majority and Laggards. The following sections describe these three segments.

Early Majority

The Early Majority segment consists of customers who seek incremental improvements and appreciate the new product category for its ability to deliver value with manageable risk. They are noted as being highly value-sensitive and reasonably price-sensitive. Purchase decisions by the Early Majority are not driven by costs alone, but more by the difference between the value that they will derive and the price that they must pay to gain that value.

In business markets, the Early Majority usually is made up of people of CEO rank. They will have developed a belief that "leading edge" often means "bleeding edge," and so they have refrained from market participation in the introductory phase. However, their drive for building and capturing value will induce them into market participation once the product category has emerged from the more experimental introduction phase to the more evolutionary growth phase.

Chief executives will seek to limit the risks that they take with revolutionary products. As such, they will desire to use standardization and rely on a minority of suppliers to deliver turnkey solutions. In interacting with suppliers, they will be concerned with all aspects of the purchasing relationship, including supplier staying power, aftermarket support, and anticipation of future product enhancements and complementary products. Some of these aspects in supplier selection may create a level of network externalities as customers use their own competitors to help select market winners.

The wide scope of responsibility of CEOs will drive them to consider numerous implications of the new product category, such as organizational and process changes required to reap value from the product implementation.

Late Majority and Laggards

The Late Majority and Laggards segments include customers who would have preferred that the new product had not come into existence but have been forced by reality to adapt to the product. In essence, they like tradition and continuity and hold some disdain for discontinuous innovation.

In purchasing decisions, the Late Majority and Laggards are picky, reluctant buyers. They seek products that meet their specific needs, preferring single-function products and showing little interest in fancy features. Once they have what works for them, they will tend to stick with it and exhibit a reasonable level of brand loyalty. They have low tolerance for risk and fundamentally want the product to function like a reliable refrigerator: Open door, lights on; close door, lights off.

The Late Majority and Laggard customers are noted as being highly price-sensitive because they hold limited expectations of deriving improvements with the new product.

PRICING IN GROWTH MARKETS

Executives operating in growth markets will have less pricing latitude than in the introductory market, but they will also benefit from better pricing accuracy and practices. This will affect the methods used to price products, as well as the potential to explore new price structures for capturing customers.

In growth markets, customers will have greater familiarity with the product category than they did during the introductory market. This enables customers to make informed tradeoffs between different product features and anticipate the benefits derived from alternative product configurations. Furthermore, the number of customers participating in the market increases, enabling statistical customer research–based methodologies to deliver reasonably reliable metrics of customer preferences. As such, customer perception–based pricing methodologies, such as the conjoint analysis explored in the pricing of mango juice in Chapter 3, can be used for setting reasonably accurate prices.

Exchange value models developed within the introductory phase shift in importance from enabling price setting into becoming a sales tool for communicating the value of participating in the market. While they still predict an accurate range of acceptable prices, the variance in price points generated from exchange value models can be reduced greatly through conjoint analysis. As such, competitors in growth markets usually shift their price-setting techniques to customer preference–based methodologies.

New price structures are usually explored in growth markets. Competitors may begin to explore add-ons and versioning as means to capture a wider variety of market segments, as was executed by Intuit in the late 1990s as it launched both a versioning strategy with different levels of Quicken Home Finance and an add-on strategy with Turbo Tax. They may also begin to unbundle products that were previously bundled to serve the Late Majority and Laggards segments. Unbundling has been seen in the U.S. mobile market in the first decade of the twenty-first century, in which the market that was initially dominated by postpaid plans with long-term contracts in exchange for "free" mobile handsets, evolved to offer simplified prepaid plans with the separate purchase of mobile handsets.

Price levels within growth markets generally decline, but not every product with a growth market will necessarily be priced lower than the revolutionary products of the introductory market. Downward price pressure will be driven by the entrance of new competitors and potentially supported by lower cost structures. Upward price movements will be made possible by the expansion of the market to include different market segments, some of which will have a higher willingness to pay in exchange for the delivery of greater benefits and value.

INTERTEMPORAL PRICE DISCRIMINATION

Between the introductory and growth phases of the product life cycle, prices of entry-level products within the new category will often drop. This phenomenon can be ascribed to a pricing technique known as *intertemporal price discrimination*.

Intertemporal price discrimination is a form of price discrimination that enables a firm to capture value from those who value it the most. In intertemporal price discrimination, time itself acts as the segmentation hedge. Early customers in a new product category, such as Visionaries and the Early Majority, are suspected to be less price-sensitive than later customers, such as the Late Majority and Laggards. Executives can use this insight to price a product at a high level initially and sequentially reduce the price as new market segments enter the market.

Intertemporal price discrimination is similar to, but distinct from, price skimming. While prices may move in a similar manner, the drivers behind the two strategies are different. Price skimming is defined as pricing high relative to competing products within the category. At the launch of a new product category, there are no competing products; therefore, it is impossible to discuss relative price differentials in introductory markets. Price skimming can occur within growth markets as competitors enter, but it is an inadequate concept for explaining the intertemporal price discrimination and price-level movements observed between introductory and growth markets.

Intertemporal price discrimination raises an intriguing academic question known as the Coase problem.[5] Rational consumers may anticipate a future reduction in price correctly and therefore postpone their purchases. If they do, companies launching a product will not only suffer from lower profits due to an inability to price-discriminate, but may also fail to gain the initial traction required to achieve critical market mass. Hence, in a rational market, time segmentation would not be possible.

One solution to the Coase problem arose from considering heterogeneity in the market. As with other segmentation methods, difference in customer preferences is required to explain variations in prices. Economic arguments such as that which led to the Coase problem, based on the market as a whole, fail to explain realistic phenomena of markets with demand heterogeneity. Some customers will value having the new product first and will be willing to pay a premium for that privilege, while others will value knowing that they are purchasing a popular product and purchase later in the product life cycle and with an expectation of paying a lower price.

Maturity

In the mature phase of the product life cycle, demand growth, competitor turbulence, and rapid product evolution are replaced with more predictable industry dynamics. Further market growth is limited as product penetration reaches saturation. Rather than attracting new customer segments to the market, the market grows through overall increase of economic productivity and welfare or of the general population. While products continue to evolve, further product modifications tend to be less radical than that seen in the earlier stages of the product life cycle. The nature of competition will have been established, and firms will often pursue one of the more common competitive strategies of cost leadership, product differentiation, or niche marketing.[6]

Accuracy in price setting in mature markets improves due to better understanding of the market. Customer preference techniques such as conjoint continue to generate relevant prices in both consumer and business markets of sufficient size. For most mature markets, customer preference techniques will dominate price-setting challenges. In some more commodity-oriented industries, economic price optimization may become viable. With a reasonable track record of products within the market, it becomes possible for pricing managers to track historical variations between prices and volumes and develop statistically reliable correlations. As such, they can construct meaningful metrics of elasticity of demand, a required data point for conducting economic price optimization.

Price structures established in early product life cycle phases become somewhat more rigid during the mature phase. Customers begin to expect a standard price structure and select suppliers based on specific aspects of the structure. Meanwhile, competitors develop business models, processes, and organizations that are supportive and rely upon the established structure.

The rigidity of established price structures may create an opportunity for a strategic blow to competitors if a new price structure can be devised that profitably gains customer acceptance. An example of a price structure change creating dramatic strategic advances in mature markets can be seen in the airline market. American Airlines first introduced yield management into a somewhat mature airline industry in the 1980s. Its ability to adopt the yield management price structure evolved from the U.S. airline deregulation and advances in information technology and computerizing booking. When American Airlines switched to yield management, it achieved a dramatic increase in revenue per seat mile, which enabled it to solidify its position as an industry leader.

During the mature phase, the pressure to improve prices shifts the pricing challenge from a focus on establishing price structures and setting price levels and toward the importance of managing price variances. Due to competitive pressures and customer heterogeneity, couponing, discounting, and price promotions all become more common practices. Pricing organizations are developed to manage price variances better, yielding an incremental improvement in profit capturing. The development of price variance management organizations is typically accompanied by data management and analysis systems that automate some of the discount management techniques described in various chapters throughout this book.

Overall, industry-level profits are suspected to come under pressure during the mature phase of the product life cycle. The specific competitors may stabilize, but each will fight dearly for a single market share point. As such, companies will face price pressures throughout the mature phase of the market. Companies may also take steps to manage industry-level prices, mitigate the probability of future price wars, and manage price wars that flare up over time.

During the mature phase, companies may also enjoy some new sources of profitability. Cost advantages deriving from economies of scale, scope, and learning can be captured during the mature phase. Furthermore, some pressure is removed from innovation and can be shifted to process improvements that drive cost reduction or marketing improvements that drive revenue growth. However, in the long term, it is believed that competition squeezes prices toward the marginal costs, and further cost reductions will become elusive, reducing the potential to capture large profits.

Decline

Eventually, a product may become outdated as new products are introduced. In this case, the product category will go through decline. For instance, the industry for making stagecoaches and saddles, once common products throughout the western United States, declined rapidly after the advent of the automobile. However, not all industries will face the decline stage of the product life cycle. Demand for clean water is not anticipated to decrease during the span of the biological existence of advanced life forms.

When markets are facing decline, industry competitors can choose one of three strategies: Harvest, Consolidate, and Focus.[7] In a **Harvest** strategy, a company will slowly exit the market while extracting the remaining profits that it can from customers. During this period, the company will not invest in any plant or process improvements. A company executing a Harvest strategy can be helped out of the industry through an appropriate merger.

In a **Consolidate** strategy, a company will seek to become the last one serving the industry. Consolidation strategies often rely on establishing or maintaining a low-cost position through economies of scale or technological improvements. Consolidators often become a natural acquirer of Harvesters.

The third strategy executed during an industry decline, **Focus**, is supported by companies that are able to better serve the needs of a specific market niche that is anticipated to last. Companies executing a Focus strategy will exit areas of weakness and invest in areas of strength. Their strength may derive from advantages in cost, technology, customer relationship, or other strategic resource advantages.

While prices during declining markets tend to be volatile, it is not possible to make an a *priori* statement regarding the direction of all prices. In most industries, general competitive pressures may drive prices lower. In some industries, increased scarcity or the relegation of a product to a specific high-value niche demand may actually enable prices to increase.

Summary

- Product categories are observed to pass through phases of introduction, growth, maturity, and eventual decline. This cycle is referred to as the product life cycle. Each phase of the product life cycle can be associated with specific growth patterns, customer characteristics, and pricing challenges.
- Over the product life cycle, industry revenues are observed to start low during the introductory phase, increase rapidly during the growth phase, stabilize or grow at

the rate of population growth during the maturity phase, and decrease during the decline phase.

- Over the product life cycle, industry profits are observed to be mostly negative during the introductory phase, increase rapidly during the growth phase toward a maximum, stabilize or decline slightly during the maturity phase, and decrease rapidly during decline.
- During the introduction phase, a revolutionary product is launched that creates an entirely new market. Revolutionary products are products that satisfy a market need in a manner that hitherto had never been considered.
- Often, revolutionary products succeed by fulfilling a latent demand. Latent demand implies that the desire for the solution to a problem existed prior to the launch of the product, but that no viable solution existed.
- In the introduction phase of the product life cycle, customers have been characterized as Tinkerers and Visionaries, where Tinkerers constitute most of the earlier market and Visionaries constitute most of the later market during the introductory phase. Tinkerers are people who appreciate the new product on the basis of their revolutionary properties themselves. Visionaries are people who are seeking to deliver a quantum leap forward in terms of solving a challenge, and they are constantly searching for revolutionary products that will help them achieve their desired goals.
- Executives launching a revolutionary new product into the introductory market will have tremendous pricing latitude. To price a product within an introductory market, executives are best served by using exchange value calculators. From the exchange value model, executives may also be able to develop an understanding of optimal price structures as well.
- In the growth phase of the product life cycle, customers have been characterized as Early Majority, Late Majority, and Laggards. The Early Majority group consists of customers who seek incremental improvements and appreciate the new product category for its ability to deliver value with manageable risk. Late Majority and Laggards include customers who would have preferred that the new product not have come into existence but have been forced by reality to adapt to the product.
- Executives operating in growth markets will have less pricing latitude than in the introductory market, but they will also enjoy the benefit of better pricing accuracy and practices. Customer perception–based pricing methodologies, such as conjoint analysis, can be used for setting reasonably accurate prices during this phase.
- In the mature phase of the product life cycle, demand growth, competitor turbulence, and rapid product evolution are replaced with more predictable industry dynamics. Customer preference techniques such as conjoint continue to generate relevant prices in both consumer and business markets of sufficient size. In more commodity-oriented industries, economic price optimization may become viable.
- During the mature phase, the pressure to improve prices shifts the pricing challenge toward a focus on managing price variances.
- When markets are facing decline, industry competitors can choose one of three strategies: Harvest, Consolidate, and Focus. In a Harvest strategy, a company will slowly exit the market while extracting the remaining profits that it can from customers. In a Consolidate strategy, a company will seek to become the last one serving the industry. A Focus strategy is supported by companies that are able to better serve the needs of a specific market niche that is anticipated to last.

Amazon Kindle Case Exercise

The e-book reader market was initiated with the Sony Reader in 2006, but it didn't take off in the United States until Amazon launched the Kindle in November 2007. Since then, Barnes & Noble entered the e-book reader market with the Nook in November 2009, and more recently, Apple introduced the iPad in April 2010. Read the following reference articles concerning the e-reader market listed under item 8 and address the following questions:

1. How many Sony Readers were estimated to have been sold by the time of the launch of the Amazon Kindle?
2. What was the initial launch price of the Amazon Kindle, and how did the price and functionality compare to the existing Sony Reader?
3. In May 2008, Amazon dropped the price of the Kindle 2 to $359, and in June 2009, Amazon dropped the price of the Kindle 2 further, to $299. What did Amazon change the price of the Kindle 2 to in October 2009?
4. How many Amazon Kindles and Sony Readers were believed to be sold by 2009?
5. At what price did Barnes & Noble enter the market with its Nook, and how did it compare to the Amazon Kindle?
6. How did the functionality and price of the Apple iPad compare with the Amazon Kindle at the time that the iPad was launched?
7. How did Sony respond to the impending launch of the Apple iPad in March 2010?
8. By the time that the Apple iPad was launched, what were the models and prices of the Amazon Kindles? What were the key differences in benefits between the different Kindles?
9. By June 2010, what were the prices of the entry-level Amazon Kindle and Barnes & Noble Nook?
10. In what ways did the evolution of the e-book reader market follow the predictions of the product life cycle, and in what ways did it differ?
11. If you were advising Jeff Bezos, CEO of Amazon, what strategic actions would you suggest that Amazon take in the next twelve months to remain competitive in the e-reader market?
12. Amazon Case References
    a. Mylene Mangalindan and Jeffrey A. Trachtenberg, "IPod of E-Book Readers? Amazon Taps Apple Strategy," *Wall Street Journal* (November 20, 2007): B-1.
    b. Geoffrey A. Fowler and Jessica E. Vascellaro, "Sony, Google Challenge Amazon," *Wall Street Journal* (March 19, 2009): B-5.
    c. Geoffrey A. Fowler and Jeffrey A. Trachtenberg, "Amazon Cuts Price of Kindle E-Reader," *Wall Street Journal* (October 8, 2009): B-9.
    d. Jeffrey A. Trachtenberg, "Corporate News: B&N Holds Back Nook from Store," *Wall Street Journal* (November 30, 2009): B-2.
    e. Geoffrey A. Fowler and Yukari Iwatani Kane, "Apple's Big Push: New Device Revives Classic Gadget Debate—Consumer Electronics Makers Split Over Selling All-in-One Gizmos vs. Products with Specialized Purpose," *Wall Street Journal* (January 28, 2010): B-6.
    f. Geoffrey A. Fowler, "Business Technology: Sony Drops Price by $30 on E-Reader," *Wall Street Journal* (March 23, 2010): B-7.
    g. Yukari Iwatani Kane and Geoffrey A. Fowler, "For Amazon, Arrival of the iPad Opens Door to More e-Book Sales," *Wall Street Journal Online* (April 2, 2010);

http://online.wsj.com/article/SB10001424052702303338304575156622836258874.html?mod=WSJ_Tech_LEADTop (accessed on August 21, 2010).

h. Geoffrey A. Fowler, "Price Cuts Electrify E-Reader Market," *Wall Street Journal* (June 22, 2010): A-1.

Appendix 16 Bass Diffusion Model

Researchers have constructed quantitative models of the market dynamics during the introduction and growth phases of the product life cycle. The most explored model is a diffusion model developed by Frank Bass in the 1960s.[8] The Bass diffusion model quantifies the early phases of the product life cycle presented in Exhibit 16-1 for many product categories.

The Bass diffusion model is useful in forecasting market growth rates. It has been applied in a number of industries, including agricultural, industrial, medical, and consumer products. Furthermore, its validity has been demonstrated across various cultures.

At its core, the Bass diffusion model for new product categories divides the market into two types of customer: innovators and imitators. Innovators will buy after hearing about the product based on their own motivation. Imitators will wait for another person with direct experience of the product to buy a product prior to purchasing it themselves.

To construct the Bass diffusion model, let us define S_t as the unit sales and Q_t as the cumulative units sold at the time period t. Similarly, at the end of the next time period, the unit sales will be S_{t+1} and the cumulative of units sold will be Q_{t+1}. (The definition of the term "time period" is up to the researcher's discretion; it can be weeks, months, or years, although it is most common to use years as a basis for analysis.) The value of the Bass diffusion model is its ability to predict the unit sales during the next time period, S_{t+1}. From this metric, it is also possible to determine the next period's cumulative sale volume within the product category, $S_{t+1} + Q_t$. Moreover, the Bass diffusion model can be used to quantify the total volume potential of the market over the entire product introduction and growth phases. Let us denote the total volume potential with the variable N. N is a metric of the units that would be sold to saturate the market with one unit per customer.

The Bass diffusion model assumes that the volume of sales is the sum of the sales from the innovator and imitator customer groups. In its basic form, it also assumes that each customer in the market purchases once and only once. The assumptions make the model more appropriate for the early stages of a durable goods market than for either frequently purchased goods or for mature markets.

The volume of unit sales from the innovator group in the period of $t + 1$ is dependent upon two factors. The first factor, a, is the coefficient of innovation, a parameter that reflects the tendency of customers to behave as innovators. The second factor is simply the number of people within the market who haven't yet purchased. Because Q_t is the number of units that have been sold up until time $t + 1$, and N is the total potential number of units that can be sold in the market, the size of the market that hasn't purchased at time $t + 1$ is simply $N - Q_t$. Thus, the volume of sales from innovators is given by the product of the coefficient of innovation and the size of the remaining market:

$$\text{Next Period Innovator Sales} = a \cdot [N - Q_t] \qquad \text{Eq. 16.1}$$

The volume of unit sales from the imitator group in the period of $t + 1$ depends upon three factors. The first factor is the coefficient of imitation, a parameter that reflects the tendency of customers to behave as imitators. The second factor is a measure of the potential of imitators to imitate an existing customer. Under the model assumptions, imitators purchase a product only after seeing someone else with it. The probability that they will see another customer with the product is related to the ratio of the cumulative number of customers within the current market to the total number of potential customers. Because Q_t is the cumulative number of units sold to date and N is the total potential number of units that will be sold, the ratio of the number of customers within the current market to the total number of potential customers is Q_t/N. The third factor is, again, the number of people within the market who haven't yet purchased, $N - Q_t$. Thus, the volume of sales from imitators is given by the product of the coefficient of imitation, the probability that an imitating customer will interact with a customer who has already purchased, and the size of the remaining market:

$$\text{Next Period Imitator Sales} = b \cdot \frac{Q_t}{N} \cdot [N - Q_t] \qquad \text{Eq. 16.2}$$

The total of sales in the next time period is simply the sum of the sales from innovators and imitators. Using Equations 16.1 and 16.2, we can write

$$S_{(t+1)} = a \cdot [N - Q_t] + b \cdot \frac{Q_t}{N} \cdot [N - Q_t] \qquad \text{Eq. 16.3}$$

Equation 16.3 is extremely powerful. Given just three parameters that describe a specific new product category, N, a, and b, a marketer can predict the unit sales in any future period given the cumulative unit sales of past periods. As such, the evolution of a market can be predicted with great precision.

The remaining challenge is quantifying these three parameters: N, the total market size; a, the coefficient of innovation; and b, the coefficient of imitation. One technique that has gained popularity is to use multivariate regression analysis. With regression analysis, the researcher will rearrange Equation 16.3 into an appropriate form and regress the sales volume at time $t + 1$ against the cumulative sales at time t and the cumulative sales squared at time $t + 1$. In doing so, the research will rely only on data that reflect the units sold during prior periods within the product category to identify the required parameters and therefore predict the sales at any future time period. Bass diffusion model parameters generated from multivariate regression analysis for an assortment of industries can be found in Exhibit 16-2.

Exhibit 16-2 Bass Diffusion Parameters

Product	Period of Analysis	*a*	*b*	*N*
Artificial Insemination of Farm Animals	1942–1959	.028	.307	73.2
Ultrasound Imaging	1964–1978	.000	.534	84.8
Oxygen Steel Furnace (France)	1960–1980	.013	.374	85.2
Plastic Milk Containers	1963–1987	.021	.245	101.5
Electric Can Opener	1960–1979	.050	.126	68.0
Refrigerator	1925–1979	.017	.188	101.1
Home PC	1981–1988	.121	.281	25.8

Notes

[1] John E. Smallwood, "The Product Lifecycle: A Key to Strategic Marketing Planning," *MSU Business Topics* 21 No. 1 (1973): 29–35. See also George S. Day, "The Product Lifecycle: Analysis and Application Issues," *Journal of Marketing* 45, No. 4 (Fall 1981): 60–67.

[2] As reported in *Tech Digest*, http://www.techdigest.tv/2006/11/lgs_100inch_lcd_1.html (accessed on July 15, 2009).

[3] For a review of industry growth patterns and decision-making habits of customers in revolutionary markets, see Geoffrey A., Moore, "High-Tech Marketing Enlightenment," *Crossing the Chasm* (New York: Harper Business, 1991): 27–62.

[4] Saras Sarasvathy and Nicholas Dew, "Entrepreneurial Logics for a Technology of Foolishness," *Scandinavian Journal of Management* 21, No. 4 (December 2005): 385–406. Stuart Read, Nicholas Dew, Saras D. Sarasvathy, Michael Song, and Robert Wiltbank, "Marketing under Uncertainty: The Logic of an Effectual Approach," *Journal of Marketing* 73, No. 3 (May 2009): 1–18. Stephen L. Vargo and Robert F. Lusch, "Evolving to a New Dominant Logic for Marketing," *Journal of Marketing* 68, No. 1 (January 2004): 1–17.

[5] Nancy L. Stokey, "Intertemporal Price Discrimination," *The Quarterly Journal of Economics* (August 1979): 355–71. T. Stengos and E. Zacharias, "Intertemporal Pricing and Price Discrimination: A Semiparametric Hedonic Analysis of the Personal Computer Market," *Journal of Applied Econometrics* 21, No. 3 (April 2006): 371–86. Mark D. White, "A Simple Model of Intertemporal Price Discrimination," *Eastern Economic Journal* 30, No. 3 (Summer 2004): 487–92. Praveen Kumar, "Intertemporal Price-Quality Discrimination and the Coase Problem," *Journal of Mathematical Economics* 42, No. 7/8 (November 2006) 896–940. R. H. Coase, "Durability and Monopoly," *Journal of Law and Economics* 15, No. 1 (April 1972): 143–49.

[6] Michael E. Porter, "The Transition to Industry Maturity," *Competitive Strategy: Techniques for Analyzing Industries and Competitors* (New York: The Free Press, 1980): 237–52.

[7] Thomas T. Nagle and Reed K. Holden, "Life Cycle Pricing," in *The Strategy and Tactics of Pricing: A Guide to Profitable Decision Making*, 3d ed. (Upper Saddle River, NJ: Prentice Hall, 2002): 192–95.

[8] Vijay Mahajan, Eitan Muller, and Frank M. Bass, "New Product Diffusion Models in Marketing: A Review and Directions for Research," *Journal of Marketing* 54, No. 1 (January 1990): 1–26. Everett M. Rogers, "New Product Adoption and Diffusion," *Journal of Consumer Research* 2, No. 4 (March 1976): 290–301.

Chapter
17

Pricing Decisions and the Law by Dennis P. W. Johnson

Image copyright IgorGolovniov, 2010. Used under copyright from Shutterstock.com

- Which U.S. agencies are charged with prosecuting illegal pricing actions, and which laws govern their inquiries?
- What is the difference between horizontal price fixing and vertical price fixing?
- What policies can a firm set in the United States regarding non-price restraints that represent a low legal risk yet can strongly improve profits?
- When is price segmentation legally risky in the United States?
- How are the legal risks surrounding pricing policies different in Europe and other parts of the world than in the United States?

It would be foolish to wait until you have invested great effort and time developing a pricing strategy and only then ask whether the path you laid out is legal. Even though the rules are sometimes murky, assessing legal risks needs to inform the entire process of developing pricing strategy. The ultimate conclusion sometimes requires more detailed analysis than you can provide yourself. Your immediate goal should be to recognize the clear legal boundaries so that you can identify areas where you need to seek help early on as you develop your pricing strategy. With that in mind, this chapter provides a simple overview of U.S. federal antitrust law and identifies some constraints that it imposes on pricing decisions.[1]

Over many years now, federal antitrust enforcement has become more business-friendly. Nonetheless, familiarity with the antitrust laws remains essential because criminal violations can result in real jail time, significant financial penalties, or both. Federal antitrust statutes authorize both criminal prosecutions by the U.S. Department of Justice and civil suits initiated by the Department of Justice or the Federal Trade Commission to enjoin unlawful behavior. Criminal fines are steep—computed with a maximum limit of twice the amount of gain or loss—but prosecutions are reserved for the most egregious violations, typically price-fixing schemes among competitors. Although government civil suits may seem less of a concern, they are just as costly because they require extensive investigations. Perhaps most importantly, though, federal antitrust laws encourage private enforcement by rewarding successful plaintiffs with their attorneys' fees—at defendants' expense—and further penalizing defendants by awarding treble (triple) damages in many cases. It's a one-way street: prevailing defendants cannot make the losing plaintiff reimburse them for their fees. That said, the good news is that so-called private plaintiffs nonetheless face an uphill struggle.

The goal of this chapter is to give you a working framework for asking whether a particular pricing scheme is likely to be challenged. Unfortunately, there are very few clear-cut rules in the law of pricing, and a court's inquiry is likely to be fact-intensive. Thus, this chapter first provides a basic overview of the goals and aims of federal antitrust laws regarding pricing to help you better understand how courts evaluate challenged pricing schemes. This chapter then discusses several types of pricing behavior that the law has recognized, explaining what has generally been deemed permissible and impermissible.

The Aims of the Law of Pricing

It is important to understand both what the antitrust laws seek to police and what they do not. The general goal of U.S. antitrust law is to promote competition, not to protect competitors. The law therefore targets pricing behavior that deprives consumers of the benefits of competition. This is the conceptual starting point for any court evaluating a pricing scheme. Although it is too soon to know how future administrations may change federal antitrust enforcement, the current administration's policy statements promise a renewed focus not only on enhancing competition but also preventing exclusionary or predatory conduct that may harm competition and ultimately consumers.[2]

Price fixing is the historical core of U.S. antitrust laws. Begin with a classic price-fixing case: Two competitors selling the same grade of gasoline from adjoining stations agree that they both will charge the same price. They have agreed to stop competing, with the result that they have "restrained competition." To judge the impact of this agreement upon competition, courts began with a straightforward assumption: By its very nature, the effect of an agreement to no longer compete must be to lessen competition. Drivers who need to fill their tanks in that neighborhood no longer can enjoy the lower prices that are the fruits of competition. This assumption became the so-called "per se standard" that courts applied to analyze most types of price fixing. Although courts gave lip service to the notion that only "unreasonable" restraints on competition violate Section 1 of the Sherman Act, the U.S. Supreme Court long ago decided that an agreement to charge the same price must fall in that prohibited category. Classic cases of price fixing, such as bid rigging, still apply this conclusive presumption, as do cases involving market allocations, by which one competitor agrees not to sell a common product in the same territory served by his competitor. The two competitors may not offer any analysis of the actual effect that their agreement has upon competition or claim that it is justified by its special purpose.

It has taken decades of slow economic enlightenment to expand the exceptions to this presumption, which now largely have swallowed the "per se" rule. Those exceptions instead are judged by examining their actual effect on competition through the "rule of reason," which weighs all the circumstances in a detailed inquiry into the market impact of the restraint. When the rule of reason applies, the defendant company is permitted to demonstrate that its challenged pricing practice actually enhances competition rather than restrains it.

Over decades of evolving antitrust analysis, most types of pricing practices now fall into one of these two categories: per se or rule of reason. Some types of cases noted here have been moved from the per se category to the rule of reason. Finally, the line between the two categories is not always readily apparent. This has given rise to categories of cases that require courts to begin with only a "quick look" using the rule of reason before inferring anticompetitive effect, because it seems at least intuitively obvious.

For at least the past three decades, the rule of reason has been the starting point for antitrust analysis. Even cases that at first glance involve price fixing now receive a more careful examination under the rule of reason. Although old-fashioned, simple price fixing remains per se illegal, courts now analyze far more types of pricing systems under the rule of reason. As a result, what is prohibited by U.S. antitrust laws today depends in large measure upon the impact that the particular scheme has upon competition.

Unlawful Pricing Behavior

Broadly speaking, the law recognizes four categories of anticompetitive (and therefore prohibited) pricing behavior: (1) price fixing, (2) non-price vertical restraints, (3) exclusionary and predatory pricing, and (4) price and promotional discrimination. Each will be discussed in turn in the next sections.

PRICE FIXING

Price fixing may be horizontal (by competitors selling to common customers) or vertical (by firms in the same chain of distribution). Manufacturers of competing products that both sell to distributors (horizontal competitors) may not agree to set or maintain the price or terms of sale of common products. This is the clearest single example of conduct that will land you in jail.

Vertical price fixing ("resale price maintenance") involves an agreement between a manufacturer and its distributors to sell at a stated price. Unlike horizontal price fixing, these vertical pricing agreements are not illegal per se, as described later in this chapter. The first conclusion is that despite the language of Section 1 of the Sherman Act, not every "contract, combination, or conspiracy" is one considered "in restraint of trade" without further analysis. Courts decide which agreements restrain trade rather than promote it by applying the rule of reason and determining that the economic impact of the particular agreement contributes more to competition than it takes away.

Horizontal Price Fixing and Other Agreements

Competitors cannot agree upon prices. However, Section 1 has never prohibited unilateral decisions to fix prices. You can refuse to sell to anyone who declines to pay your price. But Distributor A cannot agree with Distributor B (its competitor) on the price at which both will sell to Retailer C. Nor can they agree that neither will sell to Retailer C. Although not formally "price" fixing, other non-price agreements among competitors to boycott suppliers or to refuse to deal with particular customers are likewise illegal per se. The same is true of agreements not to compete in certain geographic areas.

Agreements can be proved in several ways. Courts do not require a written contract between competitors ("direct" evidence) to demonstrate a collective agreement. Price-fixing conspiracies, like any other type of conspiracy, can be proved by a mosaic of indirect ("circumstantial") evidence without an explicit agreement. Courts even may infer an agreement where entities are imitating their competitors—known as "conscious parallelism"—if additional factors are present. These additional factors may include circumstances where the pricing behavior would be against an entity's self-interest if acting alone, but beneficial if acting in concert and where the given entities had been in communication or otherwise had the opportunity to agree ("collude"). One competitor's conscious following of another's price alone is insufficient to demonstrate a conspiracy.

The law is relatively straightforward: Competitors cannot agree to fix prices. When courts pronounce these schemes per se illegal, what they mean is that the agreement without anything more violates the law; no effect has to be demonstrated. Bookseller A cannot call up Bookseller B down the street and set the price that both will charge for the same book. Both are free to charge the publisher's list price; but they cannot, for example, agree to discount the publisher's list price to a specific amount, or by a specific percent. This includes agreements, like those described previously, that can be proven only indirectly. In addition, per se illegal agreements are not limited to agreements between competitors to fix prices; they also include agreements to fix terms affecting price, such as warranties, discount programs, financing rates, and production quotas.

Vertical Price Fixing

The law as it pertains to vertical price fixing, including resale price maintenance, is more nuanced. Courts test the legality of agreements to fix prices within the supply chain under the rule of reason by, as described previously, balancing the anticompetitive effects of a given scheme against its pro-competitive effects. Vertical agreements to set maximum resale prices ("ceiling" prices) have been tested under the rule of reason for more than a decade; yet agreements between manufacturers and dealers to set minimum prices ("floor prices") were subject to the per se rule until 2007. The latter agreements usually are addressing discounting. By allowing manufacturers to reward dealers for providing point-of-sale services (for example, knowledgeable salespersons, showrooms, and higher inventories), these agreements enhance interbrand competition by eliminating the advantages that free-riding competitive retailers otherwise enjoy. Remember, however, that the rule of reason is a balancing test—the positive effects on interbrand competition resulting from agreements to set resale prices must, and will, be balanced against any negative effects on competition that the agreements might also engender.

Manufacturers also may unilaterally set either maximum or minimum resale prices by announcing their policies and refusing to sell to any reseller that will not comply, so long as there is no agreement between the parties. Resellers may lawfully adopt similar policies as well. Unilateral resale pricing policies, in which compliance is truly voluntary, are legal and are not even tested for anticompetitive effects under the rule of reason.

However, any and all suggestion of agreement must be avoided, and the law can prove tricky in this respect. Not only must obvious forms of agreement, like contracts, be avoided, but behavior that is less intuitively indicative of agreement must be avoided as well. For example, suppliers wisely simply choose to cease selling to a noncompliant reseller without warnings, threats, or probationary periods because those techniques suggest that the supplier has coerced an agreement with the reseller. In other words, the policy must be implemented on a "take it or leave it" basis. Conversely, resellers should avoid any communication that may be taken as an assurance that they have agreed to comply with the supplier's demand.

Genuine consignment, agency, and brokerage arrangements allow suppliers to dictate resale prices unilaterally because they retain title. Supplier and reseller alike must maintain a bona fide consignment to prevent the arrangement from being perceived as per se vertical price fixing. Courts examine whether the reseller has assumed the risk of loss and other indicia of ownership of the product, the supplier's purpose in adopting these systems, as well as whether the reseller willingly entered into the arrangement rather than being coerced into it.

Manufacturers may provide suggested resale prices to dealers in writing or through advertising to the dealers' customers can even provide preticketed resale prices on the product. In these instances, the dealers must decide independently whether to follow them but also must remain free to reject them. The manufacturer may encourage dealers, but some arrangements will require a jury to decide whether the supplier crossed the line between persuasion and coercion. Thus, risk-averse manufacturers may choose less-aggressive approaches. Tactics that the reseller's competitor views as coercive but do not yield some sign that the reseller assented are not signs of agreement. A manufacturer in theory may even terminate a dealer in response to complaints that the dealer has not observed "suggested" resale prices, but lawsuits that require trial to decide whether the manufacturer's action was truly unilateral rather than the product of its agreement with other complaining dealers are high prices to pay and result in long periods of uncertainty. An illegal agreement between manufacturer and distributor to maintain resale prices requires proof that the manufacturer sought the distributor's acquiescence or agreement and that the dealer somehow communicated its assurances in response, even if by a lesser means than an explicit agreement.

Resale Price Encouragement

These techniques are also called vertical non-price restraints. Rather than directly dictating particular resale prices to their dealers, suppliers can induce their adherence to a desired resale scheme through various incentives. Such incentive schemes are judged under the rule of reason.

These incentives often take the form of advertising allowances. For example, many suppliers use Minimum Advertising Price (MAP) programs. Under a MAP program, a retailer must agree to a supplier-determined lowest price at which the supplier's product may be advertised to receive advertising allowances from the supplier.

Similarly, a manufacturer may:

- Provide rebates directly to its dealer's customers or even reimburse dealers who paid it to their customers, if the dealer remains free to set its own price
- Provide promotional allowances to reduce wholesale prices, if the dealer remains free to determine whether to reduce its resale price
- Offer dealer assistance programs that require the dealer to pass a manufacturer's price reduction down to the dealer's customers, if the dealer continues to set its own prices
- Use cooperative advertising programs that deny reimbursement to dealers who failed to conform to the manufacturer's directions to include its suggested retail price or no price at all
- Agree with one dealer that the prices that the manufacturer charges will be no higher than those that it charges to other similarly situated dealers
- Use voluntary national account pricing among its dealers, so long as independent dealers remain free to solicit those accounts outside the national account program

However, manufacturers may not impose a price maintenance scheme together with territorial or customer restrictions because the latter restrictions are per se illegal.

NON-PRICE VERTICAL RESTRAINTS

Manufacturers also may use various non-price restraints on dealers to control the marketing of their products and combat against discounting and dealer free-riding. These include the customer or territorial restrictions or product restrictions discussed later in this chapter, which are evaluated under the rule of reason applied under Section 1 of the

Sherman Act. Courts uphold such a restraint if its pro-competitive effect on interbrand competition outweighs its anticompetitive effect on intrabrand competition. In addition, when the seller imposing such restraints enjoys substantial market share, plaintiffs may challenge the restraint under a second antitrust law—Section 2 of the Sherman Act. Section 2 of the Sherman Act makes it unlawful for a company to "monopolize, or attempt to monopolize," trade or commerce.

Customer and Territorial Restrictions

Sellers may mandate that dealers sell their product only to certain customers or only within certain geographic territories. Courts will uphold these arrangements if the pro-competitive effect on interbrand competition outweighs the anticompetitive effect on intrabrand competition. These arrangements are rarely invalidated, so long as they are purely vertical. Different standards apply than those relating to vertical price restrictions, although the practical effect of both price and non-price restrictions is similar.

The risk of running afoul of the law arises when a seller enjoys a substantial market share. The greater the market share, the greater the potential for an anticompetitive effect from customer or territorial restrictions. Such sellers are advised to consider methods to control marketing short of outright restrictions. For example, a seller might consider implementing a "primary area of responsibility" arrangement, wherein its dealers are permitted to sell outside their primary area but must exercise their best efforts to increase sales within it. Quotas can be implemented to give these programs teeth. Another arrangement that sellers may use is known as the "profit passover" in which sellers permit dealers to sell outside their designated primary territory but require that they split revenue with the dealers in those other territories. These are both effective ways to minimize discounting that stems from free-riding on the marketing efforts of other dealers.

Product Restrictions

Refusals to Supply. Generally speaking, suppliers may refuse to sell to whomever they choose—manufacturers or customers—so long as the decision is not part of a horizontal agreement with competitors or part of a strategy to acquire or maintain a monopoly. Thus, for example, a supplier may lawfully agree to sell only to a particular dealer within a given territory.

Exclusive Dealing Agreements. Manufacturer-imposed product restrictions on dealers are also typically upheld. Manufacturers use "exclusive dealing contracts" to prevent retailers from purchasing a certain type of product from other manufacturers. Courts widely recognize that these agreements have the pro-competitive effect of creating dedicated dealers that actively promote the seller's product. For example, they provide attractive stores, well-trained salespersons, long business hours, sizable inventory, and warranty plans. These agreements also simultaneously prevent discounters or online sellers from free-riding off those dealers. Courts generally uphold these agreements when they result in retailers providing extra services to customers. The legality of an exclusive dealing agreement is most likely to be questionable—as is true for most non-price vertical restraints—where manufacturers enjoy large market share. For example, courts are not likely to uphold an exclusive dealing contract by a powerful manufacturer that results in competing manufacturers being denied access to enough retailers to sustain a viable amount of sales. Such manufacturers are advised to implement less legally risky methods of creating dedicated dealers, such as requiring dealers to purchase minimum quantities of their product.

EXCLUSIONARY OR PREDATORY PRICING

Other pricing arrangements involve various means of using a manufacturer's market power to either force additional sales or drive competitors out of the market.

Tying

In a tying arrangement, the seller conditions the sale of one product (the tying product) on the simultaneous purchase of a second, usually less-desirable product (the tied product). Several different antitrust statutes apply to these arrangements, and services, franchises, and trademarks can also serve as the tying "product." Older cases treated tying arrangements as per se illegal, but the test that courts now apply to most arrangements closely resembles the rule of reason. The seller must have sufficient market power with respect to the tying product to restrain free competition in the market for the tied product, and must use it to coerce the sale of the tied product. The tying arrangement must affect a "not insubstantial" amount of commerce. The seller must have enough power to force the purchaser to do something that he or she would not do in a competitive market, but it does not need to have monopoly power. Even a seller with a patented product is not assumed to have market power. In addition, just what dollar amount of commerce constitutes a "not insubstantial" amount is determined on a case-by-case basis. Cases in which the seller demands an exclusive dealing relationship with the buyer or forces its full line of products on the buyer apply similar analyses.

Predatory or Below-Cost Pricing

Predatory pricing is one means by which a seller may use its monopoly power unilaterally to preserve or attempt to gain a monopoly. Both are violations of Section 2 of the Sherman Act that require definition of the "relevant" market in terms of the products and geographic boundaries. A seller that already has monopoly power may not maintain it through anticompetitive conduct, as distinguished from robust competition. The line is not clearly drawn, and courts attach conclusory labels to distinguish "exclusionary conduct" from mere "vigorous competition" by examining whether the seller intentionally acts without other business justification to exclude competitors from the market, with the likely effect that monopoly power is maintained, enhanced, or acquired.

Pricing below the seller's cost of production for the purpose of eliminating competitors in the short run is prohibited. However, courts explicitly recognize that price cutting to increase business is classic competition; what distinguishes predatory pricing is the seller's dangerous probability of being able to recoup its short-term losses by long-term profits after it has driven a competitor out of its market. This requires pricing below marginal cost or average variable cost, after first determining which costs are incremental rather than fixed. The analysis is further complicated by the need to replace accounting labels with principles of economics. The federal courts of appeals have applied various and sometimes conflicting analyses of these issues. In addition to defining what the predatory act is, courts struggle to measure its scope and duration, the predator's financial ability to endure short-term losses and the whether the market is one that will sustain monopoly pricing after the victim has been driven out. These cases often involve claims that what the seller defends as promotional or temporary discounts are in fact maintained for sufficiently longer periods of time to become predatory, but no firm tests of these principles exist. Price squeezes invoke power that the predator has in one product that is an input or component and it sells at a supra-competitive price in one market while charging an unjustified lower price for the finished product in a second market. Under current cases, the defendant seller must have either monopoly power or a dangerous probability of it in the downstream market in which the plaintiff competes.

PRICE AND PROMOTIONAL DISCRIMINATION

When Congress first passed legislation directed at price discrimination, World War I had not yet begun. In 1936, the Robinson-Patman Act amended Congress's first effort, but it left businesses with a counterintuitive, if not outright competitively harmful, law that requires some patience to traverse. Congress has never fixed this statute. The good news is that only some of the practices prohibited by this Act may be criminally prosecuted, and that has not happened in about the last fifty years.[3] In fact, the Department of Justice has essentially left enforcement to the Federal Trade Commission, and its enforcement activity has been minimal. Plaintiffs also have a lower likelihood of succeeding with these claims, but that is no guarantee that you will not be sued and exposed to the high cost and serious distraction of a competitor's or customer's suit. Thus, you must still understand and comply with the civil prohibitions that your customers or competitors may try to use against your promotional and other pricing activities.

The Robinson-Patman Act prohibits:

- Sellers from discriminating between different buyers when it adversely affects competition, unless the sellers are matching a competitor's price ("meeting competition")
- Buyers from knowingly inducing or receiving such a discriminatory price
- Sellers from granting and/or buyers from receiving certain commissions or brokerage fees except for services actually rendered
- Sellers from providing or paying for promotion or advertising in a product's resale unless they offer equivalent terms to all competing buyers

Some basic coverage issues often lead to the failure of those few private suits attempted under this law. Discrimination of course requires more than one sale. Any prohibited sales must result in injury to competition (meaning the process of competition, not just lost sales to a single competitor). Competition is assessed based on what "level" is involved: competition among sellers is labeled "primary line" competition; competition at the buyer's level is "secondary line" competition. In some cases, the distinction between the two levels determines whether the pricing action violates the Act. Both sales compared and challenged must be made in interstate commerce—at least one of the sales involved must pass from one state to another. The connection to interstate commerce for Robinson-Patman cases is applied more narrowly than in price-fixing cases.

Price discrimination requires that a single seller sell two products to two purchasers at different prices. Services are not commodities. The items must be of "like grade and quality" based upon characteristics of the product itself rather than brand names and labels, packaging, or warranties. Physical differences in products place them outside this test.

The price difference must cause competitive injury, another thoroughly litigated concept. The injury may more than a reasonable possibility or a probability. It either (a) may substantially lessen competition or tend to create a monopoly or (b) injure competition with anyone who grants or knowingly receives the benefit or with customers of either of them. As has been the case with other antitrust concepts, the competitive injury requirement has shifted to a more objective predatory pricing standard. Whereas older cases focused more upon the seller's intent, since a 1993 case, the Supreme Court has rejected a purely subjective intent test and replaced it with the cost-based test that is applied to predatory pricing cases under Section 2 of the Sherman Act (that also prohibits predatory pricing). There is still plenty of room for disagreement and litigation: to perform this test, the Supreme Court only required use of "an appropriate measure" of the seller's costs.[4]

As noted previously, injury to competition may be measured not only at the seller's own level (primary line), but also at the buyer's level (secondary line). The latter requires competition between favored and disfavored purchasers, who must compete in the same geographic market. You might reasonably expect that to prove injury to competitors, a plaintiff would need to prove that it lost sales; but often the inference of injury is enough. It may rest on a substantial price difference over a substantial period of time on a product that is resold by sellers involved in "keen" competition. A challenged company may defend its pricing scheme by rebutting this inference of injury to competition via showing that the very customers who might be inferred to have suffered declines in sales and profits instead have prospered.

As if these undefined tests were not already hard enough to apply, the Supreme Court has required plaintiffs who bring such lawsuits to begin them with allegations that go beyond accurately stating the required legal conclusions put in terms of correct labels; they must allege sufficient facts at the outset to at least suggest they will be able to prove the required elements. However, even though it is unlikely that your company will be sued for violating this statute and lose, the uncertainty of these tests make it difficult to decide for yourself whether a price that you want to charge is legal. In addition, the different federal circuits do not all agree on how to decide key issues like those previously discussed. Thus, even if you asked a lawyer to assess the legality of your prices, the answer may come out differently in different geographic areas of the country simply because different courts apply different standards. Even beyond this, the Supreme Court has left unresolved basic uncertainties such as whether the injury to be proved must be an actual injury, rather than the inferred injury that has been sufficient historically.

International Antitrust Enforcement

In addition to enforcing U.S. antitrust laws against firms whose conduct has domestic competitive impact, the Department of Justice's Antitrust Division currently emphasizes the importance of consistent enforcement of common antitrust prohibitions, so that firms operating in the global economy will be evaluated under consistent standards.[5] This requires a level of coordination with other countries' laws that prohibit anticompetitive actions similar to those prohibited under U.S. law. For example, in the European Union (EU), Article 81 of the Treaty of the European Communities (the European Community's competition law) prohibits cartels and vertical agreements that restrain competition within the common market. The statute also prohibits price fixing and market sharing, but it exempts collusion that promotes distributional or technological innovation if the restraints are not unreasonable ("disproportionate") and do not risk eliminating competition. Article 82 prohibits dominant firms from abusing their position by price discrimination and exclusive dealing, similar to U.S. antitrust laws. EU law prohibits mergers that might significantly impede effective competition, similar to U.S. law. Canada and Japan have similar provisions.

Intel Rebates Case Exercise

On July 28, 2007, the European Commission (EC), an antitrust authority, accused Intel Corp. of abusing its market dominance over rival Advanced Micro Devices (AMD) in the chip market. After conducting an investigation, the European Commission leveled a € 1.06 billion fine against Intel on May 13, 2009. Intel felt it had followed the law and believed the claims against it were false. As such, Intel chose to appeal to the European Court of First Instance. Read the following reference articles concerning Intel and the European Commission's investigation (listed under item 10) and address the following questions:

1. What were the allegations against Intel regarding its rebate program?
2. What were the positive commercial purposes of Intel's rebate program in terms of generating sales for Intel?
3. What were the positive and negative commercial aspects of Intel's rebate program for its customers?
4. What were the negative commercial aspects of Intel's rebate program for its competitor, AMD?

5. Was Intel's rebate program an abnormal practice for industrial firms?
6. In light of your research and analysis, what advice would you provide a CEO of an industrial firm regarding rebate programs specifically, and price structures that cannot be matched by competitors in general?
7. When should a firm use a legal price structure that cannot be matched by competitors, and when might it avoid such a price structure even if it was anticipated to improve profits?
8. Discussion Question: How would you analyze whether to run different programs in the United States as opposed to areas governed by EC standards?
9. Discussion Question: To make the decision for the U.S. market, would you need to answer the same questions given previously? Explain why or why not, and if not, what questions would you want to answer?
10. Intel Case References
    a. Don Clark, "Intel to Face Antitrust Charges in Europe." *Wall Street Journal* (July 27, 2007): B-4.
    b. "Intel in Euro-Land," *Wall Street Journal* (July 31, 2007): A-14.
    c. Jennifer L. Schenker, "Intel's in Hot Water in Europe," *Business Week Online* (September 2007); http://www.businessweek.com/globalbiz/content/sep2007/gb20070921_968706.htm?chan=top+news_top+news+index_businessweek+exclusives (accessed on August 21, 2010).
    d. Charles Forelle, "Intel Confronts EU Antitrust Allegations; AMD Says Chip Giant Used Illegal Discounts, Rebates to Fix Market," *Wall Street Journal* (March 12, 2008): B-12.
    e. Don Clark and John R. Wilke, "FTC Begins Formal Inquiry into Intel's Chip Pricing; Case over Incentives to Makers of PCs Could Benefit AMD," *Wall Street Journal* (June 7, 2008): A-3.
    f. Charles Forelle, "EU Says Intel Paid to Hinder AMD Products," *Wall Street Journal* (July 18, 2008): B-6.
    g. Nikki Tait and Richard Waters, "Brussels accuses Intel of retailer pay-offs," *Financial Times* (July 18, 2008): 21.
    h. "Business: A billion-euro question; Intel's antitrust ruling," *The Economist* 391, No. 8631 (May 2009): 70.
    i. Charles Forelle and Don Clark, "EU Shows Its Cards Behind Intel Case—In Emails, PC Makers Feared Retaliation by Chip Giant; 'Best Friend Money Can Buy,'" *Wall Street Journal* (September 22, 2009): B-1.
    j. Nikki Tait, "E-mails central to EU's case against Intel," *Financial Times* (September 22, 2009): 20.

Notes

[1] State antitrust laws typically mirror the federal ones discussed here. Differences among states can be significant, and you should assume that any product sold in the United States is subject to one or more state laws. International antitrust laws are beyond the scope of this chapter. Articles contained in the Treaty of the European Communities are comparable to the Sherman Act prohibitions of price fixing and other "concerted" activity among competitors and monopolization (the EC terms are "abuse . . . of a dominant position within the common market"). However, the results reached by the EC in specific cases—for example, applying these provisions to rebates and imposing stiff fines on Intel in May 2009 for rebates in exchange for future exclusive purchases—may be more harsh than U.S. rulings on the same facts would be.

[2] Christine A. Varney, Assistant Attorney General, Antitrust Division, U.S. Department of Justice; "Vigorous Antitrust Enforcement in this Challenging Era," Remarks as prepared for the U.S. Chamber of Commerce on May 12, 2009 (withdrawing a portion of a Bush administration policy statement that provided greater latitude to dominant firms to avoid so-called over-deterrence).

[3] The criminal provisions include charging "unreasonably low prices for the purpose of destroying competition or eliminating a competitor," but the Supreme Court has interpreted that to prohibit below-cost prices implemented with predatory intent. *United States v. National Dairy Products Corp.*, 372 U.S. 29 (1963). Criminal provisions also prohibit territorial price discrimination "for the purpose of destroying competition or eliminating a competitor and failing to make discounts, rebates or allowance available to the recipient's competitors in the sale of goods of "like grade, quality, and quantity."

[4] *Brooke Group v. Brown & Williamson Tobacco Corp.*, 509 U.S. 209 (1993). Lower courts have used different measures of costs for this test, including average variable and marginal costs.

[5] Christine A. Varney, Assistant Attorney General, Antitrust Division, U.S. Department of Justice; Remarks as prepared for the 36th Annual Fordham Competition Law Institute Annual Conference on International Antitrust Law and Policy (September 24, 2009).

Index

Note: Page numbers in italic type indicate the presence of figures or tables.

Q

R

S

T

U

V

W

X

Y

Z